Video Game Writing

Second Edition

VIDEO GAME WRITING

FROM MACRO TO MICRO

SECOND EDITION

Maurice Suckling
Marek Walton

MERCURY LEARNING AND INFORMATION
Dulles, Virginia
Boston, Massachusetts
New Delhi

Publisher: David Pallai
Mercury Learning and Information
22841 Quicksilver Drive
Dulles, VA 20166
info@merclearning.com
www.merclearning.com
800-232-0223

This book is printed on acid-free paper.

Maurice Suckling and Marek Walton. *Video Game Writing, 2E.*
ISBN: 978-1-683920-29-8

Library of Congress Control Number: 2016915233

171819321 Printed in the United States of America

To Neil Richards of The Mustard Corporation—
teacher, writer, script doctor, and friend.

Contents

FOREWORD

What is game writing?

No, I mean the question seriously. What do we really think *game writing is?*

For many years—can we say decades?—it was virtually an oxymoron. Games. Writing.

As if . . .

Some game companies dabbled with writers; others used people drafted from their development team who may have seemed to have a 'flair' for writing, or story, or dialogue. (And needless to say, such a flair was often more perceived than actual.)

But a few games' success and critical acclaim showed that a game that used a professional writer could not only elevate the story, not to mention the dialogue, but also lead to something even more important.

What is that?

At the risk of sounding preposterously optimistic . . .

Nothing less, boys and girls, than the integration of gameplay and story into a new narrative *entity*.

And let's go a step further.

Not just a new narrative entity, which seems to bring images of gleaming cylons holding their six-shooters—but a new art form.

As potentially powerful as film, television, and that old standby of we quaint story folk . . . the book.

Now reinvented as the e-book.

But I digress.

A different medium where someone called the 'player' can interact with other players, and characters, and story, where they can even shape and alter story, impact the world, other players . . . their whole experience.

Tall order.

So who the hell is going to do that? Sounds . . . mighty challenging.

Well, there is good news in what's been this long and rather slow march to our new entity/art form.

Writers have come along—not a lot, not an army of them—but still . . . new writers, who not only have the professional skill to craft story, to shape dialogue—who have, as we say, the 'chops'—but also completely and totally get the wide spectrum of needs for gameplay.

These new writers emerged over the past decade, slowly, inexorably, until—in my opinion—most major companies know that, along with the hundred people doing everything else that goes into creating a AAA console title, we sure as hell need a game writer.

Someone who can write.

I mean—really write.

And someone who can build interactive experiences in a dramatic and exciting way.

Someone who can mesh those two things.

The evidence is indisputably out here that it can, in fact, be done. We live in fortunate days, gaming-wise. Things are changing, and will change even more. To go . . . way back, to paraphrase a line from the birth of another new medium . . . "you haven't seen nothin' yet."

Which brings us to the book you have in your hands.

To say that it is needed is obvious. It deals with both the art and craft of exactly what I'm talking about. It deals with the inner thoughts of a number of practitioners of this new art form.

But more importantly, it is written by two key practitioners of it.

Marek Walton and Maurice Suckling belong to that brave new group of creative people that I mentioned earlier. That they get gameplay almost goes without saying; spend mere minutes with them, and you will hear insights and a dissection of interaction worthy of the best college lecture that money can buy. Their work globally sets a standard for game writing.

But they both bring a writer's sensibility and, yes, more importantly, a real writer's talent to the game medium.

They not only analyze what works and what does not.

They can show how it's done, and for anyone staring out, wanting to embrace this new world, there can—without a doubt—be no better place to start than here. Need to understand how to outline? They take us through it. NDAs and the business end of dealing with old IP and new IP? Totally covered. And of course, the methods of actual interactive scripting.

We are lucky to have this book.

In a very small shelf of key tomes on game design and, yes, game writing, this book easily takes a prominent, even necessary, place.

And not only that . . . what a great read.

But then, it *was* done by writers.

Matt Costello, writer.

Credits include games such as *Rage, Just Cause 1 & 2, Doom 3, Just Cause, Pirates of the Caribbean, and 7th Guest. novels such as Vacation, Missing Monday, and Beneath Still Waters.* Matt also works in movies and TV.

www.mattcostello.com

ACKNOWLEDGMENTS

Many thanks to the following people and organizations for their help, contributions, and/or permissions in relation to the publication of this book:

Ernest Adams, Cumron Ashtiani, Jim Banister, Allison Best, Niel Bushnell, Simon Callaghan, Tom Bowtell, Charles Cecil, Tassos Stevens and Annette Mees at Coney, Greg Childs and the Children's Media Conference, Matt Costello, The Provost and Scholars of King's College Cambridge, The Society of Authors, and Houghton Mifflin Harcourt as the Literary Representatives of the Estate of E. M. Forster, EA Games, Rick Gibson, Denby Grace, ITV, Hal Marienthal, Michael Mateas, Tim McEvoy, Mindscape, Eiji Ohnobu, Bruno Patatas, Penguin Books and the estate of T. S. Dorsch, Denise Penn, Rhianna Pratchett, Brittany Rank, Neil Richards, Now Production Inc., Matthew Seymour, Andrew Stern, Haru Takahashi, Jordan Thomas, Ubisoft, Valve, and Erik Wolpaw.

And thanks to our fellow games writers who took the time to send us their contributions for the final chapter of the book.

Thanks also to David and all at Mercury Learning.

ADAM MURPHY

Many thanks to Adam for his art and illustrations; it was great working with you. Hopefully we'll get the chance to work with you again. Please visit his site: *www.adammurphy.com.*

INTRODUCTION

Why the title? A writer seems to be constantly shifting lenses between looking very far out, at the macro level, and looking very close up, at the micro level. *What does the story mean?* is a question you ask yourself at the macro level. How it evolves to mean what you want it to mean comes down to the actions, sometimes very tiny actions, you have occurring within it at the micro level. Likewise, a story's theme is a consideration at the macro level, but how you lace this theme into the story can often be a matter of placing objects or tailoring dialogue, or scripting the tiniest of facial expressions at the micro level. As they're writing, a writer has to be able to zoom in and out seamlessly in their mind to see the script as a whole. They have to be able to operate at both levels at the same time. They can't focus solely on the big picture, because the detail will not sort itself out—where is a script without its dialogue operating at precisely the functional pitch intended, or without the detail of the object everyone is hunting for being defined? Try seeing what happens if you keep calling the thing on which the fate of the world hangs and everyone is looking for nothing other than "the thing on which the fate of the world hangs and everyone is looking for." Similarly, if writers focus purely on the detail, the pace and plot of the story begin to evaporate, and with it, an audience's attention. So macro and micro seemed apposite to the writer's craft, and so, to our book as a whole.

In addition, if Part I—an overview of the history of games writing —is the macro, and Part II is the micro, the detail of what games writers do, then Part III comprises the adventures between these two levels as well as those beyond. We might see Part IV as the application of a composite macro-micro lens, as we take another leap beyond the perspective the authors have offered over the course of the book, and look to the detail of personal insights reflected in short form from a variety of other voices. Because this book is really four books in one volume, each section has a different focus, a different target, and, as a result, many of the parts have a different approach.

First, it's important to be clear, this is a book with its focus squarely on games writing, that is, with its focus on writing that supports, supplements, enhances, and entwines with gameplay. There is much to be said for and about interactive storytelling beyond and—very clearly away from—the world of games. But this is not the book in which to find these discussions to any real extent.

When the publishers first approached us about writing this book, discussions were focused on what would make this book different from other titles tackling the topic. This was of no less importance to us because Maurice had recently contributed a cowritten chapter on writing in teams to *Professional Techniques for Video Game Writing*, as well as a chapter on driving games and another on sports games to *Writing for Video Game Genres: From FPS to RPG*, both published by A. K. Peters. This is the origin of the four-books-in-one. We wanted a book that would give an account of games history seen from the perspective of games writing, which could be used as a reference tool for both students and professionals, and which could help place games we frequently found ourselves referencing in some kind of context. Such an account would also be an opportunity to rescue games that had fallen out of our frames of reference.

We wanted Part II to appeal to students and to the curious, be they games fans, professional writers from other media, or nascent games professionals learning their trade in other games development areas. For the students we enclosed practical exercises, research projects, and discussion points, with a view to supplementing courses, and included appendices to give sample industry NDAs and contracts for the benefit of those who had never seen them. We wanted to take the hand of the reader and lead them through responses to the joint questions: *What do games writers do and how do they do it?*

But we also wanted a section that would take things beyond the basics and address what, to us, appear to be the most pertinent issues for practicing games writers today, looking at storytelling developments and different approaches. We wanted this section, Part III, to lift the book further away from similar-sounding titles by also writing what, in effect, would be like a mini-reader—comprising a number of essays, less clearly instructional in intent than preceding chapters, and often more theoretical or discursive in inclination, as well as being more varied in terms of approach. We wanted to capture the conversations and thoughts circulating around our working lives as games writers beyond the purely and immediately practical. This would be a section very much aimed at practitioners, at our peers and contemporaries in the industry, and at those who had graduated beyond the basics with a thirst to know more.

We also wanted to find a way of addressing what it was like being a games writer early(ish) on in the twenty-first century. But it seemed to us that the way to answer such a big and near-open-ended subject was to approach a large field of fellow writers and listen to what they had to say. Only with a large number of writers with experience stretching not just decades chronologically, but amounting to several hundreds of years collectively, did we feel we could present something that hoped to give some kind of worthwhile answer. Given that many of these writers would be professionally active, we decided we would also offer them the option of anonymity. This idea took shape much as we had planned. We asked over 100 writers this question: *What is it like being a games writer? Please could you tell us something good, and something bad, even just a sentence or two on each. Or—if you only have something good, or only have something bad, that's fine.* We heard back from quite a range of names, and the results, which took several months to arrive and process, are given in Chapter 24.

Our hope is that, having read this book, *the why* of it will make sense, whether you're a games student, a games designer, a curious TV writer, or a hard-nosed professional games writer with a list of war stories as long as your list of credits and a mind still sparkling with inspiration and wonder at how little we have yet mastered of this still new and growing craft we call games writing.

Note on the Second Edition

Entwined as it is with technology's ever rapacious evolution, the world of game development and of game stories continues to move in new, exciting, and often groundbreaking directions. In this Second Edition we've taken the welcome opportunity to reflect some of these directions, the new thinking, and the new games as best we could. In particular we've updated our chapter A Brief History of Game Stories to take us from 2011 to 2016, allowing us to mention the likes of *Borderlands 2, GTA V, Skyrim, The Last of Us, The Stick of Truth, The Shadow of Mordor, Her Story, Life Is Strange,* and *Until Dawn.* With the help of our U.S.-based educational consultant, Brittany Rank, we've also expanded the exercises, discussion points, and projects to be found at the end of most chapters. We hope people will find them even more useful this time around.

Maurice and Marek

About the Authors

Maurice Suckling

Maurice's first game was *Driver,* in 1999. Since then he's worked on over 40 published video games, including *Borderlands: The Pre-Sequel, Mafia III, Civilization* 6, and the *Wii Fit* series. He's worked as a producer, a designer, and a voice director, but most often as a writer. Between 2013 and 2015 he was Narrative Director at 2K Australia. Outside of games he works in TV and fiction, co-writing *Alphablocks* for BBC TV, and publishing a collection of short stories, *Photocopies of Heaven*. He holds a PhD in Creative Writing from Newcastle University, UK. *mauricesuckling.com*

Marek Walton

Marek got his break as a writer on *Driver: Parallel Lines*, in 2004. Since then he's worked on story, script and dialogue on a wide variety of games including *Borderlands: The Pre-Sequel*, *Fable Legends*, and *Wonderbook: Book of Spells.* Marek also voice directs, having worked on titles such as *BioShock 2*, *Sonic and SEGA All-Stars Racing*, and the *Wii Fit* series. He holds a Masters in Creative Writing from Edinburgh University and is currently a senior narrative designer at Crystal Dynamics.

Part I GAMES WRITING IN CONTEXT

How do we know where we're going if we don't know where we've been? Mapping the past can describe a trajectory for the future. So, where have we been? And with what lens should we regard these past endeavors? Game stories are tied to a medium that sees frequent new hardware cycles, which is fantastic news for the present and future, both creatively and commercially. But what about the hardware devices that fall off the other end of this conveyor belt? Countless games, and with them game stories, once deeply loved, are either difficult or impossible to enjoy again as devices become obsolete (though it should be noted that there is a resurgence in some "historic" titles as developers seek to recycle content for portable media that are more than capable of playing *Tales of Monkey Island* and the original *Doom*).

In this sense game stories can be much more transitory than those in other media, only remembered for as long as the players who enjoyed them exist, or for as long as people collect game stories in some of those other media. Even if simulation programs can be found for some of those older games, the historical context can never be recreated. And context, as we all know, is everything.

The history of game stories is one of pushing through contextual limitations—not just in technology, but also limitations in comprehending what we creatively could do and wanted to do with game stories in conjunction with game design, as well as limitations in our comprehension of what players wanted from game stories. The history is worth recalling because these battles were not all lightly won, and even if technology-driven limitations are eroding before us, those other limitations are still a daily feature of the development process. Modern games are not restricted to 32 kilobytes of memory like 1984's *Elite*, but that game still has something to teach us about telling a story within a game design system without cut scenes. Indeed, all the games we look at in the ensuing chapter have something to tell us about overcoming one or more of these limitations and are insights into some form of contextually wrapped comprehension relating to what is truly possible.

Chapter **1**

A Brief History of Game Stories

Thus in the beginning the world was so made that certain signs come before certain events.

— Marcus Tullius Cicero

VIDEO GAMES: DISTRACTING US FOR LONGER THAN YOU MIGHT THINK...

BRIEF TERMS

VIDEO GAME An electronic game, presented on one of a wide variety of technological platforms and in a wide number of genres, requiring the user to interact with it in order to solve problems.

MUDs Acronym for "Multi-User-Dungeons," virtual network worlds in which players can role-play within a text-based environment; precursors to massively multiplayer online role-playing titles such as *Guild Wars™* and *World of Warcraft™*.

GAMEPLAY The specific interaction between a player and the unique rule set of the video game he is playing.

DEVELOPER The term for a company that develops video games.

INTELLECTUAL PROPERTY (IP) Intangible assets owned by an individual or organization, which can include copyrights, trademarks, and patents; this term can refer to video game titles, series, and/or characters.

DEVELOPMENT CYCLE The structure imposed upon the video game creation whereby all in-game and external game elements are created and prepared. Typically, a mainstream video game title development cycle lasts between eighteen months and three years.

PUBLISHER The company that promotes and distributes video game titles on behalf of a developer.

SANDBOX Term given to a game title that allows the player a wide degree of freedom with which they can experience the gameplay and/or solve its content.

NON-PLAYER CHARACTER (NPC) A video game character or creature controlled by the game, rather than a human player.

PLAYER VERSUS ENVIRONMENT (PvE) Referring to the "artificial gameplay environment" in which a player combats problems or creatures presented purely by the game developers.

PLAYER VERSUS PLAYER (PvP) Gameplay in which players compete against one another either individually or in groups to achieve success.

For as long as humans have been able to communicate, we've told each other stories. Stories permeate all aspects of human activity; they teach, inspire, allow us to step into other worlds, and give us a way to try to make sense of our own, so naturally we also find them within video games. In this chapter, we'll look at game stories that have helped define and refine the parameters and levels of excellence and possibility of interactive narrative over the last few decades.

Two key elements have affected the evolution of story in games from their beginnings in the 1970s to more modern iterations: technological advances (in hardware, software, and networking) and the continuing development of the games writers' craft. Although the two are inextricably linked—technology has opened up and continues to open up possibilities for the writer's craft—the second factor can't be understated in its own right. Games writing is, when compared to other storytelling areas, a young craft that can force its trailblazers to work under often unforgiving and frequently shifting limitations. In Figure 1.2, fellow games writer Neil Richards sums up this challenge.

FIGURE 1.2. The challenge POSED BY GAME STORIES

Regardless of how many titles a games writer has worked on, when approaching a new project, hopefully near its inception, they must always devote a meaningful amount of time to exploring not only what should be written for the story but *how* it can be written into the gameplay. While it's wise to apply appropriate principles and lessons learned from experience, no two titles—even if they're sequels—are likely to have precisely the same requirements and limitations embedded within them. Every job a game writer works on is its own entity. This point highlights the core issue here: our craft has evolved, and will continue to evolve, primarily through the evolution of our understanding of it, not the power of the technology available to us. This is illustrated by the number of contemporary titles that, although boasting excellent games design, impressive graphics, and superb audio, still fail to make a meaningful impact with their story. Linked to this, how many twentieth-century games titles boast stories that remain fondly lodged in the hearts of those players fortunate enough to have experienced them? Technology assists good games writing but is never a substitution for it.

The titles discussed in this chapter all found a way to accommodate the particular limitations of their time and, we believe, helped change the landscape of stories within games in one of two ways: either as trailblazers—groundbreaking games that pushed story in new directions—or shining examples of what can be done with the right combination of skill, talent, technology, time, and budget. While not being evolutionary titles, this second category features games that have, nevertheless, proven themselves to be influential to subsequent practitioners. These games have overcome the inherent difficulties in combining stories within games—a problem that is always present no matter where technology leads; it simply gets recast.

Our list contains titles some might feel don't deserve recognition and has omissions others may feel are unjustifiable; this is inevitable in the highly subjective worlds of story and list-making. It's important to stress that we've chosen titles we believe to aptly illustrate something of value in the universe of game story. It's not our contention that all games we fail to list are distinctly inferior to those we have; we simply had to restrict ourselves to a limited number of choices.

Also note that we've focused on the rise and evolution of game story in the Western market; while this doesn't mean we totally exclude Eastern titles, they're only included if they've impacted the Western gamer in a meaningful way.

GAME STORY: THE 1950s, 1960s, AND 1970s

Major Hardware Developments

- Digital Entertainment Corporation PDP-1 (1960)
- Atari® 2600™ released (1977)

The first computers were huge and imposing slabs of hardware that—to most—were perceived as extremely serious tools for use on extremely serious projects. These technological titans were devised for useful and important computational tasks such as code-breaking and data analysis, not entertainment. While computational creations that could arguably be termed "games" did briefly flicker on the early computing scene, they were small in number and attracted limited attention. Perhaps the most famous game during this period was the NIMROD token-based computer game, *Nim*, exhibited at the 1951 Exhibition of Science in London. Two decades later, early computer game creators usually plied their illicit craft under the radars of the powers that be who judiciously hunted down any programs seen as a waste of time and, more importantly, extremely limited computer memory storage. We will never know what brave, early game stories were potentially deleted by these computational caretakers who unwittingly erased what would have become fascinating digital fossils of gaming history. But thankfully, this attitude changed.

One of the first ever graphical video games was created by students, Steve Russell, Martin Graetz, and Wayne Witaenem, in 1962; enthusiastically titled *Spacewar!* it pitted two player-controlled spaceships against one another in a battle to the death, each equipped with limited fuel and missiles, both trying to avoid being pulled into the gravity of a nearby dwarf star. Written on a DEC PDP-1, *Spacewar!* is a purely arcade experience with no story (beyond the framing just outlined) and no characters but is noteworthy for helping to shift attitudes. Its popularity among DEC PDP-1 users helped seed the idea that video games could be seriously fun and more than mere oddities created to illustrate computational power. *Spacewar!* also featured the first ever realistic game universe after programmer Peter Samson created a star display for the game called *Expensive Planetarium* (an apt name as a DEC PDP-1 in 1962 cost $120,000), which accurately emulated a portion of the night sky to be used as a backdrop for gameplay.

While *Spacewar!* opened the door for later games development, the massive cost and limited technology helped hold back any real progress for over a decade. Then, in 1974, Gary Gygax and Dave Arneson created the first commercially available tabletop Role Playing Game (RPG). *Dungeons & Dragons™ (D&D)* was inspired by modern fantasy fiction and allowed players to enter fantastical, imaginary worlds created by dungeon masters who acted as hybrid storyteller/referees. Players would take part in exciting adventures, their actions guided by the story and governed by detailed rule books and random dice rolls. Soon, legions of enthusiasts spent their evenings gathered around tables crowded with maps, tiny characters, and dice, hungry to experience new worlds, the color and vitality of which were predominantly held within their own imaginations. And while *D&D* was a purely lo-tech experience, it helped ignite the imaginations of a new breed of programmer who saw how easily the rule-driven tabletop gaming universe could make the transition to the rule-driven digital universe.

Created in 1975 on the PLATO computer system by the visionary Rusty Rutherford, *Pedit5* was a simple dungeon exploration game. Named after a bland file repository in an ultimately unsuccessful attempt to hide its presence from the university powers that be, *Pedit5* allowed players to experience the bare bones of fantasy role-playing on a computer. Once they had created a character defined by attributes similar to those found in *D&D*, they were free to explore a single-level dungeon, killing monsters, finding treasure, and saving their characters for later sessions. This was all managed on a mainframe terminal only capable of generating a simple interface with minimal graphics. Before it was discovered and unceremoniously deleted, *Pedit5* became extremely popular with the PLATO community. Beyond the allocation of randomized monsters and treasure to a set character, there was no core story to explain events; players made their own stories simply by playing. Despite its unfortunate demise, *Pedit5* helped inspire further, more sophisticated Computer Role Playing Games (CRPGs), which would eventually evolve to form one of the most popular modern video game genres.

The following year further proof that CRPGs were heavily influenced by their pen and paper RPG counterparts came in the form of *dnd*. Created by Gary Whisenhunt and Ray Wood, also for the PLATO system, *dnd* was a dungeon crawler that challenged players to enter the deadly Whisenwood Dungeon in search of treasure and powerful relics. Like *Pedit5*, it mimicked many of the features of *D&D* and, despite being run on technology considered crude by contemporary standards, sported a basic text and graphics interface; however, what makes *dnd* particularly noteworthy was that it also included a final boss for players to find and defeat in the form of the mighty Golden Dragon. This small story-based tweak provided a subtle, but vital, focus to events. Players suddenly had a tangible goal to reach that—once overcome—gave them license to proclaim they'd "beaten" the game. Until then, the few games that had emerged were, in effect, endless—they invariably finished with the player hoping at best to achieve a high score. The boss battle was born.

Also created in 1975, *Colossal Cave Adventure* was the first ever computer adventure game. Written by caving enthusiast Will Crowther as something he could play with his two young daughters, it faithfully recreated sections of the Mammoth Cave system in Kentucky. Using a fully text-based interface that bypassed the need for graphics and crafted the world with words, *Colossal Cave Adventure* is a game in which the aim isn't to build up character statistics and plunder dungeons, but, instead, solve puzzles and overcome obstacles. This is achieved through the judicious use of objects and knowledge gained from playing the game. While crude by modern standards, it paved the way for several variants based on the same game (most simply called *Adventure*), as well as opening up a new genre to be explored. *Colossal Cave Adventure* also provided players with a basic three-act structure that serves to enhance the story: in the initial prologue section they experience the above-ground world before descending into the confining cave-based world for most of the game and then moving to a climactic confrontation in the final act. However, while groundbreaking with its presence, *Colossal Cave Adventure*'s prose was utilitarian. Two years later a new title appeared to carry forward the story torch.

A direct descendent of *Colossal Cave Adventure*, *Zork*™ was written by Tim Anderson, Marc Blank, Bruce Daniels, and Dave Lebling between 1977 and 1979, before being released in 1980. Another dungeon crawler, *Zork* is noteworthy in part because it was a text-based title that featured a higher standard of writing—players explored a world that was more finely crafted than its enthusiastic, but more basic, predecessors. *Zork* was also revolutionary because it let players type commands that went beyond the simple verb-noun systems seen up to that point (*get lamp*, *hit orc*, etc.). Players were able to use more complex commands that included prepositions (*put sword on table*, *hit orc with magic axe*, etc.). Thanks to *Zork's* enhanced interactivity, players were suddenly able to interact with the game world in a more realistic, deeper, and intuitive manner, which served to enhance the story experience.

Interestingly, due to computer memory restraints, when *Zork* was eventually released commercially in the 1980s, it was split into three parts, giving the youthful world of computer games its first episodic title. But while it was a more sophisticated game, *Zork* still presented players with a world in which they were the only living, sentient creatures. This limitation was about to be addressed.

In 1978, British university student Roy Trubshaw, inspired by both *Colossal Cave Adventure* and *Zork*, as well as the increasingly popular *Dungeons & Dragons* tabletop RPG, created the first computer Multi-User Dungeon (MUD) and therefore the first ever virtual world. These real-time environments allowed people to interact with one another online using a text-based interface, and as with earlier titles, places, objects, non-player characters, and other players were all described rather than seen. The aim of the first game variant was to obtain sufficient points to acquire the esteemed rank of "wizard," which in turn granted the player special powers over the virtual environment. The game world's designers had, in a single stroke, created a universe that, while free enough to allow real players to interact with one another in a virtually infinite number of ways, still provided a focus to the gameplay though the inclusion of a simple, compelling goal—all this using the limited technology and networking bandwidth available at the time.

Soon other MUD environments were being created by those with the necessary skills. Upon completing his degree, Trubshaw passed care of his MUD to fellow student Richard Bartle, who added new locations and puzzles that helped garner the revolutionary game a wider audience. Over the following years, official MUDs became big business and paved the way for online gaming, especially Massively Multiplayer Online Role Playing Games (MMORPG, often shortened simply to MMO) behemoths such as *EverQuest*® and *World of Warcraft*.

Computer games and computer game stories took their first meaningful steps forward in the 1970s despite most relying on text and even the more sophisticated offerings providing only the most basic of graphics. While it's tempting to look back at the early days of video games and video game stories as "quaint," it should be noted that these worlds formed of words and crude graphics evoked real emotional responses from players who had never before experienced interactive narrative. As computers and networks increased in power, text would soon give way to increasingly sophisticated graphics but, for the time being, game stories enjoyed a more literary feel in which to "see" and "hear" and "smell" their virtual surroundings players had to exercise their imaginations. Over the decades this need would diminish, gradually eroded by Moore's Law (which states that the number of transistors that can be cheaply placed onto an integrated circuit will double roughly every two years, thereby continually increasing the amount of raw computational power available) and game makers eager to push the youthful medium forward into new territories.

But, while giving birth to video game story, the 1970s couldn't provide the kind of technology that would let it grow beyond the realm of hardcore programmers with access to serious computers. The rise of the home computer, and with it the bedroom programmer, changed all that. Suddenly games could be written by anyone with the patience to learn a computer language on systems that, only a few years before, had been beyond the reach of the average person's wallet. The heady and experimental decade of the bedroom coder coupled with the rise of the video game arcade gave birth to several classic story-based titles and helped cement the presence of video games as a part of the digital landscape.

GAME STORY: THE 1980s

Major Hardware Developments

- Intellivision™ (1980)
- VIC-20™ released (1980)
- BBC Micro™ released (1981)
- Atari 5200™ released (1982)
- Commodore 64™ released (1982)
- Sinclair ZX Spectrum™ released (1982)
- IBM PCjr™ released (1984)
- Nintendo Entertainment System™ released (1985)
- Commodore Amiga™ released (1985)
- Atari 520ST™ released (1985)
- SEGA Genesis™ released (1989)

Released in 1980, arcade hit *Pac Man*®, while being a purely gameplay-driven experience, created the game world's first ever iconic character. Originally called *Puck Man*, his name was quickly changed when Namco realized how easy it would be to "edit" arcade machine logos to something a lot less family-friendly. Gameplay was simple to pick up but hard to master—players guided the circular, yellow Pac Man around a maze, gobbling dots and avoiding the four ghosts out to capture him. Interestingly, the differently colored pursuers had their own names (Blinky, Pinky, Inky, and Clyde) and subtly different pathing instructions (i.e., code that dictated their movement patterns) that not only enhanced gameplay but lent the illusion of their possessing differing personalities. Pac Man's massive popularity still endures today and showed video game developers (and marketers) just how capable games were of capturing the public's imagination when addictive gameplay is married with a memorable character. Suddenly video game characters were big business, opening the door for the likes of Mario and Link.

While Pac Man ate his way into the global consciousness, CRPGs continued to evolve. Inspired by these and adventure games, a young man named Richard

Garriot wrote *Ultima 1: The First Age of Darkness*™. It features a simple story in which players take on the mantle of The Stranger, tasked with destroying the Gem of Immortality and defeating the evil wizard, Mondain. While Garriot, by his own admission, is not the world's most gifted writer, what made *Ultima 1* special was that it presented the player with different graphical worldviews that, for the first time, used different colors. Traveling between towns and cities presents players with a top-down view that allows them to see their character as they navigate the world and encounter obstacles along the way, but entering a dungeon shifts the player's perspective into an isometric, first-person view, which serves to provide a more immersive environment. Garriot pushed the boundaries of what had been done before, giving the fledgling gamer community a new, more varied CRPG that took the marriage of game design and game story a step further.

Published by California Pacific Computer Company, *Ultima 1* was one of the first CRPG titles to be commercially marketed and sold with the aim of making a profit. Until then, story-driven games titles had been created by gifted hobbyists eager to flex their creative muscles and test the boundaries of what was possible on new technology. Such was the atmosphere of friendly exploration; it was common for one programmer to take another's game and re-code it for their purposes to see if they could improve upon the design (often with the other's blessing). This level of cooperation between developers is unthinkable in today's fiercely competitive games market.

As video games became increasingly popular, it was natural that forward-thinking marketers would seek ways to tie in potent intellectual property (IP) from other media to provide further revenue streams. In 1982, one of the first movies to make the jump from the big screen to the video game console was Steven Spielberg's *E.T. the Extra-Terrestrial.* Purchasing the video game rights for a cool $25 million, a young video game company, Atari, gave the task of creating the title to Howard Scott Warshaw. Despite the movie being well-received, the game was a huge failure. Warshaw created a story and gameplay that revolved around the player guiding E.T. through environments in a quest to piece together the technology necessary to "phone home" and be rescued, while avoiding capture by the authorities and staying alive. The core goal (phone home) and obstacles (avoid the authorities) did fit with the movie's story, but the game was panned by critics for featuring poor graphics and crude gameplay. The extremely short development cycle, which lasted only six weeks, played a major role in ensuring the game didn't match the quality of the movie. While Atari's *E.T. the Extra-Terrestrial* did manage to sell 1.5 million units over the 1982 Christmas period, massive production costs coupled with millions of excess unsold games cartridges meant Atari suffered huge losses that helped contribute to its downfall and eventual breakup in 1984. *E.T. the Extra-Terrestrial* is often listed as one of the worst games of all-time and thought to have contributed to the destabilization of what had, up until that point, been seen as a fairly stable market. This incident illustrates how talent, opportunity, and a strong, universally popular IP are not sufficient to create a successful story-driven game. Time, thought, and careful design planning must also be present.

While the importance and use of story in games was becoming more widely appreciated, a small development team in the United Kingdom was writing a title that would let players loose in a universe where they were free to create their own stories. In 1984, before the term *sandbox gaming* was coined, space trading arcade game *Elite* let players travel where they wanted and do whatever they liked within a wide set of parameters. This amazing sense of freedom was granted by a game that, in some incarnations, only took up 32 kilobytes of memory. Written originally for the BBC Micro by David Braben and Ian Bell, players started life with a basic Cobra Mark III spaceship, 100 credits, and a cuddly "Harmless" rating. They could then choose to spend their time trading peacefully, traveling between planets, amassing huge profits, and upgrading their ship with a variety of weapons, defenses, and other technology. At the other end of the spectrum, they could become space pirates, preying on traders and anyone unfortunate enough to cross their path. Any choice came with consequences: trade peacefully and risk being attacked by pirates, become a pirate and run the risk of being attacked by law enforcement ships. At a time when game stories typically contained players with walls, roads, or both, *Elite* let players find their own way. While no story was woven into the gameplay, the game universe allowed players to create their own tale, and many chose to try and attain the lofty rank of "Elite" pilot, which took time and dedication. Interestingly, copies of the game came with a mini novella, *The Dark Wheel* by Robert Holdstock, which served to both deepen the universe and provide readers with a primer on the game, neatly sidestepping the tight hardware constraints that prevented more content from being present within the title itself. *Elite* was eventually released on a variety of other platforms including the Acorn Electron, Commodore 64, ZX Spectrum 48K, Atari ST, and Amiga.

That same year the potency of more linear stories would evolve further in Sierra Online's adventure game, *King's Quest*™. Initially released on the IBM PCjr, players took on the role of Sir Graham, a knight tasked by the king to save the land by acquiring three lost treasures. Written and designed by Roberta Williams, the world of Daventry was presented using color graphics that could be interacted with through a combination of text, input, and movement commands. Players could walk up to a rock and, should they choose to, push it aside to reveal a hidden dagger. This form of graphics-based "live" cause-effect interactivity was a new tool that helped immerse players in a world more immediate and visual than any adventure game that had come before. *King's Quest* was a huge success for the fledgling developer, who went on to release the title on a variety of platforms and create several popular sequels.

Until this point, game story in the West had been driven by developers based in the West, but this was soon to change as Eastern developers became more prevalent. Japanese video game developer Nintendo® entered the world of the console action-adventure game with the well-received *Legend of Zelda*™ in 1986 (released a year later in the West). Shigeru Miyamoto and Takashi Tezuka gave the games world one of its iconic characters in the form of boy-hero, Link. Combining action, exploration, and puzzle-solving, *Legend of Zelda's* story involved helping Link piece together the eight fragments of the Triforce of Wisdom. The top-down viewpoint and fast-paced action were inspired by older RPG games but featured a more evolved world, improved graphics, and the freedom to explore. The game cartridge also shipped with an internal battery, which enabled games to be saved. This simple addition gave console game makers the freedom to make the story far more expansive—in the past, console titles couldn't provide the save system computer games had routinely provided its gamers with as far back as the 1970s for titles like *dnd*. Suddenly, when the console's power was switched off, the world remained frozen, not reset. This enhancement was a huge step forward for story-based console games.

Nintendo wasn't the only Japanese developer working hard to release quality story-based console titles. One of the most influential early console RPGs came in the form of *Dragon Warrior*™, developed by Chunsoft and originally published in 1986 by the publisher that would eventually become Square Enix®. A year later it was released in the United States to not only give many gamers their first taste of a Japanese RPG (JRPG) but also pave the way for one of the most successful games franchises of all time. Also featuring a top-down interface, players guide their hero on a quest to rescue kidnapped Princess Gwaelin before defeating the evil Dragonlord. Combat is turn-based and requires that players use strategy rather than reflexes to defeat opponents. *Dragon Quest* (renamed *Dragon Warrior* in the West until 1994 to avoid trademark conflict with tabletop RPG *DragonQuest*™) helped set the tone for many fantasy console RPGs that followed. While crude by modern standards, both the game and story design of *Dragon Quest* are still mimicked by more recent titles.

Japan appeared to be on a roll that wasn't about to stop; Square Enix, not content with creating one successful console-based JRPG, gave birth to another the following year. Developed to provide RPG players with a deeper storyline and more involving gameplay, Hironobu Sakaguchi's *Final Fantasy*™ won a legion of fans when released in 1987. Another top-down JRPG, *Final Fantasy* was initially released on the Nintendo Entertainment System and follows the adventures of four Light Warriors on a quest to rekindle their elemental orbs and save the world from evil. Here was a compelling RPG created not for a home computer (which, naturally, all come with a keyboard) but a console. Featuring a deeper and far longer story experience, players traveled a land filled with random encounters, turn-based combat, and the ability to modify their characters.

The first *Final Fantasy* game was written while Square Enix were on the brink of bankruptcy (hence Sakaguchi's grimly humorous use of "Final" in the title, which today, given the dizzying number of "sequels," has shifted to being ironic), but its critical and commercial success helped save the company. Each features a long, some would argue, indulgent, story in which a group of characters are drawn together and journey across a fantasy land in a bid to end a great evil. While not to everyone's taste, no one can deny these tales have a depth that works hard to make the writing core to the experience. Today, the *Final Fantasy* franchise is one of the most successful in the gaming world, boasting numerous sequels on almost every gaming platform, as well as numerous forms of spin-off merchandise, and critics have hailed Square Enix's games as pushing the boundaries of storytelling, graphics, and audio.

While Japan was creating exemplary story-based games that often took place using a top-down camera or third-person perspective, a revolutionary game was being written that would plunge players into a more immersive (and frightening) first-person story world than ever seen before. Released in 1987, *Dungeon Master*™ was a CRPG created by FTL Games initially for the Atari ST before later being ported to the Commodore Amiga. It has players choose four party members from a pre-set roster before they enter a dungeon in search of treasure. It was the world's first ever fully 3D real-time action RPG, and it arguably provided players with a more immersive story experience than anything that had come before. While basic 3D had been used before in games, for example by Richard Garriot's *Ultima*, *Dungeon Master* took the visual experience to the next level, shifting the action so it takes place in the first-person and forcing players to empathize more with their unseen avatars. The use of subtle ambient audio capable of letting players hear when creatures were close, coupled with an early form of dynamic lighting, further enhanced the experience. While the game story was minimalistic in its approach (challenging players to heed the call of the Firestaff and face the challenges set out for them by the legendary Dungeon Master) like *Elite* three years earlier, the game came with a short story to help lend players a feeling of place in the games world, again bypassing the limits laid out by technology.

The 1980s saw game story beginning to be used in new and potent ways. While technology in the 1970s had been embryonic, increasingly powerful computers and consoles gave developers the ability to render more realistic story worlds for players to experience. If the 1970s had seen the sparks of game story, it was the 1980s that saw some fires lit. Towards the end of the decade, it was arguably the Japanese developers who were showing the West just what could be done with story-driven games, but Western developers weren't far behind.

GAME STORY: THE 1990s

Major Hardware Developments

- Super Nintendo Entertainment System™ released (1991)
- Sony® PlayStation™ released (1994)
- Nintendo® 64™ released (1996)
- SEGA® Dreamcast™ released (1997)

Released in 1990, *The Secret of Monkey Island*™ was a seminal "point and click" adventure game created by Lucasfilm Games (now called LucasArts®) for the PC. It follows the adventures of hapless wannabe Guybrush Threepwood as he tries to prove he's got what it takes to be a pirate. While it wasn't Lucasfilm's first adventure game (they created three others between 1986 and 1989) it was their first real commercial success and served to illustrate how a compelling story can give a game a unique sense of identity and character. Still seen as one of the greatest adventure games of all time, its fusion of intuitive gameplay, engrossing non-linear story, and a well-written, witty script ensure its place in gaming's hall of fame. Part of the title's novelty lay in the fact that it was designed to empower the player by often allowing him to tackle challenges in a flexible order, and *The Secret of Monkey Island* remains a beacon of good writing that helped cement LucasArts' position as a quality games studio. While its graphics are basic, they are colorful, fun, and present a world as humorous as it is imaginative, making excellent use of the computational power available at the time. Over subsequent years they continued to push the boundaries of adventure game story, releasing a string of well-received titles including *Secret of Monkey Island 2: LeChuck's Revenge*™ (1991), *Sam & Max Hit the Road* (1993), and *Grim Fandango* (1998). Charles Cecil's classic *Broken Sword*® series of adventure games (beginning with *Broken Sword: The Shadow of the Templars*™ in 1996), which follow the exploits of the resourceful George Stobbart, also deserves an honorable mention here.

The graphical bar was constantly being raised as technology improved, though players were still used to seeing cartoon-like representations of game story universes—but this was about to change. Released in 1993, first-person graphic adventure game *Myst* was written by Robyn and Rand Miller originally for the Macintosh PC (though it would later be ported to other platforms). *Myst* puts players in the shoes of The Stranger (unrelated to Richard Garriot's character of the same name, we assume) who is transported to a surreal world after having read the last page of a mysterious book. There, they are challenged to solve a variety of cryptic puzzles, each granting access to hidden pages that in turn help The Stranger communicate with two brothers, themselves both trapped in separate books, each warning of the other's duplicity. While *Myst* does have an interesting story that challenges players to both explore and deduce with a minimum of hand-holding, it was the game's graphics and audio that made it stand out. While most adventure games of the time—notably those created by LucasArts—wisely chose to introduce the player to worlds best described as cartoon-like, *Myst* presented them with a game that comes close to photorealistic. While the worlds are essentially rendered as a series of interconnected stills, each containing interactive elements and, where useful, atmospheric audio, skillful visual blending was sufficient to allow players to lose themselves in a series of unlockable story-based environments. The creators of *Myst* sidestepped the contemporary difficulties of rendering people and animals in any way that came close to realistic, choosing instead to present worlds which, while devoid of life, were beautiful to behold and rich with mystery. *Myst* was a significant step forward for video game storytelling as it gave the world a taste of the visual future and the emotional possibilities that lay ahead.

Released a year later, in 1994, *System Shock*™ was a first-person action adventure game created by Looking Glass Studios for the PC and Macintosh. Set in the year 2072, it puts the player in control of a nameless hacker destined to battle with rampant Artificial Intelligence, SHODAN. While the visually stunning *Myst* gives players a series of beautifully rendered worlds to explore, it is still limited to representing them as essentially a series of static slides. *System Shock*, while more basic graphically, presents the player with fully 3D environments through which to move in a continuous, analog fashion. Praised for its immersive world, compelling story, and excellent antagonist, *System Shock* (and its sequel, *System Shock 2*™) influenced future games, including *BioShock*™, and helped illustrate the power of game engines that permit movement in three dimensions.

The 3D baton was about to be picked up by someone destined to become one of the games world's most recognizable characters. Released in 1996, *Tomb Raider*™ is a third-person action adventure game by developers Core Design, initially solely for the Sony PlayStation. It follows the adventures of the aristocratic (and acrobatic) Lara Croft as she travels the globe in search of rare, ancient treasures. A mixture of puzzle-solving, platforming, and combat, *Tomb Raider* gets a lot of things very right. While the game features intuitive gameplay and a story that leads players through a variety of exotic locations, it is its striking protagonist who really shines; strong, driven, and sexy, Croft captured the imaginations of gamers and critics alike, who quickly elevated her to an iconic status. Sparking several sequels and a wide range of media products, including two films, *Tomb Raider* morphed from a single game into a brand. Lara Croft was—and remains—an icon hailed by some as a strong, independent woman who goes against the traditional "blonde bimbo" trend gaming is accused of favoring, but derided by others as blatantly designed to appeal to men and boys alike. Regardless, there's no doubt the *Tomb Raider* franchise, despite having created the occasionally poorly received title, remains a potent brand that in recent years has undergone a successful reboot.

Another major franchise that first surfaced in the same year, *Resident Evil*™ was also destined to spin off multiple video game sequels, films, novels, and other assorted merchandise. One of the first ever third-person survival horror games, created by Japanese developer Capcom® for the Sony PlayStation, players follow the adventures of Chris Redfield and Jill Valentine, members of Racoon City's elite Special Tactics and Rescue Service (STARS) outfit. Sent to investigate a series of murders, they uncover corporate corruption on a massive scale and a city overwhelmed by the undead. Despite featuring somewhat stiff dialogue and voice acting, *Resident Evil*'s use of fear and tension helped draw players into one of gaming's more terrifying story worlds of the time, evoking genuine fear in those not expecting to see undead dogs burst through a boarded up window or giant spiders swarm towards them down a grimy, dimly-lit corridor. *Resident Evil*'s emergence was further proof games had gained sufficient visual fidelity to evoke genuine fear through action. To help do this, Capcom wisely chose to present their world as a series of fixed-camera, faux 3D scenes, in which characters and creatures could move freely. These scenes, presented as stills, meant not only that the world could look more realistic, but that the majority of the PlayStation's limited processing power could be spent on both moving and movable elements.

Until then, online gaming universes had remained fairly niche affairs with few players able to access them or even that willing to experience worlds that were—when compared to offline games—visually very basic. The evolution of technology would once again help provide the impetus for games to evolve. Richard Garriot's *Ultima Online*™ was released in 1997 and, while not the first ever modern MMO, it was the first to achieve a meaningful measure of mainstream popularity. Created by Origin Systems® for the PC, it allowed players to adventure in a 2D fantasy world which, at the height of its popularity in 2003, boasted 250,000 paying subscribers. Although its roots lay in text-based MUDs and older, offline *Ultima* titles, *Ultima Online*® was a leap forward graphically for network games; players were free to interact and choose to experience their own stories in an environment that wasn't merely described in words or represented with blocky graphics. Richard Garriot's title helped pave the way for later MMO offerings including the hugely popular *EverQuest Online* and *World of Warcraft*, which are both discussed later.

Released in 1997, *Final Fantasy VII*™—the seventh game in the series of the same name discussed earlier—was the first of Square Enix's blockbuster titles to be officially released in Europe, underlining the growing fan base for Japanese RPGs in the West. Despite initially being destined for Nintendo's N64® console, cartridge storage limitations caused the developers to release it on Sony's more capacious CD-ROM-based PlayStation console instead. It follows the adventures of protagonist Cloud Strife as he battles an evil mega-corporation with the help of his friends. Lauded for its engaging characters and deep storyline, *Final Fantasy VII* was the first in the series to use 3D graphics, which served to make the world feel more realistic, the story more immersive, and the gameplay more compelling than any of the previous titles. *Final Fantasy VII* remains a revered title among gamers, some of who still feel it represents the pinnacle of the series.

While story was evolving in a variety of genres, the first-person shooter (FPS) had, until this point, remained a primarily action-driven experience normally providing players with the minimum amount of story necessary before setting them loose on worlds begging to be obliterated. Players of developer Id's hugely popular *Doom*®, released in 1993, know only that they're a marine trapped in a space base, fighting an army of demons in a bid to escape. This simple motive is sufficient to give a clear sense of what they are doing in the game and why but does little to motivate proceedings. It was 1998's seminal *Half-Life*™ from Valve™ that showed PC gamers the real power a well-crafted story has to drive FPS gameplay. Its masterful, highly cinematic opening scene turns players into passengers, able only to observe the various events inside the top secret Black Mesa research facility as they journey along a monorail, listening to the monotonous spiel of the computerized induction. Each scene which unfolds in the distance hints at gameplay to come—a helicopter landing, a robot moving crates around a radioactive bay, soldiers running in formation. Despite the player being rendered somewhat impotent, Valve still allows them to move around the carriage and choose what they watch before it slides inexorably from view. This use of foreshadowing, while commonly found in movies, had not been used in an FPS until *Half-Life*. It's also a superb example of early environmental storytelling in which the very world helps weave the tale being told, moving it beyond being just graphical window dressing. The remainder of the game's opening section has players experience a relatively normal working day for silent protagonist Gordon Freeman, before an accident tears the fabric of reality and causes all manner of problems. Seeing the hero's "normal world" is a standard story tool, as it serves to highlight the very "otherness" of the journey they're forced to eventually undertake and makes it easier to see the changes the character will undergo, but until this point, it had not been seen in video games.

While Valve chose to provide players with a fully immersive story experience that never pulls them from the gameplay universe to watch a story cut scene, another series was about to arrive that would provide offerings hailed by some as featuring groundbreaking stories and criticized by others as touting glorified films. Video games had become big business; budgets continued to swell and the world began to see titles with stories branding themselves "cinematic." Released in 1998, *Metal Gear Solid*® is a third-person stealth shooter created by Konami's Hideo Kojima for the Sony PlayStation. Not the first in the series (this was *Metal Gear*® for the MSX2 home computer in 1987), it follows the adventures of retired soldier, Solid Snake, as he infiltrates a compound captured by terrorist organization FOXHOUND. The intense stealth-based gameplay is interspersed with long cut scenes that serve to weave a story some love and others feel is overly long to the point of indulgence—and then just keeps on going. The *Metal Gear* series, thought to have popularized the stealth genre, is a divisive one; many feel Kojima and his team sacrifice too much time delivering gameplay-disrupting cut scenes and conversations that turn the player into a viewer. It's worth noting the series continues to sustain a large and loyal fan base who appear to enjoy its opulent story-based nature. Regardless, no one can deny *Metal Gear Solid*'s story (and those told in sequels) has made a meaningful impact on the gaming universe—if nothing else because they help drive the debate on just what makes good game story, and whether there's room for both games that feature stories and those that feel, to some, like interactive movies.

Gamers continued to value deep, epic narratives, which helped encourage developers to deliver titles that pushed game story boundaries. *Legend of Zelda*™: *Ocarina of Time*™, released in 1998, was a seminal action-adventure game by Nintendo EAD® for the Nintendo 64. It again follows the adventures of Link as he travels the land of Hyrule on a quest to stop evil King Ganondorf from gaining possession of the wish-granting Triforce relic. The game took the series to a new level of presentation, introducing 3D graphics, context-sensitive actions, and a lock-on targeting system, all of which, when combined with an epic storyline, helped provide players with one of the most intuitive and memorable game story experiences to date. Released on the largest cartridge Nintendo could muster at the time (a capacious 32 megabytes), *Legend of Zelda: Ocarina of Time*'s design team managed to create a fresh experience for fans of the series, both visually and from a control perspective, which did not distract or detract from the game story. The title has achieved almost legendary status as one of the best, most polished stories ever told in the games universe and was re-released on the Nintendo 3DS™ in 2011.

Meanwhile, technology's continuing evolution gave players access to faster network connections, improved graphics, more memory, quicker processors, and better audio that helped enable the creation of more advanced MMOs. Released in 1999, *EverQuest* (known simply as *EQ* to many) drew in a fresh MMO audience, attracted to its more refined, story-driven experience. Suddenly players could interact with one another in a 3D world, rather than one that was text-based or 2D, which proved alluring. Created by Sony Online Entertainment®, players enter the fantasy world of Norrath, leveling characters through a mix of questing, dungeon exploration, and Player versus Player combat (PvP). Where *Ultima Online*® peaked at 250,000 subscribers, Sony figures state that in 2003 they had over 430,000 paying *EverQuest* players. Such popularity came at a price though, as some gamers found the lure of existence in a virtual story world difficult to resist. They began to spend the majority of their time on a game which is, in essence, designed to be endless. This "addiction" was, and still is, the subject of heated debates among a variety of groups not just concerned with *EverQuest*, but a number of subsequent MMOs and other video game genres.

Subtle, horror-based storytelling had, until this point, not been accomplished in a mass-market game. Released in 1999, *Silent Hill* is a refreshing take on a survival horror title created by Konami's Team Silent for the Sony PlayStation. It follows the adventures of Harry Mason as he searches the rural town of Silent Hill for his missing daughter, uncovering a terrible conspiracy along the way. It was inevitably compared to Capcom's *Resident Evil* horror franchise, though it uses different devices to induce fear in players. Team Silent's main protagonist is a "normal, everyday man," inexperienced with guns and ill at ease in combat situations. This simple but important story and design decision hugely increases the tension felt while exploring Silent Hill, a place as full of quiet, brooding darkness as explosive, often supernatural, violence. This is in sharp contrast to

Resident Evil, which empowers its players by placing them in a military unit, supremely at home with all kinds of combat hardware; pistols, rifles, and even rocket launchers can be unleashed against undead creatures, making Capcom's story world a more action-oriented, less suspense-based offering that pushes story in a different, arguably less subtle direction.

While MMOs were growing in popularity, allowing players to adventure in relatively open worlds online, a revolutionary offline console title was about to be released that offered a similar, yet single player-focused experience. Arriving in 1999, *Shenmue*® is an open-world (or "sandbox") adventure game created by SEGA for the Dreamcast console. It follows the adventures of Ryo Hazuki, a young man on a quest to unravel the mystery surrounding his father's murder. From a storytelling perspective, *Shenmue* was ahead of its time and a hugely ambitious undertaking, the finished game being said to have cost over $70,000,000 to make. *Shenmue* allows the player considerable freedom as they explore the Japanese city of Yokosuka; Yu Suzuki, the game's director and producer, created a detailed, living world that allows players to ignore the core storyline if they so choose. Cinematic in the extreme, *Shenmue* is a superb example of a sandbox story universe both simple enough to be played by a child and deep enough to satisfy an adult gamer curious to uncover the rich backstory.

By the end of the decade games had become a huge, evolving market, with budgets sometimes stretching to millions of dollars. While this meant developers faced growing competition, with increasing amounts of money at stake, game story had proven its value in helping drive gameplay and the future looked bright for this newest of mediums.

GAME STORY: 2000–2005

Major Hardware Developments

- Sony PlayStation 2™ released (2000)
- Microsoft Xbox™ released (2001)
- Nintendo GameCube™ released (2001)
- Nintendo DS™ released (2004)
- Sony PlayStation Portable™ (PSP) released (2004)
- Microsoft Xbox 360™ released (2005)

First released in 2000, *The Sims*™ is a life-simulation game by games industry legend Will Wright, whose previous work also includes *Sim City*™. Developed initially for the PC but later ported to other platforms, it places the player in the role of a digital god empowered to create and influence virtual people known as "Sims" as they go about their virtual lives and pursue their virtual dreams. What makes *The Sims* special is that the story is driven purely by the actions of the Sims who populate a world made unique by the player's decisions. The freeform nature of the story, combined with its breadth of appeal to gamers of all kinds, not just those who like their titles driven by twitch-based mechanics or only set in fantasy or science fiction worlds, has helped make *The Sims* into the world's best-selling video game to date.

While Wright's popular offering is as much "god game" as "life simulator," UK-based Lionhead Studios® offered the world a novel take on the former in 2001 with *Black & White*™ for the PC. The title has players take on the role of a newly formed god who must defeat a rival, evil god, Nemesis. They achieve this by gaining worshippers and rearing special totem creatures that can be trained to carry out tasks on behalf of the player. While *Black & White*'s core story is basic, it bravely explores the concept of morality and, in doing so, actively encourages the player to express himself within the liberal framework provided. Should they be a kind and benevolent god, their villages and worshippers will eventually reflect this in white, glowing temples and a happy, content population. Players who choose a darker path will find their people terrified and temples more shadowy, frightening places. The game's creator, Peter Molyneux, would later further explore the theme of morality and choice in the fantasy adventure game *Fable*™ (mentioned later in this chapter), and morality would become an increasingly explored topic for story-based games, which critics claim often simply glorify violence. This discussion only intensified after another UK-based studio, Rockstar North (known as DMA Design at the time), released their masterpiece in 2001.

Grand Theft Auto III™ (often known simply as *GTA III*) is a third-person sandbox action adventure game initially for the PlayStation 2. Based in the fictional Liberty City, it follows the adventures of an unnamed antihero as he works his way up the criminal underworld's ranks before finally confronting an ex-girlfriend who betrayed him at the beginning of the game. Stylish and fun, Rockstar's third installment of the franchise was its first foray into a 3D, grittier universe that felt far more immediate and visceral than their previous, top-down offerings. *GTA III* was a huge hit as players found the combination of comic book characters, parody-rich writing, and ultra-violent gangland crime a heady mix when combined with the freedom to drive (or fly) around a large city replete with numerous elements with which to interact. This liberal, empowering design is tempered with a core story waiting to be experienced that serves to lend structure to what could otherwise feel like a hugely entertaining, but ultimately unfocused experience.

While *GTA III* and its numerous sequels boast sales figures numbering in the millions (*GTA III* sold in excess of 12 million units), for many the title quickly came to represent the ultraviolent nature of some games. Around the same time, a far more subtle and poignant game story was released. *Ico*® is an action-adventure game created by Team Ico for the PlayStation 2. It follows the adventures of a young boy, Ico, and Yorda, a silent princess, as they attempt to escape the confines of an uninhabited castle, both having been left there to die by unseen and uncaring antagonists whose cold presence permeates the world. Possessing a minimalist approach to both gameplay and story, *Ico* provokes strong feelings in those who have experienced its subtle but profound charms. As Ico guides his mute charge through a bleak castle populated only by ghostly specters, players are slowly drawn to care for the understated pair. *Ico* is a confident, quiet, but powerful example of superb game story married to simple, but compelling gameplay, which was later to be replicated by the Japanese team when they released *Shadow of the Colossus* in 2005. Originally destined to be a sequel to *Ico*, it follows the adventures of young adventurer, Wander, as he journeys the land on a quest to defeat sixteen huge creatures, known as colossi, to save the life of a young girl. A simple, compelling story was once again combined with intuitive game design to create a title that is still lauded as a masterpiece.

Released in 2001 as part of the Microsoft Xbox console launch line up, *Halo: Combat Evolved*® sparked one of gaming's most popular FPS franchises and proved that the genre could work outside the traditional mouse/keyboard platform. A large part of that success was due to Bungie's writers presenting a lean, punchy story packed with great characters, which beautifully complemented the superb gameplay. Gamers were drawn into the heroic struggle of super-soldier, Master Chief, John-117, as he battled valiantly against an almost overwhelming tide of enemies on an alien habitat. Sequels to the game, while selling in vast numbers, feature stories that arguably lost much of the simple purity featured in the series' first outing. Despite this, *Halo* helped ensure the fledgling Xbox enjoyed a successful launch.

Despite sometimes spawning offerings of questionable quality, gaming's popularity meant action movies were sometimes accompanied by titles eager to tap into the potent marketing potential offered by a more widely accepted medium. Most simply seek to find ways to turn elements of the movie's story into gameplay, but in 2003, one developer sought to take a different approach. *Enter the Matrix*™ is an action-adventure game by Shiny Entertainment for the Xbox, PlayStation 2, and GameCube. It follows the adventures of rebel fighters,

Ghost and Niobe, as they play their part in humanity's battle against machines that have taken over the world. While *Enter the Matrix*'s gameplay received mixed reviews, what makes its release interesting is its story; rather than written to echo or mimic elements of the plot in both *The Matrix Reloaded*™ and *The Matrix Revolutions*™, *Enter the Matrix* is designed to *enhance* a player's understanding of events in both films through transmedia storytelling. Players are able to experience events not seen by moviegoers and are therefore privy to background pieces of plot that serve to further enhance their appreciation of the trilogy as a whole. This complementary approach was a noteworthy and brave step, especially for a mass-market title. However, disappointing sales seemed to indicate that, ultimately, people just wanted to "be Neo," and so *Path of Neo* was the more predictable console title that followed.

While the *Star Wars* franchise has, unsurprisingly, spawned numerous titles on almost every platform conceivable, precious few have held up as excellent games in their own right. *Star Wars: Knights of the Old Republic*™ (known as *KOTOR* to fans), created by BioWare for the Xbox and PC platforms, is an RPG released on the Xbox in 2003 that takes place in the *Star Wars* universe (many years before the events of the movies) and manages to deliver on a number of important levels. Players take on the role of a mysterious character who, while imbued with the Force, initially suffers from amnesia (a common ailment in many game story universes) and is unable to remember their true identity. As they work to defeat Sith Lord, Darth Malak, a booming, disfigured individual hell-bent on taking over the universe, the player is joined by other, memorable characters; prickly Jedi, Bastila Shan, deadly, sarcastic assassin droid, HK-47, and Mandalorian mercenary, Canderous Ordo, are among those who work to save the universe from disaster, each approaching events with their own perspective and motivation. KOTOR successfully infuses a very well-known universe with satisfying RPG gameplay (and, in fact, simultaneously, the far harder task of infusing RPG gameplay with a satisfying depiction of a well-known, and loved, universe) and an interesting story in which the player can express his morality through his actions. It remains one of the titles often pointed to by those seeking to prove great games can spring from existing IP.

While fantasy-based MMOs were proving popular, a science fiction title had yet to capture gamers' imaginations. First released in 2003, Icelandic developer CCP's MMO, *Eve Online*™, arguably became the first and, to date, only title to successfully do just that. Adventures occur in a universe where humanity has spread to the stars, and players take on the roles of spaceship pilots, able to explore, trade, and battle their way through the game in any manner they see fit, in a style reminiscent of *Elite*, except on a huge, multiplayer scale. While

Eve Online shares a lot of its game design features with other, more standard MMOs, it differs in that each geographic gaming region, in essence, exists on a single server. Normally, to ease population burden and ensure satisfactory technical performance is maintained, MMO universes are "sharded," with each game world replicated in separate servers as many times as necessary. A drawback to this system is it divides the player base—two players of the same MMO cannot play together if they're on different servers. There are solutions, but none are ideal; while it's possible to pay for server transfers, most players build meaningful relationships on the "shard" they're on, which they're often understandably reluctant to abandon. Another option is to create a new character, but many players build strong emotional ties to their "main" and want to experience the game through them—and, of course, the time implications of building and "skilling-up" (i.e., enhancing the skills of) characters mean this can be seen as prohibitive, or, at the very least, highly undesirable. The story ramifications of allowing tens of thousands of players to exist in the same universe are huge—*Eve Online*, of all modern MMOs, comes closest to creating a truly living universe in which players are empowered to instigate in-game events. CCP are openly *laissez faire* about their handling of the game universe they've created; while they do enforce a basic level of conduct, players are mostly left to their own devices. Normal Player versus Environment (PvE) gameplay is available in the form of quests and encounters, but it's the PvP element that has come to capture the headlines.

The following year an accomplished game story would once again contribute to evolving players' abilities to express themselves. Released in 2004 and mentioned earlier, *Fable* is a third-person action RPG created by Lionhead Studios (of *Black & White* fame) for the Xbox and PC platforms. Players take control of a small boy who, near the beginning of the game, sees his family brutally murdered before he's taken in by the leader of the Heroes Guild. After a short training section, the character grows up and is free to pursue his family's killers as a fully paid-up member of the Heroes Guild. In a manner similar to BioWare's *Knights of the Old Republic*™, *Fable* encourages players to express their morality in a game world that tries to react accordingly; spend your time rescuing those in danger and generally being an all-around good guy, and people will react positively as you pass—some may even find you attractive. Play the part of the villain, however, and while your character might gain people's respect, you'll be feared and perhaps even hated (though there are still those who might find you attractive). Morality is so firmly anchored into gameplay it also affects how your avatar appears—the truly pure of heart eventually sport a glowing halo, while their evil counterparts grow horns (a system which is, again, similar to that seen in *Knights of the Old Republic*, which also visually illustrates the morality of the choices you make). Giving players the tools to express themselves within the gameplay and game story in this way has helped create a durable, if flawed, franchise that spawned three sequels before the studio was unfortunately closed by Microsoft in 2016 shortly before it was due to release *Fable: Legends*™.

While *Ultima Online* and *EverQuest* serve as examples of successful MMOs, both would eventually be eclipsed. One of the most popular Western video games to date was first released in 2004. *World of Warcraft*™ (known simply as *WoW* to the initiated) is an MMO created by Blizzard Entertainment® for the PC platform. Set in the fantasy world of Azeroth, first seen in their popular 1994 real-time strategy game *Warcraft*™, *WoW* is, in a design sense, closely related to predecessors such as *Ultima Online* and *EverQuest*. *WoW* has players choose a race and character class from one of two opposing factions before releasing them to experience a virtual realm filled with quests to complete, dungeons to explore, and battles to be fought against other players. The first iteration of *WoW* built upon the successes and mistakes of the past but, it should be said, didn't feature *revolutionary* gameplay. At its peak *WoW* boasted over twelve million paying subscribers worldwide, despite having to weather attempts from some of the world's largest studios to provide worthy alternatives.

Blizzard's phenomenal success is subject to much debate, but no one denies they provide a supremely refined, accessible gaming experience set inside a universe that enjoys a rich story and character backdrop. Players can choose to battle some of the game world's most memorable NPCs and explore a rich lore-based game. Anyone who's witnessed the mighty Molten Core raid's final boss, Fire Lord Ragnaros, explode from a pool of lava, ready to do battle, will agree it's a difficult moment to forget. It's this superb use of story that's helped *WoW* become one of the most successful game titles ever released. Being an MMO, *WoW* also provides players with the tools to interact and create their own stories, which is a huge part of the draw; being told a pre-set story and, to a limited extent, taking part in it (as players do, for example, when they defeat an important boss who features in the narrative tapestry of the world) can be fun, but forming stories through relatively unfettered interaction with real people is arguably the most compelling way to experience a game world.

The issue with an MMO such as *WoW* in 2004 was that while players could dive into a story world and spend countless hours completing quests and looting dungeons with friends, any changes they effected on the world were temporary, fleeting things that reset after a set period of time in a style not unlike that experienced by Bill Murray's character in the movie *Groundhog Day*. If a group of adventurers battle and destroy a major boss creature, such as the powerful dragon, Onyxia, while their victory was celebrated by NPCs and her head was somewhat gorily strung from the relevant faction's city gate, return a few days later to her lair and she will have resurrected, ready to do battle once more. While this is a shame, it's also understandable; MMO games are designed to have no solid end point and provide content playable by all, which is part of what makes them the subject of much scrutiny by those who view the genre as a dangerous time-sink for players who find it hard to resist the lure of almost endless goals. Gameplay is roughly divided into two parts—"leveling gameplay" experienced while raising a character to whatever the current level "cap" is and "endgame" where players either battle one another (PvP) or attempt to defeat the game's most powerful creatures (PvE "raiding"). This means that while the story world can be experienced, it could not—during the early days of *WoW*—be affected in any permanent, meaningful way. This issue would eventually begin to be addressed by Blizzard in later expansions. While the world of online games was becoming an increasingly compelling place to exist, consoles were about to get one of their most compelling protagonists to date.

God of War™, released in 2005, is an action adventure game created by SCE Studios for the PlayStation 2. It follows the adventures of the mighty (and angry) Greek warrior, Kratos, as he battles to stop Ares, God of War, from destroying the City of Athens in return for forgiveness for the terrible deeds of his past. *God of War*'s high-quality storytelling helped propel some of the most exciting—and gory—gameplay yet seen on the PlayStation 2 platform. Opening with the apparent suicide of Kratos, players are faced with a powerful question to pull them through the gameplay: why does he kill himself? *God of War* is another title that combines excellent cut scenes, fantastic audio, and the compelling journey of a conflicted antihero to make it one of the benchmarks of storytelling on that platform. Another example of polished-more-than-revolutionary, it's worth noting *God of War 2* was awarded the British Film and Television Academy (BAFTA) award for best video game story in 2008.

The following year saw the release of *Fahrenheit*™ (also called *Indigo Prophecy*™ in the United States), an adventure game created by Quantic Dream™ for the Xbox, PlayStation 2, and PC. While the gameplay has players switch between a variety of characters, the story primarily follows IT manager Lucas Kane as he investigates cases of normal people suddenly exploding into seemingly random killing sprees. *Fahrenheit* pushed story boundaries in part because it provides players with a game universe that, while following a core linear story, features a design able to accommodate and reflect players making a variety of different decisions from a variety of perspectives while controlling a variety of characters. Quantic Dream also sought to provide a more intuitive control interface using the consoles' twin analogue sticks, enabling players to "gesture" contextually, allowing a more immediate feeling of opening a door, for example, or picking up an object. This is in sharp contrast to most games that simply have players press a button to interact with an object and would later feature, albeit in a more refined manner, in Quantic Dream's PlayStation 3 title, *Heavy Rain*®.

GAME STORY: 2006–2010

Major Hardware Developments

- Sony PlayStation 3 released (2006)
- Nintendo Wii™ released (2006)
- Nintendo DSi™ released (2009)
- Apple® iPad™ released (2010)

Released in 2006 (2007 in Europe and Australia) *Ōkami*™ is an action adventure game created by Clover Studios® for the PlayStation 2. Through skillfully combining the myths and legends of classical Japan, it follows the adventures of Sun Goddess Amaterasu, who takes the form of a white wolf to go on a quest to save the land from darkness. Praised for its stunning cel-shaded art style, *Ōkami* illustrated how story, gameplay, and visuals can combine to tell a haunting tale that would help Clover Studios reap a large number of awards. Players travel a world both dynamic and wistful, slowly unwrapping a tale that clearly took time to create. The story also lends logic to one of the game's main design features, the celestial brush, used to draw characters on the screen, each with a different combat or other gameplay effect. Despite this, the game sold poorly in all territories, perhaps suffering as a result of being released so close to the arrival of Sony's new PlayStation 3 console, though it remains a critically respected title.

In 2006, Blizzard released *World of Warcraft: The Burning Crusade*™ (*TBC*), the first expansion pack for their 2004 blockbuster MMO, *WoW*. It added two new playable races, increased the level cap from 60 to 70, and provided several new quest areas that form part of the world known as Outland. What makes *TBC* special is that it was Blizzard's first attempt to evolve not just the gameplay available to its players, but also the world, through expanding the story featured so far; a difficult game design-balancing act. For high-level characters a new threat emerged in the form of the ancient and terrible Burning Legion, a host of demons bent on destroying Azeroth. Interestingly, the release of *TBC* also saw two character classes previously only available to their specific factions (the Horde-based Shaman and Alliance-based Paladin) cross over so players could choose from the full range of options, regardless of their allegiance. Blizzard used story to help lend this fundamental game design decision a sheen of logic, though they still managed to irritate some fans who felt their reasoning distorted the existing lore (for example, claiming that the Horde faction had been able to capture an Alliance paladin to drain his power and harness it for their own use, thus enabling the production of their own paladins, was not universally popular). Also, Blizzard changed some of the game's backstory, turning the previously benevolent titan, Sargeras, into the malevolent force behind The Burning Legion. This also didn't sit well with lore purists and illustrates how important a game's story can be to many players.

The year 2007 saw the release of several excellent story-based games. *Assassin's Creed*®, a third-person action adventure game created by Ubisoft® for the PlayStation 3, Xbox 360, and PC platforms, follows the adventures of bartender Desmond Miles, who's kidnapped by a mysterious organization and forced to replay the genetic memories of his ancestor, Altaïr Ibn-La'Ahad, an assassin alive during The Third Crusade. *Assassin's Creed* provides the player with three cities in which to carry out assassinations, as they work to win themselves back into the good graces of the Creed of Assassins: Jerusalem, Acre, and Damascus. Each is meticulously created, with detailed buildings and bustling residents that help create a richly historic atmosphere. Through the use of the Animus machine (the technology enabling Miles to travel back to the Third Crusade), *Assassin's Creed* manages to successfully evoke two distinct eras, allowing players, through game story logic married seamlessly with intelligent game design, to experience a compelling past, while subconsciously still in a contemporary game setting. This clever juxtaposition enables Ubisoft to weave a complex story that would later be expanded upon in further successful sequels.

Third-person action adventure game *Uncharted: Drake's Fortune*™ was also released that year by developers Naughty Dog™ for the PlayStation 3. Players step into the boots of roguish treasure hunter Nathan Drake as he journeys the world in search of the lost city of El Dorado. *Uncharted: Drake's Fortune* is neither evolutionary nor revolutionary from a game story point of view, but is instead a supremely polished example of what can be done by a studio intent on seamlessly marrying great game design with a well-written story. Naughty Dog unfolds the linear plot through a series of in-game cut scenes that feature cinematic quality writing and work hard to seamlessly blend story with gameplay. They also pepper in-game action with dialogue that serves to flesh out both minor story details and character, providing the player with a constant stream of tiny story and character moments, almost unconsciously absorbed as the game is played. A sequel, *Uncharted 2: Among Thieves*™, was released by the same studio in 2009 and boasts a similar polish to storytelling fused with, and complementary to, the overall gameplay experience.

Less lighthearted, but just as skillfully crafted, *Call of Duty 4: Modern Warfare*™ is an FPS created by Infinity Ward™ in 2007 for the Xbox 360, PlayStation 3, and Nintendo Wii. Players primarily experience the story through the eyes of SAS soldier John "Soap" MacTavish, as the authorities try to stop the nefarious plans of Russian ultranationalist Imran Zakhaev. What makes *Call of Duty 4: Modern Warfare* noteworthy from a story point of view is its clever use of different perspectives to tell its tale. At the start of the game the player is put into the body of President Al-Fulani, and, while they view everything from his perspective, they are powerless to do anything but look around. Dragged from a building, thrown into a waiting car, then driven through the war-torn streets of a dusty Middle Eastern town, the sense of helplessness is tangible and, to a certain extent, echoes the opening sequence of Valve's *Half-Life*. Infinity Ward's sequence ends with Al-Fulani being tied to a post and shot by a soldier as Zakhaev looks on. Experiencing this part of the story firsthand, rather than having it delivered as mission intelligence, serves to make the rest of the game a more personal experience for the player. While these events are both well-written and executed, it's worth noting the role played by the audio—from ambient sounds to the incessant, strident speech delivered in the background as opening events unfold—which further deepens the immersion felt by the player as they traverse the Middle Eastern towns' dusty streets and alleys. As the game progresses, players become familiar with Sergeant Paul Jackson, a U.S. marine, while completing several missions. Jackson's story ends with his helicopter being blown from the sky by a nuclear explosion, and we experience *his* final moments as he crawls from the wreckage to die in the aftermath. This powerful use of perspective helped *Call of Duty 4: Modern Warfare* win the 2009 BAFTA award for best video game story.

Also released in 2007, *Mass Effect*® is a third-person action sci-fi RPG created by BioWare for the Xbox 360 and PC platforms. It follows the adventures of human soldier Commander Shepard, as he (or, if the player chooses, she) travels the galaxy, recruiting a variety of fearsome and skilled individuals to help uncover the deadly plans of a shadowy species known only as The Reapers. What makes *Mass Effect* a fantastic story experience, worthy of inclusion here, is its varied array of interesting characters, ability to play either the hero or the scoundrel, and the cinematic feel that interactions are given due to the conversational response wheel. The wheel allows players to choose responses quickly, using a thumb stick to rotate an arrow so it points towards the gist of what will be said, should the player decide to pick that option. Selecting *I don't trust you* on the wheel (a fictional example) might result in Shepard saying *Something about your story stinks, want to try that again?* This intuitive system, coupled with great voice acting, intelligent use of camera angles, and a well-written script, makes conversations in *Mass Effect* a supremely cinematic blend of story and game design. BioWare, the consummate storytellers, weave a potent story that allows the player significant freedom to approach sections in any order they desire.

Another 2007 release, *BioShock*® is an FPS created by Irrational Games® for the Xbox 360, PlayStation 3, and PC platforms. It follows the adventures of Jack Ryan, the only survivor of a mid-ocean plane crash, as he battles his way through the fallen subaquatic city of Rapture. Set in an alternative 1960, the underwater dystopia has just exploded in a civil war and teems with deadly "Splicers," warped individuals granted special abilities by a drug called "Adam." One of the biggest video games of the year, *BioShock* remains a superb example of environmental storytelling. Emerging into the beautifully presented tatters of Rapture, the player is presented with a tangible sense of a world gone wrong; protestors' billboards scatter the floor of the underwater bathysphere station, along with suitcases and children's toys—silent testament to the chaos and panic that so recently spread through the city's hidden society.

That year another seminal title was set to emerge, though this one is set in an alternative future. *Portal*® closely resembles a FPS, but may perhaps, more accurately, be described as a puzzle game, or an FPS-puzzle hybrid, in which the player fires one of two colors of portal rather than bullets. Created by Valve for the Xbox 360, PlayStation 3, and PC platforms, *Portal* originally came bundled as part of the *Half-Life Series Orange Box* but can now be purchased as a stand-alone title. It follows the adventures of captive lab subject, Chell, as she solves a series of portal-based puzzles presented by eccentric AI, GLaDOS, and is another superb example of environmental storytelling. As players work their way through the increasingly difficult challenge rooms, a subtle, minimalist story unfolds as the initially benevolent GLaDOS gradually changes in tone, becoming increasingly unbalanced and eventually hostile. What makes *Portal* work from a story perspective is not only what is included, but what is not. We never find out who is behind the experiments, or what they want, and this serves not to frustrate, but to add to the air of mystery.

In 2008, Blizzard launched their second *WoW* expansion, *Wrath of the Lich King*™ (*WOTLK*). Once again, it added new questing zones, NPC characters, and dungeons for players to experience, as well as raised the player level cap from 70 to 80. What made this expansion unique, from a storytelling viewpoint, was its inclusion of a new design technology known as "phasing." This alters the world seen and experienced by an individual player based on their game accomplishments. As discussed earlier, one of the great limitations faced by MMOs is the difficulty of providing players in control of powerful avatars a feeling of agency in the virtual world where they adventure. Saving a town from certain destruction at the hands of outlaws loses much of its emotional power when, moments later, the area resets to its former state, ready for the next hero to "save it." Phasing, initially created by Blizzard to fix a game bug, is a tool that gives players a greater sense of relevance, of really making a difference in the world as they move through it. Arguably the most notable use of phasing in *WOTLK* is in the Death Knight character class starting zone that leads players through a series of quests telling the story of how their characters, sickened by the evil Lich King's wanton destruction of a nearby town, eventually break free from his evil control. By the end of the chain, the area players at first viewed as a thriving town becomes a terrible, blackened shell, infested by the undead, which serves to provide a potent story motivation for breaking free of servitude to Arthas (the Lich King). Phasing is used in other areas of the expansion, but Blizzard would really push the storytelling potential of this technology in their next expansion.

Also released in 2008, *Fallout 3*™ is an action adventure game created by Bethesda Game Studios® for the Xbox 360, PlayStation 3, and PC platforms that takes place in an alternate, post-apocalyptic hi-tech future heavily inspired by the 1950s. The player steps into the shoes of an underground "vault dweller" on the trail of their escapee father. *Fallout 3* presents players with a stunning level of choice once the introductory and tutorial levels are complete. One literally finds oneself standing on an outcropping of rock, blinking in never-before-seen sunlight. As the avatar's virtual eyes adjust, a vast landscape comes into focus, stretching away in all directions, dotted with interesting structures, each promising the chance of adventure. A feeling of real freedom washes over the player at this point. While it's possible to simply pursue the main game story, following the father's trail and unraveling the reasons behind his sudden disappearance, players can also opt to explore randomly, discovering pockets of narrative dotting the landscape. While a large number of story-driven titles allow one to travel "off-track," Bethesda has created a game world in which the design provides a greater degree of freedom than normally presented—almost everything inside a house, for example, can be picked up, sold, or used. This is in stark contrast to the typical game that provides "furniture-shaped objects" which, while pretty, often can't be interacted with in any way, making rooms and spaces feel less realistic and immersive.

Another 2008 title, *Left 4 Dead*™, is an FPS released by Valve Corporation for the Xbox 360 and PC. Focusing heavily on cooperative play, it follows the adventures of four survivors of a zombie-like apocalypse as they battle to reach various pockets of safety before being permanently rescued. While *Left 4 Dead* (and its sequel, *Left 4 Dead 2*™) are both highly refined, well-executed FPSs capable of providing an evolved cooperative experience, Valve once again raised the bar with its environmental storytelling in two ways. They first provided a landscape littered with unspoken tales of the recent and powerful tragedies that had taken place as a result of the terrible undead uprising. The numerous safe houses between levels display messages scrawled on the walls by survivors either trying desperately to reach loved ones or warn the living of impending doom. The experience feels vividly fluid and cinematic, characters talk to one another as the action unfolds, warning of danger, pointing out ammo drops and chastising poor marksmanship, towns and cities bear the subtle and not-so-subtle marks of places tragedy has struck in a variety of terrible ways, and all this is underscored by an audioscape that adds to the ambience of tension. While the story is an extremely simple one (the protagonists battle from point A to point B) it's the freeform, yet cohesive nature of events that take place during the telling of the story that makes *Left 4 Dead* a standout title. This is assisted by the inclusion of an unseen "director" who acts as a puppeteer/undead general behind the scenes, sending forth fresh waves of enemies when it judges the action flagging and lending us an early example of a simple form of procedural storytelling.

The horror theme was to be further explored by Finnish developer Remedy® when, in 2010, they released third-person psychological action thriller *Alan Wake*® for the Xbox 360. It follows the adventures of horror writer Alan Wake who, in a bid to overcome his writer's block, goes on vacation to the town of Bright Falls with his wife, Alice. When she's apparently kidnapped by dark forces, he sets out to rescue her and try to understand the source of the mysterious Dark Presence that threatens the area. While *Alan Wake* is a purely "corridor experience" in which the game story is released in a tightly controlled manner, Remedy provides us with a visual and auditory experience among the most deeply atmospheric to date. As Wake battles his way through the various forest and small-town locations (inspired by the beautiful Finnish city of Espoo), the wind howls, tugging at forest trees, and the darkness feels alive as it pushes in wherever it can, driven back only by the protagonist's flashlight and occasional street lamp. Remedy tells an interesting story set in a horror universe championed by a protagonist who, while not a combat powerhouse like *Resident Evil*'s Chris Redfield, is also far from helpless in a fight. *Alan Wake* also plays with the idea of foreshadowing, leaving pages of a novel littering locations which, when read, foretell events about to take place. While making for some interesting moments, these pages are hopefully not representative of Wake's final work, as they're often badly in need of an edit.

That same year, a superb example of what can be achieved in story with a well-designed sequel rocketed onto shelves. *Mass Effect 2*™, Canadian developer BioWare's sequel to the highly successful *Mass Effect*, available initially on the Xbox 360 and PC but later ported to the PlayStation 3, continues the adventures of human super-soldier, Commander Shepard. Tasked with assembling another deadly group of adventurers, Shepard travels the universe in a quest to thwart the far-reaching plans of the mysterious race known only as the Reapers, who seek to destroy all sentient life in the universe. BioWare created a game that provided players with a unique universe where decisions made in *Mass Effect* had tangible consequences for players who moved to the sequel; allow a species to survive in the first game and you might encounter their messenger in the second, though if you destroyed them, you most certainly wouldn't. Relationships and events from *Mass Effect* tangibly and meaningfully link into the continuing story of *Mass Effect 2*, though they are handled in such a way as to make any group of previous choices fit. This level of cause-and-effect storytelling requires skill and time to successfully implement.

The vital impact of choices on a story was also the subject of another interesting addition to the game story universe, in the form of *Heavy Rain*®, released in the same year and perhaps best described as an interactive drama or an interactive fiction game. Created by Quantic Dream (the makers of *Fahrenheit*) for the PlayStation 3, *Heavy Rain* follows the interwoven stories of four characters as they become involved in the murders carried out by the Origami Killer. In a sense the title is the spiritual successor to *Fahrenheit*, in that it follows the parallel journeys of several core characters as the story unfolds and uses an immersive, context-sensitive control system to help pull the player into the experience. (To open a door you don't simply press a button on the control pad; you move the analog sticks depicting a shape similar to the movement of pushing down on a door handle and pulling.) Hailed by critics as a uniquely cinematic experience, *Heavy Rain* features several different endings, which are dictated by choices made by the player (as they control the various characters) earlier in the game. The manner in which players interact with the story world, while oddly limited in that they are most certainly steered in specific directions, is still immersive. The ability to pick up a cup or open a door at the pace you wish, rather than one set by the game engine, lends a feeling of direct connection between yourself and the character you're controlling. Details like this pepper every level, each serving to pull you deeper into the world, linking you to the emotional paths of the people whose lives you are experiencing.

The year 2010 also saw Blizzard release its fourth MMO expansion, *World of Warcraft: Cataclysm*™, which became one of the fastest-selling PC games of the decade, selling 3.3 million units in the first week alone. While it added five extra character levels for players with "level capped" characters, as well as five new high-level zones within which to quest, *Cataclysm* pushed the boundaries of story content in other ways, literally tearing apart the original *WoW* zones that had remained untouched since the game's launch in 2004. Using the explosive rebirth of a dragon, Deathwing—who erupts from the depths of the world, tearing it asunder in the process—Blizzard reshaped old story and quest content, much of which felt outdated since the release of two expansion packs featuring more compelling, varied, and polished quest content. Blizzard also made far greater use of phasing than ever before. Rather than using it in a handful of standout moments that marked significant story moments, Blizzard use phasing liberally to empower players with a feeling of greater agency as they move through the game universe. A chain of quests might find the player seeing an area shift and change permanently several times as a direct result of their actions. The main issue with this system is players can find themselves "trapped" in different layers of the same zone when trying to locate friends who haven't completed the right number of quests to ensure they're at the same story stage. Despite this, the increased use of the technology was greeted positively by most players and critics.

GAME STORY: 2011–2016

Major Hardware Developments

- Nintendo 3DS™ released (2011)
- Sony PS Vita released (2012)
- Nintendo Wii U™ released (2012)
- Microsoft Xbox One™ released (2013)
- Sony PlayStation 4™ released (2013)
- Microsoft Xbox One S™ released (2016)

An area often overlooked by games but core to other visual storytelling media involves facial expressions. A line delivered with a scowl can have a totally different meaning to one delivered with a subtle smirk. In real life, the visual difference between these can be minor, which makes expressions all the trickier to successfully achieve in games. Additionally, most titles can't spare the system resources or the time and money to gift characters with detailed, nuanced expressions outside the rarified realm of the cut scene. This, however, is changing.

Team Bondai chose to put facial expressions at the core of its action adventure title, *L.A. Noire*™, when it released in the spring of 2011. Released on the Xbox 360, PlayStation 3, and PC, *L.A. Noire* is a third-person action-adventure game set in 1940s Los Angeles in which players take on the role of Los Angeles police detective Cole Phelps as he cracks murder cases and rises up the law enforcement ranks.

Gameplay not only includes gunfights, car chases, hand-to-hand combat, and crime scene investigations; crucially it includes face-to-face interrogations and interviews in which players ask suspects questions and decide, in part from reading facial animations, who is telling the truth.

This is possible through the MotionScan™ technology developed and used by Team Bondi's sister company, Depth Analysis. It uses thirty-two motion scan cameras to fully capture actors' performances in scenes that help players 'read' intentions more realistically than ever before.

The high level of attention paid to facial animation helps bring the game's characters to life and enables some interesting investigative gameplay related to interviewing witnesses and suspects and was noteworthy for the time. Sadly, in September 2011, a few months after *L.A. Noire* was released, Team Bondi entered into administration.

Bethesda Game Studios, well-known (and loved) for releasing several sprawling sandbox games, were to arguably release their most successful installment to date in the Elder Scrolls franchise in the same year. The *Elder Scrolls V: Skyrim*™ (typically just called *Skyrim*) was released on the Xbox 360, PlayStation 3, and PC to generally critical acclaim.

In it the player takes on the role of The Dragonborn, a potent being able to consume the very souls of dragons in order to fuel their own power. This proves a timely ability, as these impressive creatures of legend are in the process of rising from their scattered graves and wreaking havoc on people across the land. Players freely travel the region, exploring dungeons, helping (or killing) those in need and, if the urge takes them, pursuing the main quest to discover who is behind all the mysterious resurrections.

Vast, beautiful, and rich, *Skyrim*, while not the first game its kind, or even in the series, provides players with one of the most refined open-world experiences to date. Years later, players still creep through its dungeons in search of treasure and wary of traps, helped in part by Bethesda's so-called Radiant Quest system, that enables the game to generate theoretically infinite missions in a variety of game regions using a set list of variables. This freedom came at a price though, as early versions of the game were famous for being buggy, a not-unknown issue in titles as vast and complex as *Skyrim*'s.

Valve's sequel to their 2007 acclaimed slice of puzzle-solving perfection, *Portal*™, was also released in 2011. *Portal 2*'s basic premise remains the same—escape a variety of testing rooms with the aid of a device that shoots portals. What's particularly interesting is that, in order to support a far longer gaming experience, Valve presented an expanded story in which players initially work their way through a ruined complex ravaged by years of neglect, but which, as the game progresses, visibly begins to repair itself, lending the game world a palpable sense of being alive. Silent protagonist, Chell, meets chatty robot, Wheatley, in her struggle against rampant (and catty) AI, GLaDOS, and, as the game progresses, players see more of a world only hinted at in *Portal*. Once again, Valve manages to present gameplay enhanced by excellent writing and environmental storytelling, designed to be as non-intrusive as possible.

In 2012 Gearbox released a sequel of its own on the PlayStation 3, Xbox 360, and PC that would arguably prove just as popular as Valve's. First-person "loot-'em-up" *Borderlands 2*™ fuses a competent first-person shooter with addictive RPG elements to create one of the most popular titles of the year.

As in the original *Borderlands*, players take the role of grizzled vault hunters who scour the deadly world of Pandora for loot while, in this instance, butting heads with Handsome Jack, the evil, charismatic head of mega-corporation Hyperion. Jack's hell-bent on harnessing the deadly power of a mysterious entity known only as The Warrior.

Borderlands 2 is a potent reminder concerning the power of memorable characters. Gearbox took the already exaggerated, twisted world they created in the original *Borderlands* and, to name a few, added the charismatic (but psychotic) Handsome Jack, tragic (but deadly) Tiny Tina, and loud (but gentle) Mr. Torgue. It provided a powerful fusion of fun gameplay with memorable individuals capable of delivering a coherent story that helps drive gameplay.

As proof of just how powerful *Borderlands 2*'s characters are, arguably its most successful DLC came in the form of *Tiny Tina's Assault on Dragon's Keep*™, a piece of content largely driven by the tragic tale of a little girl's struggle to accept the death of a loved one.

Around the same time BioWare finally concluded its highly successful *Mass Effect* space opera with the release of *Mass Effect 3*™. Released on the Xbox 360, PlayStation 3, and PC, it sees Commander Shepard finally uncovering the power behind the mysterious, deadly Reapers and ultimately deciding the fate of the universe.

Another strong story-led installment, it was originally marred by an assortment of endings many felt were confusing and anticlimactic, especially in light of the fact that events were—until that point—increasingly shaped by player-based decisions. This led to a player backlash and BioWare hurrying back to the storyboard. Their second efforts were more warmly received. While *Mass Effect 3*'s original ending debatably sported one of BioWare's rare missteps, the final game perhaps balanced the scales somewhat by releasing one of the best-received DLC packs in the series in the form of *Citadel*.

Ideally experienced shortly before the game's climactic act, *Citadel* is a more lighthearted offering that sees Commander Shepard and her (or his) crew taking some well-earned shore leave on the Citadel shortly before taking on the game's final mission. Naturally all plans to relax are cut short when a surprising enemy decides now's the best time to wreak revenge against the commander. *Citadel* raised the bar in what one could expect from BioWare's DLC. The antagonist manages to deliver a touch of tragedy while keeping things relatively lighthearted. This helps contribute to a fun "ripping yarn," which provides some much-needed, albeit blood-spattered, levity against which to balance the universe-ending main story. It's a timely reminder that smaller, more intimate stories can be just as potent as larger ones.

By Telltale Games, and released on pretty much every modern platform you can shake a gore-covered stick at, *The Walking Dead*™ was another impressive reminder that the episodic interactive drama game was far from dead—as it were. Players take on the role of Lee Everett, a university professor and convicted murderer who befriends a young girl called Clementine in a world where the dead return to life and hunger for the flesh of the living. The first of several high-profile story-driven RPGs from Telltale, *The Walking Dead* illustrates the power of simple, skilled writing to draw us into caring about Lee and Clem's perilous journey to find her parents and reach safety.

Gameplay doesn't focus as strongly on solving puzzles or combat; the player's main challenge often involves making story decisions relating to how best to protect Clementine in a world that's slowly being overrun by undead. A simple tale following one little girl's struggle to reach her family, *The Walking Dead* is further proof that "small stories," with their focus on personal relationships, can often provide people with a more potent, personal experience than stories with "save the universe"-type stakes. Events never pull far enough back for us to really see how they are unfolding in the world as a whole; instead, Lee and Clem experience other people's smaller stories on their journey: a husband and wife's struggle to protect their child from brutal reality, a family fallen to cannibalism, or a young couple's struggle to survive. Through powerful, subtle writing and some standout performances, Lee and Clementine form a powerful bond over the first season's five episodes, which makes the final installment all the more moving and helps drive events in the following season.

Love it or hate it, there's no denying Rockstar North's *Grand Theft Auto* action adventure series has made an impact on the gaming landscape. *Grand Theft Auto V*™ (also known as *GTA V*) was initially released on the Xbox 360 and PlayStation 3 in 2013 before later coming to the Xbox One, PlayStation 4, and eventually PC. It puts players in the collective shoes of three criminals as they plan and execute a series of increasingly daring heists in the fictional state of San Andreas.

The main story is arguably not the strong point here; Michael, Franklin, and Trevor are not that likable, though the plot is noteworthy because it nimbly switches between all three of their plot strands. While *GTA V*'s narrative mileage may vary for many—not everyone enjoys spending time with three violent cop-killing criminals—moving between their stories so fluidly is fun. The star of the narrative show, however, is the game world. The main city of Los Santos and its surrounding environment is detailed, beautiful, and—above all else—alive. Here is a game that successfully manages to provide players with a highly populated, busy, and loud backdrop against which to experience the narrative. At the time of writing *GTA V* remains a solid favorite of game streamers everywhere, as Rockstar North has also provided a large number of multiplayer game modes for groups of players to enjoy in their graphically lush world, which all exist to one side of the single player story.

Rockstar North's universe also reminds us that humor is a highly subjective matter and remains something rarely 'nailed' in games. Around the same time as *GTA V* shipped, small development house Galactic Café released first-person "walk-'em-up" *The Stanley Parable*™, in which the player travels through a mysteriously deserted office building searching for a way out. Originally released in 2011 as an expansion to *Half Life 2*, it was more formally released in 2013 as a stand-alone title.

Unusually, the game doesn't feature any combat. Instead, the player guides mute protagonist Stanley through the building, accompanied by a narrator who takes great pleasure in making fun of him at every opportunity. The seamless blend of witty, Stanley-reactive writing and exploratory gameplay allow players to uncover a variety of story endings, all of which serve as a form of reward. Rather than being channeled into a virtual story corridor, the player is allowed to choose a variety of paths, some of which force the disembodied narrator to change the story it appears he expected to relate. This lends the player a feeling of empowerment not often experienced in video games. *The Stanley Parable* manages to subtly explore the nature of choice and, perhaps, the illusory nature of agency. Add to that some excellent voice acting and a space full of amusing environmental storytelling, and you have a rare title that even managed to make a cameo appearance in the third season of *House of Cards*™.

Also in 2013, Naughty Dog, a studio long associated with cinematic gaming thanks to its *Uncharted* series, released perhaps its most successful story-driven game to date in the form of *The Last of Us*™. Originally released on the PlayStation 3 (and, in 2014, the PlayStation 4), *The Last of Us* is a third-person action adventure game set in a world ravaged by an infection that turns normal people into ravenous beasts. Players take on the role of Joel, a smuggler who's forced into escorting a teenage girl, Ellie, across the United States. Mysteriously immune to the virus that's ravaging the planet, Ellie's blood could hold the key to humanity's salvation.

The *Last of Us*, while set against a grand post-apocalyptic backdrop, instead, in a manner that echoes *The Walking Dead – Season 1*, focuses on exploring both the relationship Joel and Ellie build over the course of the game, and the relationships they have with themselves. We quickly learn Joel is still in mourning for a teenage daughter he lost years before in the first throes of the infection and, later, that Ellie has ghosts of her own to wrestle. A fusion of excellent, patient writing, art, audio, design, and performances made *Last of Us* one of the year's most successful titles.

Also of note is the excellent *Left Behind* DLC released the following year. Set weeks before the events that take place in the main game, players control Ellie as she explores an abandoned mall with old friend, Riley, in a bid to rekindle their relationship and briefly recapture the magic of their fleeting youth. Once again, excellent pacing and performances help Naughty Dog deliver a story that was loved by players and reviewers alike.

But, as we've seen, AAA game development budgets aren't always necessary for a game's story to get under a player's skin. *Papers, Please*™ is a small, simple game developed by independent developer Lucas Pope and released on PC, iOS, and PlayStation Vita. In the game players take on the role of an immigration officer working at a small crossing on the border of fictional country, Arstotzka. Players have the power to decide who is allowed to enter the country and who is turned away. *Papers, Please* forces players to carry out increasingly complex checks while balancing the needs of their suffering family with those of the poor souls who shuffle through the border-crossing booth. Each has a reason to plead for special dispensation if a photo doesn't fit or a piece of paperwork is missing.

Does a player accept a bribe that'll help feed their family and keep the heating on in their tiny apartment, but risk the ire of the Ministry of Admissions, or do they stick doggedly to the rules, safe but poor? Tension inevitably mounts between the needs of a player's fictional family and those of the souls who drift through their tiny island of power. *Papers, Please*, is a small game that, thanks to providing a powerful stream of personal tragedies for players to deal with while balancing the needs of their own impoverished family, punches far above its weight in the narrative department.

Few television shows successfully make the jump into games, especially comedies. In 2014 Obsidian Entertainment, in partnership with South Park Digital Studios, released their *South Park: The Stick of Truth*™ RPG on the PC, PlayStation 3, and Xbox 360. It was to prove the exception to the rule. Based on the popular animated adult entertainment show that first aired in 1997, players take on the role of The New Kid who's just moved to town only to become embroiled in an epic struggle to recover the fabled Stick of Truth when it's stolen by a rival faction of kids. Gameplay involves a mix of 'pretend' fantasy turn-based fighting and exploration. *South Park: The Stick of Truth* is a powerful reminder that game developers need to stay true to the narrative soul of an IP, know what makes it popular, and know how to transfer it intact into the game they make. The title's success was no doubt helped greatly by the presences of Matt Stone and Trey Parker, who were heavily involved throughout the development process.

Another game that made effective use of a beloved IP, this one lighter on laughs, was released in the same year. A game world often features antagonists restricted to a predetermined set of actions; players quickly learn how to defeat NPCs who, once triggered, carry out the same attacks in the same order. This makes them increasingly less dangerous, and less interesting. Set in Tolkien's famous fantasy realm, *Middle Earth: The Shadow of Mordor*™ aims to set enemies free of such restrictions. Developed by Monolith Productions and released on PC, PlayStation 3, PlayStation 4, Xbox 360, and Xbox One, it also released in 2014. Players take on the mantle of Talion, a ranger who, along with his family, is murdered at the start of the game by the nefarious Black Hand of Sauron only to be resurrected by the spirit of the Elf Lord Celebrimbor. The pair set out to claim revenge.

While *Middle Earth: The Shadow of Mordor*'s main story boils down to a simple one of revenge, Monolith created a piece of technology they called the Nemesis System. It's basically an Artificial Intelligence that inhabits the game world's orc bosses (minor and upward), which enables them to remember player-driven events that occur and react accordingly. If an orc is attacked and almost killed by the player but manages to escape (fear is also evident in your enemies, which does a great job of making the player feel both dangerous and rewarded), then they remember the fight and comment on it when they next see the player. If an NPC manages to kill the player, they're not only made more potent themselves, they remember Talion and take great pleasure gloating about his defeat when they see him next. Monolith's Nemesis System helps the world feel reactive and unpredictable, which not only adds to the challenge and excitement, but also the value of a second playthrough.

Further proof that unpredictable antagonists, free from the usual shackles imposed upon them by more traditional game design, can make fearsome opponents was to arrive in the form of survival horror game *Alien Isolation*™. Developed by Creative Assembly and released on PC, PlayStation 3, PlayStation 4, Xbox 360, and Xbox One, players take on the role of Amanda Ripley, daughter of Ellen Ripley, as she seeks to uncover the truth behind her mother's disappearance fifteen years earlier. Played from a first-person perspective, players quickly find themselves trapped on the Sevastopol, an aging space station owned by the Seegson Corporation, trying to escape the clutches of an alien eager to kill everything on the station. In *Alien Isolation* players struggle against an essentially unfettered, terrifying enemy free to move around the environment and capable of adjusting its tactics, which results in memorable emergent story moments. While Amanda's story might not possess a rich arc, Creative Assembly manages to deliver a tense, thrilling experience echoing that of Ellen Ripley in the first *Alien*™ film.

As hardware becomes more powerful, developers can create ever-larger story sandpits for gamers to frolic in. A lesson taught by open world masters Rockstar North is that the trick to creating a large world is it has to feel alive. CD Projekt Red's third entry in their *Witcher* series, *The Witcher 3: Wild Hunt*™, features one of the largest, most richly realized RPG worlds to date.

Released on the PC, Xbox One, and PlayStation 4, players are Geralt of Rivia, a monster hunter known as a witcher, who travels the Northern Kingdoms in search of his missing stepdaughter. CD Projekt Red provide players with a vast, rich, and adult world to enjoy that helps remind us that gamers are getting older and more mature. The game's writers and designers provide players with skillfully crafted quests that often ably illustrate the value of the plot point—all is often not what it seems in Geralt's world, which is all for the better. The developer is also well-known for providing players with a generous amount of free post-launch content, in the form of new quests, animations, and armor sets. This generosity serves not only to enrich the gameplay and story experience further, but earns loyalty from gamers used to development houses charging for extra content. It's worth nothing CD Projeckt Red's two *Witcher* expansion packs, *Hearts of Stone* and *Blood and Wine*, were both met with critical acclaim and successfully extended the game's already lengthy story.

While some games grow larger to help deliver their story, the independent game scene is proving fertile too. *Her Story*™, created by independent developer Sam Barlow and released on PC and iOS, has players search though a video database of police interviews to help find the whereabouts of a missing man. The interviews are of the missing man's wife, Hannah Smith, who may or may not have been involved in a crime.

Her Story is proof that story, if skillfully woven, can be delivered in small pieces and players can enjoy piecing it together for themselves. The very act of solving the puzzle helps draw us in and make us feel involved. Its intriguing, refreshing gameplay delivers the narrative in an intriguing, minimalist fashion.

2015's *Life is Strange*™, by Dontnod Entertainment, released on the PC, PlayStation 3, PlayStation 4, Xbox 360, and Xbox One, tells the tale of Maxine Caulfield, a student of photography who discovers she can rewind time. Also apparently given the gift of prescience, Max shortly after that has a vision of her town being destroyed and sets out to ensure that such a grim future doesn't come to pass.

Telling a complex, time-traveling story through the eyes of a teenage girl and making the former interesting and the latter likeable takes skill. Dontnod's episodic tale explores the themes of love and guilt in a refreshing, low-key manner complimented by a subtle use of beautiful music.

While *Life is Strange* allows players some freedom in how the story plays out, another narrative-driven game by Supermassive Games and released on the PlayStation 4 in 2015 puts more flexible branching narrative at the very core of the player experience. *Until Dawn*™ follows the story of eight teenagers who make the inevitably dangerous decision to spend the weekend at a luxury lodge on (the fictional) Blackwood Mountain to mark the grisly anniversary of the mysterious disappearance of two of their number. Inevitably, bad things start to happen, and it's up to the player to help everyone survive until dawn. Often through providing players with simple decisions (agree or disagree, be nice or be funny), *Until Dawn* manages to provide a storyline that reacts meaningfully to decisions, causing the plot to evolve over time. Whereas many game plots allow somewhat restricted expression on the part of the player (e.g., you can take one of two paths but eventually they'll often join again), *Until Dawn* allows both small and large decisions to stack up over the course of a single playthrough.

Upon finishing the game it's entirely possible to have saved all eight of the group, though by the time the credits roll it's likely a least a few will have met a variety of grisly ends. This freedom and flexibility not only rewards further playthroughs, it lends players a strong sense of narrative agency.

Remedy Entertainment, creators of *Alan Wake*, continue to push the envelope of cinematic storytelling with the release of action-adventure third-person shooter *Quantum Break*™. Originally an Xbox One exclusive but then released on PC too, it tells the tale of Jack Joyce, heroic everyman who vows to stop his old friend, Paul Serene, from helping usher in the End of Time after a failed time machine experiment.

On balance a mostly linear experience, Remedy pushes the narrative boundaries by fusing gameplay with live-action story to a degree never before seen. Levels are capably bookended by high-quality live action narrative that both helps further the story and provide glimpses into the background of several of the individuals arrayed against, and allied with, Joyce.

Interestingly, at the conclusion of every act, players take control of Paul Serene in order to make a decision that will impact the upcoming plot. In one instance Serene must decide whether to kill a group of witnesses or spare them; leaving them alive lets Serene have help fronting a PR campaign against Joyce, while killing the witnesses to tie up loose ends will ultimately result in the public turning against Monarch, Serene's corporation. These decisions don't greatly impact the overarching story but they help shade it, which makes their inclusion meaningful and refreshing.

CONCLUSION

There is an unfaltering thirst for stories in games, and there's no reason to suggest this is doing anything other than continuing to grow the more it is fed. To date, interestingly, no hard figures have been compiled that tell us just how many unique console and handheld video game titles have been written over the decades. While carrying out research for this chapter in 2011, one well-placed industry source speculated the number to be in the region of over 60,000 (with a meaningful percentage available only in the Japanese territory). If one were to include Flash® games, core PC, MMO titles, mobile, and other casual games, that number could climb as high as 500,000. Though these figures are speculative, few would perhaps disagree with the key point being made—we have already seen, despite the youth of the medium, a great deal of games created, and the rate at which they are being made is accelerating. Of these titles, the majority will either feature story as a core feature of the gameplay (i.e. the game will be "about" something), or as an aspect of it (i.e., the game will feature distinct characters but will not tell a story).

History also shows that, within the limitations of contemporary technology, there have still been stories that have succeeded in captivating audiences. Just as the world of literature has its tales of readers waiting at the docks in New York for the next installment of Dickens' *The Old Curiosity Shop* to arrive from England, with more recent examples in the *Harry Potter* and *Twilight* series, and the music and movie industries have had their tales of lines of customers outside shops or cinemas and prodigious presales, so too, the world of games has its tales of first week sales of games and burgeoning subscription numbers. During its first three days of release in 2015, *Call of Duty: Black Ops 3*™ made over $550 million, a figure that clearly points to the fact video games are no longer a minority interest; since January 2009 games have been outselling DVDs and Blu-Rays. Stories in games and the characters within these game worlds have been instrumental in generating and channeling the emotion fans evidently feel and wish to express. (The costumes you see people wearing at events such as the Tokyo Games Show or Blizzcon are potent evidence of this.) Games are mainstream, and to those of us working within the industry, it feels as if their potential has so far barely been scratched.

But this history also seems to speak to something else, something even more interesting that gives rise to a more essential conclusion. Although technology continues to help drive the medium forward, its advances do not mean storytelling in games is merely encroaching on being ever more capable of approximating storytelling in movies. Instead, in conjunction with a growing body of knowledge about the complexities and techniques germane to the craft, technological advances are helping to offer story-related experiences that stand apart from other sources. There is much more than "movie-likeness" to aspire to. There is something utterly new to aim for.

To suggest that game stories are in all cases unique is to overstate the matter. We've seen, and continue to see, choice-driven story/character progression-based games that have their roots in conventional narrative forms, in books in which you choose your own adventure, and in role-playing games. We've seen, and continue to see, environmental storytelling inspired by theme parks, curated art exhibitions, theater, Augmented Reality Games (ARGs), and Live-Action Role Playing Games (LARPs). We're also seeing increasingly lush and ambitious graphical representations in conjunction with the broader world of animation. But when these older and parallel elements are re-appropriated and combined in any number of fresh combinations, then cast in the fire of interactivity, a sort of alchemy of forms takes place, where the sum of the parts exceeds the whole. Perhaps the most exciting place this alchemy may take us is the space where the excitement between a writer and a player creates a story not *told* in any true sense, but *experienced interactively*—something far beyond the capacity of movies or other conventional media in their past or present forms. Virtual reality hardware such as Oculus Rift™ and HTC Vive™ aren't just technological and design innovations; they are also opportunities for games writers to pull players into ever-deeper interactive experiences. Environmental storytelling, as we currently know it, may only be the gateway to what it's possible for us to imagine, create, and experience within game stories. This combination of evolving technology with varied storytelling elements that are recycled, re-applied, and occasionally added to looks set to continue to deliver game stories that often feel, in some sense, familiar (and can be evidenced as such when traced back to initial sources) but can, nevertheless, also drive surprising and somehow utterly new experiences. Perhaps we're really just on the cusp of history and what we've experienced so far is the pre-history.

EXERCISES

1. To what extent has technology played a part in helping game story evolve? Or, has the medium been driven by our evolving understanding of how story fits into games?
2. Given that a greater variety of genres are available today, which offer more compelling gameplay experiences, on a far wider selection of platforms?
3. Of the games listed in this chapter, which three had the greatest impact on how game stories were perceived and created?
4. Is there a game listed previously in the chapter in which story is clearly more important than gameplay? If so, why?

PROJECT

Create a short presentation no longer than ten minutes that explores the core reasons your title should have been included. It should contain the following sections:

Introduction

Game story and plot summary – why they work

Main character summaries – why they work

How the game design works with the game's writing

Conclusion (summarizing your core points)

If possible, include visuals to support your presentation

Part II

WHAT DO GAMES WRITERS DO? AND HOW DO THEY DO IT?

What indeed do games writers do? Have they wandered into games by accident? Is their purpose to give producers another plate to spin, or deprive designers of a juicy chunk of fun they've been rubbing their hands over since way back? The role of games writers is not always well understood in the wider world. Not only are writers *not* responsible for writing code (and coders, just as accurately, can be described as the writers or authors of a game), but there are also *game scriptors* (or *game scripters*) who write the script for a game—but these are also not the game's writers. Confused? Games scriptors are often level designers working with game design tools to create and edit extended sequences of gameplay.

The role of games writers is not always well understood within development either. Are they there to check the spelling of the games designers who write the story? Are they there to flesh out the story idea written by a games designer and turn it into dialogue and a recording script?

There are lots of different kinds of games, and even sequels of the same game will often, for various reasons, be substantially different projects. It depends on the project, but not all games need a dedicated writer. (A cinematic set piece replete with branching dialogue between each move in a game of chess is unlikely to improve the experience for the majority, and less likely to be worth the extra budget. Mind you, it does call various Koei games to mind.) And those games that do need a writer frequently need something different, delivered in a different way, at different speeds with different timings and different parameters in play. Every project is different; understanding it, and what makes it different, is what enables you to do your job.

The potential tasks of a writer cover a whole spectrum, from originating stories and engaging in game design at one end, through to writing outlines and treatments, narrative design, and writing scripts, all the way to script doctoring, writing manuals, and providing back-of-box copy at the other.

This section is intended to help walk the uninitiated through the range of these tasks, giving a sense of what and who is involved, and how to approach each in hand. Where appropriate, we've included case studies and sample exercises for the purposes of demonstration and clarification. Of course, there's more than one way to cook an egg, and we're not suggesting the approaches we outline are the only way to tackle each of these tasks. Our focus in these ensuing chapters is on the processes involved in handling these tasks, to introduce principles, rather than to derive definitive answers. As Confucius said: "Give a man a fish and he will eat for a day. Teach a man to fish and he will eat for a lifetime."[1]

[1] *http://www.egreenway.com/taichichuan/kft1.htm*

Chapter 2

DECODING AND DEVISING THE BRIEF

A journey of a thousand miles begins with a single step.

— Lao Tzu

BRIEF TERMS

BRIEF The document, documents, or verbal presentation that details the work required of—in this case—the games writer or game writing team on a specific project.

UNIQUE SELLING POINT (USP) Marketing term that refers to the unique quality of a given good or service that differentiates it from the competition; in a games title, it often refers to a unique gameplay element.

DOWNLOADABLE CONTENT (DLC) Additional content that can be downloaded to enhance a games title; DLC often takes the form of new equipment for characters, added gameplay, and new storylines.

HEADS-UP DISPLAY (HUD) A title's gameplay-oriented display of information presented on-screen in a format deemed most appropriate by its designers. Often includes information indicating an avatar's health and abilities.

CUT SCENES Cinematic sequences where players are shown story elements central to the game world, plot, and/or gameplay.

A brief is information passed from a client to a writer or team of writers, either in documented or verbal form, possibly of a formal or informal nature, designed to clearly outline what is needed from them. As a result a brief takes no standard form; it may feature many pages of detailed (quite possibly contradictory) requests with complex and intricate parameters, or it may, in essence, be the written equivalent of a shrug, accompanied by phrases such as "I don't know, just give us a story." When they do exist and are well-thought-out, they help clearly define the work a writer is tasked with completing and ensure contracts and milestones are understood by all parties. Thus, like any professional, the surest way for a games writer to court disaster is to fail to understand what's being asked of them. If you're just five degrees out at the start of Lao Tzu's journey of a thousand miles, then you end up about eighty-seven miles from where you were trying to get to.

(π times the diameter; a circle with a radius of 1,000 miles has a diameter of 2,000 miles. 3.14 x 2,000 = 6,280 miles. Divide that by 360 degrees = 17.4 miles off course for every degree, so 87.2 miles.) That's the difference between leaving New York and landing safely at Orlando airport, and ditching the plane into the North Atlantic. You could argue that that's sort of close enough, depending on what kind of risk levels are acceptable to you, but there's a more compelling argument that it's better to aim to get it right in the first place—with games development there are always plenty of other things along the way to blow you off course in any case. So your first task is to ask the vital question: What do you need from me?

There are a number of reasons why clear and enlightening answers to that question are frequently not forthcoming. For one thing, games development is often an inherently iterative and dynamic process. Things can change frequently and radically; a game might acquire or shed key elements that have

FIGURE 2.1. The difference between "right" and "close enough".

a considerable, even devastating impact on the story. If you find out halfway through writing your story that the design now allows characters to fly, and you're suddenly being instructed to make this core to the story, then you're pretty much going to have to start over. Except—most likely—characters and environments have already started being built and now you're stuck with at least some of them and therefore forced to retrofit your ideas around game elements that have become immovable.

BRIEFS AND EXPECTATIONS

Sometimes it's not just the iterative nature of games development that makes it hard for teams to express what they want; it's also the fact that they may be actively looking to innovate, explore, and experiment, so the last thing they want to do is pin things down too early and impose restrictions when they're searching for ways out of them.

On other occasions development teams can't be clear about what they need you to do precisely because you're the writer and they're not. It's a little reductive to hire an architect only to draw up intricate and full plans yourself. We hire professionals with experience beyond our own because we want to tap into that experience. We may have ideas, and targets in mind, and other restrictions such as time and money, but we're asking for the professional *not to do exactly what we say*, but, ideally, to help guide us and to show us possibilities beyond our own vision.

Sometimes the problem can be an assumed shared language that takes time to be exploded—whereupon you come to realize you haven't quite been talking about the same thing since the conversation began. Unlike many other games development disciplines, writing appears to be accessible to everyone; after all, everyone can write, right? However, this isn't about being good in English class and having perfect spelling and grammar; those things don't hurt, but that's not the point. The most important prerequisite is storytelling *ability*. But what is story?

It's not uncommon to find people on a development team talking about "story" when they seem to mean "plot," or using the word "narrative" when they seem to mean "story." The meanings of these terms are still debated in academic circles and there are no universally accepted and non-contested definitions. Nevertheless, academics are still picking these terms apart in order to examine the distinct delineations in meaning, whereas games developers are often unaware that there are different delineations and simply think of them as synonyms. It's like trying to build a wall not just with bricks, but also using shoe boxes—"they're the same shape"—and lobsters—"they're the same color"—and afterwards wondering how imperfections crept in. It's not important (or actually that desirable) for everyone to start quoting Roland Barthes and Seymour Chatman, but it is important for people to understand the ways in which certain words are being used in order to have a constructive conversation. (This topic of definitions is something we'll return to in due course.)

At other times the problem is a lack of understanding of how to deliver briefs and a failure to register what constitutes a meaningful reply to the core question: What do you need from me? The composite bad story brief we've had given to us on more than one occasion while sitting in design meetings with new clients runs something like this:

It's got to be cool. And dramatic. I don't want anything cheesy—I only want cool dialogue. Like Pulp Fiction. *And it's got to be new. And it's got to be edgy. And gritty.*

As a writer you're onboard because you've got skills to bring to the development team. Those skills not only need to include an ability to write—that's a given—they also need to include ways of deciphering a brief, decoding what a development team needs, and thinking about what's feasible and appropriate, given a project's unique constraints. Further, you may often find that part of decoding a brief, and the only way to check that you've decoded it correctly, is to roll up your sleeves and help the team by devising the brief with them.

There's no set way to go about doing this; it depends on a variety of factors, such as the development stage at which you're having these discussions, what kind of game you're working on, and, of course, the needs and preferences of individuals. One of the first questions you need to ask is *what kind of game is it? What kind of genre is the game?*

GAME GENRES

Movies are usually categorized into certain genres, such as a "romantic comedy" or "horror," due to the primary nature of the content one is presented with as a result of watching it. This basic label can help people quickly know the broad kind of story they'd get if choosing to watch a film. In a similar way, a game is usually categorized by the primary nature of the gameplay experience it provides the player. However, given the pace of change the game design universe is currently enjoying, these definitions are constantly being tested, changed, and hybridized. Is a title like *Broforce*™ for the PlayStation 4 and PC primarily a platformer or an action-shooter game? It might be a platform-action-shooter, if you're talking to a friend, but who can say for sure? While defining genres provides a useful set of basic descriptive and navigational tools, they by no means provide a solid basis for understanding the sheer number of gameplay experiences that have emerged, and will continue to emerge, over time. With this in mind, take the following list only as a useful starting point.

List of Genres

Action

A game in which the primary focus is normally on combat, either with weapons or bare-handed. Sometimes known as a "twitch game" due to the need for swift reflexes, action games encompass a broad swath of game subsets; *Pac Man* and *Double Dragon*™, both arcade classics, are early examples of action games. Given the prevalence of titles that feature combat of one kind or another, this could be thought of as a "meta-genre."

Fighting

A subset of the action genre, these titles often focus on martial art-based combat-oriented gameplay. Examples include arcade classic *Street Fighter*®, *Virtua Fighter*™, and the *Super Smash Bros.* series of titles.

Shooter

Another subset of the action genre, often known as First-Person Shooters (FPS) in which the action is experienced from the avatar's perspective, or Third-Person Shooters (TPS) in which the avatar is visible to the player on-screen. These titles base their primary gameplay experience on gun-oriented combat. It's an extremely popular genre; examples include the *Overwatch*™, *Gears of War*™, *Halo*, *Killzone*™, and *Call of Duty* series of games.

Adventure

More cerebral in nature, adventure games rely on puzzle, story, and logic-based gameplay to entertain, rather than reflexes. *Colossal Cave Adventure* (mentioned in Chapter 1) was the first such game and used a text-based interface to present the player with a series of intellectual challenges that had to be overcome to progress. Later examples include *The Secret of Monkey Island* and *Full Throttle*™. Modern examples of "pure" adventure games are rare, but the popular *Broken*

Sword™ series of games illustrate there's still a market for the genre. This utilizes a "point and click" interface in which the player uses the mouse, or other pointing device, to navigate and interact with the game's environment.

Survival Horror

These often present the player with an atmospheric world that plays on more subtle psychological fears to evoke a feeling of dread in which their avatar continually faces death at the hands of various supernatural creatures and/or a deadly environment. Rather than equipping the avatar with a variety of potent weapons, the emphasis is instead on avoidance and ammunition conservation in the face of forces far more powerful than the player; the *Silent Hill* and *Dead Space* series are renowned examples in this genre.

Stealth

These focus on stealth-based mechanics to provide the main gameplay thrust, where the player must avoid detection in order to progress. These games often include other elements (such as combat or puzzle-solving) to round out the experience. One of the most famous examples is the *Metal Gear Solid* series, which successfully combines third-person, stealth-based gameplay with a TPS mechanic.

Role-Playing

One of the most popular genres, RPGs focus on providing the player with a story-based experience in which one or more avatars must be successfully guided through a variety of obstacles in the name of a meta-quest. Based on older, traditional role-playing games such as *Dungeons & Dragons*, players upgrade their characters as they progress, evolving them in-line with the story so that, by the end, they have experienced both a story and gameplay arc. Noteworthy RPGs include *Skyrim*, *Baldur's Gate*®, *Fallout*, *Mass Effect*, and *The Witcher* series of games.

Puzzle

These require the player to solve or navigate a variety of puzzles in order to succeed. Puzzle games can extend beyond pure puzzles in their own right, such as crosswords and Sudoku. Puzzles are often a key element of adventure games and can be used to supplement gameplay in other genres, such as in an FPS game, like *Portal*, or a casual title like *Jewel Quest*™. Puzzles are intrinsic to games such as the highly popular *Professor Layton* series on the DS, or *The Witness*, which are both, in essence, a series of puzzles linked by plots.

Simulation

These titles aim to simulate an experience or activity to varying degrees of realism. Early examples of simulation games came in the form of flight simulators (*Flight Simulator* being one of the first) and city-building games such as *Sim City*. Gameplay centers around players managing a finite set of resources in order to build, evolve, or progress in a variety of ways. This genre can also include the "god game" in which players take on the role of invisible deity, able to decide on the fate of their worshippers (as in *Populous*) or a species (as in *Spore*).

Strategy

This genre focuses on gameplay that requires strategic planning to successfully achieve gameplay objectives. Players can find themselves in control of a civilization that they must guide thorough centuries of development (as in the *Civilization*® series of games) or in command of an army that hungers for victory (as in the *Total War*® series).

Music

Music-based games often require the player to successfully navigate rhythm-based challenges in order to succeed. Titles often require extra equipment, such as plastic game guitars and drums (as in *Rock Band*®), though they can rely simply on existing input methods (*Patapon*™ for the [PSP®] only requires the player to use existing buttons to play).

Party

This genre of game aims to provide a series of short, easy-to-play mini-games that can tie into a loose meta-narrative. Games such as *Rayman Raving Rabbids*® and *Mario Party*™ feature short challenges that can be played in multiplayer mode, with several people taking part at once.

Educational

These titles' primary goal is to teach players specific skills and knowledge as a result of their experiencing the gameplay. These are often simple titles for younger (subteen) players and can revolve around learning to read (such as *Teach Your Monster to Read*) and learning basic spelling and arithmetic. The BBC's *Bitesize* Website contains excellent examples of educational games for children aged between four and sixteen.

Casual

Arguably another meta-genre, these are titles that can incorporate any of the genres discussed above, but in a manner that allows a very low barrier to entry and provides satisfaction after a relatively short period of time (under one minute, in some cases). Examples include *Angry Birds*™ (now, somewhat surprisingly, also a film) and *Fruit Ninja*™.

Activity

Games such as *Wii Fit* with its dedicated balance board peripheral began to encourage players to exercise. Increasingly, mobile titles such as *Zombies, Run!* and *Pokémon Go* directly connect real life activity to gameplay, sometimes meshing stories into the experience too.

Story

Although many games in other genres possess story, and often great deals of it, we may, perhaps, say that games such as *Heavy Rain, Beyond Two Souls, Life Is Strange, Until Dawn*, and much of the output of Telltale Games, constitute a genre of their own, where story is not just central to the experience but actually, to a lesser or greater extent, drives the gameplay, arguably even being the gameplay itself. Perhaps this kind of experience approximates more to an interactive drama than what some would comfortably define as a game. This kind of experience harkens back to the Choose Your Own Adventure and Fighting Fantasy type books on the late 1970s and early 1980s.

Online

Not a genre, strictly speaking, all of the above game types can possess an online element in which interaction with other players is either core to gameplay (as in MMOs such as *Guild Wars*®) or an optional extra (as in some RPG titles, such as *Dark Souls 3*™). If online is core to gameplay, you will need to explore how it will impact the game's story.

As mentioned already, games can be, and today often are, hybrids of two or more of the above genres. Each genre brings with it its own set of potential players who bring certain expectations that either need to be delivered on or knowingly and skillfully subverted in ways that will still create a satisfying play experience.

Knowing what kind of genre the game is, or if it is intended to be a combination of existing genres or an attempt to formulate something new, will be key to your attempts to understand what the client wants. What follows is the checklist we use when trying to understand what a development team needs from us. To be clear, this list isn't the form a client brief usually takes, though a good brief might very closely resemble it. This is a list we use to help us ensure, over the course of discussions and/or other correspondence, we have a sufficient grasp of what's required in order to begin work in earnest. In a sense, it's a tool we use to help us devise our own brief in cooperation with the client.

CHECKLIST FOR BRIEFS

- *What genre is it?*

  (See the discussion earlier in the chapter.)

- *What platform is it for?*

  PC, Xbox One, PlayStation 4, smartphone, tablet, for example, and if for PC what range of specifications of PC are you aiming at?

- *Who is it for?*

  Age, gender, dedicated interest groups, countries, and cultures are all things to consider.

- *What rating is it?*

  The United States and Canada use the ESRB system (Entertainment Software Rating Board), Europe uses the PEGI system (Pan European Game Information), and there are a number of other systems used worldwide, such as the ACB (Australian Classification Board), CERO (Computer Entertainment Rating Organization) in Japan, RRB (Game Rating Board in South Korea), the CSRR (Computer Software Rating Regulation) in China, the DJRTQ (Department of Justice, Rating, Titles and Qualification) in Brazil, and VET (Finnish Board of Film Classification), and all these systems have their own specific classifications (see the Appendix A for further details).

- *When does the story have to be finished?*

  How long do you have to complete your work and to get it into the game? Are there studio recording sessions and/or localization deadlines or submission dates to work around?

- *Who is responsible for signing off deliveries?*

  Who is your line manager? A producer, designer, lead writer, studio boss?

- *What are the delivery milestones?*

  Do you have requested word counts, or scene numbers, or are you required to complete a draft of a complete script (or sections thereof) by a certain date? It's vital to clarify milestones, as they not only help structure the work that needs to be done, they act as safety points that help ensure both parties are satisfied with the progress being made.

- *How long should the story be?*

  Are there required page lengths, word counts, or "screen times"?

- *How many characters can we have?*

  Are there pre-existing characters that are essential to brand identity? Are there pre-existing character meshes that push your character development in certain directions? If there's no brand IP to be faithful to, is there a pre-existing maximum number of characters available defined by budgetary or technological limits?

- *What are the mo-cap, animation, and audio restrictions?*

  Are there pre-existing character meshes and/or motion capture that prevent you from creating characters with significantly different physiques and ways of moving? Are there limits on the kinds of (convincing) voices you have access to?

- *What are we trying to do? What kind of experience are we seeking to create?*

  What core experience are we hoping to deliver to the player? Can someone explain the ideal sensation or sequence of events that build to a sensation that best explain this experience? Think of this not as broad and thorough as a walkthrough, and not as dry and business-oriented as a Unique Selling Point (USP) list for advertising copy, but instead as an opportunity to hear someone explain in a few sentences or so in an accessible language that communicates the essence of what makes the game exciting to them. You may get different kinds of answers from different people on the project, and that is quite understandable given the range of people with varied disciplines you will be working with, but it is also helpful to hear. These different answers may not be mutually exclusive, and you may see a way to bring them all together in a cohesive whole.

- *What's the tone of voice?*

  Is the tone dramatic? Epic? Tragic? If it is comedic is it parody or slapstick, urbane wit or farce? Tone is often a highly contentious issue, and instead of reaching for synonyms, the most uniformly useful approach has proved to be, for us, to speak in terms of content that works as a universal reference—this may be a game, a movie, a TV show, a book, a play, a musical, or something else that people have broadly experienced and so can quickly understand what is meant by way of example. Often you will find you combine various kinds of media together to try and approximate a descriptor for the sort of tone you are aiming for. Avoid stopping at simply "dramatic" or "comedy," since without further clarifiers these terms are of almost no use at all. You're attempting to understand the world your story takes place in, the kinds of characters who live there, and the kinds of dramatic action that should be expected/demanded within it, as well as a sense of the kind of themes and meanings you should be tailoring your storytelling towards.

- *Do we have just sound or just text? Or both?*

  And where can we have both, or where can we have just one or the other, and what are the limits of each?

- *Are there different player modes?*

  For example, is there only a single player mode or is there also a multiplayer mode? And can the player ever play with more than one other person? Can the player play split screen and/or on other machines? Are any of the modes restrictive of content, and if so what?

- *Does the game have a relationship with predecessors in the same series?*

  Is it a sequel? A prequel? Is it a sequel in spirit but not in narrative chronology? Does it share one or more characters with a previous game? Are previous stories to be wholly ignored or taken as integral to the ensuing action, or somewhere in-between?

- *Does it have a relationship with anything else that's planned, either in the same or a different media?*

  Are there future comics, movies, toys, or a TV series in development? Is there any DLC planned? Does your story need to leave sufficient room for parallel or future stories to take shape? Do you need to make sure you leave certain characters alive you would otherwise have planned to kill off?

- *What references are we drawing from?*

  Similar, in a sense, to the question on tone of voice, however, this question needs to be asked because sometimes references are pulled from sources without there being any conscious attempt to draw on that source. You're seeking to understand what references are already being drawn on and why—what do these sources offer the development team in terms of inspiration? Are there missed opportunities to mine these sources further? Are there confusing admixtures of conflicting sources? Which of these sources can you rationalize?

- *What's the relationship between the game and the story?*

  How does the game structure break down? Are cut scenes required? If so, how many, where, and how long? Is the storytelling to be wholly environmental? Are there any other technical approaches informing the storytelling? Are the game systems, the HUD, the UI, or menu screens going to provide storytelling real estate? Is the story taking precedence over gameplay at any point? This last question is not one you will usually ask, certainly not when involved with conventional games development, but there are occasions, such as when you work at the more experimental end of the spectrum, of game-related interactive storytelling where you do need to ask this. There may be occasions where the answer is yes, however, and at such times you need to understand the ramifications.

- *What are the player's gameplay motivations?*

  How does a player win in the game or progress? How do they understand these objectives? What feedback does the game give them to mark their progress, if they are winning or losing? Is it a driving game? In which case, how can you build a story around the player driving well? This doesn't have to mean you can only tell the story of a racing driver, as the *Driver* series shows. Is it an FPS? In which case, how can you build a story complementary to your gameplay motivations of shooting a large number of enemies? Whatever the game, you need your story to run in the same direction as the player's motivations.

- *Are there any other design implications or requirements?*

  This refers, by way of example, to *James Noir's Hollywood Crimes*, a 3DS game by Ubisoft. Nintendo's desire to highlight the design features of their new console required that the story use the accelerometer and camera, beyond the original design parameters; in essence this game began as, and still is, a puzzle game. But it was the marketing needs to optimize the profile of new technology informing the design that created a new section of the storytelling brief.

- *Does the controller configuration have any bearing on the story world?*

  This is likely to be rare. However, if your controller configuration, or the UI, is closely tied to something your character can do in the game (for example, double jump, turn invisible, or transform into a winged-kangaroo), then it's clear these are primary attributes, and so your story may need to address them, to explain why they exist. At the very least, your story will need to be aware that it's knowingly avoiding explaining them.

- *What triggers can the game detect?*

  If you're writing commentary script for a tennis game, can the game detect if the ball was hit out by a distance or a margin? It's better feedback and more immersive for a player to hear "just out," if the ball was just out, rather than another generic "that was out" spun out a hundred different ways by an ingenious writer and inventive recording sessions. Again, it's better feedback and more immersive to hear "that went very long," or "almost in a different court!" if the ball was out by a large margin than the same "that was out" line. If you're writing commentary script for a boxing game and an avatar is taking hits, it's better feedback and more immersive to hear *where* the punches are landing. Can the game detect the difference between a head shot and a body shot? Can it detect the difference between a blow to the kidneys and one to the ribs? If appropriate to the genre and the story context, it's often better for the player to know the direction from which they're taking fire—in which case you need to know how accurate the game can be about this. Does the game know if an avatar is heading down the wrong corridor in an underground sewer complex? Can an intercom voice from an NPC teammate character tell a player to turn their avatar around and take the first turn on their left? There's no point writing these lines unless the game code can detect the levels of differentiation you're aiming to write for. But, if you can write them (inside other restrictions, such as time, budget, and memory space), they invariably improve the level of experience—the feedback and immersion—you can bring to a player. Not only that, but the more specific the script can be in relation to the player's progress, the more *helpful* this feedback and immersion can be from a gameplay perspective.

- *What art style(s) are we working with?*

  Instead of descriptions, can you see samples of this artwork? It could help inform your thoughts on tone of voice.

- *Is there a specific budget or a budget range to work within?*

  If you understand what budget a developer has you can help them meet it in the most appropriate and cost-effective way. Perhaps there are tasks they are requesting which experience tells you are unnecessary or best left alone until technical or other elements are definitely included in the game. Perhaps character biographies a developer has requested can be revised so that, instead of being three pages long, they are three paragraphs long. (Writing fewer words can, in fact, take longer as it requires more thought to enable fewer words to contain the same amount of meaning.) Perhaps the budget is the most instrumental factor in your decision to advise re-casting the story from being a five-act structure with six subplots and fourteen main characters to being a three-act structure with two subplots featuring four main characters.

A good brief will address those questions posed above, and your job with a bad brief is to ask the right questions to turn it into a good one. And *whom* do you ask? Well, that's what Chapter 4 is about.

DISCUSSIONS

1. What game genre do you consider a poor fit for a small screen size? List three reasons.
2. Are there any games you think are inherently a better fit on a small screen than on a larger one? Give three examples.

EXERCISES

1. Imagine you're a freelance games writer who's just been given the brief to help write the story for a game—but the brief, in your opinion, needs to be changed as the story contains characters whose motivations seem deeply problematic and need revision. Discuss how you would do this if the senior games designer you're working with feels there's no issue at all. Would you seek to put together evidence to illustrate your points? Would you provide alternative ideas that would help solve the problem? Also, who would you approach and how?
2. Take a popular game you have played (preferably to completion) and reverse-engineer a story brief for it. Imagine yourself the head of the design team in need of a writer to help bring the gameplay to life. Choose from three of the following headings and put together a one- to two-page descriptive brief without the title, or any other reference to the game, at the top:

Platform or platforms

Demographic

Genre

Story length

Player's gameplay motivations

Broad – non-specific – story beats

Tone of voice

How the game title's story links to others

Different player modes and how they impact the story

The player's gameplay motivations

Art style

Then, when you've finished, exchange your story briefs with other students or groups and try to figure out which games you've been describing.

Optional: Each individual or group is allotted three minutes to present a brief to the class (using no direct references to their chosen game), after which students are challenged to guess which title the brief is referring.

Chapter 3 NDAs & Contracts

Make fair agreements and stick to them.

— Confucius

BRIEF TERMS

NON-DISCLOSURE AGREEMENT (NDA) A legal document designed to ensure any privileged information regarding a games title remains out of the public domain. Writers signing an NDA are obliged to not reveal any sensitive information, or risk facing legal action.

MIDDLEWARE Computer software designed to integrate with a game engine to provide specific functionality; for example, Havok™ Physics is middleware that can provide a game with collision detection and other physical simulation tools.

CONTRACT A legally binding agreement that a games writer (especially freelance) often enters into prior to starting work on a project, designed to clearly state each party's obligations regarding a given project and the legal penalties for not honoring them.

NON-DISCLOSURE AGREEMENTS

As you might expect, you'll see more paperwork (or Word™-based documents) than just those relating to the story or game design. Games, unlike some other creative media, have a little preliminary dance ahead of the contract stage. This is the world of non-disclosure agreements or, as they're normally called, NDAs. These mutual agreements are legal documents used to protect sensitive commercial and design information. Invariably a publisher or developer will put them in front of a writer prior to providing information relating to the brief. In theory, these NDAs also protect the writer as they disclose potentially sensitive information, such as pay rates, or ideas in relation to the brief they have been contacted about. However, pay rates are often universally known, though they do vary from region to region, with different publishers or developers, and depending on the writer's experience and profile. (The IGDA, the Writers Guild of America, and the Writers Guild of Great Britain are all good sources to find out current rates.) And anything creative a writer offers while under an NDA doesn't stop a potential client from using it, or developing it, it only protects the writer's right to also use that idea. (In practice, few writers have access to a development team to take advantage of such an idea should they decide to unleash it, and if they did, they would have been foolish to have said anything too revealing to a potential competitor in the first place.)

Of course, if you're an in-house writer, hired on a salary working as part of a development studio, or by a publisher, you won't see these kinds of documents, unless it's as a result of subcontracting other writers. These do vary, but not, in our experience to date, considerably. In essence, they all say you can't tell anyone any details about a project, and, in some cases, you can't even tell anyone there's a project and that you have anything to do with the developer or publisher, unless that party first provides written permission. The reason for this cautious, arguably slightly neurotic, approach seems to lie in the game industry's heavy reliance on technology. Clearly, without technology, the games industry would not exist as we know it. But what is fascinating to consider is that so few of the contemporary titles released every year boast considerable amounts of technology that lift them clearly away from their competitors—purely in terms of that technology. Arguably, contemporary design elements can be, and often are, just as significant—if not more significant—in terms of attracting players and, therefore, revenue. There will always be titles that push technological boundaries, but the increasing prevalence of middleware (in-game engines such as Unreal™ and Unity™) seems to suggest the industry is as much about game design as technological innovation.

Apart from the smallest of development studios, very few won't push an NDA your way before they reveal anything meaningful about their upcoming title. Of course, you should read it carefully, and potentially have a professional lawyer check the details and ask to make changes if you feel reasonably motivated to do so, but don't expect too much by way of a response—these documents are usually standard format, and developers and publishers do not encourage any amendments to them. You can always not sign it, but that's most likely saying goodbye to the job, depending on what your status is and to what extent they specifically want you onboard.

Here's a sample NDA we've taken the liberty of dissecting in places it's useful to pay particular attention to (we don't comment on sections that are pretty self-explanatory). Please note comments, suggestions, and thoughts provided below are not intended as substitutes for legal advice from a qualified lawyer; they're there to provide an indication, from a games writer's perspective, of what to expect from a document of this nature. The NDA below is also presented, unedited, in Appendix B.

SAMPLE NON-DISCLOSURE AGREEMENT

THIS AGREEMENT is made on the 25 day of July 2016

BETWEEN

Mark B. Hardington IV, whose address is at **222 Long Street, Denver, Colorado 80215, USA**

AND

ABC Games Writing Company, whose address is at **999 Dawson Street, Denver, Colorado 80210,** hereinafter jointly referred to as the "Parties" or individually as the "Party"

Basic information that clearly illustrates who the agreement is between; sometimes the client you're signing up with is actually a parent company to the developer, and this is where that will be apparent.

Introduction

(A) The Parties wish to discuss **possible transactions between the parties.** The discussions will necessitate the disclosure of information concerning the business and affairs of each other and of other companies in the same group of companies as each of the Parties ("the business and affairs of the parties").

(B) Each party requires such disclosures to be treated in confidence and to be protected in accordance with the terms of this Agreement.

This section basically sets out the broad purpose of the document.

IT IS AGREED as follows:

1. Information disclosed under this Agreement will include, but not be limited to, commercial, financial, technical, operational, or other information in whatever form (including information disclosed orally) that concerns the business and affairs of the Parties and is of a confidential nature, including any such information disclosed prior to the date of this Agreement ("Confidential Information").

This defines the parameters of the agreement—the example above illustrates that most NDAs also seek to cover incidental information the writer might become privy to during the course of their work (the act of simply walking through an office space can result in any number of chances to pick up interesting, and sensitive, information). Section 1 makes sure that anything you find out, even when it doesn't directly involve the game you're working on, is covered by your signature. In addition, this section is explicit that information accrued prior to the agreement (not just the signing of it, but the date of it) is also covered.

2. Each party will:

   2.1 keep in confidence any Confidential Information disclosed to it by the other party and will not disclose that Confidential Information to any person (other than their employees or professional advisers, who need to know the Confidential Information) without the written consent of the other Party;

   2.2 use the Confidential Information disclosed to it by the other Party only for the purpose for which it was disclosed;

   2.3 ensure that all people to whom the Confidential Information is disclosed under this Agreement are aware of the terms of this Agreement; and

   2.4 make copies of the Confidential Information only to the extent strictly necessary to the purpose for which it was disclosed.

This defines the manner in which the parameters set out in Section 1 will be adhered to.

3. The parties will keep the existence, nature, and content of this Agreement confidential, together with the fact that discussions are taking place concerning the business and affairs of the Parties.

Section 3 ensures all elements of the work being entered into remain confidential (even the fact that an NDA has been signed). If a writer is hired to work on the sequel to a big game that hasn't been confirmed as in the development pipeline, Section 3 ensures—in theory—that the writer can't even say they've signed an

NDA, as even this would basically confirm the game's impending release, stealing much of the marketing department's thunder before they're ready.

4. Paragraphs 2 and 3 will not apply to:
   (a) information which has been published other than through a breach of this Agreement;
   (b) information lawfully in the possession of the recipient before its disclosure under this Agreement took place;
   (c) information obtained from a third party who is free to disclose it;
   (d) information independently developed by a Party;
   (e) information which a Party is requested to disclose and, if it did not, could be required by law (including a regulatory body) to disclose.

Section 4, important, defines what is not covered by the agreement (such as information provided by a third party who is allowed to pass it on to the writer, for example).

5. No licenses or any rights under any patent, registered design, copyright, design right or any similar right belonging to either Party are implied or granted under this Agreement.

Again, this section clarifies what isn't granted by either party as a result of signing the agreement (copyright, design rights, etc.).

6. The obligations and restrictions in this Agreement will last for a period of 2 years from the date of the last disclosure of Confidential Information under this Agreement.

7. The receiving Party will on request either:
   (a) return all copies of the Confidential Information to the disclosing Party; or
   (b) destroy it and confirm in writing to the disclosing Party that this has been done.

8. The disclosure of Confidential Information under this Agreement does not oblige either Party to enter in to any further agreement with the other Party.

9. Neither Party will export directly or indirectly any technical data acquired under this Agreement or any products produced utilizing any such data to

any country to which the U.S. Government or any of its agencies requires an export license or other government approval, without first obtaining such license or approval.

Section 9 ensures any technology used by either party is not basically stolen or used for projects other than the one covered by the agreement. Given games writers don't get involved with middleware or programming technologies, this section isn't really that relevant and is often left in for safety, or simply because the legal department didn't see the need to remove it.

10. This Agreement is governed by the Law of the United States.

Areas allotted to signatures normally follow, but we'll skip them as the entire document is available in Appendix B.

CONTRACTS

Contracts are the next step after NDAs. They may be predicated on day rates or fixed fees in line with specific milestones. It's in everyone's interests for these milestones to be as specific as possible. It's always prudent to pay particular attention to the details of the contract, and, if you can, to help speed up this process wherever possible—because you are unlikely to ever get paid until it's in place. As with NDAs, read the contract carefully and take issue with anything you find hard to accept (though again, the bigger the prospective client the more likely you are, depending on your own relevant size, to get a slightly confused response as they explain that's *just the way it is* and you can *take it or leave it*—if you get any response at all). In addition, writers, whether freelance or in-house, should pay particular attention to their credit provision. Try to ensure there are clauses that contractually guarantee you an appropriate credit for your work on the game—as a writer, narrative designer, consultant, and so on. (More on the difference between these roles later in this section.) If it's not yet clear precisely what the full nature of your role or roles may be, then try to ensure the contract recognizes your right to address this at an appropriate moment later on, or, at the very least, ensure your contact, most often a producer, is made aware of your desire to refine this at a later point. (Though do expect this to be very low on the producer's list of priorities for the rest of their life.) In addition, try, if you can, to have the contract guarantee you a copy of the game on release—although often developers will say this is beyond their power to grant, and will be at the discretion of the publisher.

Here's a sample contract, which, once again, we've dissected to point out particular areas that are useful to take note of. It does not contain provision for milestones, credits, or payment schedules—which should always be included. As before, comments made below are from the perspective of the professional games writer, not a qualified lawyer—always seek professional legal advice if in doubt about the meaning of a section or clause. This sample contract appears in Appendix B.

SAMPLE CONFIDENTIAL SERVICES AGREEMENT

THIS AGREEMENT (this **"Agreement"**) is entered into as of 25 July, 2011, by and between (1) **BIG CLIENT** of Glass Building Centre, 145 Long Street, Los Angeles, CA 90255, United States of America (**"Big"**); and (2) **ABC GAMES WRITING COMPANY** of 999 Dawson Street, Denver, CO 80210 (**"ABC"**).

As with the NDA earlier, the first part of the document is concerned with clearly specifying who the agreement is between; basic, but vital.

1. **RECITALS**

1.1 Big is a developer of high quality video game software.

1.2 Big is considering the possible development, publication and release of a currently untitled quiz-based video game featuring quiz show questions (the **"Game"**) for play on console platforms.

1.3 Big wishes to engage the services of ABC to create two sample story proposals to help Big to decide whether to proceed with the development of the Game and for possible utilization in the Game. ABC has agreed to provide these services upon the terms and conditions set forth in this Agreement.

Section 1 clearly outlines who Big is as a company, what they require from ABC, and that the latter has agreed to follow the terms and conditions set out in the contract.

2. **ADDITIONAL DEFINITIONS**

"Acceptable Form" means that all of the Deliverables are: (a) in the reasonable opinion of Big are of a nature and quality that are suitable for the proposed Game; and (b) free from typographical and grammatical errors.

"Commencement Date" means the date of this Agreement set above.

"Deliverables" means two distinct and appropriate story proposals, to be prepared by or on behalf of ABC and provided to Big in accordance with this Agreement.

"Fee" means the sum of four thousand dollars ($4000).

"Services" means the preparation and supply of the Deliverables in accordance with this Agreement.

"Target Completion Date" means the date of the fifteenth day after the Commencement Date.

"Term" means the period commencing on the Commencement Date and expiring on the first anniversary of the Target Completion Date.

Section 2's definitions help ensure both parties are clear as to the nature of the agreement's terms.

3. **SERVICES**

3.1 With effect from the Commencement Date, Big engages ABC to provide the Services in accordance with the terms and conditions of this Agreement.

3.2 ABC shall prepare and supply the Deliverables to Big in Acceptable Form no later than the Target Completion Date.

4. **INTELLECTUAL PROPERTY RIGHTS**

4.1 ABC unconditionally and irrevocably assigns to Big with full title guarantee all present and future legal and beneficial right, title, and interest, including all copyright and other intellectual property rights, in and to the Deliverables throughout the world absolutely to the fullest extent permitted by law.

4.2 ABC shall procure unconditional and irrevocable waivers in writing for the benefit of Big of any and all moral rights existing in or relating to the Deliverables throughout the world absolutely to the fullest extent permitted by law.

4.3 ABC agrees that it shall not have, nor claim to have, any right, title, or interest in or to the Game or the Deliverables, nor any promotional ideas, announcements, phrases, titles, music, or words originated, supplied, and/or used by Big in conjunction with the Game, and that all such rights in the Game and the Deliverables are recognized to be in Big.

4.4 ABC agrees to do any and all such acts and things and execute any and all such documents as Big may reasonably require in order to give effect to the intended operation of the provisions of Clauses 4.1, 4.2, and 4.3, including where necessary to vest in Big any right, title, or interest in or to the Deliverables.

In essence, Section 4 ensures that anything ABC creates while working on Big's game is Big's property. This is important as it ensures that no gameplay, story element, or technology used or generated while ABC is on the project is removed to potentially be used in service to a rival games developer.

5. **FEE**

5.1 In consideration of the full and proper performance of the Services by ABC in accordance with all of the terms and conditions of this Agreement, Big shall pay the Fee to ABC in accordance with this Clause 5.

5.2 Upon supply of the Deliverables to Big in Acceptable Form, ABC may submit a written invoice to Big for the Fee. Big shall pay the Fee to ABC within thirty (30) days following Big's receipt of such invoice. Big shall have no obligation to pay the Fee if ABC fails to supply a written invoice to Big. Big shall pay the Fee by wire transfer into ABC's bank account, details of which are set out below:

Account number: **12341234**
Sort code: **12-23-12**
Bank: **Writing Bank of California**
Branch address: **1223 South Vermont Avenue, Los Angeles, CA 90054, USA**

5.3 The parties acknowledge and agree that the Fee and any other sums expressed to be payable under this Agreement shall be inclusive of all taxes, including value added tax.

One of the most important sections of the contract for obvious reasons—make sure the schedule of delivery, amount to be paid, and bank details are all correct.

6. **FIRST REFUSAL RIGHT**

6.1 The parties acknowledge that Big has engaged ABC to supply the Deliverables solely for the purpose of helping Big to decide whether it wishes to proceed to develop and publish the Game. Accordingly, Big is under no obligation to develop and publish the Game, nor is it under any obligation to use the Deliverables (or any of them) within the Game should it decide to develop and publish the Game.

6.2 Notwithstanding Clause 6.1, and provided that ABC supplies the Deliverables to Big in Acceptable Form, if Big decides during the Term to proceed to develop and publish the Game, then:

(a) ABC shall have a right of first refusal to create appropriate text for the Game (the **"Writing Services"**) in accordance with this Clause;

(b) promptly following the date on which Big decides to proceed to develop and publish the Game (whichever is the later), Big shall notify ABC and for the period of thirty (30) days following the date of that notice (the **"Exclusive Negotiation Period"**) Big and ABC shall negotiate in good faith the terms on which ABC shall provide some or all of the Writing Services for Big; and

(c) during the Exclusive Negotiation Period, Big shall not negotiate with any third party for the provision of the Writing Services. If, at the expiry of the Exclusive Negotiation Period, the parties have been unable to agree commercial terms on which ABC shall provide the Writing Services to Big for the Game, then Big shall be free to negotiate with any third party for the provision of Writing Services and to appoint any third party for the provision of the Writing Services.

6.3 Nothing in this Clause 6 shall operate so as to prevent or restrict Big from: (a) discussing or negotiating with any third party or engaging any third party for the provision of services with respect to the Game that are not Writing Services; or (b) discussing or negotiating with any third party or engaging any third party for the provision of Writing Services at end time following the termination or expiry of this Agreement.

This section makes it clear who drafted the contract and whose interest it best serves. In hiring ABC, Big is not obliged to ever use any of the material ABC creates, nor is Big prevented from talking to other companies about other services (for animation or music, for example), or within the area of writing services once the term of the contract has expired.

7. **TERMINATION**

7.1 Term. This Agreement shall commence on the Commencement Date and, subject to earlier termination as provided in this Agreement, shall continue for the Term. This Agreement shall automatically expire upon the end of the Term.

7.2 Breach. If either party commits a material breach of this Agreement, and if such material breach is capable of remedy and not cured within thirty (30) days after written notice of the breach is given by the non-breaching party to the breaching party, then the non-breaching party may give notice to the breaching party of its election to terminate this Agreement. However, such right of termination shall not be exclusive of other remedies available to the non-breaching party.

7.3 Survival. The following Clauses shall survive the termination or expiration of this Agreement: Clauses 4, 7.3, 8, and 9.

This section covers the natural means by which a contract comes to completion and the rights of each party in the event of a contract breach.

8. WARRANTY AND INDEMNIFICATION

8.1 Authorization. ABC warrants and represents that it has the right and power to enter into and perform this Agreement, that ABC is free to enter into this Agreement and provide the Services pursuant to this Agreement, and that ABC is not under any agreements or obligations to any third parties that would preclude or interfere in any way with its entering into and fully performing its obligations under this Agreement or the full and unrestricted exercise by Big of the rights granted to Big under this Agreement.

This section ensures ABC is in a position to enter (legally) into the contract, which is another layer of protection for Big.

8.2 Deliverables. ABC warrants and represents that: (a) none of the Deliverables shall be libelous, defamatory, or obscene; (b) the supply of the Deliverables shall not infringe the rights (including intellectual property rights) of any third party; and (c) the Deliverables shall be free from all known viruses, spyware, and other malicious software.

8.3 Indemnification for Breach. ABC shall indemnify and hold Big harmless against all losses, claims, demands, liabilities, and expenses, including reasonable attorney fees, which may arise from its breach of any term, covenant, representation, or warranty of this Agreement.

Vitally for Big, 8.3 ensures any costs arising from a breach instigated by ABC isn't passed on to them (i.e., they don't have to pay a small fortune in fees if ABC messes up).

9. GENERAL PROVISIONS

9.1 Recitals. The recitals in this Agreement constitute an integral part of the Agreement reached by the parties and are to be considered as such.

9.2 Captions. The captions contained in this Agreement have been inserted for reference and convenience only, and do not define, limit, or describe the scope of this Agreement or the intent of any provision.

9.3 Independent Contractor. The parties, by this Agreement, do not intend to create any partnership, principal/agent, master/servant, franchisor/franchisee, or joint venture relationship and nothing in this Agreement shall be construed as creating such a relationship. Neither party nor its agents or employees are representatives of the other party for any purpose except as expressly set forth in this Agreement, and neither party has the power or authority as agent/employee or other capacity to represent, act for, bind, or otherwise create or assume any obligations on behalf of the other party for any purpose whatsoever.

This section makes it clear the agreement doesn't mean Big is hiring ABC permanently and that the two parties are in no way bound in any kind of professional relationship outside the immediate project.

9.4 Non-assignability/Sublicensing. ABC shall not sell, assign, delegate, charge, sublicense, or otherwise transfer or encumber this Agreement or the rights granted in this Agreement or the obligations undertaken in this Agreement, without the prior written consent of Big.

This basically gives Big the right to make sure ABC only provides writing services of the high quality expected. Hiring third parties brings with it the issues of quality and trust; how can Big be sure that writing work carried out by Joe Freelancer (hired by ABC to work on the project) is going to be of the same standard as ABC's core writers? Additionally, Big would want to be sure that Joe Freelancer is also legally bound in the same way as ABC. This clause ensures Big is covered in this respect.

9.5 Waiver. The waiver by any party of a breach or default of any provision of this Agreement by the party shall not constitute a waiver by such party of any succeeding breach of the same or other provisions; nor shall any delay or omission on the part of either party to exercise or avail itself of any right, power, or privilege that it has or may have hereunder, operate as a waiver of any such right, power, or privilege by such party.

This is, in essence, an extremely thorough way of saying that a breach of any single clause does not constitute a breach of any other clause. This is to ensure matters are kept separate and clear—in the event of several clauses being breached by either side, each instance would be handled separately.

9.6 Governing Law and Jurisdiction. This Agreement shall be governed by, subject to, and construed under the laws of Colorado. The parties shall submit to the exclusive jurisdiction of the courts of Colorado.

9.7 Unenforceability. In the event that any term, clause, or provision of this Agreement shall be construed to be or adjudged invalid, void, or unenforceable, such term, clause, or provision shall be construed as severed from this Agreement, and the remaining terms, clauses, and provisions shall remain in effect.

This clause makes sure that, even if one area of the contract is deemed unenforceable, then both parties are still legally protected in other respects. If this was not the case, then the entire contract and all its safeguards would be rendered worthless should there be an enforceability issue with even one clause.

9.8 Notices. All written communication under this Agreement (**"Notices"**) shall be considered given when the same is: (a) delivered to the party(ies) entitled to such Notice, (b) deposited with a guaranteed courier service to the person(s) and address(es) stated at the beginning of this Agreement; or (c) transmitted by facsimile with an original sent concurrently by a guaranteed courier service. Notice shall be deemed effective upon the earlier of actual receipt or two (2) business days after mailing or transmittal.

This clause clarifies just what constitutes verifiable communication between parties. If this wasn't defined, then there might, for example, be a risk of one party feeling a matter agreed upon verbally (perhaps with a handshake thrown in for good measure) constitutes a binding agreement. Section 9.8 makes it clear this is not the case.

9.9 Confidentiality. The parties are to maintain the existence of this Agreement strictly confidential unless and until an appropriate formal announcement of this Agreement has been released by Big. Also, the parties are to maintain the underlying terms of this Agreement strictly confidential at all times unless the parties agree in writing to release such information. However, to enable Big to carry out the terms of this Agreement, Big may discuss the present Agreement in confidence with other companies in the group of companies of which Big is a member, the game development companies that will assist Big in the development of the Game, and Big's public relations firms.

This section provides basic legal cover regarding a project's confidentiality; however, by this stage, most companies or freelance writers would have already signed an NDA anyway.

9.10 Integration. This Agreement constitutes the entire agreement between the parties relating to the subject matter of this Agreement. All prior negotiations, representations, agreements, and understandings are merged into, extinguished by, and completely expressed by it. Neither party shall be bound by any definition, condition, warranty, representation, modification, consent, or waiver other than as expressly stated in this Agreement, unless set forth in writing executed by the party to be bound.

This section basically tidies up any loose legal ends by making it clear that the proverbial legal buck stops here—any previous agreements or discussions are superseded by this contract (which keeps things simpler for both parties).

Again, areas allotted to signatures normally follow, and these can be seen in the full sample in the appendices. Both NDAs and contracts can be time-consuming to take care of, but they provide both parties—not just the client—with assurances and practical guidance to help shape the scope of the work.

Note that the documents above are examples and should by no means be considered more than that. It's possible to have all manner of clauses in a contract additional to those listed that fulfill a variety of purposes; they might define game writing credits, include copies of the finished game, or allow provision for unforeseen additional work. Always identify what you need to have covered and make sure it's included in the contract.

EXERCISE

1. Is an NDA is an outdated piece of paperwork, or a practical step that provides vital, mutual legal protection? Discuss. Consider the fact that breaching a current or potential client's confidence regarding future IP will mean a loss of reputation and future work being a great deal harder to obtain.

PROJECT

1. Research the typical clauses found in games writing contracts—what do they cover? Pick the one you consider most important and rewrite it in layman's terms. If you're unable to obtain documents that pertain specifically to games writing, try to find contracts that cover either other game development fields or involve writing in another medium.

Chapter 4

COLLABORATION: TEAM US

If I have seen further than others, it is by standing upon the shoulders of giants.

— Isaac Newton

BRIEF TERMS

TESTING The process by which all software elements of a games title are checked to ensure the minimum number of bugs are present when it ships.

BUGS The term given to any software issue that causes unintended problems with any aspect of a given game title's content or services.

MOTION-CAPTURE (MO-CAP) The process by which real-time movement is digitally recorded in a specially equipped studio, then translated into movement within a game world. A "mo-capped" character normally moves in a far more realistic manner than one whose movement is programmed.

MILESTONES Term given to important delivery points within a game title's development cycle; used to ensure a project is on-schedule and on-budget.

REFERENCES Term given to creative influences used by a writer or team of writers while creating a game's story, plot, characters, or dialogue. Can include books, movies, songs, and pictures.

CODE The name given to the computer language in which the game software is written.

PART OF THE TEAM

There are many different genres, projects, and, of course, writers. Exceptions can always be found, but broadly speaking, for the vast majority of writers who work in games, you will find it to be one of the most inherently collaborative disciplines in which you can be involved. No lonely garrets, no hilltop communing just you with nature, and no deadly embrace with a tempestuous, disloyal muse to the exclusion of the rest of creation. And if you bury your head in a script draft until it's completely finished, you are likely to regret it as the extent of the irrelevance of what you've created becomes apparent within seconds of seeing or playing the latest version of the game. Writers are part of a team on a project that is dynamically developing at a pace entirely of its own, with production, design, code, and art issues all pulling in certain directions—and sometimes conflicting directions at that. Try playing a resource management game quarrying nothing but stone to the exclusion of all else and you'll soon see the kind of mess this approach gets you into; so with games development, and so with writing. Your job as a writer is to handle the opportunities and limitations of your project and slalom between them in such a way as to put together the most appropriate writing solution possible. To keep working this particular skiing analogy, the course you're on isn't running parallel to production, design, code, and art—*those elements* are *the course.* There's little point in pulling impressive tricks if you're off-piste.

WHO ARE WE?

A games development team comprises a number of key roles. In smaller teams people take on multiple roles. In larger teams there are multiple people taking on each of these roles, and there are often more diverse aspects to these

FIGURE 4.1. The team.

roles, in line with more complex projects handling more complex technology. Let's take a closer look at who's on the team.

FIGURE 4.2. The writer.

The Writer

Also Known As: Story Medic. Story Robot. Script Monkey. The Words Person.

What Do They Do? That's what this section of this book is all about . . .

Distinguishing Traits: Most likely to be one of the few people on the team who can spell *lose* correctly. (*Loose* is generally the popular choice, albeit wrong.)

Most Likely to Say: Oh, that seems to have changed since yesterday . . .

FIGURE 4.3. The producer.

The Producer

Also Known As: The One Who Looks Most Strung Out.

What Do They Do? Organize and coordinate schedules, staff requirements, and delivery milestones.

Distinguishing Traits: Most likely to be one of the few people on the team who owns or wears a shirt with sleeves and a collar.

Most Likely to Say: We need it as soon as possible, and the budget's tight this time.

FIGURE 4.4. The designer.

The Designer

Also Known As: The Oracle.

What Do They Do? Design the game, manage the design team and, once the game enters testing, run around a lot with a worried expression frantically trying to update large complex spreadsheets.

Distinguishing Traits: Still secretly harbors the belief/hope that easy difficulty settings on games are a fad and will eventually be phased out.

Most Likely to Say: Gameplay is king.

The Coder

Also Known As: Programmer. Code Monkey. The Brains. Nerd. Geek. Techie.

What Do They Do? The clever math-related stuff, talking in 1s and 0s, which their computer seems to (sometimes temperamentally) understand.

Distinguishing Traits: A most pronounced fondness for science fiction. Least accomplished socialite.

Most Likely to Say: I should have it working tomorrow.

FIGURE 4.5. The coder.

The Artist

Also Known As: Art Monkey.

What Do They Do? Create the environments and/or game characters.

Distinguishing Traits: Most likely to have a child called Max or Maya. Or one of each.

Most Likely to Say: *How* many polys?!

FIGURE 4.6. The artist.

The Others

There are more people on Team Us. You may also meet a Creative Director, who may be part designer and/or part producer and/or part writer. There are also Concept Artists, Narrative Designers, Animators, Managers, Sound Designers, Testers, Quality Assurance (QA) people, and admin staff. There may also be researchers, music composers, and consultants in many shapes and guises, advising on general game design, or controller configuration, cinematography, motion-capture . . . the list goes on.

So, how does this team of people relate to what a writer does? Remember that list of questions in Chapter 2? Well, one way or another you need to collect those answers from somewhere. It depends on the studio and the individuals as to where you might best find these answers, and you won't always find them neatly divided into their respective disciplines. Most often the producer and/or the designer will be your most likely source of divination, and most likely your main, or only, point of contact. However, you might find the answers to your questions from the following people:

Producer

- *What platform is it for?*
- *Who is it for?*
- *What rating is it?*
- *When does the story have to be finished?*
- *Who is responsible for signing off deliveries?*
- *What are the delivery milestones?*
- *How long should the story be?*
- *How many characters can we have?*
- *What are the mo-cap, animation, and audio restrictions?*
- *Is there a specific budget or a budget range to work within?*

Designer

- *What are we trying to do?*
- *What's the genre?*
- *What's the tone of voice?*
- *Do we have just sound or just text? Or both?*
- *Are there different player modes?*
- *Does the game have a relationship with predecessors in the same series?*
- *Does it have a relationship with anything else that's planned, either in the same or in a different media?*
- *What references are we drawing from?*
- *What's the relationship between the game and the story?*
- *What are the player's gameplay motivations?*
- *Are there any other design implications or requirements?*
- *Does the controller configuration have any bearing on the story world?*

Coder

- *What triggers can the game detect?*

Artist

- *What art style(s) are we working with?*

But, equally, some of these questions can easily come under the purview of different development disciplines. What the code can and can't do is so closely related to what the gameplay is that it's only of limited value for the writer to tease them apart. Additionally, some questions—such as the platform type—clearly impact all areas of development (memory space, screen size, etc.). Taking another step further back, none of these creative, technical, and production-oriented endeavors occur in a vacuum. The project's business considerations—the budget, timescale, team, existing technology, price point, distribution method, likely target market, and so on—all shape the development process. If the writer's slalom course is defined by other disciplines of the development process, then the latitude, longitude, topography, weather systems, and planet are defined by the business context. Of course, writers are seldom offered such a macro view of what they're contributing to, and it's seldom appropriate for them to be afforded it. Nevertheless, being a games writer is still a very long way from writing a long prose poem, which you can wholly accomplish on your own.

A TEAM WITHIN A TEAM

On some occasions you may find yourself part of a writing team—a team within a team. This has its own challenges and opportunities. The key, as with working within the larger development team, is to create and maintain an atmosphere as shorn as possible of egos and political subtext, so people feel free to contribute ideas without needing to be certain that they come fully formed as *cool* and *not cheesy* and *utterly practical* and *exactly the right solution*. It often takes a lot of wrong ideas to get to the right one and not being afraid to share yours with others, regardless of how crazy they might be, can be key to moving forward creatively. This often proves itself when people work on games stories together, and it's more apposite to consider the process as a relay, passing the baton back and forth to different hands, rather than as a first-past-the-post race where winner takes all.

It's no mean feat acquiring such an atmosphere, especially when the pressures of an almost certainly ominous schedule are bearing down on everyone. It can be helpful to consider the mantra *there are no bad ideas.* Although in truth there invariably are, and most often in a creative group there are far more bad ideas than good ones—identifying then eliminating the bad ideas has a way of liberating the team, enabling progress to be made. In addition, the bad ideas are often the funniest, because they're the least appropriate, and everyone knows you can't keep following up something funny with something that's not as funny—so the only available course of action is to figure out what will work, and what the project really needs (and is actually practical).

As writers who have frequently worked in a writing team within games, we would offer this particular piece of advice: as much as possible, talk among yourselves, and draw your own conclusions before you talk to the larger team or the producer/designer single point of contact. The last thing the team needs are further opinions cutting across each other. That's not to say you have to draw only firm conclusions—if the writing team still thinks there are a range of valid options then you ought to present them. But it doesn't benefit the wider team to hear another set of meandering, disparate thoughts. Often the writing team is formed precisely in order to pull a development team out of just such a phase.

FIGURE 4.7. The micro team.

EXERCISES

1. Choose one of the roles explored above. Consider the various training routes a person deciding to fulfill your chosen role can take in order to be considered a professional in their field. Create a simple step-by-step path illustrating the training and experiential route or routes, and keep the following questions in mind:

   Which member of the team requires the most training to be considered a professional?

   Which role requires the greatest skill and/or most training to perform?

   Which role requires the least skill and/or training to perform?

   Which role requires the greatest degree of interpersonal skills?

   Which role is evolving at the fastest rate?

2. Choose a game development team role—list the top three skills needed to carry out that role.

3. What three qualities do you think are necessary to be a good creative leader on a game project? Consider those qualities and try to prioritize them in order of descending importance. How important do you think it is to have skill in one or more creative disciplines?

PROJECT

1. Choose a game development role and research in detail the route or routes taken by those established in the industry to reach that position. Try to contact individuals who are actually performing your chosen role to find out how they moved into that position (though be sure to keep any communication succinct).

Chapter 5 NARRATIVE DESIGN

Before beginning, plan carefully.

—Marcus Tullius Cicero

BRIEF TERMS

STORY SPACE The area, or areas, within which a video game's story exists.

FRACTAL GAME STORY STRUCTURES Video game story design structures that provide the player with choices that take the story and/or gameplay in totally new directions.

MODULAR GAME STORY STRUCTURES Video game story design structures that provide the player with choices designed to give the illusion of choice and player agency but which, in reality, don't significantly change a story's main route.

AVATAR A virtual creature or being through which the player experiences and interacts with the game world.

DEFINING STORY SPACE

There are two broad definitions of narrative design we're accustomed to within games development. One—the subject of this chapter—is about defining the space in which, *and the means through which*, the story can be told. Here, narrative design is first about assessing and clarifying the story "real estate" available for you to build on (i.e., making sure there's ground underneath where you plan to build, how much there is, its dimensions, and the type of ground it is). Are you telling a linear story, such as in adventure game *The Last of Us*, where the plot unfolds in a totally predetermined manner, requiring the player only to successfully navigate terrain, solve puzzles, and defeat enemies when required? Or will your story space be far more open, able to accommodate players who want to leave the main plot thread to explore side missions whenever they desire, as in Gearbox's popular FPS/RPG crossover *Borderlands*? Inextricably linked with this definition is another that's commonly circulated—explored in Chapter 15—which also applies to other storytelling media, and concerns the actual structuring of narratives, the designing of the story's basic shape, and the construction of the plot architecture (even if *narrative*, *story*, and *plot* are not truly synonyms—but more on this in that later chapter).

Marcus Cicero ably points to the vital importance of planning, but this may create the false impression that narrative design is as straightforward as planning and building according to specifications. This particular task of the games writer is substantially more dynamic than that, because the length of story, the nature of its relationship to the game design as a whole, and the means through which the story is delivered all have a bearing on the kind of story you will tell. If, for example, you only have six cut scenes through which to tell the story, none of which can be longer than three minutes, with only two locations, both of which must be interiors and contain no more than four characters, you're going to need to scale back your ambition to tell a story packed with over fifteen major reversals replete with sensational vistas and a large cast of extras told across sweeping open landscapes.

We're squarely in both macro and micro territory here—there's the macro picture of the overall game design structure, theme, and the way players win, or at least progress, and woven into that, the macro of story design itself, working down into the micro levels as you take inspiration from what could be a very particular element—a character, an idea for a scene, or further down into a scene setting, a piece of music, an accent, an object, a character's demeanor, expression, or a line of dialogue. At this stage it's a question of keeping an eye on the micro and being aware of how this will be shaped, but focusing on hewing out the broad outlines within the space in which you're about to work. A sculpting analogy seems rather apt here—where sculptors have been known to take inspiration for the final sculpture not so much from a pre-existing idea but from the block of stone, marble, or other sculpting material itself—the size, shape, and nature of the pre-sculpted material suggests the ultimate form was there all along and the sculptor doesn't so much make the sculpture as *release* it. In the same way a games writer enacting narrative design will become attuned to structural shapes and, by defining them and examining them, come to see them not just as limitations and boundaries, but, within them, hints, possibilities, and even clear indications of dramatic shapes and the way to tell a particular story. If that's all starting to sound a little arcane to be useful, let us backtrack a little by saying that the story's theme will almost certainly already be set by the general intentions of the game design and the gameplay within it—so you already broadly know what kind of story to tell. Further than that—and here let us jump ahead a little—if you're working with cut scenes, you're looking for as many of those scenes as possible to contain reversals or revelations—because these are *the two most fundamental structural means through which storytellers engage interest and retain it*. The nature of these reversals and revelations, and the number of them you can deliver shall, to a large extent, be defined by what the player will experience in the game between them, so this is now starting to tell you more about the pacing of your story and, tied to the attributes of your characters (which also come from theme), you have a greater sense of what the revelations and reversals might be. So, if you know the theme, and you know how many scenes you have, how long they are, where they occur, and what the player will experience between them, then you will begin to get a feel for some of the more micro elements of that story—that is, what happens in the scenes.

There's no set way to go about defining the space in the game design wherein the story can be told. Sometimes game designers will have already defined it completely; at other times you will be asked to start from scratch and carry ultimate responsibility for this whole area. More often than not it'll be somewhere in-between and a highly collaborative process, working with game design documents, designers, other team members, design instincts, design experience, and an awareness of how to tell stories. Imagine trying to design a shoe on a foot that's not only constantly growing and shrinking but also frequently turning into a hand, a leg, an arm, or something completely different, and you'll be getting close to a sense of how this process can feel.

Since every project comes with its own specifications, objectives, resources, time limits, and so forth, each needs to be approached on its own terms. Let's look at DS puzzle game *Unsolved Crimes*, which is also featured in Chapter 11 on editing, as it excellently demonstrates some important points.

CASE STUDY: *UNSOLVED CRIMES*

The project first came to us as a puzzle game Now Production was developing principally for the Western market; as a Japanese developer, they wanted to dip their toes into the Western market. The design focused on mini puzzle games, interaction with 3D environments to collect clues, and ultimately came to include quizzes as a means whereby to progress through levels and solve cases. In addition, there were eventually a number of action-based mini-games that came to include a driving game, a shooting game, and a maze game. Connected to this, the story, as it first came to us, consisted of the following, relatively simple, brief:

- 1970s New York setting
- The final case is to involve a kidnapping
- The player is to be a character in the story, and yet without an onscreen presence
- This character is to have a partner or guide who would talk to them and help provide tutorial instruction to guide the player
- The cast of characters should be as small as possible
- The player will often pick up "missions" at the police HQ, so a boss character will be required
- The story is to be delivered in text, without any audio
- The story will not be delivered in movie form, but as freeze frames onscreen, which the player taps through
- The text of the scenes should reflect dialogue and not the internalized thoughts of the characters, and there is no narrator to help tell this story; the story is told through the scenes themselves
- Make the scenes as short as possible
- The number of text characters onscreen at any time will be restricted (to a value yet to be defined), and the number of screens composed of text is to be kept to a minimum, so the player is tapping the screen as infrequently as possible except when engaged in gameplay
- Make the story dramatic
- Make the story emotional

In addition, there was a story outline already in place, and our first task was to assess and work with it. We won't provide it here, but our initial response was that we were concerned by the outline's apparent complexity, in terms of the actual story and the way to deliver it, as well as the intricate nature of the interrelationship necessary between multiple cases to make this work. Further, we were concerned this story would be hard-pressed to generate any emotional engagement. An avatar that would never be seen was a cause for pause. How could we ensure there was any level of emotion without seeing evidence of it? Novels, of course, can introduce characters that aren't in a scene by reference to internal thoughts or through the narrator's voice, but here we would not have access to those kinds of tools. All our text was to simulate dialogue, effectively aping the medium of movies. This was a problem. Additionally, all the other characters would be visible, and so our central character, the player's avatar, would be the least potentially fertile of everyone with regard to any kind of emotional resonance. There was the clue; the kidnapping had to mean something to a character we could see on-screen, a character with whom some kind of relationship could be built. The most suitable character would seem to be the partner and mentor. In connection with this, and perhaps as a result of the intricacy of the proposed outline, the target demographic and the tone were also unclear to us, so we asked for greater clarification.

Following (long) conversations on-site, the developers understood our concerns and we were asked to write a new story that would meet the earlier brief, with the following amendments:

- Allow for a narrative structure that could accommodate around twelve cases, most of which needed to be independent, but at least one was to contribute in some way to the final case
- The cast of characters had to be as small as possible, but should include the assistant, the police boss, and at least one bad guy
- The target demographic was to be the broadest range of Western gamers—working with the fact that the gameplay and the story itself would involve solving a series of murder cases (the nature and details of which were to be devised by the design team)

Given the subject matter involved solving murders, we knew the title's rating would not be low, but there did seem to be room to move to help broaden the demographic. The 1970s afforded us reference to a lighter tone in tackling crime, as seen in cop shows such as *Starsky and Hutch* and, pushing into the 1980s, *Cagney and Lacey*. Channeling these ultimately helped us to reduce the rating to "Teen" in the United States and "12+" in Europe.

After working through early ideas and exploring them further, we arrived at an outline both we and the client were happy with. Even at this point we were mindful of the "story real estate" we would be dealing with and the ultimate structure of the story and its relationship to the cases—the key elements of the gameplay. However, as we turned the outline into a treatment, the narrative design began to take shape. Ultimately, the narrative design for that treatment came to be depicted as illustrated in Figure 5.1.

Our own preference is always to sketch structure to visualize it and make it clear for us and for the team so there is mutual understanding, and we would strongly recommend this as a technique and a practice for all writers tasked with narrative design. In a word, when tasked with narrative design: *draw*. Get the structure clear in your head and show it to the team. If they have feedback, get them to amend your drawing, and, of course, talk about their suggested changes as it's always vital you understand the views of others and they understand yours.

OTHER DESIGN STRUCTURES

As you will see, the narrative design for *Unsolved Crimes* is very straightforward. Many games employ far more byzantine structures that may include branching options and multiple endings, both different ways of making progress through the game other than the purely sequential and linear; the more complex a structure, the greater the need to visualize it.

Where branching structures are employed we recommend a process known as "defensive design," whereby there is a core *spine* to the story and any branches are expendable *limbs*. The spine should be prioritized in development, and if production demands cuts have to be made, they should always be made first from the branches. This way the structural integrity of the story is retained for as long as possible. Take a look at this notional structure in Figure 5.2, which closely resembles the one we used for *Don King Presents: Prize Fighter*™.

The circles represent "missions"; the "b" missions here should be prioritized in development, with the "a" and "c" missions being developed later, only once schedules, performance issues, and testing permit. In order to progress from a set of missions on the same "level" to the next scene, some or all of the missions may need to be completed, depending on how many missions the game ultimately has and what the game's approach is to difficulty settings.

Of course this basic structure could be extended and run for longer, but it could also be deepened in a number of ways. More missions could be added to each "level." Additionally, some or all of the branching missions could be designated as optional, possibly providing skill or equipment upgrades or other incentives, which may relate to each other or the story in some way that moves them beyond simply

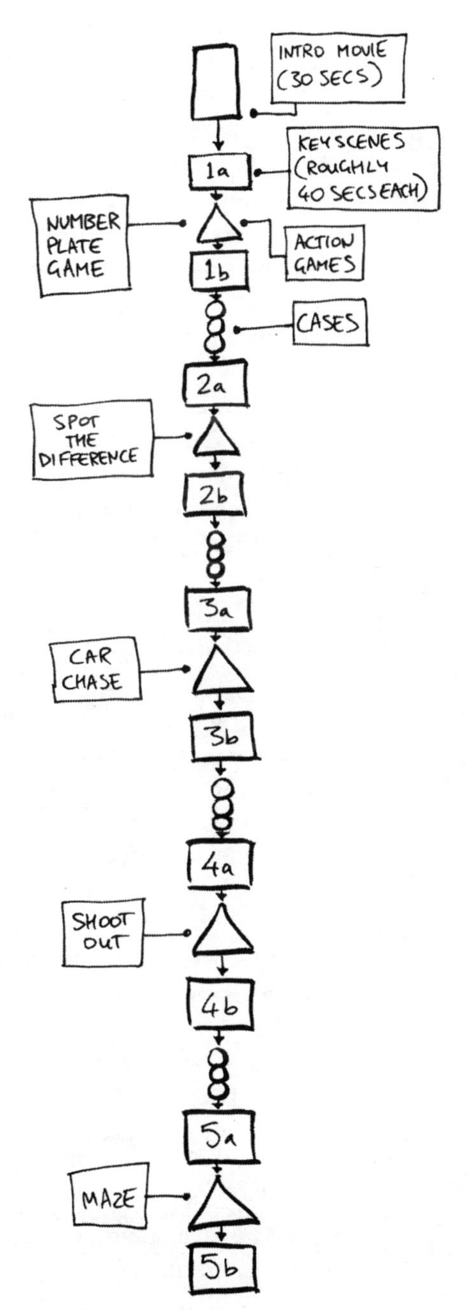

FIGURE 5.1. *Unsolved Crimes* narrative design structure.

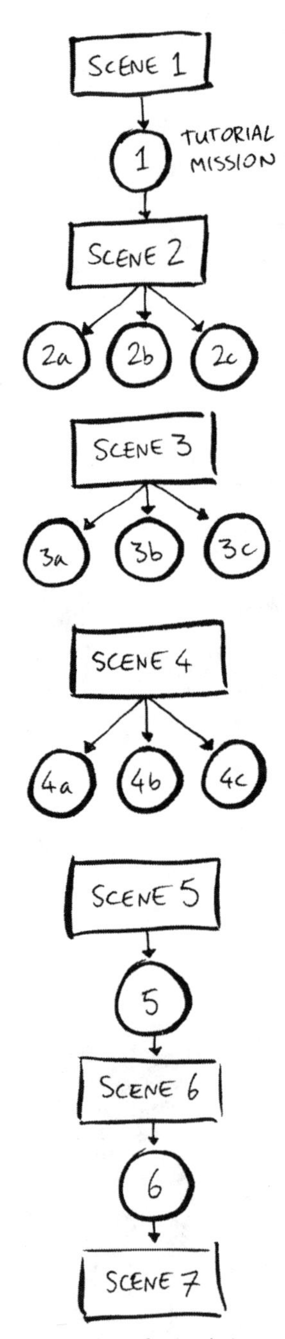

FIGURE 5.2. Defensive design structure.

elements to be completed in order to progress (so, for example, they may be re-playable and contribute to semi-independent mini-games or subplots). Any of these missions may also include characters or themes that relate to the central story, bringing added depth and resonance to both in the process.

However, there are times when no matter how you design the story, the proposed cuts will always be problematic, in which case you hope you can contain them sufficiently to prevent them from becoming catastrophic; failing that, you need to make sure you alert the development team so they understand as best they can what the impact will be on the game as a whole, time lines, budgets affecting audio recordings (or re-recordings), and any other issues affecting the project's likelihood of hitting the release date in good shape.

In addition, *Unsolved Crimes* may not use cut scenes as such, but it is still structured around scenes of a sort (or, at the very least, storytelling *nodes*) and notional definable missions, and this is not an example of environmental storytelling narrative design. (See Chapter 8 for more on environmental storytelling.) In environmental storytelling neither scenes nor missions (or gameplay objectives) may be discrete in the same way and might not be so easy to place within a structure that lends itself readily to visualization. Locations, characters, and the events themselves may well be in flux. However, even environmental storytelling is still storytelling, and so still relies on a meaningful sequence of events. Therefore, any visualization should demonstrate an understanding and explanation of the nature of the relationship between the events—no matter how and where they are initiated.

The final point we'd like to make here is in reference to the term *node*. A storytelling node is a "plot point" if you're Syd Field, a "cardinal function

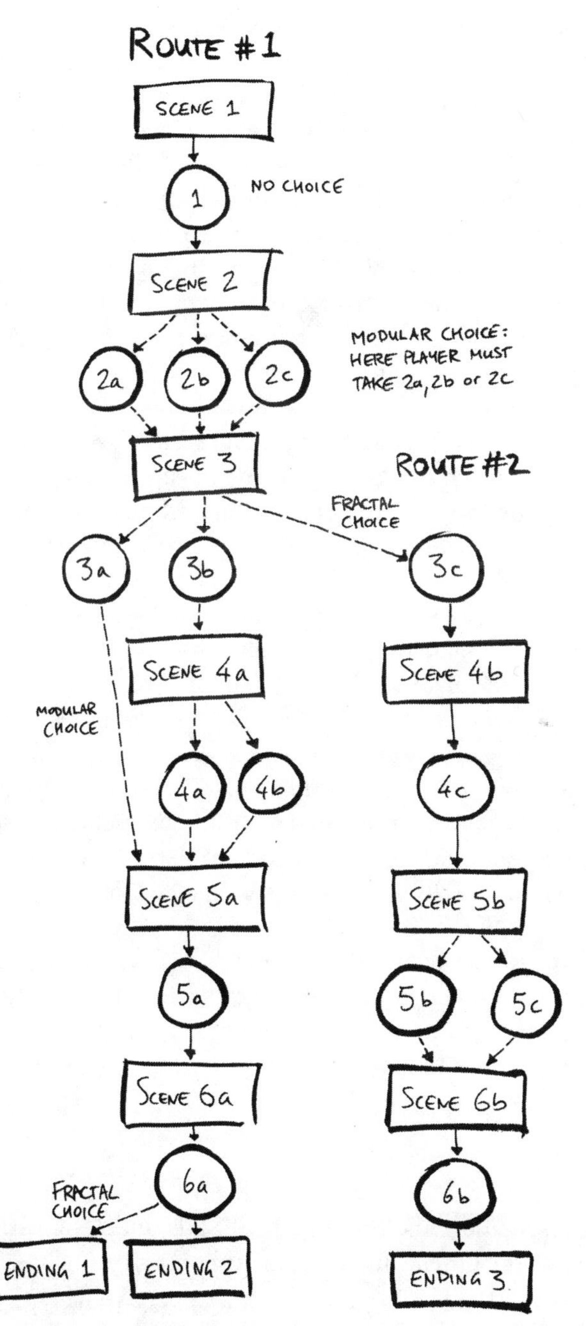

FIGURE 5.3. Sample modular and fractal interactive structure.

or nuclei" if you're Roland Barthes, and "events or kernels" if you're Seymour Chatman. Interactive storytelling has two basic forms, what we term *fractal* or *modular*. As seen in Figure 5.3, fractal choices afford the greatest and most significant levels of choice within a structure, and modular choices are more constrained. Yet fractal choices are far more problematic for production, possibly resulting in effectively hiving off your production efforts into a whole new strand and a whole new experience. This is not solely a production issue, since if your story may be substantially different in Route #1 and Route #2 (not to mention Routes #3+), how do you know what to market? If you create a sequel to the game, how do you know where to pick up from if you're taking the story further forward (as opposed to a prequel)?

Generally, writers working in narrative design work with a very restricted set of fractal choices, if indeed they have any at all. When they do have them they are often restricted to very late in any linear sequence. Games writers will more often be armed with a number of modular choices, attempting to mask their inherently restricted nature, employing smoke and mirrors to create the effect that each is more structurally significant than it later transpires to be, or, *even better*, the player is never aware that the choice was modular, and it had the feeling to them of being fractal. However, the narrative design of video games does *not necessarily* mean working with choices, modular and restricted or otherwise. In the case of *Unsolved Crimes*, the player makes no choices at the story level at all (other than choosing to continue playing the game "successfully" in order to progress, just as in *BioShock Infinite*™, *Bulletstorm*™, and any other linear FPS). And although games writers are concerned with storytelling in an interactive environment, it's a false assumption that they necessarily structure stories that are intrinsically dependent upon offering choice. The first task of a games writer is to offer an engaging story that encompasses and ties together the gameplay that is the substance of the story's form. Perhaps though, to consider interactive storytelling as, by definition, a matter of offering and exploring choice, is to veer close to the limits of game writing where it meets interactive storytelling independent of the world of video games, and that is really a whole other book.

EXERCISES

1. Choose a specific game genre (e.g., FPS). Is one design structure more desirable than the others? Justify your response.
2. Build a basic "defensive design structure" for Chapter 6's *Code Obsidian* game.

PROJECTS

1. Take an existing, preferably well-known game and visually illustrate its design structure. Don't worry if you've not completed the game, either go as far as you can with what you know or create what you think would be a great structure for the rest of the game (marking the point your "creative input" begins). Once complete, compare it with the types of structure discussed previously and answer the following questions:

   Does your game structure conform to one of the structures discussed in the chapter?

   Did the game's developers use the best design structure possible to support the gameplay and story, or should they have chosen a different one?

   If the game, in your opinion, would have benefited from using a different structure, which would you recommend and why?

2. Create a story using Twine (*www.twinery.org*) with no more than two choices at a time (i.e., on the same page), and no fewer than five pairs of choices for the player to experience from beginning to end of your story. The setting, characters, and plot are all up to you. (If you want, you can link to previous choices, and not every choice has to be unique; the important thing is that the player experiences five pairs of choices over the course of your story.) Discuss what you learned in a group.

Chapter 6 OUTLINES & TREATMENTS

No great thing is created suddenly.

—Epictetus

BRIEF TERMS

OUTLINE A document designed to provide the broad structure of a game's story.

TREATMENT A larger document normally based on an outline that expands upon the story giving greater levels of detail; it normally precedes the actual writing of the game story script.

PROJECT STAKEHOLDERS Individuals or corporate entities that possess a creative, managerial, and/or financial stake in a game project.

PROTAGONIST The "hero" of the story.

ANTAGONIST The "villain" of the story.

SUBTEXT Implicit, rather than explicit, information contained in a scene or gameplay that is revealed as events progress.

PITCH DOCUMENT Short document, often less than two pages long, designed to quickly and skillfully illustrate a game's core story, often to gain permission to proceed further with a given direction; frequently read by a publisher's marketing department.

THE OUTLINE

One of the most frequent tasks a games writer is required to carry out is creating a story *outline* and, following that, a *treatment*. These documents are designed to take you from a core story idea that has been largely agreed on—or, at least, the merit in exploring and developing that core idea has been agreed on—to the stage where you're ready to start actually writing the script.

An outline maps out, in broad strokes, the basic flow of your story. It can be any length, but generally the shorter the better—within three to five pages is usually about right for most projects. At this stage you're looking to break the story into rough approximations of scenes and acts, each containing a line or two that describes what happens. As you're doing this you need to ensure that the story and gameplay are working together and aren't at cross-purposes.

Keep in mind that the outline is there to be played with, finessed, torn down, built up, changed, tweaked, poked, and prodded. Now's the time to experiment with a range of story ideas and see where they take you; developing these on paper is relatively quick and cheap, but the further down the production line a story travels, the harder, and more expensive, it becomes to make meaningful changes. Use this development time to work through as many of the problems and opportunities your story setup and game world appear to give you. Changes can happen pretty much all the way through a project, and sometimes they can be profound and wholly story-breaking ones, but the outline is a development stage designed to try and minimize risk and to attain appropriate sign-off from all the project stakeholders. It prevents you from disappearing for three months then emerging with a script based on a futuristic supernatural sub-oceanic species when the team needed a gunslinger story set in the Midwest in 1882. Clear, simple steps ensure everyone is seeing the same picture and that work heading in the wrong direction is kept to a minimum. You wouldn't build a house without first drawing up architectural plans, and you shouldn't start trying to write a script without knowing where you're going—even if you have a natural and instinctive feel for story structure, you still need to be sure your team is happy with what you intend to write and how you plan to approach it.

So, how do you go about writing an outline? First, as mentioned earlier, check the brief, and if you don't understand it (perhaps you weren't involved with its creation), meet with people again and ask more questions until the task in hand is as clear as it possibly can be. At this stage talking to the team might not only reveal what people want, but, perhaps more interestingly, what they don't want. It's fairly common for team members to harbor intentions or agendas they aren't fully aware of themselves, so the more you can do to try and understand the team, the better chance you'll have to deliver what they want. There are a number of ways your outline can broadly map the story. A good place to start is by writing nothing at all. Instead, ask high-level, macro questions: Whose story is it? What's their motivation? Who or what's trying to stop them? How? How does any of this fit into the gameplay? How does a player win, or progress? What's the story about?

Who's in Our Story?

Think about the characters you need to make your story and gameplay work. At the beginning we concentrate mainly on the protagonist(s) and antagonist(s). Keep in mind that your brief (and budget) might set a limit on how many characters you can have in your game world, though a few restrictions can be a useful thing as having too many can lead to a confusing story. We'll talk more about characters in the next chapter, but for now paint them with a broad brush and concentrate on finding conflict between your protagonists and antagonists.

What Do They Want (and Why)?

Think about what motivates your characters, as knowing this is the key to understanding them. Create some details about what they want. Why does it mean so much for them to have it? What will happen to them if they don't get it? Ask this for most of your major characters, but the more you can ask it, and find answers to your minor characters, the deeper and more interesting you can make them too.

What Do They Need?

The emotional distance between what a character wants (for example, revenge for the brutal murder of their wife) and what they actually need (perhaps redemption or forgiveness) is a space in which skillful writing can create a compelling emotional journey, which is what most game stories are about. If you know what they need, and what they want, and the distance between the two, then you can start to ask yourself what's in the way of the character getting what they need and want. Are there many obstacles? Are they complex? Are some external and others internal? Are there things the character needs to know about themselves, or other people, or the world? Or perhaps all three?

How Do They Fit into the Gameplay?

Make sure your characters fit the gameplay universe—if you've got a FPS set in a futuristic world, the protagonist should belong there and have goals that can be realized within the framework of your game. The obstacles, the things stopping the protagonist from getting what they want, also need to be considered in relation to the opportunities the gameplay affords. The player obstacles (game "tasks," "objectives," "goals") are natural places to align character obstacles wherever you can, and will help knit the story and gameplay together in the most seamless way. They may not always afford you easily identifiable internal obstacles, but they are certainly the first places to examine. Try to capitalize on as many game obstacles as you can and give the player additional motivation for achieving them, and additional benefits in doing so.

What's the Story About?

This might seem obvious, but at this stage you can get held back worrying about specifics—resist the temptation to explore micro details. This is the time to break out the big story brush and paint in broad strokes; are you writing about a highly trained explorer on a quest to uncover a long-lost treasure (as in many of the *Tomb Raider* series) or an ex-con, out for revenge against the people who betrayed him (as in *Driver: Parallel Lines*™)? Keep things as simple as possible at this stage.

What's the Story Really About?

The answer to this important question will probably be less obvious and require thinking about, as it needs you to go beyond "mere" plot and delve into the more abstract areas of theme and meaning. Good stories contain subtext that's deeper than action and dialogue—keep this in mind during the whole story-writing process. On the surface, Ninja Theory's *Enslaved*™ tells the tale of a dangerous convict forced to help a woman with the ability to end his life if he doesn't cooperate; the subtext, however, could involve the dangers of technology (as the pair travel through a perilous wasteland populated by robots designed to destroy intruders) or the nature of relationships and interdependence (as the leading characters come to understand one another's needs as their journey progresses). Whatever your story's deeper meaning, it needs to be carried in the action in order to be present; if not, it's just an idea for a meaning you have as a writer, or an idea for a meaning one of your characters has in dialogue. Dramatic action is the testing ground for the existence, strength, and clarity of a meaning.

From here begin working with possible story beats and getting a first sense of a rough act structure and possible scenes. Don't start at any particular "end" of this spectrum and work through it in a consistent or regular fashion; instead, constantly shift between the micro of the beats to the macro of the acts and the place in between with the scenes, touching all elements of them lightly with the goal of trying to arrive at an overall act structure. Remember, an act structure devoid of key details held in scenes and beats is little more than a plot paradigm lacking tangible identity.

Acts

At the outline stage initially break a story into usually three or five acts giving a rough structure of a beginning, middle, and end to the game. The first act (sometimes called the setup) is used to introduce the dramatic premise, world, characters, and events that will drive the story forward. The second act is where the hero must face and overcome a series of obstacles in order to reach their goal. The third and final act involves resolution where you decide how things end. Not all games lend themselves naturally to a three-act structure and may incorporate preludes or epilogue stages, but it is useful to think in broad terms of a beginning, middle, and end when starting to shape the story. As an example, RPG *Mass Effect*'s first act involves the player as Shepard discovering the existence of a strange ancient beacon and reveals the treachery of rogue Spectre agent Saren Arterius. The second act involves Shepard gathering evidence of Saren's betrayal, information about a strange race of beings known only as "The Reapers," and enlisting the aid of a highly specialized group of individuals to help counter a plan that could bring about the end of civilization. The third and final act involves a race against time to stop The Reapers, who are assisted by rogue agent Saren, from bringing their deadly plan to fruition.

Scenes

Each *act* is broken into *scenes*; these can be defined as meaningful story moments. It's up to you how many you need in a given act, and it is normally decided partly by gameplay length and partly by the needs of your story.

Beats

The smallest element in an act structure, a screenplay "beat," is a pause in dialogue to underline a moment of significance. A character might suddenly, in the midst of a conversation, realize a vital fact they've missed up until that point. The moment of realization would be illustrated by a "beat" written into the script. An example of such a "micro moment" can be seen in *Mass Effect 2* at the beginning of the mission to recruit the dangerous (and incarcerated) biotic warrior, Jack. If the player, as Shepard, refuses to give up his weapons to Warden Kuril when his team visits the private prison ship holding Jack, the refusal is followed by a silent beat as the pair size one another up, before Kuril finally breaks the deadlock and agrees to let the player's team keep their armaments.

To help break the story into acts and scenes, keep reversals and revelations in mind. The use of reversals and revelations ensures that the story contains sufficient "bumps in the road" and "twists" to keep things interesting.

Reversals

Reversals are events that send your story in a different direction. They often help you define an act break and help set up the new trajectory of the subsequent act. You might alter the course of a relationship, a motivation, or an assumption; the hero's closest ally could turn out to be their worst enemy, or the jubilation in leading orphans to safety through a dangerous mountain pass to a haven city could turn to distress as you realize that the city arrests all children and has them work in mines. Be sure to underpin a reversal with logic—don't turn an ally into an enemy without a solid reason for this deep change or the player will feel cheated. Towards the end of Lionhead RPG *Fable*, it is revealed that the player's ally, Guild Leader Maze, is really an enemy in thrall to the individual responsible for the murder of the hero's parents at the game's beginning who now must be defeated—this is a potent reversal that helps propel the gameplay and story into the final act, making it clear to the player that little is as it seems in the land of Albion.

Revelations

Revelations are moments where a character learns something important they didn't previously know. Perhaps the hero suddenly has their memory restored and realizes he was once the scourge of the universe (as in *Star Wars: Knights of the Old Republic*) or a key member of your party discovers they're actually a robot, not a living, breathing child searching for his parents as originally thought (as in *Final Fantasy IX*). Revelations change the perspective of the story or the perspective of a character.

So, to recap, ask a series of essential questions about your story and its characters. Think in terms of acts and scenes (or blocks of scenes), use your key tools of reversals and revelations, and you are ready to write a draft of your outline. Resist the temptation to write too much; save the hefty word count for the treatment and calm your creative excitement by remembering that skillful writers tend to use fewer words. When you judge the time right, run ideas for the outline past other team members, in particular the creative lead, and use feedback to iterate until you have a document people are happy with *at least for the moment.*

Once a draft is complete we typically put it through something we call the "But Test." This is a quick and simple way to gain a solid idea of how strong a fledgling outline is. Remember, compelling stories are conflict-driven and filled with interesting obstacles our hero or heroes must overcome. An obstacle test is a simple yet effective way of checking that a story is, at least on the surface, replete with sufficient problems and that there are reversals within the story structure. Fellow games writer Neil Richards explains it eloquently in Figure 6.1.

FIGURE 6.1. The obstacle test.

To illustrate Neil's point, let's visit the fictional world of Dave, energy scientist extraordinaire:

> *Dave wakes up in his hotel room beside a beautiful woman* ***and*** *smiles smugly, remembering the previous evening. He gets dressed, heads out to get a coffee,* ***and*** *returns to find the woman still asleep, that afternoon's fuel cell presentation papers right where he left them.*

The absence of any conflict—signified by the presence of **ands**, but lack of **buts** – results in a pretty dry story so far. Who cares that Dave got lucky the night before? Sure, we might be slightly interested to know more about who the woman is, but our hero clearly feels on top of things, so there's no conflict there. Let's try that again:

> *Dave wakes up in his hotel room beside a beautiful woman,* ***but*** *can't for the life of him remember what happened the night before or who she is. Worried, he fingers his wedding ring, quietly gets dressed, then heads out to grab a coffee,* ***but*** *returns to find the place trashed, the mysterious woman gone, and his company's top secret prototype fuel cell plans missing.*

In one short paragraph, we're already seeing conflict illustrated by the two **buts**. If an outline contains a lot of **ands**, we take that as a sign it needs work. While the examples above are a bit extreme, it's amazing how frequently **ands** creep into outlines where there should be **buts**.

A few years ago we were hired by 2K to work on their foray into the boxing world, *Don King Presents Prize Fighter*. Here's part of an early outline we put together for it.

OUTLINE SAMPLE

Working Title: Fighting Chance – Outline

ACT 1

Scene Block 1

The Kid's coming into the ring—the glitz, the glamour, a world title fight. Fight stops, we travel back in time. The Kid coming off the street—wants to be accepted into the gym. Needs to win to prove himself worthy of a spot but they're tough to get. Is supported by established boxer, Dawson.

Gameplay: Low-level fights

Scene Block 2

The Kid gets enough wins to be taken on but ruffles feathers, has a run-in with top dog, Ramón Silva—there's a scuffle, Dawson saves The Kid from a beating, but now our hero's going to have to work extra hard to prove to the owner he's worth the trouble.

Gameplay: Low-level fights

Scene Block 3

The Kid's on fire, impressing everyone but Silva, who hates him with a passion. Bitter about his humiliation at Dawson's hands, Silva ends up killing Dawson in the ring—perhaps by accident. He leaves the gym, disgraced but unrepentant, but now The Kid's free to try for the top spot.

Gameplay: Low-level fights

Scene Block 4

Word hits the street that Don King's looking for fresh talent, but he's only after the most promising boxers. The Kid has to work his way up the rankings if he's to get noticed.

Gameplay: Mid-level fights

Each section of this outline was designed to provide both the logic and motivation to help drive the player along; they not only need to know the reasons underlying what they're doing, but, ideally, why they should care about it too. Outlines can also function as a pitch document for your proposed story further up the production chain, with possibly marketing and senior execs having to sign off on the concept at this stage before you get green-lit to develop it further. Therefore, try to avoid making them too dry and descriptive (though don't sacrifice clarity and brevity). If you can, slip in some of your story world's tone as you describe events; it'll help bring things to life.

You might go back and forth many times at this stage, taking on feedback from many sources, which is great as this is precisely what the outline is designed to do. Reservations (especially poorly expressed or, even worse, unexpressed ones) at the outline stage have the potential to become major problems at the script stage, so now's the time to work through the concerns of the team and your own issues with the story too. You can save yourself and the team months of rewriting and heartache if you can get things right at this highly macro stage, so resist the temptation to move beyond an outline of a few pages until everyone is signed up to a single version of that document. (Of course, this may not be possible in development environments where the design is in considerable flux, but, nevertheless, you should still seek to capture a snapshot of the game story as best you can, and an outline is your best chance of that.)

THE TREATMENT

Once your outline has been signed off on, you're ready to move onto the next step, writing the treatment. Much like the outline, this is a development tool designed to minimize wasted work and maximize sign-off from the team. But with a treatment you're going to move into more detail. Where before you may only have had a line or two in an outline covering the events of perhaps a few scenes, in the treatment you will turn those into more clearly identifiable discrete scenes—perhaps by name, or at least by clear implication, so you can see more than just the broad strokes of the story; now you can also get a sense of how many scenes there are and how you intend to tell the story within them. Treatments should remain prose-based. They're not the place to start writing full scenes, although the occasional dialogue insert can be a useful way of giving a sense of both tone and character.

At this stage we apply more detailed thinking to the way we are going to tell the story. There are two key techniques to draw on—dramatic tension and dramatic irony—with others less common, but nevertheless sometimes useful—telegraphing, foreshadowing, dangling clause, analepsis (flashbacks), and prolepsis (flash forwards).

Dramatic Tension

Dramatic tension occurs when a character, or set of characters, wants something and is prevented from getting it. The more a character wants that something, the more it means to them, so the more insurmountable the obstacles in their path should be. This results in a more emotionally loaded story, with a greater sense of satisfaction for the character and the player if they finally achieve their goal. In *BioShock 2*, Subject Delta's quest to find and rescue Eleanor Lamb from the machinations of her tyrannical mother, Sophia Lamb, is beset with numerous obstacles all designed, in part, to heighten tension and enhance the feeling of success once she is saved.

Dramatic Irony

This occurs when the audience knows more than a character or set of characters inside the story. It may generate suspense in the audience as they fear for a character, knowing and seeing more than they do. It may also generate laughter in the audience as they enjoy the disparity in the comprehension of a character in a given situation and the reality. A classic example of dramatic irony in action can be seen at the end of Shakespeare's *Romeo and Juliet*, when Romeo assumes Juliet lies dead before him when, in reality, she is merely drugged—a vital fact known only to the audience that results in Romeo tragically taking his own life and ultimately causing Juliet to do the same when she wakes shortly after the terrible deed has been done.

Telegraphing

This is where the writer is explicitly clear to the audience regarding what will occur later within the story. There is also "false telegraphing," where the writer tells the audience, but delivers something different (a telegraphed reversal). In *Half Life*'s opening journey through the Black Mesa Research Facility, developer Valve telegraphs future gameplay moments, as people, machines, and places slide by, beautifully, though fleetingly.

Foreshadowing

Where telegraphing is explicit about what's going to occur in a story, foreshadowing merely hints. This can be useful in a more subtle story and, if handled well, can leave the audience feeling rewarded for successfully "reading" the clue left by the writer.

Planting

Planting is the placement of critical information (perhaps in the form of an object, ability, or character) that will later become essential in the way the plot develops. (When something is foreshadowed it's not essential the audience grasps its eventual meaning, when something is planted it's important enough that the audience notices it, or the story logic is compromised - the storytelling will feel clumsy or overly convenient.)

Dangling Clause

A dangling clause is an expression of intent, which could be a warning, or perhaps a clearly demonstrated hope, fear, or prediction that leads the audience to question the ultimate outcome, yet keeps them guessing until later on.

Analepsis (Flashback)

A moment in the story when the viewer is taken back in story time to view an event or events that can serve a variety of purposes. The analepsis typically sheds light on events or motivations previously not known about or fully understood by the viewer, character(s) affected, or both. The popular television series *Lost* often used these to explore a character's motivation and history. *Mass Effect*'s story features several flashbacks (in reality, one single flashback, but one that is initially fragmented) in which Shepard glimpses the destruction of extinct race the Protheans. This gruesome montage serves to not only shed light on the past, but acts also as a warning as to what might happen if an impending invasion led by The Reapers is not stopped.

Prolepsis (Flash Forward)

A moment in the story in which the viewer travels forward in story time to view a future event or events. The prolepsis is typically used to provide the viewer with a tantalizing glimpse into what will happen, though they must watch until the end to have all elements of the story fully clarified. Foreshadowing may allude to future events, perhaps with imagery or other metaphorical devices, but a prolepsis actually presents them.

Let's return to the world of boxing to take a look at a section of the treatment that sprung from the outline we saw earlier. The section below is built on the outline's first sentence (*The Kid's coming into the ring—the glitz, the glamour, a world title fight*), which illustrates just how concentrated story can be in documents of this type.

Act 1

SCENE BLOCK 1

Don King's talking to camera—subtitles tell us who he is and that we're watching a documentary. *Good fights, bad fights, struggles that shall go down in the books of legend, I have seen them all—but that night I bore witness to such extreme spectaculosity as to render me almost speechless. Two titans, but only one throne!*

We're inside a jam-packed boxing arena. It's the ultimate showdown—glitz, glamour, it's all here, the height of boxing showbiz—add to that a personal grudge between the two fighters and you get a fight only one place on Earth has agreed to stage—Las Vegas. The crowd's going wild, they can smell blood about to be spilled, scent history in the making. The wisecracking, smooth-talking kid from Atlantic City versus the obliterating power of the unstoppable, brutal fighter from the depths of Malawi.

They roar with excitement and derision as we swoop down to capture the vicious and menacing Bomani enter the arena. This is a being no one has been able to stop—who has killed in the name of this sport and some think should be in prison. Many wonder if he'll kill again tonight.

Inside the tunnel at the arena entrance *The Kid* waits patiently, the hood of his satin robe keeping his face deep in shadow. He's an island of calm in a sea of reporters trying to get that historic picture and handlers struggling to simply keep a path clear.

GAMEPLAY: PLAYER CAN LOOK AROUND AND THROW PUNCHES TO "WARM UP." HE'S OCCASIONALLY JOSTLED BY HANDLERS WHO BARELY MANAGE TO KEEP BACK A HUNGRY CROWD.

A treatment, in its role as "master story document," could also contain some, all, or none of the following elements:

- Story high concept
- Tag line
- Notes on story structure and design
- Story structure diagrams
- Character documents

Story High Concept

Sometimes known as "The Elevator Pitch," this is the story condensed into a succinct, punchy, and clear line or two. It's useful because it provides readers with a basic idea of what the story is about without having to read the whole document. It may also help attract the attention of the marketing department, so everyone concerned can clearly see what the game purports to be about, giving all parties involved the chance to consider if this really is what they want to make.

Tag Line

You might want to include a suggested tagline or slogan for your game, which relates in some way to your game's story or gameplay (for example, *Enslaved: Odyssey to the West*™, *Dragon Quest IX: Sentinels of the Starry Skies*™).

Notes on Story Structure and Design

Stories by themselves can be complex creations, and working out how to marry them to a game's design can be an interesting challenge. A good treatment may include thoughts and instructions on how your story will fit into the gameplay.

Story Structure Diagrams

Related to the above information, including one or more diagrams to illustrate your current thinking can be extremely useful. Take a look at Chapter 5 on Narrative Design to get a sense of what these might look like.

Character Documents

Characters are, of course, key to your story, and so are key to your outline and treatment. You may feel your story is too embryonic to allow you to create a full character document at the outline stage, and our detailed character documents are usually created in tandem with our treatments—although we don't embark on an outline without at least having core characters sketched out. See Chapter 7 for a detailed look at character documents.

The treatment is another important opportunity to reiterate until you've got a document the team is happy with and can readily be used to write the script. This will require you to provide steady work for team members on which to provide feedback (preferably in group meetings, as these help everyone reach a consensus faster). Once again, this section of the process acts as another vital safety valve that helps ensure the game story moves forward in as efficient and risk-free a manner as realistically possible, which in turn helps make everyone's life on the team that much easier.

PROJECTS

1. You've been asked to put together an outline by a design team based on the client brief below. Keep in mind that these come in a variety of styles, but should always clearly explain what is needed from the story. Our fictitious game, *Code Obsidian*, is in the early stages of development, so not all the game design details have been worked out yet. Briefs are often written before all of the game design decisions have been made, so be aware that at the early stages in particular you will probably be building your structure on shifting ground.

Introduction

Code Obsidian (CO) is a first-person stealth shooter set in the deadly world of 1960s international espionage and corporate piracy. We're in the world of Jason Bourne meets Harry Palmer. We need an outline that pitches a great story to go with our fantastic new game design document.

The player takes on the role of an operative at a secret agency tasked by the UN to work off the radar, behind the scenes, to preserve the peace. Using their cutting-edge skills our hero will travel the world to uncover and stop a rival organization plotting to take over small governments and undermine global stability. As they unravel a dark mystery that will turn the political world upside down, they realize all is not as it seems—even for them.

Code Obsidian is a cool, realistic, and gritty world, though we'd like there to be some humor present to lighten the tone (avoid anything cheesy).

Platform: Xbox One, PS4, PC
Target Market: 15–34-year-old male
Rating: 15+

CO's gameplay will be divided into three sections, each taking place in a different country. We expect your outline to suggest possible places for the action to go down.

Gameplay for the main campaign will last between ten and fourteen hours and be spread over twelve missions. Each mission can begin and end with a two-minute in-game cutscene (IGCS). Also, there's enough in the budget to have a two-minute intro movie and two-minute closing movie.

There will be a multiplayer component to the game, but this is still in development and shouldn't affect the main story (though we will use elements from it to help lend events a basic story shape).

Characters

The game must contain the following four characters for gameplay purposes:

Player Character

- Elite agent
- Male/Female, 20s–40s
- Physically capable, combat- and stealth-trained

Mentor/Ally

- Older, experienced, capable but no longer able to do the things the player can
- Acts as source of missions and information

Rival Agent

- Physically capable, combat- and stealth-trained
- Accompanies player on some missions, though true loyalty in doubt

Antagonist

- Physically capable, combat- and stealth-trained
- Serves as puppet master, is confronted in the final level

For story (and potentially gameplay) purposes, we have the budget for one further main character to be suggested.

Briefs often come with some story elements embedded. This is common practice as designers have to create a basic story framework to flesh out their gameplay ideas. But briefs that come pre-loaded with large quantities of story matter need to be handled carefully. Be sure there is an understanding between all parties as to which elements *must* be retained and where there is room to maneuver. Part of your responsibility is to help explain the consequences of any story elements and make it clear where and how this causes restrictions and has an impact on the rest of the story and, wider, the game itself.

2. Write a treatment for fictitious console game, *Arcadia*, using the following brief and outline documents.

Arcadia Brief

The world, at first sight, appears normal. It's a traveling fair, a carnival, a circus that's pitched up outside town. Our hero Adam and his date Helena find themselves enticed onto a ride like no other—a strange ghost train run by a strange character called The Host. The ride sucks them into darkness and Adam wakes alone in a twisted, darker version of the fairground, a carnival world of the dead . . .

Arcadia is a downloadable third-person action adventure game that puts players in the shoes of 15-year-old Adam English as he tries to rescue his date and escape a bizarre fairground world holding them captive.

Platform: Xbox One, PS4
Target Market: 8–14-year-old (male and female)
Rating: 7+

Gameplay

This is a Tim Burton-like universe, macabre, humorous, and faintly disturbing. At its heart is the Big Tent. All around the Big Tent are a number of other "attractions," each constituting a mini-game. The structure is simple and illustrated in Figure 6.2.

Guided through Arcadia by the mercurial, enigmatic figure known only as The Host, the player must successfully beat increasingly twisted fairground-inspired

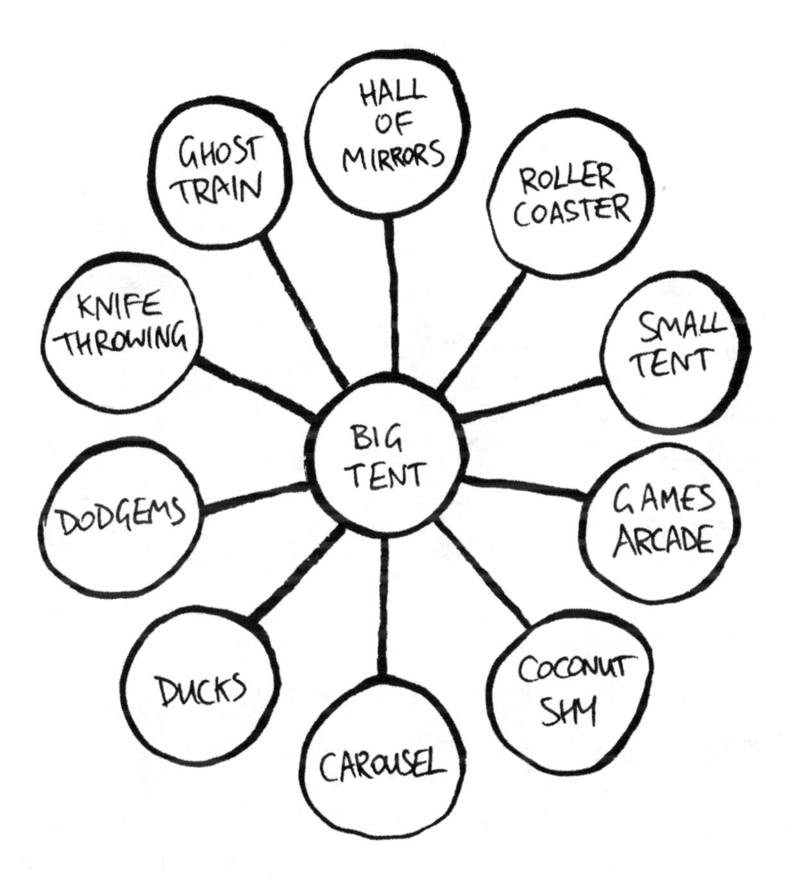

FIGURE 6.2. Arcadia's basic structure.

games to collect enough Escape Tokens to grant passage back to reality. Once they have collected these tokens they must face a final challenge in which they battle The Host to win freedom and return to the world of the living.

Current games being tested include the *Hall of Mirrors* (player must destroy warped versions of Adam as his reflection morphs into monsters) and *Rollercoaster* (player must avoid being thrown from the ride for three minutes by leaning in the appropriate direction, avoiding a variety of missiles and, whenever possible, grabbing power-ups).

To help him complete the games successfully (and provide gameplay variety), Adam will be able to transform himself into a range of carnival world creatures to help him defeat his foes and beat the challenges laid before him. These forms have yet to be finalized, but currently, the following are being experimented with:

Ape-Acrobat:	Gains 50% chance to dodge attacks for 30 seconds
Strongman:	Can throw objects 50% faster/harder for 30 seconds
Ghost:	Unable to be attacked, but unable to touch anything for 30 seconds
Juggler:	Has ranged attack capabilities

Characters

The game must contain the following three characters for gameplay purposes:

Player Character – Adam English

- Average 15-year-old boy
- Initially hates fairgrounds, only there because of date
- Develops courage over course of game

Ally/Date – Helena Simons

- Pretty 15-year-old girl
- Main reason Adam feels driven to escape Arcadia
- Can help Adam win some games

Guide/Antagonist – The Host

- Dark, twisted ringmaster who guides the player through trials
- Arrogant, impatient, and mercurial; Batman's Joker meets Jim Carrey's Count Olaf, though gender currently undetermined
- The power at work behind the scenes

Outline

Act 1

Scene 1

Faded trucks and vans rumble from the mists, montage of a grand fun fair swiftly being built, then people there, enjoying the rides. Adam's on a date, desperate to impress a bored Helena. They walk past the Ghost Train, the creepy old guy persuades them to give it a try. But the ride sucks them into blackness and Adam wakes, the old man leaning over him, shimmering, turning into The

Host. Adam's told the rules of Arcadia and how he needs to win Escape Tokens if he wants to escape. He's also told Helena wasn't transported, that he's alone. Adam's terrified, but decides to play the games and escape. The Host offers to help.

Gameplay: Player wins three basic games.

Scene 2

Adam's starting to understand the crazy world of Arcadia, feeling more confident, but stumbles upon a hidden room, finds Helena tied to a chair with unbreakable candy floss rope. The Host tells Adam he needs to beat the new games to win enough tokens to free her. Adam's newly invigorated and gets to work.

Gameplay: Player beats three more difficult games (perhaps using shape-changing power).

Act 2

Scene 3

Adam manages to win enough Escape Tokens to free Helena. The Host appears to be really pleased by Adam's victory, but when they arrive to release Helena she turns out to be furious, blaming him for their predicament. Adam persuades her to come with him to help gather Escape Tokens.

Gameplay: Player beats more games, gathering Escape Tokens. Once 1,000 have been gathered, next scene is unlocked.

Scene 4

Adam's really getting the hang of Arcadia, collecting tokens, shape changing, and even managing to impress Helena along with the mercurial Host, but his success appears to awaken a great evil. The Host tells them they need to hurry if they're going to escape, as his boss, The Dark, won't stand for someone actually escaping his universe. Adam redoubles his efforts.

Gameplay: Player beats more advanced games. Gets 90% of the Escape Tokens they need.

Act 3

Scene 5

Adam and Helena can taste freedom, they're close to getting enough Escape Tokens, but The Dark finds them and steals back Helena. Adam gives chase through the crazy world, The Host close behind, giggling insanely. They end up in a scarier part of Arcadia, with new, dark games The Host tells Adam not only give Escape Tokens, but—if beaten—will weaken The Dark and force him to release Helena.

Gameplay: Player beats top-level games, gets the rest of the Escape Tokens.

Scene 6

Helena appears, safe. Having earned enough escape tokens to win freedom for both himself and Helena, Adam demands they're set free, but The Host, menacing now, reveals there was no boss, that he was only trying to encourage our hero to work harder. Turns out the escape tokens are really fragments of The Host's soul, scattered throughout Arcadia. Adam has succeeded in earning The Host's freedom and now must take his place. They begin to swap bodies, The Host laughs and jumps down a huge slide, eager to finish the transformation. Adam tells Helena to get out if she can, then gives chase.

Gameplay: Chase game – if he succeeds in catching The Host, Scene 7 plays.

Scene 7

The Host, firmly back in his body, is sucked into Arcadia as Adam surges towards light, along with Helena. Suddenly they're stumbling into the fresh night air. Almost no time has passed. People still bustle around, enjoying the rides and winning prizes. The Ghost Train now dark and unmanned behind them, Adam and Helena hold hands and hurry towards the fun fair exit, talking about their crazy adventure.

GAME END

Chapter 7 Character Documents

All the world's a stage, and all the men and women merely players: they have their exits and their entrances; and one man in his time plays many parts, his acts being seven ages..

— William Shakespeare

BRIEF TERMS

GAME CHARACTER An individual being that exists within a game universe.

MELODRAMA Plot characterized by exaggerated emotions, or with characters whose emotions are unsubstantiated by their actions.

BIBLE Term for a document that defines in detail an aspect of gameplay or the story—can include "Design Bible" or "Story Bible."

Characters are *always* core to story and *often* core to gameplay. A character document is used to help create, edit, and change the characters that will eventually populate your game world. (Sometimes to keep track of the characters you decide to scrap too.) It exists because it's vital to have a space dedicated to defining characters and is often created in conjunction with the outline and treatment it evolves in-line with. A character document is not only an essential resource for writers; it's used by a variety of teams to ensure there's a shared understanding across disciplines.

A compelling story will always need compelling characters to drive it. When James Cameron wrote the movie *Titanic*, he created a fictional romance around which to base very real events. Cameron understood a cruise liner hitting an iceberg and sinking, while tragic, would lack heavyweight emotional punch unless the audience was invested in some way. Thus were born Jack Dawson and Rose DeWitt, doomed to spend a single night of passion together before being forced apart by cruel circumstance. Cameron added further conflict in the form of DeWitt's fiancé, antagonist Caledon "Cal" Hockley, played by Billy Zane. His character represented elitist social attitudes and served to provide the early part of the story with a measure of tension. To be invested in your story, an audience needs to care about what happens to the characters. The most cataclysmic and visually stunning of occurrences still only operate at the level of melodramatic spectacle without something emotional and personal to make us care and continue to care about what happens next. Characters are story, and story is character. You do not have one without the other. As E. M. Forster said on story:

It has only one merit: that of making the audience want to know what happens next. And conversely it can have only one fault: that of making the audience not want to know what happens next.[1]

Similarly, you cannot make your audience care about what happens next in your story unless they care about at least one character. In most media, characters exist to serve the story and are core to how events are experienced by the viewer, listener, or reader. While this is also true in most games, characters have two further, more vital roles: to act as vehicles for the player or players to interact with their environment in meaningful, coherent ways, and to act on occasion as targets to compete against, aim at, or protect.

HOW TO CREATE A CHARACTER DOCUMENT

Before getting started, be familiar with the requirements of your brief; some don't contain very specific instructions on character, preferring to leave the details to you, though they ideally should at least outline who is needed to make the basic story and gameplay work. If in doubt, always check with your team leader. Once you're clear on gameplay and story needs, list out the core story and gameplay jobs you know require characters. Your list might be fairly short to begin with and feature just two entries as follows.

[1] E. M. Forster, *Aspects of the Novel* (London: Penguin Classics, 2005), 42.

Protagonist

The hero—the person, creature, or object through which the player is likely to experience the majority of the game and therefore its story—Mario, Lara Croft, Gordon Freeman, Link—take your pick. Your protagonist should not only fit the needs of your story, but the needs of the gameplay, so be sure to imbue them with the qualities necessary to thrive, or at least survive, in the game universe.

Antagonist

The villain of your story, a being against whom your protagonist must struggle with every ounce of their willpower to achieve their goals—Emperor Tachyon, Frank Fontaine, Bowser, Vass—to name a few. Be warned: a weak antagonist makes for a weak story in which the player will not feel driven to push themselves to the edge of their abilities to overcome; a protagonist can only be as interesting as their antagonist allows them to be.

To build your characters you need to ask some key questions; answering these will let you form the nucleus of each:

- What is their gameplay function?
- What is their story need?
- What is their external world?
- What is their internal world?

What Is Their Gameplay Function?

What function does that character have in the game? Does the player get to play as this character or not? Do they have a major role or a minor one? What must they need to be capable of doing in order to satisfy the gameplay requirements? If *Portal 2*'s protagonist, Chell, didn't have Aperture Science's Handheld Portal Device, she wouldn't be capable of traversing the numerous challenges forced upon her by rampant Artificial Intelligence GLaDOS. Not every character you create will necessarily have a specific, direct gameplay purpose. Some might simply exist to help propel the story forward, never making an appearance when the player's in control.

It's important to understand the significance of a character's place in the story as this helps inform you of the kind of character needed. Does the game require you to create someone or something capable of being a boss to battle with at the end of the first act (who then may later change to being an ally), or does the game require you to forge a character who, irrespective of where else they occur in the game, *must* be a boss at the end of a level? As mentioned in the last chapter, *Fable's* initially benevolent mentor, Maze, leader of the Hero's Guild, eventually reveals himself to be a powerful enemy, worthy of "boss" status due to his high station.

What Is Their Story Need?

Knowing what a character needs is vital. It doesn't matter if you've created the most vividly detailed individual, complete with an array of artists' drawings to accompany them—if you don't know what they want and why they're in your universe, they will remain artificial and empty, devoid of drive. If they're a main character, your story will feel empty too. Desire, need, want—these are the fuels that will propel your character through a scene and through your story. These can be physical, emotional, or both. Remember, what a character wants and what they really need can be two very separate things. As stated in the previous chapter, the space between them can underline a lesson that needs to be learned over the course of the story and can be an exciting place to explore as a writer that provides the basis for a compelling character journey to help fuel the plot. *BioShock*'s egotistical city-builder, Andrew Ryan, is fueled by such a powerful ego that his desire to live is outweighed by his desire to dictate the terms of his death, which results in him forcing the player to end his life.

Another way of thinking about a character's story need is to think in terms of *character arcs*. A character arc is a way of describing a character's emotional journey from one state to another, not just from happy to sad, for example, but perhaps from thwarted ambition to ambition realized. An arc is a dramatic demonstration of how a character changes, or how their story need has played out. Not all characters in a story will have an arc, but major characters usually will. You can think of a story as *the means* by which a character, or a series of characters, change. RPGs often take a character of low (or even the lowest) status and provide them with a story that sees them rise to a significantly higher status perhaps from a lowly apprentice to a mighty magic user.

What Is Their External World?

How does your character appear to the rest of the world? How are they seen? What kind of universe do they come from? Knowing this can give the art team some great pointers that will let them begin work. Again, your answers should serve the needs of the game.

- What do they look like? Are they tall or short? Is their build athletic and lean, that of a chubby couch potato, or somewhere in-between? Are they physically attractive, plain, or perhaps ugly? How do they dress? Are they flamboyant, snappy, and expensive, or muted, grubby, and cheap?

- How do they physically move through the world? Are they agile, graceful, and deadly, or slow, clumsy, and stiff? What's their walk like? Do they take long, confident strides, or skitter along, eager to avoid being noticed?
- How do they sound? Do they have a strong accent? If so, what's it like? Have they perhaps worked to change it or are they proud of their roots?
- Do they wear a lot of makeup or sport other unique markings that make them stand out?
- Are they rich and famous or poor and unknown?

What Is Their Internal World?

Who is your character on the inside, beneath their virtual clothes and digital skin? Spending some time thinking about the internal world of your character will pay dividends later on as knowing them emotionally and intellectually is core to knowing how they'll act in any given situation.

- How do they think? Do they possess a sunny disposition that leads them to often see the bright side of a situation and the good in people? Or do they tend to brood over every little upset and perceived slight they encounter on the journey of life?
- Are they smart, educated, and sensitive, able to see to the truth of things quickly, or slow, uneducated, and irascible, unwilling to look below the surface of a situation? Or perhaps the majority of their lessons were learned on the streets, making them tough and cynical, though well-connected.

NOTE *A character's backstory can form an important part of your document. This is basically the story of where they came from, the salient parts of their childhood and life in general that, while not necessarily directly important for the purposes of your game, can really help you understand them in deeper detail.*

RESEARCH

To help answer these questions and create interesting, consistent, and compelling characters takes time, skill, and—vitally—research. Nothing can implode the suspension of disbelief necessary for one to be drawn into a story more so than characters that don't feel real. If your antagonist is an ambulance driver by day and an assassin by night, you'll need to delve into the worlds of both. In the case of the former, find out what sort of shifts they work, the language they'd use, and the kinds of situations they might find themselves in. Details are what matters. If you need them to refer to their medical equipment, find out whether they do that with precision or with nicknames. Anything and everything they say is significant and tells us something about them. In the case of their being an assassin—what kind are they? Do they have particular equipment, or specific methodologies or particular philosophies?

Identify what you need to know, and then plan your research strategy. This stage will typically involve delving into a number of areas in order to add that vital veneer of authenticity. But be aware of what could be termed the "research trap." Not everything you discover during the course of your research necessarily needs to be overtly featured in the game. Although it might be tempting to show just how much you know about a subject, cluttering your story with too much detail can slow it down and make things feel pretentious. You may have heard people use the phrase "the research is showing." This is what they mean when you've fallen into the research trap—you've succumbed to the temptation to show what you know because you know it, not because it is dramatically essential. It's often useful just to know something as the writer; you don't have to prove it to the rest of the world. Start your research by looking into the following areas:

Background

What social class do they belong to (if it matters)? Working class, upper class, somewhere in-between? Are they from a rich world and used to getting what they want, or have they had to struggle to survive? What culture are they part of? Hispanic? African American? Anglo-Saxon? The list goes on, and the answer you have is likely to tell you something significant about them.

Geography

If your character lives somewhere specific that actually exists, or once existed, then it's important you understand what that could mean for your character's identity. If they live in the historic city of Edinburgh in Scotland, research will tell you the type of buildings it features, the layout and typical weather, among other things. Failing to do your research and then having one of your characters say they miss "the bonnie skyscrapers of Edinburgh and long dry winters" would have anyone who knows the city at all wondering what they're talking about.

Career

Career can be an important part of your character's identity. Whatever they do (even if their "job" is simply to be an 11-year-old girl) be sure you know whatever you need to about it. What is the typical world this career inhabits? What kind of words and slang might people in this career use? What tools, if any? What skills might this career imbue your character with?

You might need to create characters for a game story that have very little to do with a "normal world." Researching fantastical or surreal characters can still be done through source materials such as books, movies, graphic novels, art, and so on. In today's networked world it can be tempting to rely on easy-to-access online resources such as Google™ and Wikipedia™ to carry out your research, but be sure to pool from a range of sources. Depending on how much time you have to spend and what you're looking for, remember there are also newspapers, books, people, magazines, movies, music, museums, galleries, antique shops, library archives, and more, all capable of providing rich seams of inspiration and information.

EXAMPLE CHARACTERS

Here's a sample taken from early work we carried out on 2K's *Don King Presents: Prizefighter*. Jesus Silva (here still called *Jesus Espiga*; he became "Silva" later on in the writing process) was designed to be both an early barrier for the protagonist and an eventual ally whose death would fuel the third act and lead to a more emotionally charged confrontation with Bomani, our main villain.

Antagonist/Ally: Jesus Espiga

Initially symbolizes bitterness, anger, arrogance; forgetting where you came from; ambition without restraint or respect for others. Also symbolizes the betrayal of inspiration—as he was once a role model for The Kid. He represents the dark path—the path of corrupted success, the one The Kid must avoid. Espiga is who he will become if he doesn't measure his success and keep his feet on the ground. After his clash with The Kid, Espiga symbolizes the possibility of self-reinvention; that enemies can be misunderstood friends.

He is twenty-four years old, a Panamanian.

Had a tough childhood, comes from a working-class background, parents not there enough, in and out of juvie, he eventually discovered boxing. It became an avenue to channel his tremendous energy—his rage, his passion—and a place where he could taste victory and dominate.

This guy is a rarity—a big, really built Hispanic. There's something of Tyson's early twenties swagger and ferociousness about him. He trains in the same gym as The Kid. A little bit older and a little further on in his career, Espiga is a major influence and inspiration for The Kid. There's no doubt the kid models himself after Espiga—wants to be him, be like him; Espiga has shown him there's a way out.

Initially driven by anger, a feeling that the world owes him and it had better pay up. Arrogant, unwilling to admit to any real weakness, which is in itself a weakness.

The dark side of The Kid— someone who's willing to destroy anything and anyone in his way. Something changes in Espiga after his fight with The Kid; he realizes they're both alike, and instead of fighting against the world alone, they can fight it together.

Loves bling, highly ostentatious—one of those guys who, when he was poor, would spend every spare cent to show the world how fly he was. As he rises in the boxing world, his hunger for the gaudy trappings of success never wanes.

Espiga fancies himself as a bit of a warrior-poet-philosopher and can be a bemusing person to talk to. Listeners can get buried under a mountain of poorly remembered quotes that can come from anywhere, including *The Art of War* ("When you're strong, let your enemy think . . . you're strong. When you're weak, you let them know."). He might not even care he often gets them wrong, just as long as people are listening to him. While clearly not well educated, Espiga's still a savvy fighter who knows his way around the ring.

Tremendously talented boxer—his skill built on strength and physical intimidation of opponents.

There's talk of him being one the best boxers of all time . . .

Zack Harper

Here's a second sample, taken from Ubisoft's *Emergency Heroes*™ for the Nintendo Wii, that includes their three main character requirements.

Protagonist: Zack Harper, 18

Game Requirements

Someone young and inexperienced who grows as the game progresses

They develop as the player does

They are the only one capable of doing what the game requires

Young, fit, enthusiastic, and brave, Zack Harper dreamed of doing something exciting with his life ever since he was a kid. He's not hungry for attention, he's not even that eager to prove himself to anyone (he knows he's good)—he just loves a challenge and loves a thrill.

Upbeat, engaging, and fun to be around, Zack's been into sports all his life, the more extreme the better. He's too young to have driven for long, but already he's at home behind the wheel.

To say Zack's got a can-do attitude's an understatement; nothing seems to daunt him, and the scary thing is, there's not much he can't do when he sets his mind to it. Thankfully, all that confidence is tempered with a dash of humility—just enough to pull Zack back from being cocky. He's a young man who doesn't only know he's capable, he knows he's got a lot to learn.

Getting onto the EHO Cadet training scheme was the best day of Zack's life. Being kicked off it was the worst.

Ever since the EHO had been announced, Zack knew that was what he wanted to do—had to do—with his life: the EHO would push him harder than almost any job and he'd be helping a lot of people in the process—everyone's a winner, right?

Then his dreams fell apart. All it took was one terrible accident. Two years ago, but it still feels like yesterday.

Zack's now starting college, determined to make something of his life, to move on. His feelings about the accident are confused—he's not sure if he should blame himself or not. That's the one doubt that clouds his mind.

EXAMPLE ANALYSIS

As you may have noted from these samples, there's no set contents list for a character document. However, certain elements are worth drawing attention to.

Character Name

Character names carry weight. They are not just random monikers. Names tell players a great deal about the character they are ascribed to; a regular unpretentious name for a regular unpretentious character (or the opposite for comic or thematic effect), and potentially an exotic name for an exotic character. Whatever you do, try to avoid lazy naming. Try to be clear why a name is right for a character. But also don't be too precious about this, certainly to begin with—you can always come back and change it as you feel your way through the character's identity and personality.

With Espiga, we wanted a name that felt Latin American and strong, yet contained an undertone of wealth and power. Here is a character as much in love with money, women, and the world of celebrity as he is with boxing, and while Espiga was designed to be an early antagonist, eventually he would become the protagonist's ally, so using "Jesus" as his first name helped underline a slightly religious upbringing, and therefore a certain moral grounding. We eventually changed his last name to Silva, as we came to feel it said more about him. It was equally Latin American, but it brought an association of the word "silver" as a homophone, and gave off a sense of something glistening, special, potentially ostentatious, above the dross, and yet also a suggestion of worldly riches, as opposed to something spiritually higher and more noble. Silva was a man whose magnificence in the ring was to be admired, but whose horizons were ultimately limited to only this world.

With Zack Harper, we had a young character who was full of energy. We wanted the tone of the world to be naturalistic (it was a driving game with naturalistic car handling) and optimistic (the core target demographic was preteens). We also wanted our main character to sound distinctive but also have grounding in everyday life—he wasn't a superhero. So "Harper" felt like a regular enough name to not draw too much attention to itself. And "Zack" had a satisfying ring to it—the sound of it was clean and zappy, speedy and definitive, so, for us, it was distinctive and optimistic.

Quick Details: Age and Racial Background

These details are important and deserve careful consideration as they're fundamental to your character's identity. It bears repeating that you need to ensure each decision fits within the logical needs of both gameplay and story.

With our sample characters, Espiga needed to be old enough to have more boxing experience than the game's protagonist, but young enough to have realistically not "made it" yet. In *Emergency Heroes*, Harper's age again was a balancing act—while no raw cadet, he still needed to be young enough for the target age group to empathize with but old enough to have the skills necessary to play a key role in saving the city of San Mira from destruction. Interestingly, in the version above we don't specify Harper's exact age, as at that stage in the project the team was still debating this.

In the boxing game, we knew Bomani, the ultimate antagonist in the story, was going to be African, so for Espiga we wanted someone who looked different visually and came from a markedly different cultural background. We wanted the game to reflect the broad world of race in the sport (the player could choose the race of their avatar).

Story Function

This text describes what role the character plays within the story—it should move beyond the obvious (*they're the antagonist*, *they're the love interest*, and so on) and enter the realm of symbolism and subtext. Here, you can outline how they're destined to help drive your story, by who and what they represent—which, while not always that useful for gameplay, can be vital when it comes to detailing your plot.

Espiga's role in the story is outlined clearly—he's not only designed to be an initial barrier to the protagonist, there to help push him to a new level of ability before becoming his ally; he's there to provide a warning about the path of arrogance and where it leads. On a more optimistic note, Espiga also represents the potential we all have to change and comes to illustrate the power the protagonist has to turn him away from the darker route he has initially taken when the game begins.

Visual Samples

At the start of the process, it can be useful to have visual samples of a character to give the team a broad idea of what they look like. These can be pulled from any source, though typically online databases have a huge array of material that can serve as your first port of call. Two or three samples should be sufficient for readers to get a clear idea of your character's broad look and build. As your document and the characters contained in it evolve, the art department generally provides iterative sketches to zone in on their final appearance.

This section is missing in both our sample documents, though the original versions we submitted to the teams did come complete with a variety of possible visual samples for each character. For copyright reasons, it would be too costly to obtain permission to reuse them here.

Dialogue

A good way to help bring a character to life is to let them be heard. This is where dialogue samples can be great. As we stated earlier, it's important that each character looks and feels unique—knowing how they sound, the sort of slang they might use, and even the rhythm of their speech are all important ways writers can tease uniqueness from a character.

When writing sample snippets of dialogue, be sure that whatever you use stands alone and clearly belongs to that individual without having to be read out by an actor. Well-written dialogue should, without leaving the page, have a flavor that clearly marks it as having been said by the character in question. Don't try too hard, however—as with many elements of writing, getting dialogue tone and style right without making it feel overwritten is a balancing act.

CHARACTER SIDES

When the time comes to record the audio, you may need to help prepare a voice director and actors, and a full-blooded character document is not always the most helpful tool—given its size and purpose, it can take a long time to read, and longer to pick out what is useful for the session or sessions. This is where a smaller, more nimble set of character "sides" can be extremely useful to create. These are designed to give an audio director and actor concise and relevant information on a character, as well as sample lines of dialogue. It's generally sent out to all parties who might need it, so they're able to prepare well in advance of the session. When recording studios and actors can cost thousands of dollars to hire per hour, even spending five minutes to brief someone on a character is expensive.

Here's a sample side, to give you a better idea of what you might be called on to write, further down the production process.

Name:	Maria Janina Consuelo (a.k.a. Jay Cee)
Sex:	Female
Age:	13
Location:	The Bronx, New York
Ethnic Origins:	Hispanic
Accent:	Standard American, hint of Hispanic, she knows her roots
Gameplay Role:	Mechanic (helps with player's vehicle and inventory tech)

Background

Maria's a tough, not to mention smart cookie who loves her working-class family but drives them crazy with her passion for all things car-related.

FIGURE 7.1. Maria Janina Consuelo.

Ever since she could hold a socket wrench, she's spent a lot of her free time hanging out at her dad's garage, helping him and his guys fix up whatever's on the menu.

Hanging out with the guys gives her a harder edge; Maria can hold her own, but she's still a kid and knows it. Her folks make sure she's not up to her elbows in grease every day, so Maria's got a healthy circle of friends who really like how different she is. She's also not afraid to embrace "girl stuff" when it suits her (though it can make her feel a little self-conscious).

Sample Dialogue

(Response to someone criticizing her work on an engine)
Step off, Tool Monkey! I don't see you doin' any better!

(Greeting the player—they enter the garage)
Hey! Hand me that alternator over there—just kiddin'!

(Defending how she's in a summer dress that afternoon)
My mom practically forced me into it! Uh. Whaddaya think?

(Commenting on player trying to mend item in inventory using spare parts)
You sure that's a good idea? My ol' man says you can change the tires on a junker, but it'll still suck on the turns.

EXERCISES

1. Time to roll up those creative sleeves and help create some character documents of your own! Below are three sample game character sketches; either individually or in pairs, use them as the inspiration to create character documents that include the following information:

   Name

   Age

   Gender

   Story function

   Gameplay function

   Description

   Sample dialogue

Think carefully about each character's role in both story and gameplay terms, and make sure the elements fit together logically and coherently. When you're ready, present one of your characters to the rest of the class.

Character #1

FIGURE 7.2. Character #1.

FIGURE 7.3. Character #2.

Character #3

FIGURE 7.4. Character #3.

2. What should be decided upon first, a character's role within the gameplay, or their role within the game story? Are they mutually exclusive? Is one more important than the other?
3. Consider a character from a game, book, TV show, play, or movie who demonstrates the greatest range of change, from one extreme to another (for example Harry Potter). Think in terms of where the character began and where they end up, not in a physical sense, but an emotional one. Is this extreme change necessary for the success of the overall narrative?
4. Think of a story in which the protagonist has a character arc that goes nowhere, and they fail to change by the end of the story. Perhaps you consider Patrick Bateman, in *American Psycho* as just such an example, Are there any other instances when you think it would make sense to tell a story without a character arc for a protagonist. That is, are there any kinds of stories better suited to this approach?
5. Create a single-page character document using the Brief, Outline, and Treatment material from Chapter 9's fictitious game, *Code Obsidian*.

6. Create a full character document that contains all the characters involved in Chapter 9's *Arcadia* to go with the Treatment you wrote.
7. Using a character drawn from Chapter 20's game sample, *The Delivery*, create a short character "side" document, complete with sample dialogue.

Chapter 8 Environmental Storytelling

My take on games writing is if a player is playing a game they ought to be having a good time, and if I was to interrupt that player with some story or a cut scene it's kinda like knocking on the door of a couple having sex, sitting on the end of their bed, and getting them to stop while I read them my poem.

— Games Writer on GDC Austin Writers' Panel, 2009

THINGS HAD EVIDENTLY GOT OUT OF HAND AT THEIR SON'S "CHESS CLUB" EVENING.

BRIEF TERMS

GAME LEVEL A discrete area of a game map loaded separately by the hardware so as to make processing requirements manageable. Each level has its own beginning, middle, and end, and can be, effectively, an interactive story (or short story) in its own right.

PLAYER PATHING The design approach to the route and intended experience through which player characters are directed within game levels, sometimes called "*The Golden Path.*"

GATING Restricting the player's progress within a level until a specific objective has been achieved.

BOSS FIGHT An especially difficult video game encounter in which a creature or character (a.k.a. the "boss") must be defeated in order for the player or players to progress and/or be rewarded. Typically, these are placed at the end of game levels and/or a series of challenges.

CRITICAL PATH The route within a level that a player character will traverse in order to complete it.

NON-CRITICAL PATH A route a player character may optionally traverse through a game level.

THEORY

Perhaps as a result of the release of *Half Life*, "environmental storytelling" has been a term in the vocabulary of games writers since around the year 2000. Valve's famous FPS takes place in a universe carefully constructed to seamlessly enhance both our understanding of the story and requirements of the gameplay—an achievement that others have since worked to emulate with varying degrees of success. Like most terms it often means different things to different people and is accordingly used in different ways. In essence it's an approach that seeks to use the environment itself as a means to convey story. Of course, writers of all kinds have long used the description or presentation of environments to convey not only their story worlds but their narratives—foreshadowing events, symbolizing past, present, or concurrent action with physical objects, and so on. But what's significant about environmental storytelling, as it's commonly understood among many of our peers, is that it either significantly reduces or completely removes the need for cinematic set pieces altogether. This not only benefits art resources and allows a design team to have tighter control of the experience they're delivering to the player (therefore ensuring an integrated look between story and game elements) but, *crucially*, appears to promise a far more satisfying experience for the player. With environmental storytelling a player can remain a *player* instead of being frozen out of the game as they watch helplessly, so bombarded with the story they have no choice but to sit through with as much grace as they can muster. As our GDC writer's quote at the beginning of the chapter eloquently and memorably illustrates, this kind of storytelling allows the player to totally exist within the gameplay, no longer interrupted from what they're actually there to do.

The origins of environmental storytelling seem to lie somewhere between the development of theme park experiences and games allowing players a greater sense of freedom of movement within the game world—most often, though not exclusively, shooter, action, and RPG games with less purely linear paths, and sandbox games. Instead of developers being trapped into forcing a player along a certain route to ensure they receive cinematic set pieces at the correct locations at the correct story junctures, environmental storytelling frees developers from those restrictions, at least in part, which then allows players more freedom—or, at the very least, allows them a greater sense of freedom.

MISE-EN-SCÈNE

You may hear this phrase (pronounced MEES-ON-SEN) used often in the context of environmental storytelling. The literal French translation is "to put on stage," or "placing of a scene." It's a term used in theater and cinema, with many interpretations. Game developers generally use it to mean storytelling by the controlled placement of visual assets. A crime scene, with police tape and wooden sticks thrust into bullet holes in walls, is an example of mise-en-scène. From specific elements within the environment you can rapidly interpret at least part of a story—a murder, or attempted murder, the number of bullets fired, their trajectories, perhaps the number of people involved. When a mise-en-scène links to others, or to other parts of the environment and/or story, you are telling a story environmentally.

The strategic placement of a well-chosen object can save you the need to deliver a whole cinematic scene. As illustrated by futuristic RPG *Fallout 4*, should you need to convey to a player they're in a post-apocalyptic world (and let's assume they don't already know this from the marketing and screenshots they've seen prior to starting the game), a cinematic scene is certainly one way to do it. Another is to have them walk, of their own volition, past a monitor screen displaying the information as a news item. Another is to leave newspaper clippings up, or have scraps of newspaper headlines scattering the street, or discarded radiation protection gear, or have them find a survivor moments from death—because, in its broadest terms, environmental storytelling isn't just about using the space, it's also about using people or other storytelling media as conduits for what you wish to convey in much the same way you might use buildings, advertising hoardings, abandoned cars, or street furniture such as phone boxes, lampposts, mailboxes, and so on. Of course, it depends on how much detail you want to deliver and how much you feel you need to. You could convey a post-apocalyptic world (or at least a post-mysterious-cataclysmic-event world) without any news items, or survivors, simply by showing a world abandoned—it depends what your story really is and what information it's important for you to release and at which junctures. Whatever decisions you make, this method of storytelling can be more highly engaging for the player because they are proactively *discovering the story information themselves*, reaching in and interpreting it, rather than merely being information receptacles into which predetermined story segments are dropped when the game deems it the correct time. In the same way, you're looking to find fixed elements of the environment or objects or people you can attach to the environment in order to do your storytelling; often they can actually prove more useful than the environment itself—although it does depend on what kind of overall game and level design you're working with. If your game allows a player to take a few different routes to a nodal point, you may need the flexibility to attach an object, event trigger, sound sample, or whatever might suit your immediate need to multiple cars, traffic signals, or fire hydrants distributed along a variety of paths, so whichever route the player takes, you can guarantee they will trip the metaphoric wire and experience what they need to see or hear.

That's not to say that, equally, you couldn't put objects or triggers in multiple buildings along different paths. It's important to understand the player's critical path in order to interpret the relative likelihood of any storytelling moment being encountered. Those instances that are harder for a player to miss, and so have a higher likelihood of being encountered, have a higher value than those that are easier to miss. It's like the difference between building on prime land and marshland. Use the prime land for the most essential elements of your story and the marshland for more secondary or tertiary elements. Developers call this prime land, the path the player *must* pass through, the "critical path."

While dramatic writing is served very well by the mantra *show don't tell*, games writing has really developed its own extended mantra: *do, then show, then tell.* If you can get a player to participate in a manner that directly contributes to the story "telling," especially in a manner that makes them feel it's on their own terms, that is almost always preferable to showing them in a dramatic sequence, which, in turn, is almost always preferable to telling them; Princess Peach's dramatic kidnapping in *Super Mario Galaxy*™ would surely not carry as much emotional weight for the player if it had been relayed in a letter from arch-villain, Bowser, rather than witnessed firsthand by our plump plumbing hero.

There are many different ways we can compartmentalize the approaches to environmental storytelling. We could divide topics into geographical/architectural, personal, audio, and AI-based elements. We also could divide them into location- or time-based triggers. Here, however, let's approach the theory by way of the categories of orientation, a sense of a dynamic presence, characters, semi-playable cut scenes, and triggers.

Orientation

It's important that a player be properly oriented in the game world they've stepped into before they lose interest in it, and that you provide good, clear clues to do just that. Action adventure game *Batman: Arkham Asylum's* opening moments have the player guide our caped protagonist along an atmospheric journey through the still fully functioning Arkham prison facility, which allows them to view in safety the deadly world they're entering and the enemies they'll eventually face. This orientation also skillfully weaves in telegraphing and foreshadowing, in a manner reminiscent of *Half Life*'s introductory sequence.

Let the player understand where they are and you're well on your way to conveying the first part of a plot—the setup. The type of buildings, the state of the buildings, and their age and architectural design are all good places to start. Are we in the past, present, or future? Are the buildings being used for what they were designed for? Is the area affluent or poor? War-torn or a thriving commercial hub? Is it urban or suburban? Countryside or wasteland? Perhaps there are no buildings at all, only vegetation. Is it recognizably Earth or not? Is it healthy or dying? Are there people present? Do they look healthy or ill? Rich or poor? Pleased to see you or not? What era or planet do they seem to be from (which may deliberately contrast with the era and planet of the buildings you find them in)? Do they talk? Aggressively? Casually? With accents? In a language you can understand or not? Lighting, the weather, and audio, both contextual/atmospheric sound as well as music, are also elements to consider that can provide immediate or near-immediate contextualization should you wish to employ them.

There can also be an advantage in delivering the crucial contextualization in one dramatic, spectacle-laden moment. Yet there is also much to be gained from not telling a player everything at once, letting them instead gradually build a picture of understanding in their own minds, making the environment part of the story you're telling; naturally there are both advantages and risks involved in handling their introduction to the game in this way, which require you understand how and when you plan to allow the player to be oriented. It's a trade-off. Delaying explanation can build tension, but it also risks a player becoming frustrated, confused, and unengaged, and everything you are showing (*if* you are showing anything)—every building, every tree, every bird, or every absence thereof—is telling the player something. People will be able to rapidly build a picture of where they think they are (even more rapidly if the pre-release material has helped convey the game world), and you need to ensure, within the team, that the picture they have (or the one they don't) is the one you *fully intend* them to have, aware of the expectations you're already putting into play. With an excellently written four-minute, twenty-second introduction movie, the setup for zombie shooter *Left 4 Dead*™ is already well established; as a player you understand the world, the gameplay (not just shooting, but also sneaking around deadly witches, the importance of group cooperation, and the overall intention to seek rescue), the monsters (not just their appearance, but also their differing attributes), as well as the weapon types and playable characters. After this there's almost no need for any other storytelling throughout the game. Simple audio cues triggered by game events are almost all that's needed to keep things moving coherently, and, as a player, you're contributing to an evolving story that doesn't lock you behind a glass screen whenever "story happens."

Dynamic Presence

Creating a sense of a dynamic presence can be a very effective way to keep a story developing, or *a sense of a story developing* in the world, without resorting to cut scene cinematics. You can keep players guessing as to the intentions of the person or people behind the presence, just as you can keep them guessing as to their identities, and the likely culmination of their intentions and how these might affect the player—for good or ill, or somewhere in between. Game developers often use what they call "breadcrumbs," leaving a trail of items, arrows, symbols, puzzles, or sounds, for example, which need to be followed in sequence (either with or without a time limit) in order to reach the goal. In Bioware's fantasy RPG *Dragon Age 2*™, players journeying through the city of Kirkwall during an uprising don't only hear the sounds of battle nearby, they'll run past burning buildings, dead bodies, and encounter warriors to fight—all of which combine to lend a potent sense of conflict.

In essence, dynamic presence is a fully functioning quest motif—all you need to make it a more satisfying quest, at its simplest level, is to add thresholds and reversals along the way. Because although not the most complex of devices, they are nevertheless effective ways to keep the player playing as they simultaneously gain a sense of a story developing—"not here—so where next? Maybe here? No? Back where we started!?" And story-based breadcrumbs are capable of doing more than simply leading players from one place to the next. If you're planting objects, for example, they can tell players something not just about their ultimate destination, but also, as mentioned, the person they might be pursuing, or the state of the person who has been kidnapped, or even the person who has employed them to conduct the search. The objects could be ancient relics that not only point to new destinations but also contain text, images, clues, or puzzles that help expand and enrich the story world. A sense of presence can be created in other ways too, through clues like bloodstained handprints on windows, or a discarded shoe, or items that appear in a room that weren't present when the player was initially there, such as a fresh-looking half-eaten sandwich, a crackling record that springs to life on a jukebox in an abandoned room, a rusty mechanical toy that greets the player as they enter, the wail of a police siren in the distance—it depends on what story you're telling and what tone you're seeking to evoke. All these things can tell the player something—that they are not as alone as they thought they might be—and you can push this to have them believe this state to be a good or a bad thing as it suits your story and the plotlines and arcs you want to explore.

Characters

The way a character looks always tells a player a great deal, or, at the very least, appears to. Within seconds an opinion can be formed as to their threat level, likely status, and the potential contextual meaning of their current activities—are they a woman in an expensive-looking dinner dress digging in the trash? Are they a soldier without any equipment save a battered uniform and helmet traveling on public transport? Are they a homeless guy sneaking around the outside of an embassy carrying a large, seemingly empty cardboard box? The look and contextualization of such characters sparks interest and causes hypotheses to develop in the mind of the player. *Halo*'s Master Chief is entirely encased in a powerful suit of armor that not only enhances his abilities on the field of combat, but illustrates his total immersion in the world of the soldier (so much so we never see his face, in much the same way we never see the features of futuristic law enforcer Judge Dredd™).

As a writer you may choose to be clearer or more abstruse about what you want players to draw from these characters. You may wish a player to arrive at the conclusion that the woman in her fifties pushing the baby carriage is a harmless grandmother, precisely because she's about to reveal herself as a deadly Soviet marksman and you know this is going to award dramatic collateral when she does. The importance of a character's appearance and the dramatic context within which they are presented in either building or subverting expectations is evident in all stories. In environmental storytelling this importance is heightened, since it may be that this is the sole or primary means of engaging with these characters; there may be no scene to establish their dramatic role, and you may be relying solely on in-game interactions that may or may not be supported by voice samples delivered while the game is running. In this sense, environmental storytelling calls for even tighter and sharper control and understanding of the conception and depiction of characters. It's not essential to work with archetypes, but there's a good reason games writers do; archetypes are quickly identifiable as deriving from, or approximating to, culturally established character "types," and they therefore come carrying some of the "storytelling mass" or "meaning" of these characters that can be conveyed quickly, which makes them immensely efficient storytelling devices. Of course, names can also be incredibly useful and allow players to form pictures in their minds as to who characters are even before seeing them. A space pirate called "Hood" who evades the clutches of the "Sheriff" of a group of planets in the far reaches of a galaxy that goes by the name of "The Nottingham Cluster" already creates an expectation of who these people are and the kind of attributes and motivations they may have. (Expectations which, as mentioned earlier, you might fully intend to subvert.) Of course, archetypes are close to stereotypes, and sometimes the only difference is in the eyes of the beholder. The difference, at least to us, is stereotypes are used without a full understanding of the power or value of the character type's origins and are employed ineffectively or lazily, without honing to ensure they fit smoothly and appropriately into the story world. Archetypes are employed with an understanding of the power they wield and the associations they bring with them, and are more carefully integrated into the story world in which they're used. Archetypes are a little like jokers in a deck of cards; play them strategically and at the right time, and you've got the best hand possible (exposition-light characters with a clear dramatic function). Play them at the wrong time in the wrong way and you'll create stereotypes and a losing hand.

Semi-Playable Cut Scenes

Semi-playable cut scenes are a powerful tool in environmental storytelling. Instead of cut scenes being FMVs (full motion videos) rendered with higher quality graphics but non-playable (or, alternatively, in-game cut scenes which use the game engine) and stitched into the fabric of the game with possible loading screens in and out of gameplay, semi-playable scenes avoid load times as players leave and re-enter the playable game world, avoid the likely disparity in look and feel between game world and FMV scene, avoid the continuity issues that plague any attempt to coordinate between the two states, and allow players to keep on playing, with at least some control of their avatar. Action adventure horror game *Dead Space®* allows the player to maintain some control of protagonist, Isaac, during many of its cut scenes by relaying information to a screen that appears directly in front of him, ensuring it's seen and heard regardless of where the player moves while story events play out. One could argue this method offers no drawbacks, especially when you consider the production perspective of costs and time spent integrating this kind of work.

Triggers

Triggers come in a variety of types that we might categorize as event-, audio-, and AI-based. Events triggers are activated when reaching a particular location, perhaps at a particular time, or within a certain time limit, and perhaps after having completed a set of prerequisite tasks. *Dead Space* uses environmental triggers to spring a variety of events on the player—a video message from an NPC (non-player character), a full-scale attack by bloodthirsty Necromorphs, or a body dropping from the ceiling. These triggers can open up new content or possibilities for the player, with the activation of the event trigger effectively being a moment of storytelling in its own right. Audio samples are often used at the same time as event triggers, of course, but they can also be used without an event trigger, commenting on or giving help or hindrance to a player as they play without any interruption at all, seamlessly being part of that play. Sound samples can tell players useful and guiding information and help convey the sense that the player is in a world with sentient and dynamic and responsive life. GLaDOS, the catty computer AI in *Portal*, mentioned in a previous chapter, is more than a tutorial voice and guide; she also serves to convey much of the game's atmosphere and emotional weight, as well as much of the (highly dubious) backstory. While audio samples might be your sole or primary source of delivering your story, Valve's first-person puzzle game illustrates how, when used skillfully, they can still provide a compelling, subtle experience.

In a sense, all triggers could be termed "AI triggers," as they're all activated by the game at specific moments for specific effects. Yet distinguishing AI triggers from event and audio triggers is useful to highlight those responses the game makes that are adaptive to player performance in a deeper way, or in a way that requires more complex coding; responses such as melding around player performance so the game becomes easier or harder to play, depending on how a player is faring. Or a response such as bringing a guide to a player who is lost, or bringing a player who favors puzzle games more puzzles, and a player who favors more action games more action.

Cohesion

In theory it's possible to create a story that develops with the tightness of a plot, but a looseness that thrives on interactivity. *Left 4 Dead* manages to escalate dramatically as different monsters are encountered, or evaded in turn, or in combination, as waves of undead intensify or slacken off, creating a simple and similar arc across all its levels (or movies, as they are contextualized) that nevertheless feels satisfying. This variety of pace is controlled in part by Valve's "Director" AI that "watches" the players and influences events in a manner designed to keep them on alert, but not exhausted.

There is also more to think about when building interactive stories as a story that delivers dramatic satisfaction is not the same as one that delivers interactive satisfaction. They may not be mutually exclusive, but they are distinctly not the same thing. Jordan Thomas, one-time creative director at 2K Marin, feels "[an] interactively vapid story choice, no matter how dramatic . . . is creatively bankrupt."[1] Indeed, the task of a games writer is often to explore and develop ideas in the areas where they coincide so the story's themes, plot, and character arcs are all delivered at the same time as the game's interactive promises. If the player is made to feel remote and absent from core dramatic developments by having not helped to shape them, then the games writer should consider themselves as having failed to meet the player's expectations. Of course, this depends on the kind of game you are setting out to make, and the kind of game a player is expecting. At its pinnacle, environmental storytelling is not just storytelling through the game world's environment; it is also storytelling through the game's choices, systems, and designs. After all, good level and gameplay design need meaningful obstacles as much as good storytelling.

Just as storytellers consider what a character wants and what is stopping them from getting it, game designers think about what a player needs to do in order to triumph, what objectives they have, and what makes these challenging and interesting. Designers will look for complications within their level design to ensure the player

[1]Jordan Thomas, in conversation, 2K Marin Studios, 2011.

path has moments of interest, requiring a player to do something beyond simply following a straight, bland route; in effect, to deliver an interactive *but* moment. Together with artists (sometimes known as level architects) they will be considering how to route the player along the path so it's clear and difficult (if not impossible) to get lost, and yet simultaneously, how to make the route interesting and replete with surprises (interactive reversals and revelations), and to mask the funneling and largely linear nature that often underlies good player pathing. *Halo: Reach*™, Bungie's popular FPS, often allows players a certain degree of freedom, especially when missions take place outdoors; however, not only will there be a clear objective (normally pointed towards by a marker on the player's screen), but there will be only a single "real" route to take. Tasked to disable some anti-aircraft guns, the player will perhaps be presented with two or more roads from which to choose, but they'll either both lead to the same place (past some different enemies on the way) or loop back to eventually channel the player to their ultimate mission destination.

Designers will also be concerned with "gating" a player to ensure certain areas of the level are not accessible (or are no longer accessible) until certain objectives have been met, helping them control the pace and sequence of information flow and gameplay they deliver to the player. Pace and a clear sequence that can lead to narrative consequence are concerns clearly shared between a designer and a writer. A further similarity exists in the form of "boss battles," which directly equate, in storytelling terms, to threshold guardians between or within acts. Platform games such as *Little Big Planet*™ sometimes use a boss battle to end a level, as they can provide a fresh shift in gameplay as well as a rewarding challenge to underline the reward felt once the boss is defeated and the section completed.

When these shared concerns map directly onto each other, both game design and interactive storytelling are not only able to work effectively together, but they also empower and reinforce each other in a virtuous circle, where the player benefits in every conceivable way.

BIOSHOCK

The excellent FPS *BioShock* features a multilayered story that players can experience on a variety of levels so as to deliver a narrative tailored to suit a variety of play styles. Its Creative Director, Ken Levine, speaks of consciously building in three delivery levels that enable the story, and therefore the game, to appeal to a wider audience, pulling in both the hardcore gamer and meandering enthusiast with equal ease.

At the topmost, macro level, the story is designed to cater to players who want to do little more than power through the game, defeating anything its designers can throw at them, in order to successfully beat the content. At this level, story, plot, and linked gameplay motivations are kept simple, clear, and sufficiently compelling: make your way to safety; rescue Atlas's family from the submarine; and find and kill Fontaine are all easy to understand and act upon. Delivered to the player through a kind of walkie-talkie system, this level of game story is never allowed to break into the gameplay and remove control from the player. If nothing else, they are always aware of where they are, what they are meant to do next, and, broadly, why. The UI also provides a floating golden triangle that points towards the active goal for those who might not even be interested in partaking in this most basic level of story.

For a player who wants to go deeper into the story and world of *BioShock*, the developers provide audio tapes scattered throughout the fallen city of Rapture. These are essentially diaries recorded by a variety of characters (some core to the game universe, others secondary), which serve to flesh out the city's history and varied motivations of the story's key characters. While this system is simple and compelling, it still allows the player control over the level of "story flow"—diaries can be picked up and listened to later, when the player feels ready, though even if they're activated immediately upon being picked up in the middle of a battle, they release the story in as unobtrusive a manner as possible, never removing control from the player.

For the truly dedicated gamer, with a passionate desire to immerse themselves as deeply as possible in *BioShock*'s story and world, the developers sprinkle the backstory and city of Rapture with obscure clues, story complications, and props designed to provide greater insight and understanding of the world Jack Ryan moves through. Scattered placards on the floor, stacked suitcases, and a departures board filled with cancellations all whisper (or, perhaps, shout) of a place in which a desperate, angry uprising mixed with an urgent hunger to flee a city has just imploded into a bloody civil war. Wandering Rapture's shadowy corridors and spaces reveals advertisements and neon signs which, upon closer examination, each expose slivers of the decadence into which Rapture fell, as scientific arrogance and greed consumed a population eager to improve themselves and "keep up with the Joneses" in a way we may find both fascinating and worryingly relevant in today's modern society.

Regardless of the level to which a player chooses to experience the game's story, they travel through a world carefully crafted to project a sense of place, of reality, of calamitous events having just occurred, which still reverberate through a utopia turned dystopia. Skillful environmental storytelling, superb level design, audio, and art can make for a potent mix. This multileveled approach to storytelling, or perhaps *multilayered*, so as not to be confused with terminology of a "game level," also encourages players to replay the game, in search of elements missed beforehand, perhaps in the initial eager rush to consume the game and everything it had to offer.

Environmental storytelling is one of the most essential approaches available to a games writer, and anyone serious about games writing needs to understand it. Indeed, it could arguably be *the* central approach games writers need to understand as many titles continue to develop narrative designs embracing this kind of storytelling. It is certainly an area of games writing in which the potential for exciting development is fertile and promising. It's in the field of environmental storytelling where the space between the writer and the player is most highly charged with creative possibilities, as insinuation, inference, and implied meanings can create a kind of electrifying friction.

However, there is much to be said for hoarding approaches and techniques and holding onto everything available to you, because there might come a time when you need them. Even now there is still a space in game development for cinematic set pieces—whether as an opening sequence or a trailer with marketing functions, or inside the game itself. For although environmental storytelling is a technique every practicing games writer *must* be aware of, it does have its limitations. To begin with, a fixation on *never*, under any circumstances, taking control away from a player is not always practical or even desirable—even in games with an expressed environmental storytelling intent. Also, *always* letting the player have some degree of control can ultimately amount to little more than a "semi-playable cut scene" with movement disabled, but the ability to rotate a camera through a controlled range; this can result in giving you the worst of both worlds—the game has been stopped, but the story isn't even delivered from satisfying camera angles sympathetic to in-game art limitations. More importantly—*and practically*—not every game has a target demographic and/or budget that makes the total circumvention of cut scenes feasible or even desirable. You may be fortunate enough to only work on technically and creatively ambitious projects where you have the resources and carte-blanche to never need to think about them. If not, however, the chances are high there will be times when the best solution (considering technology, budgets, resources, who the player character is, information you need to convey to the player, time until release, etc.) is to use some form of cut scene.

To seamlessly integrate environmental storytelling into a games title takes time, a considerable level of team integration, a commitment to keeping writers (possibly in large numbers) on-site for extended periods of time, and no small amount of skill. Unsurprisingly, striving for the highest quality is expensive, so it is not for investors who are faint of heart. It's important not to make any definitive judgment on the use of environmental storytelling, as you can never be certain when you might need to call on older and less shiny tools in your games writer's toolbox, and the only really permissible definitive statement on games writing is that there are no definitive statements on games writing; remain open-minded and use whatever technique or combination of techniques best deliver a satisfying and appropriate experience for your title.

PROCESS

How do you *do* it? How do you tell stories environmentally? The process won't be the same for every project or for every writer, as there are a wide range of methodologies within teams and writers. Environmental storytelling may not always feel like storytelling. It may feel as akin to storytelling as arranging an exhibition in an art gallery. If it does, that's good, because that is *precisely* the point. Like a curator, you can set an entry and exit point, you can have a desired critical path through the various rooms, you can theme each room and even write supporting text by every piece, but you can't guarantee people will flow between the rooms as you hoped, that they will look at things in the order you intended, or that they will read anything at all. But be assured, being a curator of a gallery is—*beyond any doubt*—an opportunity to tell a story, even if the one you wish to tell concerns the shapelessness of things. As in a gallery, *everything* on display (or hidden with an invitation to be found) *is highly significant* and *capable of carrying meaning*, so be aware of everything a player will experience and see it as an opportunity to tell them something, or to not tell them something unintended. Don't be surprised if you seem to write very little, and that your job is to be the logic police—trying to help shape the functions and sequence of buildings, and trying to make sense of the design choices from a narrative perspective to create a coherent experience for the player—and then trying to figure out how you might deliver that narrative coherency with as little need for on-screen text or voiceover as possible.

The development process we are most familiar with and advocate is as follows:

- Understand the project ambitions and limitations, the time lines, assets, production pipelines, and the team. Games writing is by nature highly collaborative, and environmental storytelling even more so. You may find yourself working closely with designers and artists as you build levels and the game. You need to understand the gameplay and art concerns of this team and work together to build a coherent experience for the player. The multi-disciplined nature of this process means constant accommodation of others' needs and an ability to convey the importance of your story's needs to effect solutions and compromise across the whole team. Without collaboration everyone will fail.

- If you're joining a project already in progress, play the latest builds of the game as soon and as often as you can.
- Build the macro story, paying particular attention to where you can keep the player tied in to the core story developments, making choices, performing actions, developing skills, and acquiring knowledge that can match the experience of their avatar(s). Ensure the story places the player's avatar in a central or at least ultimately highly significant role within the unfolding drama. This may sound obvious, but it's not unheard of for stories to become so complex or wrapped up in backstory that a player can feel inconsequential to the ultimate dramatic concerns, even if they are tied closely to the game design. FPS and TPS games can be particularly susceptible to this, where the player takes part in the battle, but has no control over objectives—they must simply obey orders relayed to them by the game's mission delivery system, eliminating enemies as efficiently as possible to progress. Games such as Tripwire Interactive's Rising Storm™ may not make a player feel single-handedly responsible for turning the tide of World War II, and do give the impression of broader events occurring within the context of the game world, but they do still make the player feel as if they are in the heart of the action inside their own game story.
- Consider the kinds of people you could expect to find in the environment in question. What kinds of stories can they tell? Are these stories contributions to your macro story, or are these micro stories that contribute to the macro story? The macro story you are building, the story real estate, the environment(s), and available storytelling media all have a bearing on the characters you may create; they need to make sense in the place where you put them and their stories need to be compatible with the means through which you intend to tell them.
- Consider the story real estate. Do you only have levels in which to tell the story and play the game? Or are there also other parts of the game such as a user interface hub or perhaps a city or base that allow you to

conduct auctions, re-tool inventories, or other essential gameplay elements? What is the player's critical path within the levels? And what buildings are present? What stories do they tell? Is it an area growing or declining in prosperity? Is it highly populated or unaccustomed to human presence? Use the macro story to help inform you as you consider the micro stories inside the levels. Place the most essential elements of the story on the player's critical path.

- What functions do any buildings here have? Try to help make sense of their presence within the space and the relationship of these buildings to each other. Offer assistance with the logic underpinning these buildings and their functions and, where appropriate, offer advice on how to help mold them so they work with art, design, and story needs. In effect, you need to channel the skills of architects and town planners to ensure the game space is understandable and convincing; you'll break a player's suspension of disbelief if you have a medieval town with an airport in it. But, in more subtle terms, you can also destroy the player's experience by having the stables next to the Queen's throne room and having the room controlling the portcullis bereft of any machinery with which to control it. What's at stake is more than just the suspension of disbelief (vital in itself) but also causing the player serious confusion. Placing locations in a logical, easily readable sequence helps orient the player and build the sense of a coherent space they can interpret; jeopardizing coherency of interpretation is fundamentally jeopardizing storytelling.
- Consider the media available to your story's era and setting. What media is appropriate as a means for the story to be disseminated into the world? Diaries? Letters? Block print? TV? Radio? Telex? E-mails? Hieroglyphs? Poetry? Photography? Live news feeds? Wet ware? Advertising as leaflets? Advertising as hi-tech streaming movies? Does your story world allow for more than physical and technological media? Does it permit ghosts or mirages, or other kinds of apparitions or sounds? Remember that signage and anything that can "carry" text is important to you (walls, for example, can carry graffiti). But also remember much of your storytelling could well be the placement of objects, equating to a kind of choreography, and may not be dialogue or text-based at all. A car that has smashed into a telegraph pole, its front windscreen shattered, is already part of a story. Opening the car door to find the driver dead and a large poisonous snake on the front seat is an extension of that story.

FROB

"Frob" is an abbreviation of "frobnicate" or "frobnitz," meaning to adjust, manipulate, or tweak. It's fairly commonly used in games design and generally means the player presses a button on the controller to interact with the object on screen. The interaction may add an item to the player's inventory, it may bring a story media element into play (e.g., open a diary), or trigger another game element (such as a cinematic sequence or the spawning of enemies).

- How do players access the story media? Do they frob to collect the content or gather it by some other means? Do they have to frob to open drawers or unlock hidden areas, or do they simply walk past it—perhaps seeing diaries on the floor, reels of recording tape on the shelf of a 1970s recording studio, or graffiti on the side of a building? The way the content is accessed may have a bearing on the content itself. People are less likely to leave secret journals on desktops and usually hide them (unless in a hurry or taken by surprise).
- Consider whether you have any "floating" triggers that can be used at specific times to control pacing and are not tied solely to locations.
- Create an outline for each of the levels, telling the story the player will experience inside each one. Acquire sign-off from the key team members—such as design and art leads, level and art leads.
- Develop details for each level, researching specific characters and specific story delivery media, then draft scripts.
- You may also decide to write a walkthrough of the entire level, tracking where and how elements of stories are delivered, and then use this document as another safety net for acquiring sign-off from key team members.
- Play the latest build with your audio script in the game, either as proper voice recordings or a robo-voice. Try to experience the game and your scripts as if you were a player. Play as a blast-right-through player, an explore everything player, and a somewhere-in-between player.
- Rewrite your scripts.
- Repeat the last two steps (and possibly the last three or four steps, depending on the extent of your necessary rewrites), until you run out of time.

WALKTHROUGH

A walkthrough roughly equates to the treatment stage for environmental storytelling. As with the scripts for environmental storytelling, there is no set format for a walkthrough. It may include various color codes and other means of differentiating critical paths, non-critical paths, and other elements within the environment. You should aim to capture what the player will experience in the likely order in which they'll experience it. At this point you don't need to capture minor details—they can wait for the script. It is often helpful to create a list of the story beats you want to convey in a level and then transfer them into the walkthrough by finding the most appropriate locations and likely chronologies, and the most potent delivery media. Creating the list of beats first would help ensure you bring those ideas into the walkthrough and, most essentially, the script itself. When working with the level design flow and the environment, you can find yourself wrapping around the restrictions and shape of the level that, unless you remain clear and focused on your story intentions, can become subsumed and neglected.

HINTS AND TIPS

- Giving buildings and locations names is a helpful way to make sure everyone on the team knows what everyone else is referring to. The names don't need to be elaborate, and they certainly don't need to be names that the player will ever be aware of—you want the player to have to carry as little geographic information as possible as they try move around the game—but in an area filled with buildings and rooms of a similar nature (offices, labs, or aircraft hangars, for example) it's likely that at some point you will need some means of specific reference. Once you've given locations names, and the team has agreed on them, try to stick with them to avoid confusion. Remember that these are not names for the player; they are names for the development team. You need time and space to coin names for the player, and the team doesn't need to be subjected to your own changes and edits. Try to avoid names such as "First House" or "Second Barracks"—if buildings are deleted your names may end up confusing everyone after all.
- This kind of storytelling can be very involved, with numerous simultaneous elements to consider and address. But remember to return to basics and ensure the stories you are telling can be traced through arcs with a clear beginning, middle, and end. Don't be at all surprised if the char-

acterizations helping drive those arcs are sometimes people or creatures a player's avatar will never meet (e.g., we never directly meet Lara Croft's father in *Rise of the Tomb Raider*™, but his troubled relationship with our protagonist helps fuel her motivation to find the "Divine Source"). Many games, for reasons of theme, and/or genre, and/or resources, and/or code find considerable advantages in putting players in worlds where there are limited numbers of characters for their avatars to interact with.

- A sound principle is to try to keep the chronology of the story you're telling about what happened in the space the player is moving through in step with their sequential progress through that space. So, if a Roman legion was slaughtered, which gave rise to ghosts, which led to newly bereaved mother Vera being abducted into the spirit world, try to have the player discover evidence of the Roman legion first, then evidence of the ghosts, before learning anything about Vera's abduction. This may not always be appropriate or desirable, given the kind of environment you have, the kind of story, and the kind of tone and game you are working with, but this principle will help ensure that the sequence of events you wish to convey is understood.
- Sometimes you may find yourself layering recent, but still past events over the top of a location that had a function pre-dating the recent events; for example, layering an outbreak of a deadly virus on top of a nineteenth-century French shipyard. Try to ensure the shipyard is believable, that it looks and sounds like a shipyard from that era, in the right part of the world, before applying the additional layer of storytelling on top.
- Try to use as much signage as is appropriate to the art direction treatment and design concerns. Clear signage not only delivers clear player direction, but also, on occasions, delivers simultaneous mise-en-scène.
- Building connections between a variety of story elements tagged to specific environments is a highly effective way to knit pieces of your stories together and dovetail subplots into one another. Caution is advised, however, since the highly iterative nature of environmental storytelling means a more modular approach is a safer approach and requires less rewriting when sections of the level are cut, added, or shifted in placement.
- Expect the process to be writing then rewriting, rewriting, and rewriting. Level design is highly iterative and linking story so directly to the environment means it's cursed with the same serious development churn and flux (with the hope that it is blessed in equal measure in terms of final game quality).

EXERCISES

1. Choose a well-known game title and create a breakdown document that analyzes the environmental storytelling elements present in the first ten minutes of gameplay. Answer the following questions:

   What are the primary sources of environmental storytelling used by the game's developers?

   In what ways, if any, could the environmental storytelling be improved in your chosen title?

   Are there any other games that use environmental storytelling methods similar to those of your chosen title?
2. Devise an outline for a level purely utilizing environmental storytelling techniques. The level should last no longer than one hour but can be for any kind of game genre you like, with an appropriate story of your choosing, but other than the player character or characters can only include one other NPC who can talk, but may not join up and follow you or be killed by you.
3. Which game title, in your opinion—not mentioned in this chapter—contains excellent environmental storytelling? What techniques do its writers and designers use to help tell the story? Which game title, in your opinion, does a poor job of telling the story environmentally? Why? How could the writers and designers have done a better job?
4. If you have completed an outline and treatment for Chapter 6's *Code Obsidian* game exercise, create a short, three-page walkthrough sample for one of the levels or areas.
5. What types of stories do you think are well-suited to environmental storytelling?

PROJECTS

1. Select a partner. Alone, and secretly, choose an environment as a setting and place between four and eight objects in it that, to your mind, tell a coherent story. Write down your story in a few bullet points and keep this hidden. Take it in turns to be a Scene-Setter, and a Detective. The Scene-Setter tells the Detective the location and all the objects, but not the story. The Detective must try to guess at the story. The object is to conceive of a story that a Detective can guess, but to make it sufficiently interesting that it's not obvious.

2. The previous Project could be expanded into a classroom activity. Each pair of students can choose their favorite environmental story, jot it on a piece of paper, and give to the teacher. At the front of the class, the joint Scene-Setters present their story to the other students, who jointly act as Detectives. (Perhaps 2–5 minutes per story, depending on class size and time available.) Each Scene-Setter pair receives 1 point if the other students correctly guess the story, or get close enough (at the teacher's discretion); and the other students also receive 1 point for guessing correctly. No one receives any points if stories aren't worked out by the Detectives in time. The teacher may choose their three favorite stories and students can then vote on their favorite of those three: 3 points for the most votes, 2 for the second most, and 1 for the least votes, go the Scene-Setters in each case. At the end of the class all votes are totaled and a winner arrived at.

Chapter 9

WRITING SCRIPTS

If I don't write to empty my mind, I go mad.

—Lord George Byron

BRIEF TERMS

NON-INTERACTIVE CUT SCENES A story cut scene in which control is removed from the player for the duration.

SEMI-PLAYABLE CUT SCENES A story cut scene in which the player retains a limited amount of control, often movement- or perspective-based.

BRANCHING DIALOGUE SCENES A scene in which the player is presented with multiple dialogue choices that steer the conversation along a variety of routes.

SYSTEMIC SCRIPTS Scripts designed to react to specific in-game triggers (e.g., NPC dialogue or a building elevator's announcement spiel).

ENVIRONMENTAL SCRIPTS Script written using the environment to tell the story—often created when gameplay doesn't feature a highly linear approach.

As you've seen, there's considerably more to games writing than writing scripts; a great deal of thinking, discussion, and writing of outlines, treatments, narrative design documents, and character documents generally precedes the script itself. Story scripts describe the visual and/or audio action to be experienced by the players. They can take on many forms. Often, when the action is tightly controlled they can closely resemble movie screenplay formatting, but there is no set way for games scripts to be presented, because the form itself is open to multiple design interpretations and how that design relates to what is required of a writer. It's not unusual to find games scripts written on combinations of spreadsheets, Word documents, storyboards, animatics, and inside design documents, many of which may be hyperlinked to other documents of the same kind, or documents of different kinds.

TYPES OF SCRIPT

The different kinds of scripts written for games are given a variety of names and serve a range of functions. The major script types you may expect to encounter are:

- Non-interactive cut scenes
- Semi-playable cut scenes
- Branching dialogue scenes
- Systemic scripts
- Environmental scripts
- On-screen text

Non-Interactive Cut Scenes

Non-interactive cut scenes (usually called simply "cut scenes") are used when writers need to be sure a player will experience the correct story moment at the correct juncture in the game for the overall experience to remain coherent and cohesive. In short, these are scenes in which players have no control over the events about to take place. A great deal of debate surrounds the use of non-interactive cut scenes, as some feel they're anathema to games that are ultimately about taking part—about playing.

Cut scenes may occur only at the beginning and end of a game, or perhaps staggered at a number of key points throughout it, perhaps matching key act breaks. Should, for example, a key event not take place early in a story, because the player or an NPC doesn't instigate it, then an important chain of events upon which the remainder of the story rests could fail to make sense; if, at the end of *Fable 2*'s opening tutorial, the player's sibling is not murdered by the nefarious Lord Lucien, then the deeply personal motivation to work towards his downfall is lost; at the most one would feel they were defeating "someone evil who needs to be stopped." While this might be acceptable on a basic design level (the player knows what they must do and why they must do it), an opportunity would be lost if they are not emotionally invested in the core story, involving not just an evil man, but someone responsible for murdering a beloved member of the player's virtual family.

Non-interactive cut scenes are typically delivered as either FMV (as seen at the beginning of *Fable 2* or *Wipeout 2097*™) or as an IGCS (as seen in *Grant Theft Auto IV* or the opening playable race sequences in *World of Warcraft*) and can run for any length of time, even just a few seconds if deemed useful; *Mass Effect*'s mini-sequence used whenever the Mako rapid-deployment vehicle was dropped off on a new planet is a useful example of a quick burst cut scene used to illustrate a simple transition from one environment to another. Typically, however, they last a few minutes, long enough to move the story forward and provide the player with fresh motivation, though in rare instances they can run for over half an hour; SEGA's open-world Japanese gangster title *Yakuza 4*™ contains over six hours of cut scenes to tell its various stories, which illustrates the value still placed on this form of storytelling (though it is worth noting Japanese titles often contain a larger amount of cut scenes, when compared to their Western counterparts—Bioware's RPG *Dragon Age II*™ contains a mere 103 minutes of cut scenes).

FMV scenes use pre-recorded, high-quality (and usually expensive) animation to present a cut scene, whereas an IGCS seeks to do the same, instead using in-game assets and characters. Until recently, there was normally quite a discrepancy between the quality of an FMV cut scene and an IGCS (the former being markedly superior, as can be seen in both *Driver* and *Driver 2*); however, modern game engines and assets have closed the gap considerably.

Non-interactive cut scenes are useful also in that they can, should the design team require it, deliver story using preset camera angles, lighting, dialogue, and other audio, all of which can combine to provide the player with a tightly controlled, cinematic, and hopefully compelling story experience. For example, the opening moments of a game can be delivered in the form of a non-interactive cut scene that delivers a sequence introducing players to the game world, key characters, and important game design elements they are about to experience themselves. In short, it could be used as a succinct primer that serves to both inform and excite players about the environment they are about to enter. In 2004, Blizzard crafted some superb FMV cut scenes when *World of Warcraft* first launched that served to introduce prospective players not only to the huge variety of races, classes, and powers available to them, but an epic world driven by adventure and conflict. In one beautifully rendered sequence we travel from the snowy hills outside the Dwarven city of Ironforge, leaving a stoic hunter and his grizzly bear to struggle through the snow, to the mystical forests of Ashenvale to follow the speeding form of a night elf druid as she shimmers and transforms into a panther and bounds off the edge of a cliff. The scene transitions seamlessly to show us an undead warlock and his infernal minion towering overhead—and the transitions continue before finishing on a series of explosive fights erupting between the two sets of faction races. This level of *controlled* exposition, which, it should be noted, carries with it a great deal of story and design-based information, can only be carried out using a non-interactive cut scene. Non-interactive cut scenes are often written in a format that closely resembles screenplays, and we'll return to look at this structure later in the chapter.

Semi-Playable Cut Scenes

Semi-playable cut scenes are a means to convey relatively controlled story moments (that may or may not be heavily weighted with instructional content so the player understands their motivation regarding what they do next) that still grant the player a degree of freedom while events unfold, typically as NPCs "act out" a pre-set script. Excellent examples of semi-playable cut scenes can be seen while playing any of Valve's *Half Life* series of games, where the player, as Gordon Freeman, at one point finds himself free to explore Dr. Kliener's laboratory, as the professor holds a brief, but urgent conversation with Alyx, your ally, regarding the best step to take next; or, later on, listening to her talk to her father, Dr. Eli Vance over an intercom, while nearby, the enemy Citadel tower experiences its final death throes. These conversations both take place in areas in which it's impossible to wander too far away and therefore are always—to a greater or lesser extent—audible by the player. Related, in a sense, to environmental storytelling (discussed in the previous chapter), this form of cut scene has the advantage of not demoting the player to impotent viewer, forced to watch pre-set events unfold, unable to "do" anything. However, in both these examples, the conversations are totally scripted in both senses of the word, and nothing can be done to change their outcome. Granted, the illusion of freedom can be somewhat cracked should the player decide to begin dropping grenades at Alyx's feet, only to see the game universe continue on, unaffected in any way, but most choose to allow events to unfold, content to listen, learn, and wait for the signal to move forward.

Semi-playable cut scenes, while immersive, are not as cinematic because control of the camera is not taken away from the player. This does not prevent it being a potent tool in the game writer's armory, if used at the correct time.

Branching Dialogue

While non-interactive and semi-interactive cut scenes feature dialogue that doesn't deviate from a pre-set path, some games, in particular, adventure games and RPGs, feature scenes in which the player interacts directly with one or more NPCs, choosing their conversational responses from a list of options provided by the game. These responses can result in a number of consequences, from unlocking information to starting a fight. Figure 9.1 illustrates a basic example of branching dialogue.

These branching dialogue sequences allow players to steer the flow of events and relationships in whatever manner the design allows, lending them a feeling of greater freedom and power to affect change in the game and story universe. These more flexible interactions can be extremely short, perhaps—as in RPG *Dragon Age: Origins*™—to simply confirm the desire to view a merchant's goods. They can also, naturally, stretch to provide far more epic, important experiences during which key decisions can be made that affect the remainder of the game.

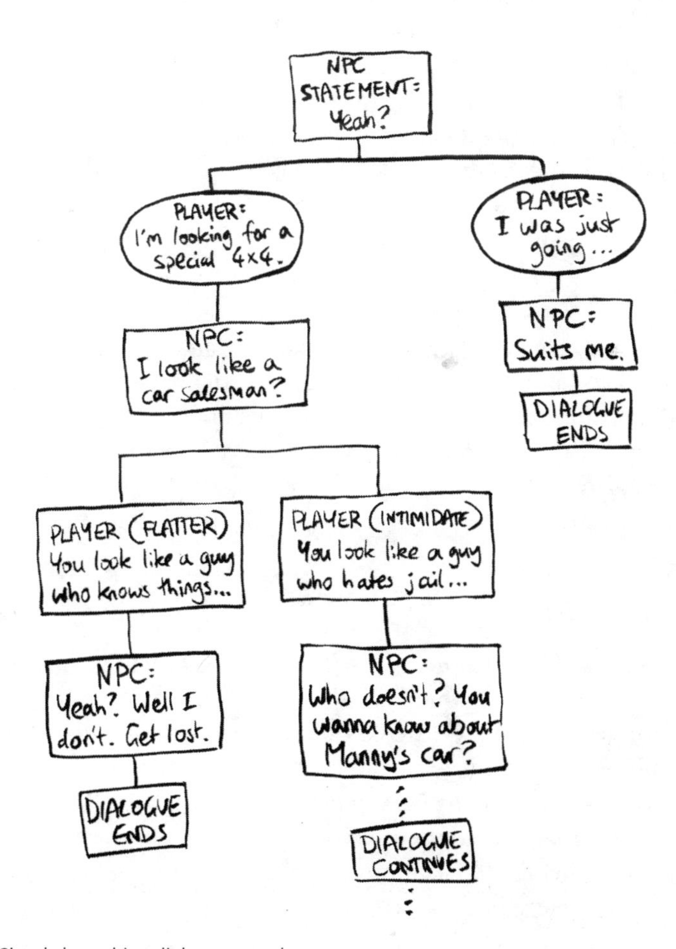

FIGURE 9.1. Simple branching dialogue sample.

A superb example of this can be witnessed, again in *Dragon Age: Origins*, when playing through the Landsmeet scene in which the player decides, in a series of interwoven branching dialogue scenes and combat-oriented gameplay, who will rule the kingdom of Ferelden in place of the slain King, Maric Theirin.

Scenes that feature branching dialogue can contain a variety of outcomes dictated by whatever choices are made by the player and can therefore create more meaningful story moments. By the end of a scene containing branching dialogue, the player may have picked up a clue to help solve a puzzle, have used her charisma to gain a valuable new ally, or offended an NPC and made a dangerous new enemy. Branching dialogue options can be based on a variety of factors; they might be based on morality (e.g., allowing the player to follow "good" or "bad" choices) or their character's style (e.g., allowing the player to interact in an often sarcastic manner, or perhaps be threatening). These basic "planes" of decision serve as starting points for where dialogue can branch from and to. *Star Wars: Knights of the Old Republic* allows players to both flirt with, and tease, fellow Jedi Bastilla at specific points in the game—if pursued, it's even possible to steal a fleeting kiss from her, all as a result of building a relationship during gameplay and choosing the right options during branching dialogue scenes.

Adventure Game Dialogue

Adventure games are not driven by statistics like RPGs, they're driven by problem-solving; as a result, adventure game dialogue is used expressly to unlock information, gain useful items, and generally move the story forward (even if, frequently, via characters). It's often more linear in its approach, letting players witness multiple interchanges between characters once a conversational path has been chosen, almost, in a sense, unlocking a potential stream of dialogue every time a choice is made.

Broken Sword Case Study

Broken Sword: The Shadow of the Templars™ (Director's Cut version) is a point-and-click adventure game from the popular *Broken Sword* series in which intrepid American tourist, George Stobbart, and determined French journalist, Nico Collard, join forces to unravel a complex web of intrigue surrounding the Knights Templar. To help chart the game's conversational flows, developers Revolution Software planned their dialogue exchanges in the body of their low-level design document using a combination of diagrams and text.

To illustrate one method of writing adventure game dialogue, let's examine a section from Revolution's design document that deals with one of the game's early scenes in which Nico interviews Imelda Carchon, whose husband, Pierre, has just been murdered. First, examine Figure 9.2, which visually illustrates the scene's conversational flow. In the body of the case study, italicized text has been added to help guide you through the section. Note that, for the purposes of brevity and clarity, we have edited the design document's text so it only includes information directly relevant to our discussion.

The initial exchange is triggered when the player chooses to approach Imelda and interact with her. This opens up the initial four exchange options.

NICO:	Excuse me, Madame.
IMELDA:	Yes. [irritated, gruff response]

Followed by the conversation below.

Now four conversational topics open up to the player to broach in any order they wish. Each is represented by a picture on the screen and results in a preset exchange taking place, each of which may—or may not—contain useful information.

Carchon 1

First Time

NICO:	I am so sorry.
IMELDA:	No you're not. You're a journalist. Journalists don't have feelings.
NICO:	Not true, Madame.
IMELDA:	We shall see.

Carchon 2

NICO:	Why did your husband send for me? What did he want to discuss?
IMELDA:	I have no idea. His business was his business.
NICO:	He never told you anything?
IMELDA:	Nothing. And frankly I preferred it that way.

Mime

NICO:	Why would a mime want to kill your husband?
IMELDA:	Pierre had plenty of enemies. The husbands of most of my girlfriends for a start.

Thierry 1

NICO:	How did your husband know my father?
IMELDA:	I have no idea.

FIGURE 9.2. Broken Sword dialogue diagram.

NICO:	You didn't know him? Thierry, Thierry Collard?
IMELDA:	Pierre knew a lot of people that I didn't know. Most of them women . . .

Now that all of the questions possible have been asked, the following exchange occurs, which both moves the conversation forward and presents the player with a choice.

When all subjects are exhausted, automatically proceed with the following:

IMELDA:	This is quite a scoop for you. I suppose you're already inventing the headlines.
NICO:	Just because I'm a journalist—
IMELDA:	Don't patronize me. You're all cut from the same cloth.
IMELDA:	Do you have any morality at all?

The following design-oriented line indicates the exchange that takes place if the player decides to have Nico tell Imelda she does have morals.

IF YES – set moral_yes flag

NICO:	Yes. That's why I do this job.
IMELDA:	Pah! You do it to see your name in print.
NICO:	As if. My editor gets the by-line. I just do the work.
IMELDA:	Well don't expect my sympathy.

The following design-oriented line indicates the exchange that takes place if the player decides to have Nico tell Imelda she is not that concerned with morals.

IF NO – set moral_no flag

NICO:	I certainly don't let it get in the way of a good story.
IMELDA:	I admire your loyalty to your profession.

Each decision puts in place a marker that notes what was decided (called, in this document, a "flag"). After this decision is made, the conversation moves forward with some set dialogue, spoken regardless of the previous choices made.

Then follow from either route with:

NICO:	The police will be here soon Madame. Is there anybody you would like me to contact? Family? Friends?
IMELDA:	No. I have no family. Pierre and I were . . .

At this point, Imelda breaks down and cries. This is a key change in the scene.

IMELDA: He was all I had really. Not much was it? The dutiful wife—that was my role. He never talked, never let me in . . .(Sobbing)

She breaks down sobbing again.

NICO: I know one thing, Madame [Nico starts to warm to her]
IMELDA: What?
NICO: If you want to find out who killed your husband then you would be better off trusting me to do the job—not the police.
IMELDA: Why? How do I know I can I trust you?

After the pre-set exchange that ends in this important question, the player can choose to either be pleasant and earnest when trying to persuade Imelda to give Nico the job of investigating the murder of her husband . . .

If Nice Person (Smiling Nico icon) – set trust_Nico flag

NICO: Your husband invited me here today because he needed me. He knew somebody intended to kill him—and he knew I could help.
IMELDA: You do yourself a disservice. I doubt it was your database he was after.
NICO: You're wrong. I think I was onto his killer already. And your husband read my article—I'm sure of it. Please . . . You owe it to him.

Or the player can choose to play on Imelda's fears, with a more aggressive argument.

If Killer (Assassin icon) – set trust_danger flag

NICO: Because you have no choice. The police will take weeks. In which time your own life may be in danger.
IMELDA: What?!
NICO: Believe me. This killer has struck before. And he will strike again. Who is to know that you are not next on his list?

Again, each decision puts in place a marker that notes what was decided, as it will impact later exchanges. The conversation then continues with the following dialogue, which is spoken regardless of previous choices.

Then follow from either route with:

IMELDA: [Trying not to cry.] I don't know . . .
NICO: All I need is a few more minutes to look around before the police come.

Interestingly, only one of the following two lines is played depending on the player's earlier choice regarding their morality.

Then play two lines that depend on choices made earlier.

If moral_no

IMELDA: I think perhaps you do have a moral sense. You're not a very good liar Nico Collard . . .

OR

If moral_yes

IMELDA: I believe that you really do have a moral sense. I feel that I trust so few people . . .

Again, the player's previous choice dictates which of the following two lines is spoken by Imelda.

And then:

If trust_Nico

IMELDA: . . . and maybe Pierre really did think that you could help. Of course it wouldn't have stopped him seducing you too.

OR

If trust_danger

IMELDA: . . . and I share your low opinion of the police.

Imelda is, in essence, saying the same thing in the final two lines—that Nico has her permission to investigate her husband's murder but, vitally, her motivations differ, depending on choices made by the player. In the line spoken if she trusts Nico, Imelda is driven by a more benign reason to grant her blessing, linked to her husband's belief in Nico. In the line spoken if Imelda feels in danger, her motivation is selfish, she doesn't want to be hurt.

The final exchange unlocks regardless of previous choices made, as the player, to progress, must have access to the item given by Imelda.

Then follow from either route with:

IMELDA: Here—take this. It's the key to the Drawing Room—next to the library at the end of the hall. It was Pierre's room. He kept it locked—even from me.

Imelda reaches out, and Nico takes Drawing Room Key.

NICO: Imelda, thank you. I promise—you won't regret this.

The conversation ends here.

Whatever choices the player makes, the final result is the same—they gain Imelda's permission to investigate her husband's murder as well as access to his private drawing room as a result of being given the key. Vitally, the player's choices change the conversational journey, not the final destination; this enables the ensuing adventure to move smoothly forwards while providing the player with a feeling of agency as they take part in a well-written, interesting exchange that provides information on a number of levels, as well as a vital item at the end.

Hub-Based Dialogue

To help ensure important information is not missed, branching dialogue is often designed to reflect a more circular conversational pattern than one might first think. This can be reflected by a more hub-based conversational structure as shown in Figure 9.3.

In post-apocalyptic RPG *Fallout: New Vegas*™, a player can return to the same question several times when conversing with a desert wanderer, always receiving the same answer, delivered in the same tone of voice, which can also be useful if specific information needs to be noted (and, for whatever reason, hasn't been). This freedom allows the player the chance to explore and experiment with an interaction at their own leisure, though arguably at the cost of some realism.

Conversation Wheels

Games that present dialogue options directly on the screen, often to be read from a list of possible responses, are still popular and used by high-budget titles such as *Fallout: New Vegas*™ and *Dragon Age: Origins*™. However, this system can result in slow, unnatural conversations bereft of any real pace, unable to accommodate many of the normal moments we're used to experiencing in reality, such as interruptions and swift retorts. Conversation wheels allow for smoother, more realistically paced conversations that typically follow a branching path.

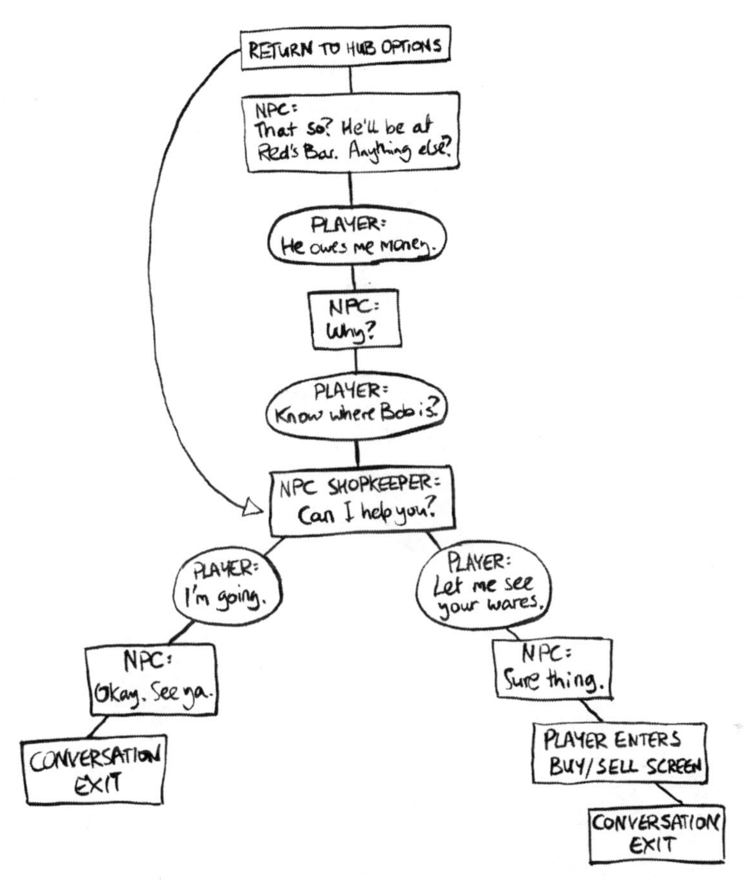

FIGURE 9.3. Hub-based conversational structure.

Instead of the player reading from a prescribed list of possible, verbatim conversational responses, they are presented with a wheel around which shorter text options are presented to provide the spirit of what would be said, but not the exact words. This system has two advantages, the first being that the player does not have to spend a great deal of time reading what can sometimes be lengthy chunks of dialogue before choosing a response (that's often not voiced). Instead, once chosen, the resulting response can be part of the reward for the player, as they're not sure exactly what will be said, only the thrust of it. Also, being faster to read means players can respond far more quickly, making for a far more cinematic experience rather than one filled with long pauses. Figure *9.4 shows a sample conversation wheel for our fictional spy game,* Code Obsidian.

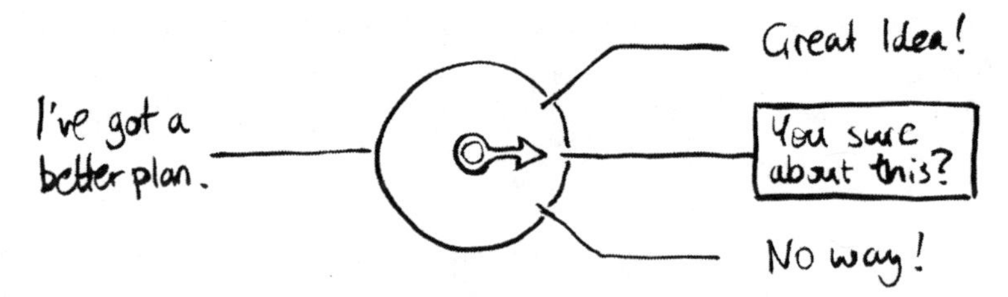

FIGURE 9.4. Sample conversation wheel.

Mass Effect uses this system to great effect, resulting in a game that can at times play more like a film. Both sequels (*Mass Effect 2* and *Mass Effect 3*) use the same conversation wheel system but add the ability to occasionally interrupt a speaker mid-flow, either verbally or through an action, which provides the player with another method of interaction that deepens the sense of realism.

DIALOGUE TOOLS

There is no single method or tool used by games writers to structure branching dialogue scripts, though often a developer might have an accepted system in place. Here are some (of the now many) options:

Microsoft Word™

Perhaps the simplest of ways to create a short branching dialogue document readable by most people is by creating the conversation in *Microsoft Word*, then threading it together using bookmarks and hyperlinks. This can, however, result in a cumbersome, text-based file that quickly becomes hard to follow.

Google Docs™

Google Docs is a free alternative (with a Google account) to *Word*, which allows multiple users simultaneous access to the same file. It also has its limitations for branching structures, although templates are often added to the software which may provide solutions, depending on what you're trying to do.

Twine™

One of the easiest ways to begin handling branching story structures, *Twine* is freeware that's extremely fast to learn with a simple visual display that helps writers see how their structures work at the macro level. Its limited functionality may not matter, depending on the script's ultimate destination; it's suited to text-based stories operating in their own right with limited graphics, not for high-end graphic or animation-rich experiences woven into physics-based game engines.

Chat Mapper™

Created by Urban Brain Studios, *Chat Mapper* allows the creation and testing of non-linear dialogue that can also be exported to *Word, Excel*™, and XML. Also, as illustrated in Figure 9.5, conversational paths can be displayed both visually in the form of a clear flow chart or as text, which is extremely useful. The main editing window contains, among other elements, the active dialogue tree, available characters, and the locations list. *Chat Mapper* also allows a writer to simulate and test conversations using the software's built-in engine.

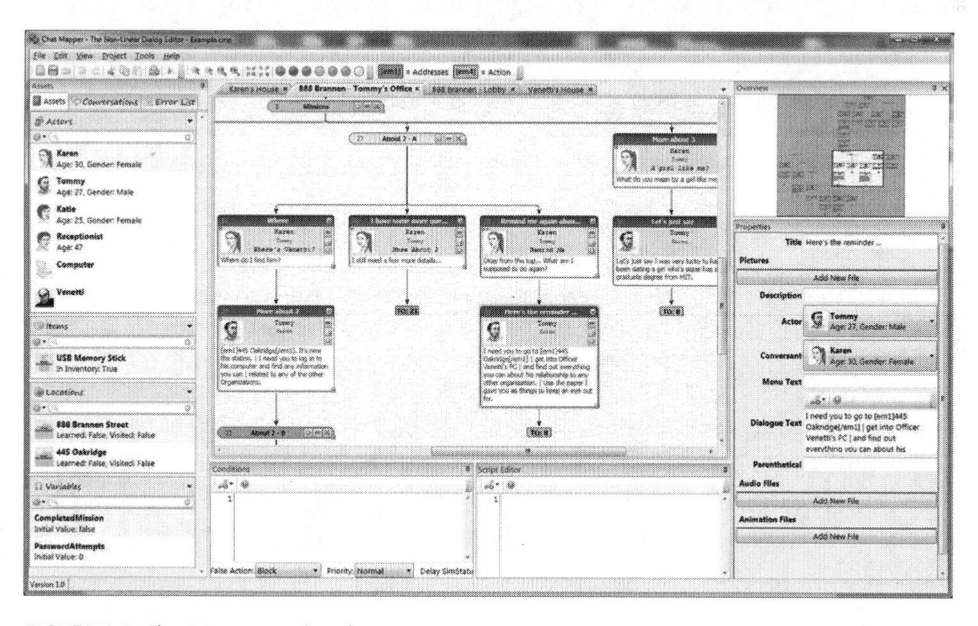

FIGURE 9.5. Chat Mapper user interface.

Articy Draft™

Articy Draft is a fully functional narrative development tool that can be integrated with high-end games engines. It presents a clear way for writers to track how sections of branching and linear dialogues and scenes connect to one another. Although certainly more daunting at first glance than *Twine*, online video tutorials are readily available that help writers wrap their heads

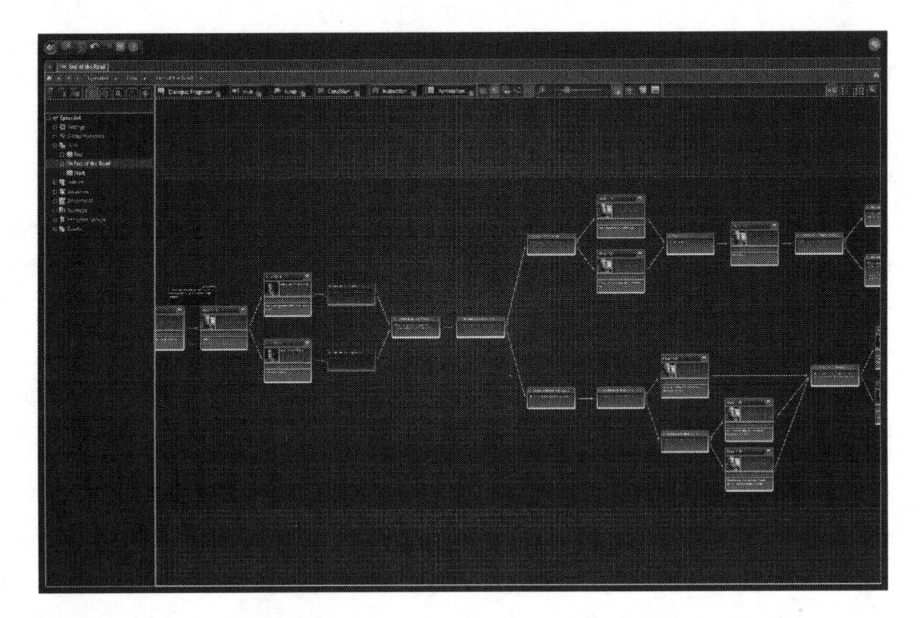

FIGURE 9.6. Articy Draft.

around concepts such as Global Variables and Condition Nodes (if X happened then go to Y, if not, go to Z). It also features a Presentation Mode which lets you "play through" the story in something like a slideshow format to get a sense of what players will experience.

Microsoft Visio™

Microsoft's commercial diagramming program *Visio* specializes in creating the kind of flow diagrams that could be used to chart the flow of a branching dialogue. Since it is not specifically built for video game writing and is a more costly option, Visio is not a common tool among games writers.

Microsoft Excel

A popular option for games writers when writing any kind of dialogue, *Excel*, like *Word*, can be set up to link sections of text through the use of macros and hyperlinks.

While writing a scene that contains branching dialogue, always remember what the player's goal will be; perhaps they want to purchase goods as in *Dragon Age: Origins*; find out what an unwilling NPC knows as in *Mass Effect*; or convince someone they've just rescued to help them fight their captors, as in

Fallout: New Vegas. Knowing this will help you know what happens if the player is successful, and what happens if they fail.

Systemic Scripts

These are scripts written to respond to specific triggers occurring within the game with enough frequency to warrant a systematized approach. They are generally created in a spreadsheet format, like *Google Sheets*, for example, with one sheet being used per game level. These can cover player character, NPCs (non-player characters), locations and effects (elevator voices, public announcements, etc.), and anything else that's audible whenever specific game states are satisfied. Sometimes the same basic phrase is rewritten many times over in different alternative versions. Sometimes specific lines aren't written, but a guide for the voice director and actor is provided instead (when the actor is required to make sounds indicating they are taking damage, etc.). These lines are often written so they adhere to strict restrictions, normally linked to the length of time necessary to say the line (some need to be punchy and fast, especially if conflict-oriented) and/or character count (especially if the game's on a handheld platform). These lines help to give a player feedback so they understand what is happening within the game and what the effects of their actions are.

Figure 9.7 shows a small sample of in-game dialogue for *Driver: Parallel Lines*. Note how the "health hit" cells (triggered when the character takes damage of any kind) require the actor to improvise—while it would have been possible to write these lines, they would have felt forced. For this work we were not set hard character limits, but needed to make each line suitably short.

Typical triggers include idle animation (triggered when the player leaves their avatar alone for a sufficient period of time), warnings, geographic (triggered when the player passes a certain point), and success-based triggers (the player manages to secure an item, dispatch an enemy, etc.). Sometimes lines delivering warnings and shouts in response to taking damage are known as "barks" due to their often inherently short nature.

Environmental Scripts

When engaged in environmental storytelling there's no set format to follow. You may use a combination of prose, screenplay, and spreadsheet formats. To an extent, it's a mixture of conventional storytelling (because certain events need to occur in a certain order) and systemic script writing (because certain triggers will occur at certain points—though more often location dependent than time dependent). Ultimately your script may be formatted in spreadsheet form and,

Trigger	Sample	Character	
		TK	Ray
Health Hit	1	Improv.	Improv.
Health Hit	2	Improv.	Improv.
Health Hit	3	Improv.	Improv.
Health Hit	4	Improv.	Improv.
Health Hit	5	Improv.	Improv.
Annoyed (at TK)	1	N/A	Cut it out!
Annoyed (at TK)	2	N/A	Stop it, will ya'?
Annoyed (at TK)	3	N/A	Hey!
Annoyed (at TK)	4	N/A	Jeez, TK!
Annoyed (at TK)	5	N/A	Enough already!
Idle (on foot)	1	I should get going.	N/A
Idle (on foot)	2	No time to stand around.	N/A
Idle (on foot)	3	What was I doing?	N/A
Idle (on foot)	4	Where was I?	N/A
Idle (on foot)	5	Man, I love New York.	N/A

FIGURE 9.7. *Driver: Parallel Lines* in-game dialogue sample.

as a result, may look at first glance like a systemic script, but if you have written it well, it should still be clear (if read in the right way) that it demonstrates a clear sense of plot progression. It can often be very helpful to provide a key within an environmental script to help readers understand its various elements.

ENVIRONMENTAL SCRIPT EXAMPLE

Context

Contemporary FPS set in United States. Player has just escaped a strange military base and is on the run from mysterious robot captors who we fear are not far behind. They move through a deserted small town. At this stage, not much is known. Player has in his possession a military comms device on which a woman calling herself Clover contacts him to offer assistance, claiming to be a friend. She's using the town's numerous cameras to observe proceedings.

Black Text - CRITICAL PATH DIALOGUE

CAPITALIZED TEXT - GAME NOTES

Italicized Text - NON-CRITICAL PATH

ON LOADING SCREEN . . .

PLAYER MOVES THROUGH MALL PARKING LOT, TOWARDS MAIN SHOPPING STREET. IT'S NIGHT. THE DOORS TO THE MALL ARE SMASHED, BUT HAVE BEEN HASTILY BOARDED UP. SOMEONE'S SPRAY-PAINTED "WATCH THEIR EYES" OVER THE WOODEN BOARDS.

CLOVER - RADIO

I know you don't trust me. Heck, I'd not trust me! But what choice do you have?

There's no time to send a resume—you got out 'cause of me, that's gotta count for something. Man, look at this place. From picture-postcard to nightmare in hours. It came out of nowhere, my men didn't stand a chance.

PLAYER HEADS TOWARDS MAIN STREET, PAST SMASHED NEON SIGNS, SOME STILL VAINLY FLICKERING IN A SHATTERED PIZZA HALL AND DRY CLEANING SHOPS. THERE AREN'T MANY CARS, THOSE THAT REMAIN ALL HAVE THEIR ENGINES EXPOSED AND SMASHED.

CLOVER - RADIO

We need to get a message to my people, let them know what's happened—that's our only chance. Make your way east, to the gas station on the outskirts of town. It's not quite what it seems. I'll explain when you get there.

[SHORTER ALT VERSION FOR SAFETY]

We need to warn my people—it's our only chance. Head east, to the gas station on the town outskirts. I'll brief you when you get there.

DIRECTIONAL ARROW APPEARS ON PLAYER'S HUD.

IF PLAYER EXPLORES BEHIND SET OF PARKING LOT DUMPSTERS - THEY FIND a HUMANOID ROBOT SQUATTING THERE, COVERED IN DENTS AND PAINT. SLOWLY, IT STANDS.

CLOVER - RADIO

You had to get all adventuresome, didn't you? Back off, it's one of them.

ROBOT

I hunger!

CLOVER - RADIO

He's faster than he looks! You've got two choices—live or die. Your call!

PLAYER DEFENDS HIMSELF SUCCESSFULLY.

CLOVER - RADIO

Good job. Now let's get back on track.

PLAYER REACHES MAIN SHOPPING STREET. IT LOOKS LIKE A RIOT CHARGED THROUGH TOWN, THOUGH EVERYTHING'S EERILY QUIET. SHOP AND BUILDING WINDOWS ARE ALL DARK, MOST ARE DAMAGED IN SOME WAY. A STREET SIGN POINTS WEST TO I40. BENEATH IT IS ANOTHER SIGN, POINTING EAST, TO "HAPPY LARRY'S GAS STATION."

CLOVER - RADIO

Stay frosty and keep to the shadows. This place still has plenty of shoppers, but not the healthy kind, if you get me.

On-Screen Text

This is text that appears on-screen during gameplay, which can be purely instructional, written in the "voice of the system" and there to help steer the player through the tutorial or the body of the game; text such as *Gather bonus items by completing special Bonus Missions!* could appear the first time a player successfully completes a gameplay task. This is, in essence, the system addressing the player directly.

A similar, guiding function can be served by using the voice of a game character, or narrator, to say something that provides essential glue between the game and the story or supports the game without stopping proceedings. This could be dialogue spoken by an ally that basically covers the same game design instructional requirements as those illustrated in the example above. So a game character, instead of addressing the player directly, would address the player's character by saying something like, *Great, completing special Bonus Missions can get you some neat gadgets!*

CUT SCENE FORMAT

The movie style screenplay format evolved during the early part of the twentieth century. The format is, at its heart, a simple one, but it's important not to let the details of script formatting distract you from being clear about the purpose of your script. Today professional screenplays are written in twelve-point Courier font, partly out of a sense of tradition and partly because it's a mono-spaced font (i.e., a font whose letters and characters are all the same width). Each page of a screenplay normally equals around a minute of screen time, which is a useful metric for producers to apply.

Professional writers may use software such as *Final Draft*™ · *FadeIn*™, *WriterDuet*, *Trelby*™ , *Celtx*™, *Scrivener*™, or *Adobe Story*™. These days *Google Docs* also provides the option of a free screenplay template. Regardless of the software, there are a number of screenplay format conventions.

Scene Numbers, if there are any, are placed on the left side of the page, as are Scene Headings. Action text runs the width of the page. Characters, when they speak, have their names in capitals, centered on the page. Their dialogue is also centered but runs in a thicker column. These rules, and others, are discussed later in this chapter.

Your script is designed to *tell your story through action and dialogue*—that's all. Script scenes are not meant to instruct the (virtual) director what to shoot, shot by shot and scene by scene. A common misconception is that a script should contain detailed camera angle instructions, when in reality deciding *how* to shoot a given scene is for the Director and Director of Photography (DP) to decide. Let that sink in, as it lightens your responsibility load considerably.

Sample Cut Scene Script Breakdown

Figure 9.8, with numbered talking points inserted for the purposes of this chapter, is a scene from *Driver: Parallel Lines*. It comes early in the game and is designed to both move the story forwards, by introducing key character, Slink, and open up a new set of gameplay missions by alluding to the impending need for the player to impress him.

(1) EXT. FUNKY RABBIT NIGHTCLUB - DAY

(2) Sexy women silhouettes on the logo, black on neon 70s cool.

(3) Subtitles: *"FUNKY RABBIT, MIDTOWN" punches across the bottom of the screen then fades.*

(4) CUT TO:

(5) INT. SLINK'S CLUB - DAY

(6) The club is closed. It's young, black, urban disco. It's not expensive or as funky as it likes to think it is, but it is cool. Chairs are stacked on tables, music plays low over speakers. A semi-clad DANCER moves on the stage - an audition. SLINK sits at a table watching the girl. He's relaxed, feeling breezy. TK walks through the tables towards him.

(7) TK

(8) You Slink? I'm the driver.

(9) Slink glances at TK, then looks back to the dancer.

SLINK

What I hear, you're just a taxi service for punks.

TK

I do okay.

Slink gestures for TK to take a seat next to him, doesn't take his eyes off the dancer. TK sits, waits.

Subtitle: *"SLINK" punches across the bottom of the screen then fades.*

As he speaks, Slink continues to look at the dancer. TK watches too.

SLINK

Ray says you got po-ten-tial ...

You got am-bition? You wanna live the American dream? Eight-track stereos, color TVs in every room, wall-to-wall pussy? You wanna **(10)** be somebody?

TK says nothing. Slink looks across to TK, then back to the dancer.

SLINK

(11) (to the girl)

Ooo, that's good, baby, do that again. Do it slower.

While the dialogue and action contained in the scene took a lot of work to arrive at, the actual format of the script is simple. Using the numbered sections, here's how to break down the important formatting rules.

(1) Sometimes called the Slug Line by screenwriters, this tells us where and when we are. In this case, outside, EXT. a nightclub called the FUNKY RABBIT NIGHTCLUB and it's DAY.

(2) Provide your succinct description of people, places, or action. These lines should be single-spaced and stretch across the page.

(3) Another double-space here. Anything that appears on-screen, like subtitles, should be clearly highlighted, in this case through italicization.

(4) Double-space. We're telling the director we're about to change location.

(5) Double-space. We've moved from outside the club (EXT.) to its interior (INT.).

(6) Double-space. Another succinct description, this time of the club's interior. New characters are always capitalized the first time they're mentioned in the script.

(7) Whichever character is speaking is capitalized and placed in the center of the page.

(8) Dialogue is placed in the center of the page so whoever's speaking creates a column of text beneath their capitalized name.

(9) Directions also tell the director what a given character does—reactions, where they look, and so on.

(10) Underline a word if a character really stresses it, as this is far clearer than simple italicization. Use this sparingly—if a character says every word with emphasis, they will end up saying nothing at all with emphasis (and you will hurt your actors in the process as they may attempt the impossible).

(11) Specific directions for a character are placed in parentheses beneath the name of the speaker. Again, these should be used sparingly.

FIGURE 9.8. *Driver: Parallel Lines* script sample.

Don't over-complicate your formatting; script format conventions are adopted so as to make your scripts as readable as possible and are a means to an end. A well-formatted script is indicative of a professional approach and understanding of how to write; overly fussy formatting is suggestive of the opposite.

Other Basic Screenplay Terms

Here are a few further key terms normally found in scripts.

VO (voiceover)

Narration heard over a scene, typically spoken by the protagonist.

POV (point of view)

Illustrates that a particular shot is seen from a character's point of view.

O/S (off-screen)

Indicates the dialogue is spoken while the speaker is not in-shot.

SFX (special effects)

Encompassing both audio and visual special effects, which in some way alter reality. When used in a film, these are added in post-production.

It's important to remember that, due to the highly iterative and collaborative nature of video game creation, the final version of your current game may contain scripts that don't exactly match those that you wrote. While it's naturally desirable for any edits and deeper script changes to be implemented by the writer or writing teams, sometimes these people are not consulted. This can be due to strict time restrictions, or because the changes needed are judged simple enough to be carried out by a non-writer. Often these reasons are given when the writers are freelance and not sitting three desks away. Perhaps worse, the scripts you wrote might make it into the final version of the game despite being outdated after shifts in design and structure. Ideally, your role as a games writer should include guarding the story's relevance when linked to gameplay.

EXERCISES

1. Write the opening scene for a game. This can either replace the opening scene of an existing—preferably well-known—game title, or create something entirely new. The scene should be no longer than two minutes long and fulfill the following requirements:

   Clearly show the player the game world they're entering.

   Introduce the main character or characters.

   If appropriate, illustrate future gameplay elements.

   Explore the following questions:

What did you find easy about writing the scene?

What was difficult to write—the dialogue, action, or something else?

Were your scenes acted and interpreted in the manner you intended them to be?

2. Write ten pages of a new script, making sure it follows the format outlined above. If you've done the Treatment exercise in Chapter 6, use that as your template.

PROJECTS

1. Write a script, using *Twine* (or another visual tool), that will give a reader at least a ten-minute story experience from (their) beginning to end, with at least ten choices to make along the way. A choice must consist of at least two options, but need not consist of more. Your story can be about anything you like.
2. Select between ten and twenty images and build a *Twine* story around them. As with your previous *Twine* story, you must give the reader at least a ten-minute story experience from (their) beginning to end, and there must be at least ten choices for them to make along the way.
3. Write a scene on the topic of your choosing using the screenplay format. The scene must be at least two minutes (i.e., two pages) long.

Chapter 10 EDITING

The present letter is a very long one, simply because I had no leisure to make it shorter.

– Blaise Pascal

Games writers are often required to edit a variety of text types over the natural course of a project, and are sometimes explicitly on a project to edit work that has already been completed to a certain stage. In the context of game story, editing is an iterative process in which we refine what has been written, improving, tightening, tweaking, occasionally adding to, and more often deleting along the way. This aspect of games writing is concerned with the micro—but even here, it's a micro that's concerned with the ultimate target of the macro. While not the most glamorous of tasks, it remains a vital one—if *BioShock 2*'s main antagonist, the clinical and intellectual Sofia Lamb, were to ever deliver an overly long, rambling speech containing the occasional grammatical error, much of her power and presence in the game would evaporate, which in turn would crack the player's immersion in an otherwise seamless world. Good editing encompasses a number of tasks. We tend to make a distinction between copy editing, covering the more "basic" elements of spelling, spacing, and grammar, and creative editing, requiring script writing and associated skills in order to effect.

SPELLING, SPACING, AND GRAMMAR

It's rare, if not unheard of, to be asked to work on a project with the express purpose of rooting out spelling mistakes. With modern spell-checking software ubiquitous, it might be tempting to think poor spelling is something confined to the dusty days of printer ribbons and telex machines (ask your parents). While those squiggly red lines we're used to seeing on-screen now do catch a great number of mistakes, they can't be relied on in all circumstances. A spelling mistake might simply result in a different correctly spelled word being used than the one intended, so no spelling error has technically occurred for the spell-checker to identify. *Feather boat* will pass muster with most spelling (and grammar) checkers, but if you meant to write *feather boa* then your scene's been accidentally shifted into a rather different, perhaps even surreal, place. It's also important to remember language is always changing—the moment a dictionary is printed it's out of date as new words are formed in the primordial linguistic ooze of our ever-evolving society. Also, a dictionary can't contain every word from every *dialect* of English you might use nor can it know a noun, adjective, or verb you might have created expressly for the purposes of your work. Granted, these programs can be taught new words, but anyone who has read the novel *Trainspotting* by Scottish author Irvine Welsh can imagine he wouldn't have gotten much use from his spell-checking software. Ultimately, you should always check your work visually before you deem it finished. Nothing looks less professional than a spelling mistake (and they're so easy to fix).

Remember to make sure character spacing is uniform, especially if there are several of you working on a project. Many writers feel a single space is all that's required post-period and others (still) argue for two. Both sides would agree, though, that whatever you decide, be consistent; the same principles apply to checking grammar. A useful way to run a grammar check is to read your work aloud as our ears are often far better at hearing mistakes than our eyes are at spotting them in text. This method also has the benefit of highlighting anything that, while not grammatically incorrect, doesn't flow properly and can be improved upon.

DIALOGUE

There are times when it might be necessary to edit a game's dialogue to ensure it is consistently clear, concise, and suitably reflective of the individual characters and overall tone required. If it feels stilted, or clipped, or perhaps just a poor fit for the characters that exist in the game, then the story will suffer. Linked to this, make sure that, if warranted, the right terms and slang are used. If they're not, the speaker won't feel real, but the opposite can be true too—if too many are used, even if they're technically correct, then the dialogue can lose its natural flow and feel forced. Generally, good dialogue in a game will use as few words as necessary. There's a saying from movies, passed on to us from fellow writer

Neil Richards: a king is allowed three lines, a prince allowed two, and every other character just one. This is a sound principle to encourage you to be critical of long speeches (and if you do write them, be completely sure you can justify them) and to ensure your characters conform to a hierarchy in terms of their importance to the story. Keep in mind that the line counts stated just now reflect a principle and should not be taken literally!

WORD AND CHARACTER COUNTS

Sometimes there can be a set limit of how much text, or even individual characters (including spaces), can appear on a game screen at a time. This is often the case with handheld games, where screen space is at a premium; without much space you need to be careful about what you fill it with. The flow of a game can be slowed to the detriment of the overall player experience if too many text-heavy screens follow one after another. After all, every time a player taps a screen on a smartphone to read more text they aren't playing a game, they're moving from one screen of text to another. But you need to ensure that any text you remove doesn't endanger any of the essential gameplay or story information. If the player needs to go to *The Jumping Bean Café on Second Street* for their next mission, it may be problematic to edit the line to just *the café*. They may still manage to get there, but gameplay information should always be clear and direct (unless ambiguity is called for, which might be the case in certain kinds of detective game).

You may find you have a specific limit of characters per line and lines per screen without an automated system in place allowing for an easy way to check. Perhaps this text has been written prior to the restrictions being set, or the restrictions have subsequently been changed.

One quick and relatively simple way to perform such a task is to use a uniform font such as Courier (in which each character, including the 'space,' is exactly the same width). The chances are the source file you'll be working from is in a spreadsheet form—and this is a good thing, because now you can adjust your spreadsheet column so it permits the required number of characters before forcing a line break.

Table 10.1 shows some dialogue and text edit examples carried out for *Unsolved Crimes*, the DS title we helped write for Japanese developer Now Productions, in which the player takes the role of a rookie detective tasked with helping solve a series of murders. Our job was to first tighten the text so the story used as few *screen taps* as possible while still being compelling and clear. It was also necessary to ensure each line of text was, at most, 38 characters long, including spaces and all other punctuation. Note that when a line appears to cut off, it indicates a need for the player to tap the screen to access the next line or lines.

TABLE 10.1. Unsolved Crimes in-game dialogue editing sample.

Format	Now Pro English	Edited English
Speaker: System Line:3 EachLineCharMax:38	File 04	File 04
Speaker: System Line:3 EachLineCharMax:38	"Murder's Examination Room"	{Death's Examination Room}
Speaker: Abbot Line:2 EachLineCharMax:38	If you don't wanna stay at home, I'll put you in the team.	I'm guessing you'd rather work than go home, right?
Speaker: Marcy Line:2 EachLineCharMax:38	Thank you. And, please promise me that	Yeah. If I don't keep busy I'll go out of my mind. Look, Captain...
Speaker: Marcy Line:2 EachLineCharMax:38	If you get information about my sister,	promise you'll tell me the moment you hear something.
Speaker: Marcy Line:2 EachLineCharMax:38	you give me the informa-tion right away and	/* Empty */
Speaker: Marcy Line:2 EachLineCharMax:38	let me handle what I can do.	I'll do everything I can.

Notice that the edit resulted in the text being condensed to the point that we actually gained a blank cell. In game terms, this is one less screen tap before being able to return to the gameplay (as well as less text to be translated, and, potentially, fewer art assets, less to implement, and less to test).

You might also be asked to edit dialogue temporally—which is a fancy way of saying edit it so that it can be spoken out loud within a specific time limit. This might be a requirement on games where audio file memory sizes have a set limit and therefore require lines to be read by actors within a certain number of seconds. You may also have to edit text to be spoken within a prescribed limit because the animation has already been created (possibly less the facial animation, or with the character's face off-screen). Remember, when it comes to both written and spoken dialogue, less is *generally* more anyway.

TONE OF VOICE

Checking story and dialogue for tone of voice to ensure it's consistent and on-track is a core editing task. This can involve a variety of elements. Ideally, the brief should indicate tone of voice, although sometimes special tone documents are created to help clarify matters.

Here's part of a tone document we wrote for developer Reflections Interactive when we worked on *Driver: Parallel Lines* (working title, *Driver 4*). It was designed partly to state where we felt the tone needed to be for the game, and partly to open a constructive discussion on the matter, as tone is the responsibility of several departments.

Driver 4: Tone Document

The physical look and feel of any game world defines the tone and voice of the story and the gameplay.

Driver 4 is a game that will take place in two real worlds—New York 1978 and 2006. Much of the design effort is going into accurately replicating the precise look and feel of those two worlds. At the same time, car behavior and physics is also being refined according to laws of "logic" and "reality."

Clearly, cartoon gameplay and story will not fit comfortably in the world we're creating. But nor, at the other extreme, will cold realism.

We all agree we're not after naturalism. We all agree that we want a lighter tone than *Driver 3*. We want the player to feel they're inside an exciting action movie when they play the game.

We're in the world of Elmore Leonard, an author who creates serious worlds and powerful dialogue for potent, memorable characters (*Get Shorty*, *Rum Punch*, and *Killshot*). We could talk movies, but what kind? *Ronin*? Or *2 Fast 2 Furious*? Or maybe *Duel*? Or do we want *Bad Boys*? How about *Con Air*? Who thinks we're actually making *Italian Job*? With a little bit of *Assault on Precinct 13*? *Man on Fire*, anyone?

Movies and other games can often be misleading when it comes to tone and voice—especially when we're trying to create something original. *Driver 4* may at any one time have elements from any of the above movies—but it won't *be exactly like* a single one of them. Nor will it be like any other game.

So here's a different way of describing how we see *Driver 4*.

Characters

These will be larger than life but not caricature. Filmic not cartoon. Immediately recognizable as types but individuals nevertheless.

Dialogue

Should be sharp, lively, energetic, urban, slick. This is not a world where humor has been banished. But we're definitely not after cheap gags . . .

Gameplay

Bruckheimer-style action within the constraints of a real world is the aim—just as long as it doesn't get silly or absurd.

Visuals/Direction/Art

Driver 3 was gritty and naturalistic, but sometimes silent and cold. *Driver 4* will be more colorful, more energetic and upbeat. In Part Two of the game the tone will change, but the pace will remain the same.

NOTE *Writing a Tone Document can be a great way to make sure everyone's on the same page when it comes to the kind of gameplay and game world that's being created.*

TONE OF VOICE IN LINE WITH CHARACTER

There are times when games writers need to edit dialogue to bring it in line with the overall tone of the game and the world in which it exists. Sometimes this need to police tone can be due to the original writer or writers not having a great deal of experience dealing with the culture they're writing about. While to most English-speaking Western games writers it might be obvious that the Vikings didn't engage in jousts or go on the Crusades, writers from foreign cultures might group them in with the Middle Ages and so stumble into historical inaccuracies.

Sometimes you may be asked to edit existing text to align it with the team's desired tone and then, once that's done, to add to the current text. For example, a designer might have written some dialogue that acts as both placeholder text and helps illustrate the kind of work that's needed on the project. This will normally be done in a spreadsheet that typically features the following cell columns.

Design Information Column

These columns show a variety of information types; sometimes bewildering, sometimes simple to read, they're usually there to let the design team know something important about the cell you'll be working on. This information might not be of use to you (especially if it's in a language you don't understand), but still check all such sections as you might be able to glean something from them. If a column is clearly totally unrelated to anything you're doing, hide it to make for a neater spreadsheet that's easier to work on. If you're unsure of a column's value, check with your team leader.

Original Pass Text

This is the text or dialogue written by someone else that you're there to check and, if necessary, edit. It's common for designers to do a first pass on text before the work gets to a games writer, as they need to ensure specific gameplay-related information is included for the player. Sometimes there's no original pass for you to work with; if this is the case, make sure you're totally clear about what's needed before you start. You might also find only some of the first pass done as it can be useful for a designer to write a few examples for you to look at by way of illustration. This might happen should a large number of variable cells be present that require basically the same information written in a large variety of ways, all essentially saying the same thing (this kind of text is known by many as "alts," for alternatives).

Resist the urge to assume every cell you look at requires alteration. Editing is the judicious application of necessary change, not change for change's sake. Changing an original line that did not require change is as bad as not changing a line that does; either way you end up without the text in its optimum condition.

Purpose-Descriptor Text

If no one has created any sample work to help you understand the tone, context, and other necessary information you need to convey in your text, then often, at the very least, a column should be present to tell you what you need to write—in a sense, a mini-brief. This will typically be short and clear, for example, in a casual game like *Sonic and SEGA All-Stars Racing*, commentator purpose-descriptor text including instructions such as *triggered when attack inbound, triggered when player passes checkpoint,* or *triggered at the close of the race.*

Edited Text Column

Rather than putting your final edits in the Original Pass column and overwriting that text, having an independent column for this allows you, and other team members, to easily see just what changes have been made to the previous pass. Having the original text also enables you to make sure you've included all the necessary gameplay information in your new edit. Keep in mind that, generally, while well-edited text and dialogue uses fewer words, the information you present, above all else, must be clear.

Notes Column

Often while editing text, it can be useful to have a column in which to leave notes, queries, and comments relating to specific cells or groups of cells for the next person to see and potentially provide feedback on. This might be a fellow writer, one of the design team, or your team leader. If a piece of work is likely to go through several rewrites, then set up new notes columns for each pass, to keep track of conversations pertaining to specific text. While these can get slightly unwieldy, using a spreadsheet's "hide" function will keep your work as clutter-free as possible.

ID Column

These are used to give each spreadsheet cell its own identity number, used by the audio team to organize recording sessions.

Localization Columns

Normally empty if you're working on a first or early pass of English text and dialogue, these columns will eventually contain the various other languages your game is going to be localized (i.e., translated) into.

Table 10.2 contains some examples of early game text and commentator edits for the game mentioned earlier, *Sonic and SEGA All-Stars Racing.* Note that due to page size restrictions, this is a cut-down version of the project spreadsheet. The original text supplied by the design team was often workable, though the majority of the job involved expanding on what was provided with totally new commentator dialogue.

Most edits result in fewer words either on-screen or being spoken as dialogue. This is desirable partly because taking less time to communicate the same information means the player doesn't have to spend longer trying to understand what they need to know in order to play the game. It's also desirable because text and dialogue is generally punchier when it's shorter. Brevity can also save money when recording the game's audio, especially when the same script is used as the basis for recording sessions in multiple languages. However, there are times when a line will warrant being edited in such a manner as to make it longer, for example if it's going to be spoken and, in its current form, is hard for the actor to say. Sacrificing brevity for flow is sometimes necessary (as illustrated by the edits done in the first and final rows of the table above). A line may also be extended so as to improve its tone, bringing it into line with the rest of the dialogue.

TABLE 10.2. Sample game text and commentator edits.

Sample	Edit	Designer Notes
Welcome to today's super battle race live from Seaside Hill.	And a big welcome to today's super battle race live from Seaside Hill!	Introduction to Sonic Seaside Hill zone setting
The hot favorite for today's race is AiAi.	Hot tip for a fruity first finish - it's AiAi!	Triggered during driver intro cams/ players character is commentator's pick of the race
Look out for AiAi, surely today's winner.	Today's winner? My eye's on AiAi!	Triggered during driver intro cams/ players character is commentator's pick of the race
They're off the line like a host of rockets!	And we have blast off!	Triggered once the race has started/good start
Get a move on! The race has started!	Whoa! Hit the gas people, c'mon!	Triggered once the race has started/poor start
You snooze, you lose, Amigo.	Amigo snoozing and losing there…	Triggered when specific driver loses a position in the field

GAME WORLD TEXT (STORY PROSE)

Sometimes games writers are asked to edit story prose. This can come embedded within the game itself and/or as part of the game's accompanying documentation. This kind of work is normally there to help flesh out the game's universe through the creation of stories that can either run in tandem with the game's events (i.e., exist in the game universe, but not involve themselves directly with events) or expand upon them (i.e., involve characters the player will know through the game, taking part in events that are directly linked to, or even mirror, the core story). Whatever the purpose of the text, editing it is, in a sense, a simpler affair than normal in that you will have to worry less about direct gameplay design considerations.

Let's take a look at a sample of original text from fantasy RTS (Real Time Strategy) game *BattleForge*™. It was destined to form part of a prose story to be gradually unlocked by the player as they progress through the game's story campaign.

Original Text

As the dungeon doors glowed in a blue light and burst open, Bren Morhold did not flinch from the horrors that poured in. Stones and an iron bar quickly got rid of those. And secure in the knowledge that he could kill whatever it was that had overrun Lyr, he moved out in search for his armor and weapons, a predator on the hunt for different game now, flexing his muscles as he slowly moved into his new hunting grounds. He smiled to himself as he left the dungeon empty behind him. Why hurry?

Our edit aimed to compress and clarify the text while pushing the fantasy tone further. "Why hurry?" also felt confusing and pushed against an intended sense of progress for the player. These story sections are contained within the game (as unlockables) and therefore read on-screen, and trimming text where possible served to make them easier to digest.

Edited Text

Moments later the thick, steel doors glowed blue and exploded. Creatures born of nightmare quickly overran the few screaming prisoners who had gathered hoping for release. As the beings tore aside thick iron bars, their eyes glowing in the semi-dark, Morhold smiled and ran at them, hungry for different game now.

Visual Style

While this is the Art Department's bailiwick, there's no harm in helping define their vision from a story perspective. If possible, include visual samples of characters, landscapes, creatures, and buildings that can be found online using any image search engine.

Inspirations and Source Material

What creative sources serve to inspire the game's universe? While movies can and do provide rich seams of inspiration for these worlds, there are other media deserving of serious attention. These include news stories, art (of any kind), prose literature, music, and TV series. Gabe Newell, Valve's Creative Lead, is documented as citing the Spanish Influenza as being one source of inspiration for him when his team created the hugely popular first-person zombie shooter, *Left for Dead.*

Define What It's Not

Stating what a game story is *not* can be as useful as stating what it is. If you're working on a game that's a contemporary cop thriller, defining it as not belonging in the universe of *Miami Vice* (serious, slick, cool) can be a useful way to start honing in on what your world is.

How Do We Do It?

In principle, editing is a process of refinement that takes practice, objectivity, and an eye for detail to master. In keeping with the theme of this book, it's important to point out that editing takes place at both a macro and micro level. On a macro level, a games writer edits story and document structures, making sure they're ordered in a manner that ensures they flow in as efficient and effective a manner as possible. On a micro level, making sure each letter of each word of each line of each paragraph is the best one for the job is vital to present quality work.

EXERCISES

1. Choose a game with a scene where the dialogue needs editing. It need not be longer than two minutes. Create a simple script that replicates what is said and done on-screen, then edit it. Make notes detailing your editing decisions and discuss them with your classmates.
2. Edit the following in-game dialogue contained in Table 10.3 for fictitious kid's murder mystery game *Death in Shadow Bay* for a smartphone in which the player takes on the role of an unnamed third friend.

   Your final text should be shorter (unless with good reason), without sacrificing clarity. Once you've finished, compare your work with our edit in Appendix D.

TABLE 10.3. Death in Shadow Bay dialogue edit.

Original	Edit	Designer Notes
Morning! Are you ready for a cool day of adventure?		Missy, greeting player (happy)
Oh, hi. I slept really, really badly last night.		Missy, greeting player (unhappy)
Urgh! It's impossible to sleep in this terrible, yucky town!		Missy, greeting player (really unhappy)
Good morning. Not sure if I'm feeling pretty today.		Missy, greeting player (neutral)
Did you sleep ok or did you have nightmares?		Caleb, greeting player (happy)
Hey. I'd say 'good morning' but that'd be a total lie.		Caleb, greeting player (unhappy)
I'm having, like the worst morning ever!		Caleb, greeting player (really unhappy)
Morning. Ready to face the world, are you?		Caleb, greeting player (neutral)
There's definitely something right there!		Missy, spotting clue
I just saw something, do you see it too?!		Missy, spotting clue
I'm pretty sure that's a clue over there!		Caleb, spotting clue
Ah ha! See you have to pay attention! I think there's something of importance here!		Caleb, spotting clue
You can't be serious about that, can you?		Missy, player guesses wrong
Nope, that's not going to be the right answer!		Missy, player guesses wrong
I'm afraid not, dearest of cousins.		Caleb, player guesses wrong
Ah, no. That's not anywhere close to correct.		Caleb, player guesses wrong
Huh. What a lucky guess.		Missy, player guesses right
Okay, that sounds like it's right.		Missy, player guesses right
Yes! A great deduction indeed!		Caleb, player guesses right
You really mastered that in no time!		Caleb, player guesses right

A quick note about the characters:

Missy

Nine years old, from California and as spoiled as she is pretty. Missy's parents are rich, a fact she never lets anyone forget. Cousin to Caleb and the player, the only reason she hangs out with you both is because there's nothing better to do. Missy's a pain, but she's smart in an intellectual kind of way and great at solving puzzles.

Caleb

Eleven years old, skinny, bookish, and a Shadow Bay local, Caleb normally can't stand Missy, but patiently puts up with her attitude as she's family. While his folks aren't rich, he's had a good upbringing and enjoys showing off his practical knowledge, even if it makes him sound a bit old-fashioned sometimes.

Chapter 11 CONSULTANCY

Patience is the companion of wisdom.

—St. Augustine

BRIEF TERMS

PROJECT RESTRICTIONS Restrictions unique to a given games development project; these can, for example, be linked to financial, manpower, or scheduling limitations, or be due to restrictions stemming from the project IP or development studio.

GAME STORY LOGIC The logic upon which all elements of a game world rest; this can pertain to character relationships, motivations, or a world's laws of physics—all need to be supported by solid reasoning, or appear creatively bankrupt.

TROUBLESHOOTING The act of identifying and then rectifying a project's problems.

On some occasions you may be hired as a consultant. What this means varies broadly depending on who's using the term and when. You may be considered a consultant when you're asked to look at one particular area outlined in a preceding chapter—to perhaps work alongside an existing team member or team without taking full responsibility for its implementation, merely in the guise of an advisor. Equally, your duties may require you to take responsibility for one targeted area. You may just as likely be asked for advice, guidance, or support across the full spectrum of what a games writer does—or be asked to be responsible for all of it—and still be called a consultant. Sometimes the reason you're called a *consultant* as opposed to a *writer* can be because the existing team already has particular roles and titles and a settled sense of inter-company politics and hierarchies.

If you are hired as a consultant, this generally involves not just assessing the current game and making recommendations predicated on ideal solutions—it almost always involves understanding the current restrictions or, more usually, solely considering solutions in relation to these restrictions; these will include scheduling, technological, team-based, and budgetary restrictions. For example, you might be working with a game story that can only support three characters, so it's not possible to create any new ones, and you'd have to work with the number you have; or perhaps you might not be able to record new lines of dialogue, as the window for that closed a week ago, but you can cut existing ones if that helps; or perhaps you're not allowed to create new scenes or change any character art but you can have lines re-recorded. Part of the skill of writing for video games is concerned with working within restrictions from the very start of a project and still finding solutions that not only fit the immediate needs, but are compelling as well—this does not change should you find yourself being asked to help locate and solve story issues further down the creative production line. It's vital to understand that your role in a troubleshooting capacity requires you to provide practical solutions that fit within the boundaries of the project you have been asked to assist on—and don't forget, these boundaries almost always change from title to title. Suggesting solutions that, although technically "correct," or in principle wholly sound, cannot be implemented for any number of reasons unique to the team and project you're working with, will not impress anyone, and could bring your career as a consultant to a screeching halt.

Perhaps one of the more familiar roles of the games writer turned consultant is as a script doctor. In this guise your task is often focused on evaluating the underlying narrative design—in both senses of the term, both in terms of storytelling in its own right, and in ascribing the space within the game where the storytelling is to occur. In terms of the title's storytelling in its own right, elements to examine range from the macro to the micro; it's generally wise to start with elements associated with the former before moving closer in and grappling with the latter.

MACRO ELEMENTS

You might begin by assessing what the story is about, if it's about what it intended to be about, and how this "aboutness" has been *dramatically* delivered (not just referenced). From here you could consider how the plot is structured, if its events are consequential, if its acts are clearly defined, if reversals and revelations keep the story interesting, if the underpinning logic bears stress-testing to support the characters and storytelling, and to what extent the story is *experienced* by the player—how tangible it is for them, and the pacing and nature of the delivery of this story. A story too deep in backstory, too far away from what the player experiences or at least witnesses *on-screen,* is likely to be deeply unsatisfying and leave players feeling detached from the experience.

Tone, too, is something to consider, though this operates at both the macro and micro register. Be clear what the intended tone is—for the demographic, the genre, the platform, and in line with other game elements—and be vigilant of tone being lost for the sake of a cute one-off line or incident which, although in its own right has merit, clashes with and jeopardizes the tone of other content. In terms of game design-related narrative design, is the structure affording the story room to breathe, or is it stifling the game? Is the approach to interactive storytelling appropriate to the project's intensions and its intended audience? If there are moments when the player is permitted less interactivity, are these moments justifiable, according to design intentions? Can the length of these periods be reduced in number or length or be better justified with the logic of the game story and/or the game design? Are there moments where granting player freedom is causing considerable problems for the game design and/or other elements of development? Is there a case for further restricting the player character in order to solve other more serious problems? Are there moments where the interactive narrative design teaches the player only by failing? (Does dying a few times make success much easier to complete the level?) Or are there times when the story fails to deliver a sense of progress and achievement to the player? Can these instances be removed or finessed so as to at least offer some mitigation for this kind of design?

Also, at the macro level, it's important to explore how the story's arcs are presented. A story arc moves a character or situation from one state to another and is vital to ensuring a journey of some kind takes place. RPG *Fable III* begins its story with the hero as the younger of two royal children, yet events move matters quickly along turning them into a revolutionary, bent on leading an uprising against their unjust older sibling, before eventually rising to rule the land as king or queen (depending on the avatar's gender); in short, the hero changes. Without arcs you have stasis—the antithesis of story. A story without change is not much of a story at all. (To be clear, there are stories that cycle back around to deliver their protagonist to a situation reminiscent or functionally the same as where they began, but at the very least the experience the character has had in going through the story is part of the point. When Alice wakes at the end of *Alice in Wonderland*, her amazing experiences are "the change.") A game's main story arc could involve the transition of a high-security prison from being under criminal control to back in the hands of authority (*Batman: Arkham Asylum*) or, if we're thinking about character arcs, exploring the protagonist's journey from unknowing puppet to free individual (*BioShock*). At this stage you may also become aware that the key story characters are jarring with the tone, or are simply not fit for the conflict the story requires of them. (Needing to become fit for the conflict is *great*—this is an arc, but never becoming fit or never being capable of ever becoming fit suggests either the wrong character in the wrong story or a story with no climax.)

"IT LOOKS BAD! WE'VE GOT A SEVERE LOSS OF TENSION IN ACT TWO, AND A LACK OF MOTIVATION IN THE ANTAGONIST! GET PREPPED, WE'RE OPERATING!"

MICRO ELEMENTS

As you move closer to the micro you may find problems in scene structures. Is a scene lacking conflict? Are there too many characters so the scene is crowded? Is the scene too long? Are the essential beats of the scene confused and overcomplicated? Are there too few beats? Does a player leave a scene knowing nothing more than when they entered it? Perhaps your story has no scenes, in the conventional sense, and you are consulting on a story told "environmentally." Are the essential beats of this story being conveyed clearly? Would additional signage, additional audio strings, additional diaries, or other storytelling devices, or other art elements help clarify the storytelling needed here? Or is it a case of less, rather than more? Are there too many stories competing for player attention? Remember, player comprehension cannot be taken for granted, and you must ensure you are catering to the player who wants to dive into the game and start running and shooting (in the case of an FPS) before you start looking after players who want more complex layers of storytelling. At least question whether a player will understand where they are going and what they are trying to do before threading in deeper layers of subtext and difficult-to-find diaries subtly hinting at heavily veiled and coded dramatic ironies.

But what can really up the ante in consultancy, aside from the multiple tasks it can comprise, is the fact your job can often be so open-ended that it's for you to define—and to do so in so many areas. If you miss something and don't identify it as an area that needs your guidance, then you've failed. Identifying something and making a mess of it is one thing—that's good old-fashioned *tier one*-type failure. But not even identifying it in the first place—that's a whole other level below. And, of course, depending on the project, you may soon run out of hands or sub-brains to help you keep on top of things. When hired to address a specific set of agendas with people who know games and know very clearly what they expect of you, this is less of a problem. But when working on games where your co-partners are in the worlds of TV or book publishing, for example, and seek to embrace digital interactivity, areas of responsibility considerably increase—the people who worked alongside you in the past who may have taken care of or warned you about certain issues or prevented you from needing to be fully aware of these issues may no longer be there. In which case now's the time to channel the best producers, designers, programmers, artists, and sound engineers you've ever worked with and ask yourself: what they would say, what they would do?

BOUNDARIES AND LIMITATIONS

Consultancy can be a curse and blessing in equal measure. At times it really is a matter of what you make of it, and a job of just a few days or a couple of weeks can develop into something far longer term as people become aware how invaluable your contributions are, not just because you identify problems, but also, of course, because you're able to offer or even implement solutions. However, a good consultant is obviously one who is cost effective and doesn't outstay their welcome. If you can get in, do your job, and get out again you'll ultimately be remembered more kindly by those you leave behind—which may mean more work in the future, either with that company or at new ones those people go to, and perhaps better longer term relationships with industry people in general. A good consultant is genuinely *efficient* as well as wise, hardworking, beloved, good-looking, etc.; in any event, unless you're loving the project, the chances are you'll have your own motivations for wanting to get the project done and get out the door—not the least of which might be to work on something new you may be about to lose unless you can start very soon, or to spend more time at home catching up on games everyone is referencing but you haven't played, instead of working hundreds, if not thousands of miles away from where you live and from the people you actually set out to try and live with.

At other times you'll be all too painfully aware you have no authority to change anything that in your very considered opinion, beyond any doubt, needs changing—and fast. You may feel like your hands are tied but your head's on the block; like you're a voice in the wilderness going ever so slowly but very definitely crazy. While this might not exactly sound uplifting, at times like this it can be helpful to remember that if you weren't needed you wouldn't be there, and the people you're working with all have their own concerns and are all trying to get their own jobs done, and they may be looking to you to help them figure out how to work with you. The chances are you may have much more experience than they do working with new people in high pressure situations with short lead times *in your specialist areas of expertise*—and so part of performing in your job is helping your new and temporary colleagues understand how best to work with you.

You should also bear in mind that you never know what may be said between colleagues and employers after you've completed your work on the project (just as, equally, you may not know before or during). This isn't mentioned to induce terminal paranoia, but because if you push through your ideas and solutions, even if you're utterly convinced of their rightness, and you do this without everyone else being onboard, then expect it to fall apart when you leave. It'll be like building a plane and expecting it to hold together with tape and string once it takes off. From the moment you start work as a consultant, you need to be projecting ahead to the time you leave. You need to try and ensure that when you do leave your coworkers have a common understanding of the areas you were hired to work on.

Ultimately, getting the job done is what you're being paid for. Getting the job done well involves ensuring it doesn't fall to pieces the moment you leave. You'll have no capacity to champion your solutions when you're not there, so you should hope to convince people who will still be there to take on that mantle—and the more people you can get onboard, the better it's going to be for the project. What you're trying to ensure is that the solutions become more than just mantles and things to be borne—you're hoping they can excite and engage the team and bring unity where before there may have been confusion, conflict, and perhaps even inertia—and at that point you'd really be earning your keep, *assuming, of course, you have the right solutions.* But if you're going to start not believing in yourself and your understanding of how games and stories work together, then this is unlikely to be the career choice for you until you do. (Of course, that's not advocating a non-critical and non-self-analytical approach to your solutions—that also, at this stage, is a given.)

EXERCISES

1. Imagine you've been hired by a large games company to consult on the story for their next blockbuster hit (which you've been told has run into trouble six months down the production line)—what are the key questions you would list before walking into your first meeting with the creative leads?
2. Some argue it's easier to consult on story elements for a game that has not yet entered production while others feel having some, or all, of a game's story already in place make a consultant's life easier—list the justifications for both perspectives and discuss which you prefer.

PROJECT

1. Choose any published game you like and create a presentation lasting no more than twelve minutes that explores improvements you would recommend to its writing. Topics may include plot, characters, dialogue, story world, and gameplay integration. End your presentation with suggestions as to why you think the developers did not pursue the improvements you recommended. Consider why you think your suggestions would have improved the game, and if you think they could be justified in terms of the extra work, time, and production costs involved (if applicable).

Chapter 12 ADAPTATIONS: TURNING OTHER THINGS INTO GAMES

Things alter for the worse spontaneously, if they be not altered for the better designedly.

—Francis Bacon

BRIEF TERMS

AAA PROJECT A games project that enjoys a particularly high budget, typically in excess of $30 million with associated expected high production values.

LICENSE HOLDERS The legal owners of an IP or brand's copyright.

SIDE-SCROLLING A games title in which the player's avatar travels through a world from left to right, or vice versa.

BEAT 'EM UP A game genre in which the primary gameplay centers around fighting enemies in direct, hand-to-hand combat.

Increasingly, games writers are tasked with turning other IP into games; movies, TV dramas, TV soaps, books, card games, toys, and characters in advertisements are all potential targets. These projects achieve mixed results. There are several reasons why so many adaptations have been poorly received by critics, fans, players, and shareholders. Perhaps most infamous of all movie-to-game adaptations, and one that still hangs over the industry like a silent specter, is the case of Atari's licensing of *E.T. the Extra-Terrestrial* from

Steven Spielberg. As mentioned in Chapter 1, it transpired that, in an attempt to bring the game to market in time for Christmas, six weeks was just not enough time to deliver very much—other than something that looked and played like it had been developed in about six (reputedly extremely fraught) weeks. As a result, sales suffered. Most of Atari's five million *E.T.* cartridges looked set for indefinite stays in warehouses. So, the decision was made to at least free the space, and they were transported to a New Mexico landfill. When people found the site, Atari crushed the games and had the landfill filled in with cement. Without definitive proof these events ever happened (at least on the scale told—instead of the millions of copies speculated, only around 1,300 copies were found in the site excavated in Alamogordo, New Mexico, when it was excavated in 2014), the story has taken on an intoxicating mythical quality that has further added to its enduring (cautionary) presence in the minds of games developers.

Some reasons game adaptations fail are likely to be specific to particular projects, but it's equally likely the majority of reasons are shared across most of them. It's worth keeping in mind that, for all the many sun-bleached and fresh carcasses of disasters littering this landscape, it's not impossible to get things right. *GoldenEye 007*™, *Star Wars: Knights of the Old Republic*, *Batman: Arkham Asylum*, and *Viva Piñata*™ are beacons of hope for all of us in the field of adaptations.

There's no doubt this kind of work can be taxing and complex for a games writer—as well as perilous. You may encounter stakeholders from media with conflicting backgrounds with different agendas, often with limited understanding or appreciation of how their respective medias work at a creative or business level. This could have been the case with successful science fiction thriller movie, *Minority Report* (itself an adaptation of Philip K. Dick's short story *The Minority Report*), which spawned a corresponding game criticized in some quarters for providing a player experience that doesn't faithfully reproduce the movie experience. Game levels were, in one review, accused of resembling a basic side-scrolling "beat 'em up" that failed to evoke the spirit of the movie, lacking many of the iconic elements first seen in the big-screen version (the gadgets, relationships, etc.).

However, open conflict from stakeholders may not be your worst enemy; glazed indifference can trump that. It may be none-too-popular a view among members of the game development community, but the argument behind the idea of turning "other things" into games remains sound, *in principle*. The marketing exposure of these brands and the mutual benefits of this kind of traction seem just too great to be resisted. However, although the principle is sound, it's very infrequently appropriately applied. While Ubisoft was said to have been given a high degree of creative freedom to create a game set in the universe of James Cameron's highly successful *Avatar* movie, the resulting title garnered some mediocre reviews that criticized gameplay for being formulaic and overly linear. One wonders the extent to which the title was beholden to a variety of voices from different camps—movie producers, game designers, marketing experts, and James Cameron himself would have all had potent voices that resulted in a title that was workmanlike and visually striking, but hardly revolutionary. No doubt scheduling and budget limitations also had significant parts to play. It's worth noting that the game still managed to sell 2.7 million units, which either illustrates how wrong the reviewers got it, or the potency of *Avatar*'s IP and Ubisoft's marketing.

Not everything can or should be a game; and those that are should very often be a very different kind of game from the one they ultimately turn out to be. In addition, the cost of securing licenses can sometimes be such that by the time one has been secured, the funds available to actually develop the game can become severely limited, presenting the perfect rendition of a games development catch-22.

FIGURE 12.1. Beware of what (license) you wish for.

So, this chapter is about how to do it right, how to know if the kinds of games you're making that derive from other media sources are taking the correct approach. The first point to make concerns integration. Just as writers are aware of the cyclical debate that revolves around the primacy of plot over character or character over plot, game adaptations draw a writer into the same kind of endless loop. Nothing you do at the creative level can truly be divorced from the business parameters of an adaptation. Everything you do as a writer on an adaptation needs to respond to what producers, coders, artists, animators, designers, and other stakeholders are telling you about the project.

KEY QUESTIONS

In the same way that any project begins with an understanding of the brief, in consulting on a game adaptation of a brand, you need to ask a series of questions of the project and those who are looking for your guidance on it. The earlier you are involved, the more of these questions you can ask and the more detailed the answers you may hope to elicit. These questions might be duly summarized as follows:

- What? Why? Who?
- Promises?
- Potential?
- Restrictions?
- Process?
- Planet Earth?

First, a tripartite question, What? Why? Who? It's vital to ask *What?* because the project may not necessarily lend itself naturally to the creation of an engaging game, and even if it does, people coming from different media often have a different understanding of what a game actually is and what the experience of playing one involves; a title centered around broadcasting the news and delivering the weather hasn't topped the charts yet, for good reason. The project could be a predominantly interactive experience, perhaps with game-like elements to it. The project could have its focus more on a social network or a community. The project could be a series of mini-games threaded together by some other possibly non-game-like element that makes sense in connection with the brand. What is the tone? This is often set directly by the brand, but are you doing a straight version of it or a parody of it? What are the aims of the project? What's the relationship between this project and any pre-existing media connected to the brand, or any media that is being simultaneously developed or that seems likely to be developed in the near or perceivable future?

Why are the license holders making the game? The answer won't necessarily be for profit on unit sales, or in-app purchases, or micro transactions. The answer might be marketing-led. The project could be intended to extend a brand that already exists in one or more other formats as part of a marketing department spend relating to another project that's intended to be the real revenue generator. For example, a movie company may decide to make a game out of its marketing budget that it distributes for free, fanning the flames of box office attendance and giving the same movie marketing profile well into the release of the DVD, Blu-Ray™, or digital download. Alternatively, a branded game may be made to reward loyal fans and to consolidate a fan base. The more you understand about why the license holder is embarking on this endeavor, the better equipped you are to tailor an appropriate solution to their needs. Be sure you have a clear answer to *why*. If a license holder does it because they can, because they feel they should, or because everyone else is doing this kind of thing, these are warning signs the project lacks clear goals or an understanding of the task in hand.

Who? Who are you making the game for? Who is the core market? Who is in the supplementary market? Be specific. If you're making a game for very young children, you need to remember that it's the parents who will buy it, so you need to appeal to their sense of what gaming activity is appropriate for their children to engage in, as well as provide gaming activity that fits with the brand itself.

Promises? What are the inherent promises that come with a brand? What is the beating heart of the property you're about to adapt? What will people expect to be included in the game once they hear of the adaptation? What do you know for certain will cause disappointment if potential players hear those things are not in the game? The answer lies within each brand itself and the way it has been, is being, or is about to be culturally absorbed. A *Ben 10* title, for example, would leave players feeling cheated if there were no transformation mechanics inside the core gameplay. In a similar vein, a game version of the classic comedy movie *Monty Python's Life of Brian* would feel lacking if it didn't deliver the same tone of voice, recreations of the movie sets, its characters, snippets of dialogue, the voices of the original cast, artwork associated with Terry Gilliam's opening and closing credits, as well as the well-known music. People may be forgiving if some elements are missing, but miss too many and you've broken too many promises. This matters because it's these promises, even if often in intangible and undeclared forms, that usually lie behind the reason to adapt in the first place; there's a belief that people will find the brand's inherent promises engaging enough to make the adaptation worthwhile.

Potential? In many ways linked to the *Promises* question, this is really a question concerned with the gameplay potential inherent in the brand, or at least the potential for people to engage with the brand in any kind of interactive way.

This may be more immediately apparent with a TV show like *Top Gear*, which is about motor vehicles, predominantly cars, a little bit about celebrities driving reasonably priced cars over a test track, and quite a lot about the delivery styles, obsessions, opinions, and interactions of its presenters. In this case you would be clear, right from the beginning, that you're looking in the direction of a driving game or a driving-themed quiz game—at the very least about something that relates to cars. This sort of potential can be harder to discern with other brands.

CASE STUDY: CORONATION STREET

In 2009 we were hired to work on a trial game concept using the brand of the popular British TV soap opera, *Coronation Street*. (Ultimately the game did not proceed to development, due to the publisher, Mindscape, re-assessing their own business priorities in the DS market.) With this brand the potential gameplay possibilities were very hard to perceive. A large cast of characters did all the kinds of things soap characters did; they talked, argued, fell in love, had affairs, lied, argued, got ill, planned murders, covered up mistakes, had babies, argued some more, got into fights, ran away, became mentally unstable, got engaged, got married, got divorced, got injured, got sent to prison, turned up late to work, got sacked, got hired, turned up out of nowhere after several years of absence, found they were unsuspectingly related to other characters, and argued again. There was no shortage of story matter, but how could this be turned into a game? The answers aren't always to be found in obvious places, and don't always present themselves in an obvious form. One game-like element we detected was linked to an association in the program with pigeons; both in the opening sequence of the show that features shots of pigeons, and through the long running and much loved (though now deceased) character Jack Duckworth, who was a renowned "pigeon fancier," that is, someone who keeps and breeds pigeons—sometimes, though not exclusively, homing or racing pigeons. (If this all sounds like an utterly implausible British oddity that's kept safely away from the rest of the world, it's reported that Mike Tyson himself indulges in this pastime.) In gameplay terms this tiny seed led to the idea of a collectible pigeon mini-game that became increasingly playable the more pigeons the player collected, which they could best achieve by being in the game for extended periods of time.

However, just because you've been approached to help turn existing intellectual property into a game doesn't necessarily mean you should hack about at that property and wildly distort it in order to deliver something that approximates a game. This is where the promises of the brand are intricately tied to its gameplay potential. After addressing the other questions thus far—*What? Why? Who?*—it's not uncommon to find the term *game* has been used by makers of other media very loosely. The term may be a placeholder one, standing in for any kind of interactive experience, until it can be more closely defined and refined, according to the various needs of the project, not least of which are the promises inherent in the brand. Shakespeare's *Macbeth* can be turned into a game. But it's hard to envisage a way of designing it and hewing gameplay potential from it that delivers on the play's own inherent *promises* and doesn't, in fact, work contrary to them—killing the very hand that feeds it. However, if a broader interpretation is permitted and a *game* is not essential, but, rather, something *game-like* that offers interactivity would fulfill the project's requirements, then this is substantially less problematic. The project can then stay closer to the text, the story, and its characters. This may not seem to be games writing in the true sense, but then part of being a games writer is knowing when something should be a game and how much of a game it should be; knowing where to use game-like elements and when not to, knowing when to open or close the valve of interactivity, to let more through or less, according to the project's needs. Many AAA projects may have a tendency to maximize interactivity and pipe it in as seamlessly as possible, with the storytelling intruding as inconspicuously as possible. But this doesn't mean this approach is right for all projects—especially when those projects are defined by their stories and elements that do not inherently allow themselves to be wholly subsumed by the nature of games. Third-person action adventure *Dante's Inferno*® is very clearly a game. Yet it is so removed from its inspiration of Dante's *The Divine Comedy* that a very different approach must be taken if the integrity of that source is the overriding concern for the developers, publishers, and customers.

Restrictions? Inevitably there are restrictions at the business, technical, and manpower levels. What is the platform, the budget, and the schedule? What are the restrictions on the code, on the memory space, on the delivery method, on the team's skill set? Trying to deliver the epic sense of adventure experienced in Tolkien's *Lord of the Rings* through a mobile platform would be a challenge, whereas creating an expansive MMO universe for the PC platform is a far better fit for the IP (as has indeed been done by games developer, Turbine). Yet there are further issues to consider. If adapting a TV show inherently linked with a specific host, how will you respond if that host does not sign up to the game? Does it mean the game cannot go ahead at all, because you're breaking a promise that's too important? Or, are there ways around the absence of that host that nevertheless still deliver on the essence of the brand? It's not always practical to wait until you have all talent agreements in place before beginning work on a project, given the length of time it can take to secure these, but embarking without them is certainly a risk to be fully aware of. On the *Coronation Street* project key promises of the brand are connected to its location, its characters, and the stories revolving and evolving in and around these characters. The location presented no particular hurdle and we had good access to set exteriors and interiors. Yet the characters and stories were far more problematic. We couldn't tell a story that would call for reinventing any of the backstory, reinterpreting any backstory already in existence, or adding new backstory that gave new dimensions to existing (or previous) characters. We couldn't tell a story that might in any way prejudice anything the TV writers wanted to explore in the future—and, keep in mind, *Coronation Street* is the longest running TV soap currently in production; it celebrated its 50th anniversary in 2010, moved to new studios in 2011, is a mainstay of ITV's program scheduling, and looks set to run indefinitely through the 21st century—so that's an awful lot of potential future to tiptoe around. We could invent new characters, but what would be the point in that? They would mean nothing to the core audience this game was to be specifically aimed at. This audience wanted to see characters they knew and loved—that's what made the game appealing to them, and that's what would make it feel like it was *Coronation Street*. This created considerable problems since the promise of the game seemed to lead to a character-led story-based game.

Process? How well do your clients understand the process involved in making games? This matters if they are to understand something of how you need to work and the kind of resources you need access to and the times and means by which you are likely to want access to them. This matters even more if the client is taking a more hands-on role in the adaptation. At any rate, it's certainly likely to matter when it comes to signing off on deliveries and paying invoices and developing a healthy working relationship, where delays and difficulties can be addressed with the appropriate levels of urgency and resources required. Ultimately it's in everyone's interest to make the game as good as it can be and to make the right kind of game for the right kind of people and get it to customers at the right time. Often TV, movie, and book publisher people don't speak the same language as games development people. From experience, some kind of executive producer role is a good solution. The person in this role should be bilingual, or as fluent in all the relevant media languages as possible, and should be able to move smoothly between the relevant camps to retain the integrity of the initial stakeholders and ensure that the game's delivered in an interactive media, while also being fully conversant with the restrictions and limitations facing the developer.

Planet Earth? In essence, check that you and everyone involved in the project are still on Planet Earth. Check that the thoughts and ideas you're having regarding your creative approach to adapting the brand are realistic. Given the time you have to make it, the resources you have, the team you have, the technology you're working with, the platform you're developing on, and the parameters of your business intentions, does your approach actually make sense? And, if it does, you need to check that no one has effectively beaten you to it and produced something so similar as to invalidate your approach. And make sure that no one is currently developing something so similar that you're going to lose out to them in the inevitable marketing heavyweight slugging match.

Understanding integration between the creative, the business, and the technical elements and asking of yourself, the project, and the stakeholders of the project these six key questions is the approach we take regarding adaptations. If you can find good answers to these questions, then all you need is inspiration and luck to ensure you never make anything that has to be buried in a New Mexico landfill—be it metaphorical, mythological, or real.

EXERCISES

1. Does every form of IP, regardless of the medium in which it was originally created, ultimately contain elements that lend themselves to the creation of a good video game, or are there certain creative channels that should simply be left alone? Discuss.

   Linked to this, is there a hierarchy of media that ranges from "highly suitable for adaptation into a game" down to "not suitable at all"? Justify your response.

2. Take a game of your choosing and write a two- to three-page pitch document that explores how it could be turned into a radio play. Be sure to consider the following:

   The core radio story and how it relates to the existing game story.

   Should you faithfully reproduce the game title's story, or change it in places?

   How characters from the game will translate into radio characters.

   The need to communicate story using just audio channels.

   How gameplay might help inform the overall plot.

3. What do you feel is the primary driving force for adaptations? Do they mainly stem from a desire on the part of brand owners to generate more awareness and demand for their products, or are more altruistic motives often at play? Are these the right reasons?

PROJECT

1. Choose a well-known TV show and, in a document no longer than three pages, describe how you might adapt it into a game. Be sure to briefly answer the following questions:

   What are the key 'promises' of this show? (What things do you think players will expect to see and be able to do in this game?)

   What sort of gameplay would it comprise?

   What platform or platforms would it be for?

   What kind of story structure would you choose?

   What characters would you use?

   What abilities will they have?

   How will these abilities link into the gameplay and are they linked to the logic of each character's personality?

Chapter 13

Other Roles of the Games Writer

Choose a job you love, and you will never have to work a day in your life.

— Confucius

THE GAMES WRITER'S PROFESSION: SOMETIMES INVOLVES ACTUAL WRITING.

BRIEF TERMS

CROSSMEDIA STORYTELLING The act of telling a coherent story in such a way that the story—or at least the story world—may be ported to a variety of platforms and formats. Crossmedia sees platforms as brand extension opportunities.

TRANSMEDIA STORYTELLING The act of telling a coherent story across a variety of platforms and formats. Transmedia uses the variety of platforms as the very means through which the storytelling is done.

FIRST-PERSON PERSPECTIVE Gameplay experienced from the avatar's point of view.

Being a games writer can and often does include working in a number of other areas of game development. Some of these roles may come your way as a result of your ability to combine words effectively. Others may come as a result of your understanding of the themes, backstories, characters, and processes behind the key story. Others may be connected to the depth of your understanding of the script itself and how to deliver the dramatic potential within what you have written. While perhaps not an exhaustive list of these various tasks, the following are among the most common:

- Additional story documents
- Back of box copy
- Instruction manual
- Guide book
- Associated prose novel
- Trailer(s)
- Audio casting and direction
- Motion capture consultancy and/or direction
- Website copy and other elements
- Other marketing copy

ADDITIONAL STORY DOCUMENTS

Besides the documents we've discussed so far, a game can benefit from the creation of other document types if the story warrants it or the team feel they're useful.

Player Journey Document

A short prose document designed to give the reader a vivid experience of what it's like to play the game for a defined period of time. It might focus on the gameplay experience, detailing how the player utilizes the UI and control system to interact with the game world and overcome obstacles placed in their path. This is useful to give the teams a clear idea how the game will 'work' for the player and how they'll navigate the UI.

Alternately, the document might present the experience of playing the game through the eyes of the player, tracking their perception of the story, the way it unfolds, the characters they may care about, the moments of gameplay that may be of special note, and the feelings they may have as they play, and the ways these feelings and thoughts may change as the game progresses. Take a look at our sample of what a player journey document might look like for popular platform-puzzler, *Limbo*.

LIMBO PLAYER JOURNEY

The screen fades up. We're in a deeply shadowed, dream-like forest torn from a flickering black and white 1920s movie. Huge tree trunks stretch skyward out of shot and the darkness is punctuated by soft shafts of gray light. The silhouette of a small boy wakes and stands—suddenly you're in control of him. Using the left thumbstick, you make him run to the right, across the shadowy terrain; the screen scrolls to follow. Pressing the A button, you jump him over a small obstacle and get the feel for how he moves. Trees pass in the background and foreground, the boy's steps crunch softly on the hidden ground, and the feeling of being totally alone presses in. After a few seconds, he encounters a huge tree trunk lying on the ground, angling upwards; pushing the thumbstick to the right, you make him run along it to find it leads to a steep drop. Pressing A, you have the boy spring into the air and plunge several yards to land on a steep bank that whisks him downward, to a small ledge abutting a ditch. Tilting the thumbstick to the right and pressing A at just the right time, you make the boy leap over it and run to the right, through more shadowy forest. The silhouette of a platform perched on the edge of what looks like a cliff slides into view; beneath it is a mine cart with a handle and, hanging from a stray plank of wood, a rope dangles over the cliff edge. The platform's clearly out of the boy's reach. Running up to the cart, you press B to have him grab its handle, then angle your thumbstick left so he pulls it out from under the platform. After a few yards, it stops, held in place by a short rope. Letting go of the B button so the boy lets go of the cart handle, you tilt the thumbstick to the right so the boy runs towards the cart; you then push A to have him jump up to grab its edge before pushing up on the thumbstick to make him clamber up onto its top. Seeing he's now high enough to make it onto the platform, you push the thumbstick to the right and press A to have him jump onto it. He can now reach the rope . . .

This can be a useful tool to check whether the on-screen story developments seem to make sense, and the release of information makes the overall, experience that's unfolding, coherent.

Character Backstory Document

This is a prose document that explores some or all of the backstory of one, some, or all of the story's characters. Creating this kind of document can be useful in developing a character's voice or understanding elements of a character that need deeper exploration to give them the requisite depth for the story they are part of. The backstory might be written in a first-person point of view, channeling their voice and giving a sense of their internal dialogues and the way they think. Alternatively, it might be written in the third person, giving a narratorial point of view on the character's moral values, opinions, ideas, actions, and relationships.

Take a look at our example below, which shows a small section from a possible character backstory for Adam English (one of the characters in our fictitious *Arcadia* game, found in Chapter 6's Projects). Here, we want to get a little inside his head, find out what he thinks about himself, his hopes, doubts, and dreams, as understanding these will help us know how he'll react when thrown into the disturbing world of Arcadia.

ADAM ENGLISH BACKSTORY

I guess a lot of my teachers think I'm pretty average, which doesn't bother me much, though I get the feeling I've never really been pushed, you know? Before he met mom, dad spent a lot of his life traveling to cool, exotic places, doing amazing things. One day I'll do something daring and maybe even a little bit crazy! Skydiving or a desert trek! What am I saying? Even my *crazy* is a bit boring . . . I'll never get Helena to go out with me, not when she's the coolest girl in school and I'm the guy nobody notices. Still, I know I've gotta stop being so negative—I've got a lot going for me (as mom keeps saying): I made the high school swim team last week and even got Terry Bradley to stop bullying me—if it's one thing I can't stand, it's someone with nothing better to do than pick on people. Still, I think Helena liked it when I called him out at lunch yesterday, right there in front of the whole school . . .

World Backstory Document

This document (or series of documents) could be created to understand philosophical, political, spiritual, historical, scientific, geographic, mythic, thematic, or any other elements of your story world, which help to underpin it, though it will not necessarily be evident within any of the scripts you write.

Environment-As-Story Document

This document helps track the storytelling that will be evident within the game's environment, such as the posters on walls, the names of shops, restaurants, gas stations, cinemas (and what's showing), the graffiti, the advertising billboards, the video displays, the road signs, and the corporate messages disseminated in a game like EA's *Dead Space*. Even if you are not inventing a world like the underwater city of Rapture from *BioShock*, and are working with a very naturalistic world, will you use real names, or names that are intended to sound real and believable? Be careful that you don't accidentally use names or elements that are already trademarked—always make sure that your newly created car brand, for example, is not the name of an existing household cleaner.

BACK OF BOX COPY

You might be asked to write the back of box copy—this is the descriptive text found on the reverse of the game box or, with the advent of digital distribution, on the sales section of a title's game site. If the project you're working on is large enough, the publisher's marketing department will normally handle this element. Back of box copy is there not only to efficiently *tell* someone about the game they're thinking about purchasing, but more crucially it's also there to *sell* it to them. It needs to be compelling and persuasive enough to convince them to buy your game over the rival titles available that week. This is, in a very real sense, the elevator pitch for the whole title.

Typically this kind of text begins with an explanatory section that succinctly details the story, and this lends proceedings a context before a second section lists, in more detail, interesting (hopefully unique) gameplay elements the player would enjoy should they purchase the title. Story is once again a useful vehicle, in this case through which to sell gameplay. Consider the following two examples, both describing the same, fictitious (before you try to buy it) game.

Box Copy Stripped of All Story Elements

Guide your avatar through a variety of environments filled with hostile avatars on a journey to reach a goal or place that doesn't really hold any meaning beyond mere personal accomplishment! Use thumbsticks and push controller buttons to make your avatar leap across gaps, climb things, avoid things, and do things to stop dynamic obstacles from being a threat to your avatar! Do this long enough and eventually the game will end!

- Unlock things that will mean you'll need less button presses to stop enemy avatars or the same number to stop more powerful ones!
- Explore environments that look different from one another!
- Take things from dynamic obstacles to help you defeat more of them!

Box Copy Using Story Elements

When disgraced mage Timothy Blast's young daughter Tabitha is kidnapped by The Evil Wizarding Organization, there's only one thing he can do—fight back! Join Blast as he learns new spells and magics his way across the world on a valiant quest to save Tabitha and the land from eternal darkness!

- Unlock a huge armory of powerful spells!
- Explore exciting new worlds, packed with fantastic creatures!
- Defeat cunning foes, use their magic to fuel your own!

Be sure to make your text succinct—it should set up the conflict and player's goal in a line or two, or risk losing the reader's interest (there are a lot of games out there, all eager to have their box copy read).

INSTRUCTION MANUAL

Normally written in conjunction with the design team, an instruction manual could involve little more than editing the text to make sure grammar, spelling, and punctuation are all flawless. But some publishers prefer instruction manuals to be written "in-character" as if truly originating from the game world—these require more careful thought and in such instances the games writer should ensure the tone is kept consistent with that found in the game. An instruction manual needs, at the very least, to feature useful gameplay and game world information laid out in a clear, concise manner. These typically provide players with the bare minimum amount of information to play the game and use its various features. Increasingly, however, this kind of content is placed online, because it's more accommodating of last minute changes and cheaper than print.

GUIDE BOOK

Guide books are typically far larger than basic instruction manuals and can run to several hundred pages long. (Though, as with instruction manuals, they're now more often online, in some form, rather than released as print editions.) They normally feature a wealth of information designed to grant the reader full access to most aspects of the gameplay and game story world. This information typically includes:

- Detailed game maps (usually illustrating points of interest, item locations, etc.)
- Information on all in-game items, abilities, strategies
- Mission descriptions and walkthroughs
- Detailed character analysis
- Information on enemies
- Game art

ASSOCIATED PROSE NOVEL

Developers and publishers might want their game accompanied by a novel, or perhaps a series of them, taking place in their title's universe. These stories might feature, or even revolve around, key game characters that sometimes take part in new adventures or simply have their game adventures retold in prose. However, it's not unknown for these stories to feature totally new characters for readers to enjoy, as they come with far fewer complications and won't need to be as carefully checked for inconsistencies with the source material or tread on the toes of potential sequels.

TRAILERS

It has become standard practice to create and distribute trailers for a game weeks and sometimes months before its release. Much like movie trailers, they feature tantalizing glimpses of future gameplay that help generate interest and hopefully excitement in the gaming community. Again, these can require the deft touch of the games writer to ensure the final trailer is structured in such a way as to ensure it's compelling and, importantly, coherent from both a story and gameplay perspective, with an added sensibility as to what spoilers to include and what teases are too oblique to be powerful.

AUDIO CASTING AND DIRECTION

Many games writers also take on the role of an audio director, as in many ways it's a natural extension from writing. This may initially involve being responsible for casting the actors needed to record the game's audio. Finding the right fit for each of your characters is not simply about locating the best voice among the submissions, it's also about finding the best actor. While someone might sound fantastic for that "hot sultry femme fatale" you've written for your game, be sure they've got the artistic range to deliver the gamut of emotions required of them. While it's relatively straightforward for a voice actor to sound good while using their normal voice, the real test exists in their ability to deliver emotions like hate, fear, and amusement convincingly, time after time.

Audio directing is a subject worthy of a book in its own right. Again, a large number of games writers have become skilled audio directors, able to successfully helm a recording session (or series of sessions) to ensure a game's character lines are recorded to quality, budget, and schedule. This is normally done working closely with an audio engineer responsible for successfully capturing the actors' reads and preparing the resulting audio files for processing. Make no mistake; this role can require the patience of a saint, the diplomacy of an ambassador, and the eloquence of a gifted orator to get what is needed from an expensive day's recording.

MOTION-CAPTURE CONSULTANCY AND/OR DIRECTION

Some developers use motion-capture technology (also known as "mo-cap") to capture the movements of real people, which is turned into animation data and then handled by the animators and programmers so the characters move in naturalistic ways, adding to the believability of the characters, scenes, and therefore immersion in the story. A mo-cap director ensures the right action happens at the right time in the right way. Since this facet of game production is closely linked to game story, some writers have also taken on this role. Even if a developer uses a separate mo-cap director, a games writer may also be present as a consultant, there to advise the director when necessary on story and character related details.

WEBSITE COPY AND OTHER ELEMENTS

A games writer's ability with words might be called upon to write Website copy for the game. This could include creating text about the game world, instructional or tutorial information, and marketing copy. A games writer might also be asked to help write and produce mini-episodic movies, perhaps with some connection to the game story (perhaps a parallel story or drawing from backstory), or movies containing development, design, or story information on the games title.

Crossmedia Storytelling

There might be times when a games writer is asked to help transfer the game story they've helped create to other media platforms—this could include helping put together comic book, TV, or movie concepts. The value of IP today means that many studios will want to make the best use of a story brand, which will include, among other things, exploring its value across a range of delivery channels. *Avatar*, the video game we mentioned in the last chapter when discussing adaptations, attempts—among other things—to allow players to experience the vibrant world of Pandora from an interactive perspective. This alternative avenue it presents is a form of crossmedia storytelling that, if nothing else, deepens the experience for movie fans and gamers alike, should they choose to both buy the game and watch the film.

Other Marketing Copy

The marketing department might ask a games writer to help them write a variety of sales-related material. This might include a game's tagline—that is, a sentence that helps brand the experience, summing up the game in a memorable slogan (such as *Driver 3*'s *Good. Bad. Both.* tagline).

EXERCISES

1. Create a sample back of box copy for Chapter 6's *Arcadia*, outlining not only the story, but possible gameplay selling points.
2. Choose an existing game title you like and create a player journey document for its first five minutes. Where possible, include the following information:

   What does the player see on the screen?

   How do they use the control system to navigate the initial stages of the game?

   What do they hear?

   What choices does the player make?
3. Create three taglines for *Code Obsidian*—these should instantly sum up the world and tone of the game, as well as work on the back of the box and in online material.
4. Create three new taglines for the real game title of your choice—these should instantly sum up the world and tone of the game, as well as work on the back of the box and in online material.

PROJECTS

1. Draft a one-page outline for a short story to accompany the release of Chapter 6's *Code Obsidian.*
2. Create eight unique in-game advertisements designed to help bring the world of *Code Obsidian* to life—these can be either audio-visual (i.e., for the Internet or TV) or purely audio (i.e., for the radio).
3. Write a three- to five-page short story for a game world of your own creation. Your story can cover any aspect of the game world—its lore or character backstory, for example.
4. Write up a two- to three-page player journey for a game of your own design you'd like to make. Cover no more than a ten-minute experience in the game. What does the player do, feel, see, and hear while playing? Convey clearly what it would be like for a player to experience your game (don't just use adjectives, try to convey details that explain why this fictional player feels what they feel).

Part III Beyond the Basics

Now, let us take a step or two back and readjust our lenses to consider the macro. The following are a series of essays or collected thoughts that move us beyond the more straightforward presentation of games writers' tasks and the ways by which they might accomplish them. These essays and thoughts combine practical topics that are current concerns among our peers and fellow practitioners, such as story layering, with theoretical topics, that seek to shed light on why a writer may do what they do, and what might change about what they do in the future. Yet, such is the nature of the constant readjustment of macro to micro that even here, in a chapter ostensibly macro-oriented, we still sometimes return to the micro, as moving beyond the basics causes us to look with greater detail and with greater clarity at what a plot is and how it works, and, in exploring possible future approaches, detail inevitably comes into play if the thoughts are to hold any water. Perhaps the preceding section could be said to contain the kind of information that, in time, practicing games writers know to such an extent they barely feel the need to think about. In which case, this section could be said to contain the kind of information they may more frequently think about, as they constantly examine and re-examine details of their techniques and explore the more experimental fringes of what they do and the creative field in which they operate.

Chapter 14

WHY HAVE STORIES AT ALL?

Integrating a plot inside game design is one of the hardest things for a game designer. If a game has an involving, immersive story but poor gameplay, it's a failed product. In this medium gameplay should drive narrative, not the other way around.

—Bruno Patatas, Creative Director, Biodroid Entertainment, Lisbon, in conversation, 2011

BRIEF TERMS

LUDOLOGISTS Proponents of ludology, the study of games and other forms of play, where the emphasis is on their abstract systems in their own right, not on anything they may incidentally represent.

NARRATOLOGISTS Proponents of narratology, the theory and study of story structure. Within game theory there is a debate between ludologists and narratologists; the latter push for an understanding in relation to story theory and storytelling.

META-STORIES Stories that are beyond the usual limits of what and where a story is thought to be.

If games are about winning and losing, and stories are more (or less) about something very different, such as insight, comfort, or sense-making, then it is pertinent to ask why games should muddy themselves with stories at all. We might further contemplate this in light of the view held by some that the parts of a game taken up with story are the parts you can't play and therefore not actually games. Although not mutually exclusive, and sharing many of the same concerns, game design goals are seldom consistently on the same trajectory as story aspirations.

STORY LOGIC VERSUS GAME LOGIC

It's far from uncommon to find a designer proposing something they know will play well in a game and to hear the games writer has problems with the story logic. "Here we can shoot sky lobsters because the way in which they swoop down and swerve provides players with a fresh form of gameplay, and the player won't have had this kind of experience for a while!" meets "But the sky lobsters are our friends and we've spent the entire game working to save them." "Here," says the writer, "we need a close, confined space to heighten the psychological tension and convey a sense of uncovering a deep, dark secret." "We need it big enough for combat," replies the designer. On some occasions story goals are wholly contrary to game goals. A story with a character who never faces any moment of failure, a story that never hits an obstacle, a setback, a *but* moment, not merely an *and* moment (as discussed in Chapter 6, Outlines & Treatments) is likely to be deeply unsatisfying, if it constitutes a story at all. Yet to force a player to fail in order to meet story demands is to break a golden rule of game design and flirt with the very real danger of the player leaving the game in disgust, never to return. Storytelling frequently reaps huge benefits in subjecting its protagonist to a "long dark night," where they are so emotionally and/or physically buffeted and battered by their antagonists and the broader antagonism of their story world that they are stripped back emotionally, spiritually, and physically to all but nothing and forced to overcome the biggest obstacles of all, shortly before the story's climax. This kind of character growth ensures the value of the protagonist's ultimate victory is as emotional and dramatically engaging as possible. Yet to deliver this kind of storytelling interactively can, in an FPS, amount to taking all a player's hard-earned weapons and upgrades away. For example, towards the end of FPS *BioShock*, protagonist Jack Ryan is systematically stripped of health and control of his powers by antagonist Frank Fontaine once Ryan discovers the truth about his past—this forces the player to work to reverse the attack and claim back Ryan's abilities and health before finally confronting Fontaine in a battle to the death. In a fantasy RPG, this can amount to returning a player's maximum-level wizard, replete with immense and hard-won spell-casting abilities, to a low-level character far less able to raise a wand, let alone do anything with it. Not surprisingly, games do not routinely take this course; it would betray a player's vast emotional and time investment in the game, investments they expect to be rewarded, not penalized for; *BioShock*, as it turns out, is quick to return the player's abilities and health once their noticeable absence fulfills its purpose. Not delivering this disabling before the enabling, this nadir before the zenith, this burning away of the hero's lesser self before the phoenix of their true potential can rise is unquestionably a considerable restriction to storytelling.

Further, the (over) familiar amnesia trope has more to do with good game design theory than it does with the execution of bad (cliché-laden) story ideas. The obvious drive to have the player *playing* as soon as possible means there's an imperative to reduce non-playable story sections at the start of a game. Yet a player's knowledge of their playable character(s) only begins the moment the game begins (and knowledge is less valuable than experience). So, to have a game that's *playable* as soon as possible and to *also have a story with any depth*, with any layers of backstory (or to begin *in media res*, in the middle of things, and therefore in the midst of an exciting moment suitable for gameplay that also provides recourse to deeper elements of storytelling later on), generally means you either create dissonance +between what the player knows and what their character knows, or you create a character you can thrust quickly into action, but burdened with amnesia to retain that player and character shared experience connection (as in *BioShock*). These aren't the only choices—game stories with depth can be built without long non-playable sections, as mosaic story structures such as those used in the *Modern Warfare*™ series demonstrate. *Assassin's Creed*® also approaches accessing memories in a way that's interesting and conceptually a non-tired approach to recycling the amnesia trope. But, purely in game design terms, there is no contest in deciding which is inferior; to disconnect the player from their avatar is to disrupt a fundamental bond of sympathy and an understanding of game and story values and identities, and is a far riskier move than to deliver another re-telling of an amnesia-based story. Again, purely in game design terms, the amnesia-based story has repeatedly shown it works—it keeps player and avatar agency in-step with one another and permits a deeper story. With these kinds of complexities, among many others, let us re-state the question: *Why have stories at all?* Answers to this come in three main forms.

THE ARGUMENT AGAINST STORY IN GAMES

The first version, in its most curt form, is *don't*. Slightly more expansively, this might be rendered as: make games for gamers and stories for non-gamers, and never combine them. For players, games are about winning and losing, and for their respective audience, stories, whatever they're about, it's not winning or losing them; games are about progress, and stories are about obstacles. Some games can only be harmed by plot lines and character development. In a strategic-level war game that simulates the decisions of commanders like Generals Lee and Grant, to insert cut scenes and attempt to tell a Shelby Foote-style narrative of the war would make for a very different kind of game, at best suspending the gameplay while the non-playable sections of the experience are endured, at worst disrupting and openly interfering with the core game mechanics.

THE ARGUMENT FOR LIMITED STORY

A second version of an answer is that games very frequently and very definitely require stories. In one sense they often need them to explain player motivations and, by seeding story throughout the experience, the compulsion to know what happens next becomes an encouragement in continuing to play the game. It's impossible to overstate the extent to which stories are compelling and powerful things. The desire to know what happens next is what keeps Shahrazad alive in the *Arabian Nights*, and by broad (perhaps even reckless) metaphorical extension, we might find it similarly in keeping to suggest this is true for humanity too. In this sense games are harnessing the undoubted capacity of plots to engage and absorb. Further, characters are a very successful and proven way to elicit sympathy from an audience, regardless of how reactive that audience is. To this end, you are considerably more likely to see an image of a character in a game on the press release material than you are to see a picture of the controller configuration or a bullet point description of the gameplay mechanics. Characters engage us, and without characters and plot, games can be nothing more than simple mechanics possessing a limited capacity to absorb us. Yet there are problems with this view in that, even should one suggest that the type of absorption from *Tetris* is not the same as the absorption in plot—perhaps it is absorption at a different *level*—plot is ultimately *about* something. But without becoming mired in that debate, the more significant issue is that even though titles such as adventure games clearly have close relationships with plots, some genres do not need plot, and even those that do use them, including adventure games, may yet find there are ways to mesh games and stories without the latter providing mere motivation to gameplay; it is possible that stories can be even more deeply entwined with gameplay.

In another sense, we might say that games may not necessarily need plots, but without *themes* they may fail to engage with an audience in any enduring way. Try imagining *Space Invaders* without the theme. Try imagining a *Tomb Raider* game without Lara Croft, and without a theme or story-world context for any of your actions. Games are generally more compelling when they succumb to our need for stories. We're more compelled to think of our avatar as needing to jump across to the next plinth and then grab onto the tree trunk to swing up onto the stone wall in order to progress, rather than needing to press forward on a thumbstick and square at the same time and then, within the permitted time range, pressing the triangle button and lower-right shoulder button at the same time, and then the circle button, then releasing it within the confluence of the correct range of angles and velocity to provide the necessary trajectory to arrive at the correct three-dimensional coordinate. Without themes, games become nothing more than game mechanics, ultimately, sets of parameters being measured in reference to each other. As a game there is clearly nothing wrong with *Tetris* (in fact, very clearly, there is everything right with it), but the number of games with themes, characters, and plots clearly suggests there is a voracious appetite for them.

A senior games designer and studio head friend of ours once remarked that when interviewing applicants for game design positions he would ask them what they felt the secret to game design was. They would invariably reply the secret was to find fresh, new, interesting mechanics and to keep being as creative and imaginative as possible. "The answer I was looking for," he said, "was that games are inherently repetitive and good games designers know how to hide that and to work with their limitations." He went on to say: "if anyone ever told me that I'd hire them on the spot." Without the game mechanics being masked by story, their repetitive and restricted nature are wholly exposed. Many games do not boast game mechanics so intrinsically transfixing that they do not benefit, at some point, from the advantages that come with using stories.

Perhaps we may say, just as there are a limited number of basic plot types (as few as seven, depending on whom you listen to), there are, likewise, a limited number of game mechanic types (insert arguable number here), and that theme, together with the way a title is delivered, are the most potent elements in engaging an audience. Admittedly, this is rather a broad view given that, in a game, the way a theme is delivered also involves the approach taken regarding game mechanics; nevertheless, *Shooting Game 7: The Same Basic Mechanics* is not as compelling a proposition on our imaginations, even purely in terms of a title, as *Call of Duty: Black Ops*™. Theme gives an understandable context to the game mechanics—the theme is what, most of the time, first draws the player in (or repels them) and the part of the game which, in the case of most people most of the time, is the one that operates at the same frequency as their imagination, helping them believe they're a racing driver, a superhero, an adventurer, or a troll. Theme continues to work beyond the setup too, and we might say it gives a game a *meta-story* that is told purely by and in the process of playing the game. Consider games such as *Elite*™ or *Civilization*™, or the campaign mode of *Total War*™. In *Elite* you're a trans-galactic pilot, in *Civilization* the leader of a civilization spanning from the time humanity could harness the land and build crude settlements until the point at which your eyes bleed, and in *Total War* you control the military, political, and scientific destiny of your chosen nation through to successfully meeting victory conditions and a short congratulatory cinematic. Here the stories are developed through playing the games, and these games have built-in obstacles and problems that must be addressed in order to progress. They may be galactic police, space pirates, insufficient funds, the wrong kinds of goods available to trade, or space ports that need to be docked with, in the case of *Elite*. In *Civilization* these obstacles and problems may be barbarians, enemy troops, deep water, insufficient resources, backwards technology, or an unhappy population. In *Total War* these obstacles and problems may be insufficient morale, the wrong kinds of troops, or not enough troops in the right place at the right time. But in all cases we can identify clear problems in these games that need to be addressed in order to progress, and we may consider them to, essentially, be meta-stories that are literally *played out* by the player. At this point we may begin to consider that everything is ultimately a story. In its own way this is as extreme a view as the one suggesting stories and games don't mix and should never be combined. Might this really extend to games without theme?

Perhaps when playing *Brick Breaker*™ we are imagining breaking out of a prison cell, or attempting to smash through a wall to save someone on the other side. It's probably more likely we're telling a less overt story, and are running a simpler one in our heads, which is a story in so far as it's making sense of the activity within the context of our own lives. So, for example that story might be about how good (or otherwise) we are at this game, or about how much time we've spent on it today when we didn't plan to, or how our competency compares with a friend's. In any event, although this may often be the case, even when uncoupling from our truly conscious selves as we get pulled into another game of *Patience* or *Scopa*—and humans cannot help but turn their lives into stories, even encompassing or in some way acknowledging the most mundane elements of it—it feels a little disingenuous, and not a little perverse, to maintain these "pure" games are truly stories. These games are stories only in so far as every human activity may be perceived to be a game, and so the value of the definition becomes limited because it is so broad.

It should also be noted here games are not just about winning and losing, as any *D&D* or MMO player will tell you. Here a game does not reach a finite win/lose conclusion that resets the gaming environment ready for another "go." These games may encompass measurable success and failure states within them, but they are essentially experiential and continue to engage beyond the mere winning or losing, and they do so at the level of story, or theme, or character as story, not because a win or lose state is being indefinitely withheld. A 49th level Paladin has stories to tell that may be deeply related to successes and failures, but aren't necessarily wholly dependent on them, and these stories do not cease to exist on acquiring a 50th, 70th, or 100th level—they carry on for as long as the person behind the character continues to engage with them at an imaginative level.

THE ARGUMENT FOR STORY AS GAMEPLAY

The third main version of the answer is along the lines that stories are not necessarily the parts of a game you can't play. As noted in Chapter 8, which examines environmental storytelling, games have objectives and obstacles to be overcome, just as characters have goals and obstacles they must overcome, and these *can* be reconciled in such a way as they amount to the same thing—at least for limited periods of a game/game story. This is why there's excitement about environmental storytelling, because the older way of meshing stories with games, with discrete cut scenes you sat back and watched (historically, as a kind of reward for your achievements and to offer entertainment while the next part of the game loaded), has huge limitations. These cut scenes stop you from playing and, however helpful they are in explaining context or as a means of subtly placing tutorials into the skein of the game design, they are far from ideal. So, what we may broadly term *environmental storytelling* is an approach that promises the best of storytelling—the engagement derived from theme and character as well as, potentially, from plot—but without the worst of it—the intrusiveness and non-interactivity.

Stories can also *be* gameplay, as developers like Telltale and Quantic Dream, and games such as *Until Dawn* and *Life is Strange* show, where players make decisions on how a story plays out. Here the lines between a story-driven game and an interactive story really do become intriguingly blurred.

EXERCISES

1. Take a video game of your choosing that has a story; list its mechanics. Use this list to create a one- to two-page design outline for a story-free game. Now create a one-page story outline for your new game.
2. Consider the mechanics discussed in this chapter. Give an example of a game that uses very few and yet still manages to remain a satisfying experience. Why was this game still satisfying? Give three main reasons.
3. What do you think is the hardest game genre to add a story to? Why? How would you do it?

PROJECTS

1. (a) Look over this list of sample game mechanics:

- Walk
- Run
- Fly
- Swim
- Stealth
- Aim
- Fire
- Throw
- Jump
- Duck
- Punch
- Collect
- Evade damage
- Synchronize
- Collect
- Protect target

- Complete pattern
- Follow
- Evade target
- Solve puzzle
- Grab/release
- Pick up/put down
- Reverse/alter time
- Reverse/alter physical density
- Reverse/alter gravity

(b) Pick five of the above mechanics and use them to create a two-page design outline. Include sections that answer the following:

How does a player win?

How can they tell if they are winning?

How many players is this game for?

Who is its intended audience?

What games platform is it for? (Only concentrate on one lead platform.)

How does the player control their avatar(s)? Try drawing up a controller configuration diagram to show which buttons on the controller do what for the lead platform. Perhaps there is no controller, or perhaps the control interface is built directly into the touch screen. In the case of the latter, provide a sketch for how that control interface looks.

If you like you can also add the mechanic of performing any or all of the actions within a time limit or add enemies to attack you.

(c) Use your design outline to create a one-page story outline.

(d) For more practice create a second story outline for a different type of story.

2. To help explore design and story development, keep a development blog/diary of the following:

(a) Find the card game Once Upon a Time, and play it in groups.

(b) Find the card/board game Mysterium, and play it in groups.

(c) Design your own card or board game, and make it purely about story choices.

(d) Play your games in groups and assess them. Give feedback.

(e) Using this feedback, re-design your game and try it again.

(f) Conclude your blog/diary. Discuss what you learned, what you enjoyed, and what your strengths are as a game developer and/or writer. Consider if any of your peers have made any contributions you found especially helpful; what did they contribute to your project that you weren't able to?

Chapter 15 WHAT IS PLOT AND HOW DOES IT WORK?

Plot is character revealed by action.

—Aristotle

BRIEF TERMS

STRUCTURALISM Intellectual movement originating in 1950s France concerned with the study of human cultural endeavor, whereby individual elements have no inherent meaning within a structure, but only through their relationship with each other.

RUSSIAN FORMALISM Literary theory originating in the early part of the twentieth century concerned with how a literary work conveys meaning within the structure and presentation of its own form.

NARRATOLOGICAL Pertaining to narratology, the theory and study of narrative structure.

MONOMYTH A journey or quest undertaken by a mythical hero of a cyclical nature, and therefore whole or unified, from the Greek "monos" meaning "one" or "single."

Linked to any work you carry out in *game design-related narrative design* is, as mentioned, the work you carry out in *non-interactive narrative design*. As suggested earlier, the former isn't always as simple as only working within the prescribed space, and can, on occasion, lead you to see possibilities in the story design and help you reshape the space you're working in. (This isn't always possible and not always desirable, especially for other members of the team, but isn't unheard of.) There are, of course, many books, articles, lectures, and courses on designing non-interactive stories, and this chapter is a brief examination of key storytelling terms, such as *plot*, *story*, and *narrative*, exploring how they function. Although fundamental to any storytelling, in a game development context, these elements can be seen as *basic*, insofar as they are not *interactive* storytelling elements at all, but the more *advanced* techniques games writers use to build upon these (which are addressed in a general sense in Part III of this book).

WHAT IS PLOT?

Let's start by asking the question *what is plot?* and delve into some literary critical history to help us. Since Aristotle's *Poetics*, if not earlier, critics have discussed the nature of story and, with it, plot. These two terms are often used synonymously in non-academic circles. And yet the critical discussion ongoing since Aristotle shows a breadth of opinions, often with careful delineation between "plot" and "story," and often with a variety of interpretations behind them. On many occasions critics also consider the issue primarily through one specific genre, poetry, fiction, or drama (theater or film), and have sought to make comments simultaneously applicable to other disciplines. In spite of this, it may yet be possible to trace unities of thought across critics, traditions, eras, and disciplines, and thereby attempt some kind of unified theory allowing us to not only explore the question *what is plot?* but also approach an answer that can be of use practically. Aristotle's *Poetics* identifies events or incidents (praxis) and states that a plot (mythos) is the way these events are ordered:

> *every tragedy has six constituents, which will determine its quality. They are plot, character, diction, thought, spectacle and song . . . Of these elements the most important is the plot, the ordering of the incidents.*[1]

The notion that the connection between events is what generates plot is also outlined in E. M. Forster's *Aspects of the Novel*:

> *We have defined a story as a narrative of events arranged in their time sequence. A plot is also a narrative of events, the emphasis falling on causality. "The king*

[1] Aristotle, "On the Art of Poetry," *Classical Literary Theory*, Aristotle/Horace/Longinus (London: Penguin, 1965), 39.

died and then the queen died" is a story. "The king died and then the queen died of grief" is a plot. The time-sequence is preserved, but the sense of causality overshadows it.[2]

Yet Seymour Chatman, writing in 1978, is unconvinced by Forster's distinction between plot and story. He notes that adding the reason the queen died (of grief) may add evident causation, but it is different narratively only in degrees of explicitness and that the causal element is present in both versions.

Indeed, Forster's insights in this regard seem limited, especially in light of the critical developments occurring around him.[3] This was the time Russian Formalism brought with it a distinction between *fabula* and *szůjet*; between events within the tale's own chronology (as they are supposed to have happened), and the presentation of the story (the way it is actually ordered in any particular narrative).

In the 1970s Genette's terms *histoire* and *discours* entered the critical vocabulary, alongside *narration. Histoire* seems wholly analogous to *fabula*, to "story" and *discours* to *szůjet*, or "discourse."[4] *Narration* is a term often used synonymously by structuralist critics with the term *discourse* (the English transliteration of the French *discours*). *Discourse* is generally used to infer the means through which a story is communicated. Umberto Eco sees story as events happening to characters in a chronological sequence; plot is the reordering of those events—not chronologically—but in terms of their presentation, so it's the release of the story material itself; and discourse is the means through which the plot is "released." So for Eco a narrative may potentially lack a plot, but it cannot be without a story or discourse. Yet to Chatman a narrative cannot exist without a plot. If we revisit his *Poetics*, we find that *discourse* or *narration* is an element that Aristotle had already identified. To quote Aristotle again: "every tragedy has six constituents . . . plot, character, diction, thought, spectacle and song."[5] Putting character, spectacle, and song to one side, Aristotle clarifies: "By diction . . . I mean the expressive use of words."[6] Under

[2] E. M. Forster, *Aspects of the Novel* (London: Penguin, 2005), 87.

[3] Curiously, however, his discussion in Chapter 5, by way of analogy involving an aunt who doesn't know what she thinks until she hears what she says, is a rather good demonstration of Foucauldian discourse in action.

[4] Oddly, direct translations of the Russian 'fabula' and 'szůjet' render, in English, the quite helpful 'fable' for 'fabula' and the almost utterly confounding 'story' for 'szůjet.' Genette categorizes five areas of narrative analysis: order, duration, frequency, mood, and voice.

[5] Aristotle, "On the Art of Poetry," 39.

[6] Ibid., 41.

thought he "includes all the effects that have to be produced by means of language."[7] While Aristotle's terms may not have the range and depth of subsections that Genette identifies, between his "diction" (*lexis* or "speech") and "thought" (*dianoia* or "theme") it seems we might well be covering what some critics term *discourse*. Further, since Aristotle made no distinction between "plot" and "story," perhaps we might argue that his "plot" (or "mythos") is actually closer in context on a number of occasions to the English word "story," which, in turn, bears similarities with the fable of the Russian "fabula." If we accept this, then Aristotle is telling us about "plot," "story," and "discourse" in *The Poetics*, without always identifying where exactly he switches between meanings. Where Aristotle talks of "The Scope of the [Mythos] Plot" in Chapter 7, if we allow that *story is causal*, we might argue he is really talking about "story":

> *Now a whole is that which has a beginning, a middle and an end. A beginning is that which does not necessarily come after something else, although something else exists or comes about after it. An end, on the contrary, is that which naturally follows something else either as a necessary or as a usual consequence, and is not itself followed by anything. A middle is that which follows something else, and is itself followed by something.*[8]

Where Aristotle talks about the "Unity of [Mythos] Plot" in Chapter 8 of *The Poetics*, if we allow that *plot concerns the way the causal events of a story are ordered*, we might argue he is referring to "plot":

> *In writing his Odyssey he [Homer] did not put in everything that happened to Odysseus . . . the plot of a play . . . must represent it as a unified whole; and its various incidents must be so arranged that if any one of them is differently placed or taken away the effect of wholeness will be seriously disrupted.*[9]

Where Aristotle talks of complications he is also referring to elements of "plot":

> *Every tragedy has its complication and its denouement. The complication consists of the incidents lying outside the plot, and often some of those inside it, and the rest is the denouement. By complication I mean the part of the story from the beginning to the point immediately preceding the change to good or bad fortune; by denouement the part from the onset of this change to the end.*[10]

---

[7] Ibid., 57–58.
[8] Ibid., 41.
[9] Ibid., 43.
[10] Ibid., 56.

And where Aristotle talks of "Thought and Diction" (Chapter 19), "Some Linguistic Definitions" (Chapter 20), "Poetic Diction" (Chapter 21), "Diction and Style" (Chapter 22), among other places, he is touching on what the structuralists would call *discourse* or *narration*. "The greatest virtue of diction is to be clear without being commonplace."[11] Oddly enough, this appears to foreshadow the formalists and their identification of "de-familiarization" as an element of literary value. Indeed, in general, it seems as if Aristotle is sketching out the contours of much of the critical discussion it took over two thousand years for others to pick up and fill in.[12]

To return to two critics working in more recent times, for all the apparent difference in their views, perhaps Eco and Chatman aren't as far apart as they first appeared. Eco sees plot as a kind of complication of the story (the content), something *that is additional to the narrative discourse employed to convey that story*. Therefore, it's possible for him to accept a story with no "complication," and in turn, no plot.[13] Chatman sees plot as an aspect of the narrative discourse employed when conveying the story (or content), which he acknowledges is inclined to be viewed in terms of how complex it makes that story. He sees the events of a story being turned into plot by its *discourse*, by the means through which it is presented. Perhaps, then, we can see "plot," *szůjet*, and *discours* as the means by which the events in a story are not only ordered, but also that which covers the various intricacies and technical subsets of *narration*. Fellow games writer Neil Richards seems to lend support to this view. He sees it this way: "For me plot amounts to the multi-changeable engine parts that a writer uses to drive a story; and plot is always subservient to story."[14] It might, then, be possible to say that across a number of critics, and across a number of years, there is some kind of consensus. Events connected by chronological consequence amount to what we might call a *story*. The presentation of those events, the various time, character, and narratological viewpoints through and from which these events are presented, amount to what we might call a plot, or narrative discourse. In his

---

[11] Ibid., 62.

[12] It is tantalizing, if specious, to consider what a fuller or second version of *The Poetics* might have contained had it not been lost.

[13] This is an acknowledged simplification of Eco's position who, more accurately, appears to see plot as not just a kind of complication of the story, but also as a complex filter through which it passes back and forth to a reader who then acquires meaning from it and gives meaning to it.

[14] Neil Richards, in conversation, June 11, 2007.

Story and Discourse: Narrative Structure in Fiction and Film, Seymour Chatman puts it in terms of a *what* and a *way*; the *what* being the nature of the story and its *way* being its *discourse*. Forster's earlier quoted, rather cute distinction is therefore out of step with modern critical theory. For, as other commentators have demonstrated, there is more at stake than degrees of causality. There is also the presentation and form of the material, which bring with them a vast range of issues relating to point of view and audience reception.

Perhaps what Forster was really doing in trying to show the difference between *story* and *plot* was to emphasize the call for obstacles (or *complications* and *reversals*). Perhaps, it might be possible to say a story is the *what*, and the plot is the *how* (and Chatman's discourse, or the *way*, is synonymous with the *how*.) A story is the *what*, which comprises the *who*, the *when*, the *why*, the *means by which characters do what they* do, and *what the consequences are of all these things*; the plot is *how* the author presents it, the *means they employ*, and the narrative techniques they avail themselves of to release the "story matter." The enormous influence the *how* has on the *what* amounts to saying as much as "the tale is in the telling." There is, then, a relationship between the construction of a plot and the construction of meaning.

HOW DOES PLOT WORK?

If it's possible to see some kind of unity in thought regarding what a *plot* is that makes it different from a *story*, and some unity on what a *plot* is in terms of its relationship to *discourse*, then a further question presents itself: *Does anyone agree about how a plot actually works?* What qualities does a plot comprise such that it may be generally considered to function effectively for an audience, as opposed to being generally considered *ineffective*? How does a plot, or how does a story through its presentation, engage an audience and bring them to emotional fulfilment? It's Aristotle who first gives us the sense of "purging" or "purifying" when he uses the word "catharsis," which contains both meanings:

> *Tragedy, then, is a representation of an action that is worth serious attention, complete in itself, and of some amplitude; in language enriched by a variety of artistic devices appropriate to the several parts of the play; presented in the form of action, not narration; by means of pity and fear bringing about the* ***catharsis*** *of such emotions.*[15]

[15] Aristotle, "On the Art of Poetry," 56. The word *catharsis* here is our own emphasis and is substituted for the translation's original 'purgation,' a transliteration of the Greek word.

The discussion regarding how plot works runs much the same course as the debate over what plot is, given how essentially inseparable the two questions are. After Aristotle it took until the early twentieth century for the debate to be substantially advanced, from the early studies into monomyths and explorations into folktales from Propp and the work of the formalists, through to the structuralists and the work of Campbell and Frye (who were, in a sense, developing their own work out of Propp and Jung's, just as structuralism developed, in a sense, out of formalism). Yet additionally, since 1979 and Syd Field's publication of *Screenplay*, there has been a tradition originating in the United States of vocationally targeted publications, lecture tours, and screenwriting software, intending to educate screenwriters practically. These non-academic works have sought to address the question of how a plot works with a range of different solutions.[16] This tradition is now filtering into academic circles with the proliferation of academically recognized creative writing courses in the United States, the United Kingdom, and beyond. It seems that both the academic and the vocational traditions have something to offer practicing writers. Academic pursuit brings intellectual rigor and more thoroughly research-based notions, while the vocational approach provides practical guidance and tangible application. While its title promises a synthesis, Michael Tierno's *Aristotle's Poetics for Screenwriters* (2002) has its emphasis squarely on a vocational application.

First, let us summarize Aristotle's views on what makes a plot function. He makes three key points:

1. A plot should have unity and basic form, developing along a linear and "logical" path, to ultimate denouement.
2. En route to denouement, a plot requires key "moments," "events," or "incidents" in time fundamentally responsible for engaging the audience.
3. Plot requires other elements in conjunction, such as characters, setting, and atmosphere, which are not directly tied to the linear causality of the "events" or "incidents," but are still essential.

The first point references the discussion in *The Poetics* on wholes having a beginning, a middle, and an end. That passage could well be responsible for the

[16] At the same time, it is arguable that they have simultaneously educated writers on how they ought to think plot works, because commissioning producers are reading the same books and thinking that plots work the way the books and celebrity script editor tours say. This is really a separate discussion, or, in fact, several, given the vast numbers of writers and producers and the large range of vocationally targeted books, tours, and software of this kind.

commonly held misconception that Aristotle advocates a three-act structure as the definitive template for storytelling. In fact, *The Poetics* makes no mention whatsoever of a three-act structure. Instead, in that passage, Aristotle appears to be making the point that a story or plot must begin, develop, and end, in some sense. This may sound somewhat glib, and yet, not only is an ending integral to meaning, but Aristotle is at pains to point out what makes for unity is not necessarily to focus on one key character, but on what he calls "an action":

> *A plot does not possess unity . . . merely because it is about one man. Many things . . . may happen to one man, and . . . not contribute to any kind of unity . . . he may carry out many actions from which no single unified action will emerge . . . the plot . . . being the representation of an action, must present it as a unified whole; and its various incidents must be so arranged that if any one of them is differently placed or taken away the effect of wholeness will be seriously disrupted. For if the presence or absence of something makes no apparent difference, it is no real part of the whole.*[17]

Aristotle is more concerned that the plot has everything it needs to reach its effect, and be shorn of anything inessential; that everything in the plot should be there for a reason, or perhaps multiple reasons. Once the central *action* has played out, according to what he termed *probable* or *necessary*, the plot, Aristotle suggests, has come to an end. Anything added is superfluous. As uncontentious as that might at first sound, it isn't. As Wallace Martin reminds us in *Recent Theories of Narrative* (1986), it is Horace who says that epics should begin in the middle of things, *in media res*. As a technique, *in media res* would appear to be open to some interpretation. Where a movie such as the original *Star Wars* may be said to start in the middle of things as Princess Leia's spaceship is attacked by Darth Vader's moments after the opening credits, it seems just as possible to describe this action as "an inciting event" or "first cause" that propels the plot forward, even if it is working off (an immense) backstory of which we later come to understand the significance (several films later). Where other plots, such as *Goodfellas*, may start with an incident and drop back in time, and later bring us back to the same point we came in, it's also possible to argue this is a "prologue" or "coda" or a "motif" that helps establish background, character, and thematic information (as well as enticing spectacle) in order to help formulate the sense of something beginning, which still must lead to development and denouement in order to be resolved. Even in an example such as *Memento*, where the

---

[17] Aristotle, "On the Art of Poetry," 42–43.

chronology of the film is so constantly unsettled, the viewer experiences a plot that presents itself through developing stages, as they come to appreciate what is at stake for Leonard, how the crisis deepens, and how it is resolved.

The rise of the three-act structure "convention" is a subject of discussion in itself and, oddly, not a well-documented one. Yet in professional screenwriting circles the term "three-act structure" is generally traced back to Field's *Screenplay* with an assumption that it comes informed by Aristotle. Field himself never makes this claim. But it is Aristotle who first gives us the terms "complication"

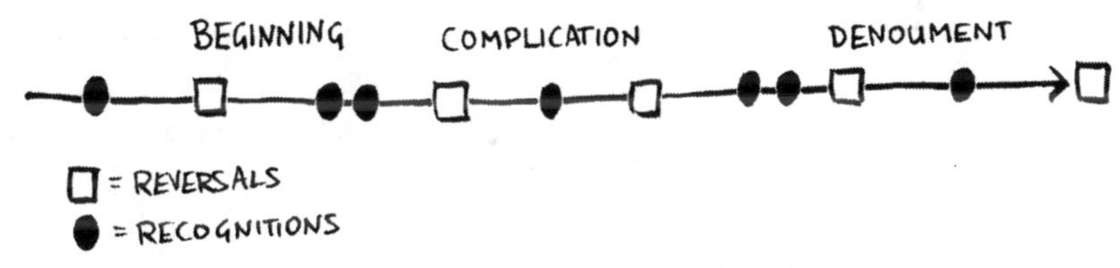

FIGURE 15.1. Linear plot route.

and "denouement." He effectively describes the linear route of a plot as "beginning," followed by "complication," then "denouement." Figure 15.1 illustrates Aristotle's view of plot visually.

Here, white squares are reversals or recognitions and black spheres are other events. The number of reversals, recognitions, other events, and their exact placement on the line are arbitrary since Aristotle stipulated no quantities or exact placements. Field describes his *paradigm*, equating the beginning with Act 1, or "the setup," the middle with Act 2, or the "confrontation," and the end

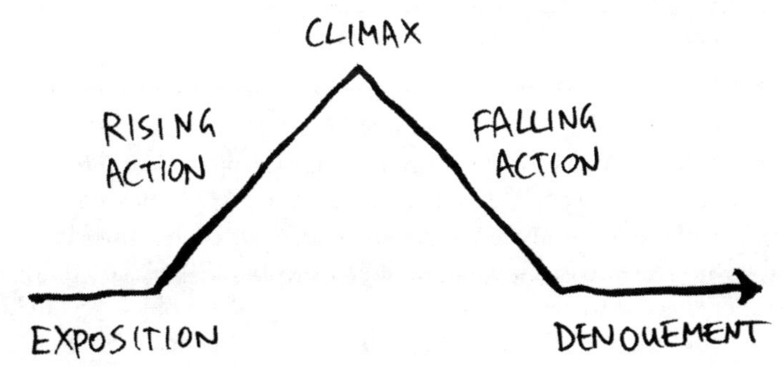

FIGURE 15.2. Freytag's triangle.

with Act 3, or "the resolution." In later works he introduces the notion of "the Mid-Point," splitting Act 2 in two. Either way, it's not hard to see similarities not only to Aristotle's delineation, but also to plot structure formulated by others, for example, Gustav Freytag, seemingly adapting Aristotle, as illustrated in Figure 15.2.

There are plenty of other presentations too, including Cheryl Klein's adaptation of Freytag's triangle, employing additional wording from Aristotle, Wallace Martin's configuration in *Recent Theories of Narrative*, and Labov's "square," all showing a similarity of not just terms, but also structural elements, with three or four key *points* on which a plot *turns*.

Although the difference between three or four points may seem significant, depending on the terminology in the examples above, they more or less amount to the same thing: there is a beginning, a middle, and an end. The middle may contain further complication, there may be a prologue (exposition, orientation), and there may be an epilogue (coda). In this way the distinction between three acts or five can often be little more than semantic, or mathematical, with the basic structure remaining the same.

There are various responses to these kinds of "general" plot structures from a range of commentators on the various merits and demerits of each, but it seems a convention of sorts has developed.[18] It may not have been intentionally founded by Aristotle, and its development from Freytag to Field may also not be clear. Even so, this basic form appears to be currently in general use (either in visual or conceptual form) among practitioners and tends to follow a similar pattern, rendering plot structure as "motivation, complication, climax, resolution," or "exposition, complication, climax, resolution, conclusion," or "motivation, complication, crisis, climax, resolution." But it appears as if by generally following these (essentially similar) structural guidelines, writers generate plots that have the chance[19] of successfully engaging an audience and bringing them to catharsis, with the full "working out" of their emotions. It is by "moving through the gears" of the plot's structure that an

---

[18] Other very different looking kinds of models also exist, such as Bremond's and Campbell's, both referenced in Wallace Martin's *Recent Theories of Narrative*, page 98.

[19] "Have a chance" in so far as plot structure itself is clearly no guarantee of engaging an audience—subject matter, character, dialogue, and countless other elements also contribute. For his part, Aristotle sees it thus: "if someone writes a series of speeches expressive of character, and well composed as far as thought and diction are concerned, he will still not achieve the proper effect of tragedy; this will be done much better by a tragedy which is less successful in its use of these elements, but which has a plot giving an ordered combination of incidents." Aristotle, "On the Art of Poetry," 40.

audience's emotions can successfully be brought to the point of despair or relief (or otherwise) as the writer intends.

With regard to the plot requiring fundamental "moments" of audience engagement to function, Aristotle, as cited above, discusses events or incidents (praxis) building towards a denouement. On the way to that denouement, "the two most important means by which tragedy plays on our feelings [are] 'reversals' and 'recognitions.'"[20] (The term 'recognitions' is used interchangeably with 'discoveries.') He defines these as follows:

> *a reversal is a change from one state of affairs to its opposite . . . a discovery is a change from ignorance to knowledge.*[21]

He further adds: "The most effective form of discovery is that which is accompanied by reversals."[22] When we come to Roland Barthes in 1978's *Image Music Text*, he talks of *functions* and *indices*. *Functions* relate to action, to events that happen, whereas *indices* relate to elements within a text that *are*, that is to say, descriptive elements. He ascertains a level of hierarchy among the functions, where some are "real hinge-points" and of critical importance to its structural integrity, because they must be consecutive and consequential, and others are more structurally expendable. The former he calls *cardinal functions* (or *nuclei*) and the latter he calls *catalyzers*. The "real hinge-points" sound close to Aristotle's "two most important means." When Barthes talks of the consecutive and consequential nature of cardinal functions, he begins to sound reminiscent of Aristotle's plot "reversals" and "discoveries," being both consecutive and consequential. Where Barthes speaks in terms of it being impossible to delete a nucleus without altering the story, this sounds even closer to Aristotle's "incidents must be so arranged that if any one of them is differently placed or taken away the effect of wholeness will be seriously disrupted."[23] There are clear similarities in these definitions in Field's "plot points" and Chatman's "kernels" and "satellites." We might use the term "acts" for each of Chatman's "nodes" or "hinges," or, equally, we might use Field's term "sequence" to denote a narrative block being a subset of an act, where a sequence is a series of scenes connected by a unifying idea. Chatman's "kernels" seem essentially the same as Barthes' "cardinal functions" or "nuclei,"

---

[20] Aristotle, "On the Art of Poetry," 40.

[21] Ibid., 46.

[22] Ibid., 46.

[23] Roland Barthes, *Image Music Text* (London: Fontana Press, 1977), 42–43.

which are also the same as Field's "plot points" at the end of acts one and two, or the same as Aristotle's "reversals" or "discoveries." Chatman's "satellites" are essentially the same as Barthes' "catalyzers," which are also the same as

	ARISTOTLE	BARTHES	CHAPMAN	FIELD
MOST SIGNIFICANT STRUCTURAL ELEMENT	REVERSAL OR DISCOVERY EVENT (OR PRAXIS)	CARDINAL FUNCTION OR NUCLEI	EVENT, KERNEL	PLOT POINT AT END OF ACTS 1 AND 2
LESS SIGNIFICANT STRUCTURAL ELEMENT	OTHER EVENT (OR PRAXIS)	CATALYSER	EVENT, SATELLITE	OTHER PLOT POINTS

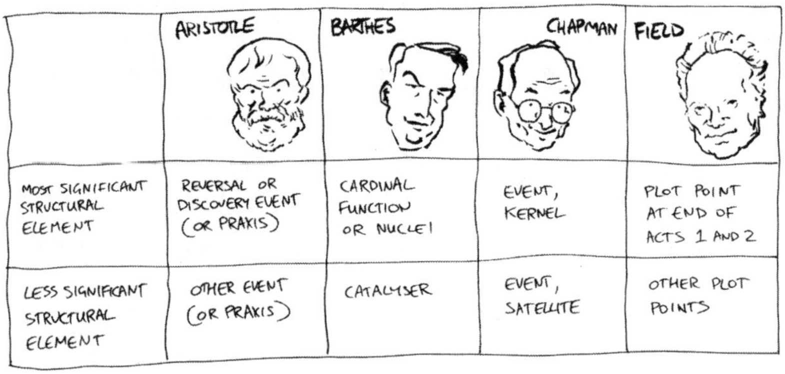

FIGURE 15.3. Key elements of plot.

Field's lesser plot points. It seems no betrayal of Aristotle's meaning to suggest within the nature of "reversals" or "discoveries" he would acknowledge some are more significant than others. At any rate he declares "discoveries" and "reversals" are "the two most important means by which tragedy plays on our feelings."[24] The parallels seem clear, and Figure 15.3 maps the views of various commentators on key elements of plot accordingly.

It's important to remember not to ascribe too much importance to Barthes' "catalyzer," which is markedly less significant than Field's minor plot points. In spite of the sound of the word in English, it really does not catalyze the plot in the way Field's plot points or Barthes' own cardinal functions do.

As far as plot requiring other elements in conjunction to be effective, Aristotle's reference to, additionally, "character, diction, thought, spectacle and song" has already been mentioned. It seems Barthes, Chatman, and Field all acknowledge the need for similar elements to support the effect of plot. In Field's *Screenplay* much space is devoted to the formation of both character and dialogue. The former, he suggests, does not only help support the plot, but can even, on occasion, lead it, suggesting that story will emerge out of character. Having already distinguished between "functions" and "indices," Barthes further defines the latter as being concerned with character or atmosphere.

[24] Ibid., 40.

Detailing the age of a character or notations of atmosphere might serve as good examples of an index. Again, Chatman's views seem to essentially mirror

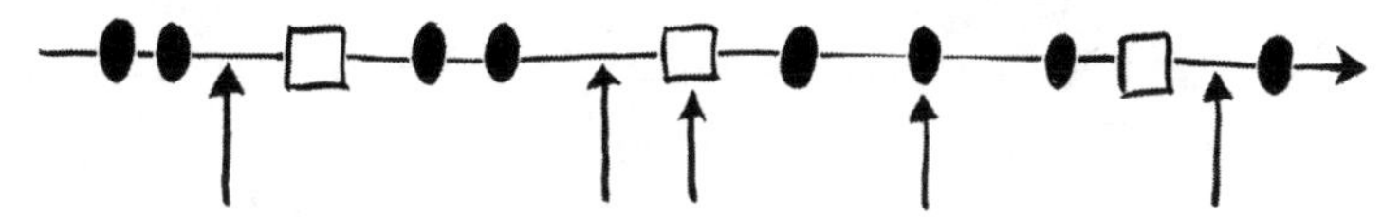

FIGURE 15.4. Barthes' cardinal and index functions.

those of Barthes. For Chatman the non-sequential elements combining with events of the story are termed "existents," subdividing into "characters" and "settings." Barthes distinguishes between the "horizontal" and "vertical" nature of the relationship between functions and indices, yet also makes it clear that a unit can belong to two different classes at the same time. That is, a cardinal function might be an index at the same time. Figure 15.4, then, visually renders Barthes' views.

The horizontal line left to right is the temporal, linear discourse, the white squares the cardinal functions (or nuclei), and the black ovals catalyzers. The horizontal arrows could be placed at any and several junctures along the "temporal" line of the plot and are the indices and informants. In addition, the same basic function can also operate as an index. This is not unlike the views of Aristotle, Chatman, and Field. In a general sense, all four are saying:

1. A plot should have unity and basic form, developing along a linear and "logical" path to ultimate denouement.
2. En route to denouement, a plot requires key "moments," "events," or "incidents" in time fundamentally responsible for engaging the audience.
3. Plot requires other elements in conjunction, such as characters, setting, and atmosphere, which are not directly tied to the linear causality of the "events" or "incidents," but are still essential.

Different terminology is used, different visual representations (and in the case of Aristotle and Barthes, none are given by the authors themselves[25]), and different emphasis for elements may be brought to bear at certain points, but these commentators are not fundamentally opposed to each other with regard to their general views on how a plot works.

---

[25] Or whoever committed *The Poetics* to paper.

Psychological proof demonstrating that stories work the way theorists suggest is a whole other realm and definitely for another chapter in another book. Yet it may suffice to say some stories are more successful in engaging audiences than others, and there is general agreement among commentators as to the reasons for that with regard to plot structures. But rules and formulas only achieve so much. Attaining and retaining audience attention is really the only fundamental criteria a writer is bound to. However, the structural conventions on which Aristotle, Barthes, Chatman, Field, and others seem to reach broad agreement appear to offer the basis for plots that function effectively, and so therefore have the potential to retain audience attention—no doubt this is because these theorists based their narrative theories on the analysis of existing "successful" plots. Nevertheless, this does give us some kind of answer to *what a plot is* and *how it works*. It also provides some insight into the different meanings and interpretations of *story*, *plot*, and *narrative*. For any writer, a games writer included, this kind of knowledge is priceless.

EXERCISES

1. What is the difference between story and plot, and why might it be useful to distinguish between them? Discuss.
2. Aside from reversals and revelations, what other key tools do storytellers have at their disposal to retain audience interest? What tools do games writers have to retain audience interest that other writers do not have?
3. Using a format of your choosing, diagram the plot of any game story you like.
4. There are sometimes said to be only seven basic plot types: quest, tragedy, comedy, rags to riches, coming of age, a stranger comes to town and mystery. What stories can you think of that are examples of each of these seven kinds? Provide a game story example for each of these seven kinds of plot.
5. List three examples of stories that combine more than one kind of plot.
6. List three examples of stories with a plot not covered by any of these plot types or plot type combinations.
7. Arthur Miller felt that tragedies are essentially optimistic, because they are attempts to wrestle with ideas concerning ultimate forces, and that comedies are essentially pessimistic because they propound the view that there are no ultimate forces. Discuss.

8. Do some plots inherently lend themselves to game stories better than others? Which ones, and why?

PROJECT

1. For each of the seven plots listed above, construct a one-page game story outline.

Chapter 16 OTHER RESOURCES FOR WRITERS: MORE THAN MOVIES

There are more things in heaven and earth, Horatio,
Than are dreamt of in your philosophy.

—William Shakespeare

BRIEF TERMS

CONVERGENCE The process by which differing technologies and platforms move towards an overlapping state whereby they're able to perform similar technical tasks to satisfy similar audience desires.

CLIFFHANGER An unresolved, potentially disastrous situation that occurs at the end of a game scene or episode that encourages players to either keep playing or purchase further content in order to discover how matters were resolved.

IAMBIC PENTAMETER Commonly used line of poetry where there are five sets of two syllables, beginning with an unstressed syllable immediately followed by a stressed syllable, with the pattern replicating until the end of the line.

MULTIPLE INTERSECTING STORYLINES Game storylines in which major characters from one story appear as minor characters in another, lending the game universes a greater sense of organic realism.

The creative world, now more than ever, is a vibrant, exciting, and evolving sphere rich in a wide variety of resources for writers to draw upon; use these to both broaden and deepen your writing where necessary.

MOVIES

There can be no serious doubt that, for games writers and developers as a whole, movies have been, and continue to be, a deep source to mine for reference and inspiration. For example, at a 2010 presentation exploring the creative impetus behind the popular *Fable* RPG series, Peter Molyneux named Australian action movie *Mad Max 2* as the inspiration for the player's canine companion in *Fable II* (as a way to both evoke emotion from the player and add an interesting new gameplay mechanic). Many game cinematic set pieces wear their inspiration thinly veiled, with compositions, camera moves, and scene settings drawing very evidently from the big screen. Likewise, many characters, in any combination of attitude, arc, attire, or speech, draw unashamedly from movies. It's hard to imagine the opening sequence of the game *Driver* without the Ryan O'Neal movie, *The Driver*, preceding it or *GTA Vice City*'s Ken Rosenberg without Sean Penn's portrayal of David Kleinfeld in *Carlito's Way*; it's also hard to imagine Tommy Vercetti in the same game without Michael Madsen's Mr. Blonde in *Reservoir Dogs* or Al Pacino's Tony Montana in *Scarface*. It's no less hard to imagine the D-Day opening of the first *Medal of Honor* game without the movie *Saving Private Ryan*, or McTavish in *Modern Warfare* without the British sergeant major meme of movies such as *Zulu* and *The Wild Geese*. The reasons for this may well lie in historical expediency—just as movies in their youth conspicuously drew from the theater and vaudeville, where pre-existing art forms helped give shape to a fledgling form, games draw from movies. "We don't know what we're doing, so we should watch what they do in movies—and do that," as one studio head once said in our presence. Presumably he was thinking they are both visual and sound-based media after all.

But matters have further developed in recent years, with the influence of games coming to bear on movies, not necessarily in just terms of movie adaptations of game licenses (*Tomb Raider*, *Prince of Persia*™, *Resident Evil*™, *Silent Hill*™, etc.) but in terms of movies that it's hard to envision without pre-existing game-like themes or concepts, such as *Avatar*, *Crank*, and *Inception*. So, peering into the future, it's hard to imagine that the two art forms won't continue to borrow from each other in some respects and rub along in a sort of improvised dance without any accompanying music, other than the backbeat of commercialism and convergence to guide and/or confuse them.

However, be this as it may, the gist of this chapter is that, for all the depth of the seams of movies to be mined, games are severely restricting themselves by not casting their gaze elsewhere. In 2009, Charlie Brooker's *Gameswipe*

TV show on the BBC included an interview with writer and director Graham Linehan (whose credits include popular UK comedy shows *Father Ted*, *Black Books*, and *The IT Crowd*). He suggested that everything in games was improving, with the exception of storytelling; his theory was that games writers have stopped reading books. Instead, he suggests, they are only watching films, and the result is stories with a lack of depth.[1] While we would certainly still contest this among our peers whose working practices we know well, and have had the good fortune to work inside development studios where this is certainly not the case, we have also worked inside studios where movie-watching does indeed appear to be the dominant culture within the team to the exclusion of other forms, perhaps books most of all. What, then, might writers be missing out on if they absorb movies to the exclusion of other sources?

TELEVISION

Move from the big screen to the small screen and look at TV drama series; through these, games writers can learn how to handle a relatively small cast of central characters often restricted to a limited number of set locations. As games writers know only too well, art resources often restrict them to a similarly small cast and limited number of set locations. Game design usually imposes further restrictions in these areas. But in TV shows like *The West Wing*, a reasonably limited cast of characters, only rarely added to or depleted, are largely contained within the physical space of a few rooms (until the campaign trail storylines begin). Audience engagement is retained through the intersecting motivation arcs as characters are variously "up" or "down," as their relationships accordingly readjust, and as sparkling dialogue dramatically delivers those characters. Indeed, many, if not most, TV series are founded on a core group of characters around a set location and/or circumstance: the Hell's Kitchen neighborhood in New York (*Daredevil*), a funeral home (*Six Feet Under*), a spaceship (*Battlestar Galactica*), or an island (*Lost*). Although many of these do venture beyond their key location, it is generally infrequently and not until after the core identity of the show (and its commercial viability) has been established.

Of course, it's very rare that games writers are afforded the time for character and plot development that TV writers are, and a seasoned games writer might also justly suggest that to have anywhere between six and ten major characters is

[1] View online at *http://www.youtube.com/watch?v=W37SjBMvZbI&feature=related*, last accessed May 2016.

still an exceptional luxury reserved for the big-budget titles. However, the point remains—there are functioning dramatic models where limited cast lists and scene locations deliver audience engagement, and it's important to remember other plot models exist beyond picaresque quests. It's in the nature of picaresque quests that multiple locations are often required, only to be used once or twice as players have to complete the same level in reverse, or with the same locations clearly re-skinned. So models that move away from these limitations of formats can give writers and design teams more options.

Likewise, sitcoms are evidence of dramas focused on even more limited cast lists and even fewer set locations. They're also a reminder that story matter doesn't always have to aspire to the epic. Sitcoms are fantastic at re-setting themselves at the end or beginning of each episode. This allows them to be unhindered by preceding events (other than when they choose to make explicit or implicit reference to them) and to head off into each episode afresh to explore the comic and dramatic potential of their characters. As long as writers see sufficient potential in their characters to begin with, they're unfettered by previous journeys they've taken them on. While this is not always relevant for games writers, it's a salutary reminder that if it fits the tone of your world, and if it gives you story mileage, you can keep re-setting it: being stuck in the same set locations can feel a lot more bearable to a player if each time they're actually experiencing different, fresh stories.

As for soaps, something they excel at is the "what-nextness" of storytelling—hooking viewers back day after day, week after week, year after year to find out what happened and to whom. If E. M. Forster felt that it was somewhat crude for *what-happens-next* to be so uppermost in storytelling, he may have considered soaps to be the crudest form of stories conceivable. But Forster brought an Edwardian prudishness and naivety to critical literary thinking that throws doubt on whether there's anything so very wrong with wanting to know what happens next. While in the late 1920s Forster was bemoaning the lack of seriousness in an audience who approached stories in their basest form, the Russian formalists were helping to shape modern critical thinking—as if Forster was a remnant of the nineteenth century (and an excellent one at that) finding himself adrift in the twentieth. In any event, Forster wholly and clearly acknowledges, in his *Aspects of the Novel* (first published in 1927), that a story is fundamentally all about making the audience care about what happens next.

But we digress. What soaps do very well are cliffhangers—or, as we have referred to them elsewhere by their critical and practical terms—reversals and revelations. No storyteller in any form will ever get very far without them, but for games writers they may take on special significance when working with episodic content—even more so when new episode downloads are dependent on audience satisfaction with the preceding installment. Make sure your episodes find genuine endings—and if you're not finding a reversal or a revelation (or both at the same time), then you haven't got an ending. Sometimes act breaks can be a little unclear and take a few scenes to play through or become apparent, but with episodic content you can't hide—an episode without a proper ending is no episode at all.

THEATER

The theater is a potentially useful model too—restricted cast list, restricted locations, a reminder to find conflict—because on the stage if you aren't delivering conflict between characters, there's nowhere to hide and you can't fool yourself that other elements are operating on the audience and taking preeminence. (Even in Beckett's plays where there is seemingly not much more than anticipation and frustration occurring, there's still conflict between the characters as their frustration spills out and is directed at each other.) In theater, as in poetry, there is a reminder that epic events can be conveyed with little or no stagecraft and carried in dialogue and the rich imagery of iambic pentameters—the Battle of Bosworth in *Richard III*, the Battle of Agincourt in *Henry V*, the circumnavigation of the globe in flight in *Doctor Faustus*. What practical use might this possibly be for a games writer? Again, we urge a less slavishly literal way of exploring these possibilities.

AUDIO BOOKS

You might think audio books have nothing to tell a games writer until you consider that purely audio-based games have been published, such as *Aurifi*™ and *Papa Sangre*™ on smartphones. Here dialogue and sound effects are the sole way through which players navigate the world and play the game. A purely audio-based game experience would seem to liberate a writer from set cast lists and set locations and free them from being a slave to art budgets. By extension, audio-based games would seem to allow you to explore time-travel themes with unprecedented freedom—as you jump to new planets and times almost to your heart's content. And there might be projects where you want to create a visual-based game and to hybridize it with purely audio elements—like an extended version of a movie scene trapped underground with no, or very little, light.

SHORT STORIES

Short stories are a reminder that a neat and well-formed plot riffing off an intriguing start-point, but not outstaying its welcome, is often a more satisfying and more memorable experience than a story that grows and bloats beyond its own inherent capacity to engage and entertain. While Bungie's well-received FPS *Halo* garnered a great deal of praise for its lean, well-told story, and compelling array of characters, some feel *Halo 2* falls prey to an over-ambitious plot that tries to do too much, expanding the universe further by adding a second storyline that takes players into the universe of the enemy. Admirable as this is, the result is a less-focused story leaving players less clear on the core truth of character motivations and events (these ideally have to be capable of shining through gameplay, which is, by necessity here, loud, fast-paced, and distracting).

Although ostensibly of limited value, and certainly to be handled advisedly, short stories are, conversely, also reminders that plot is not everything, and that the voice a writer uses can sometimes be all you need to hypnotize and engage an audience, even to the exclusion of any meaningful consequential narrative at all. It's hard to always be sure when a Raymond Carver story, for example, has really finished, but you still feel like you've been somewhere, you've witnessed something, and you've met some people. Sometimes creating an effect and evoking a feeling is more important than the specific content within your story.

Something else found in short stories, although there's no reason why it couldn't feature in other forms (and infrequently does), is multiple intersecting storylines—where major characters from one story appear as minor characters in another. Bioware use multiple intersecting storylines in both their *Mass Effect* and *Dragon Age* games to great effect. Crossing paths, however briefly, with Leliana at the conclusion of *Dragon Age 2* (a major character in *Dragon Age: Origins*) not only evokes a feeling of fond nostalgia, but the sense of a deeply interconnected story world in which meaningful events take place away from the player's presence. To an extent this is commonplace enough in movies with diverging subplots (Marvel Studios© are masters at inter-weaving a diverse family of characters, sometimes in a single film, and often throughout multiple films in their ongoing franchise), but it's a very different kind of thrill to find characters returning in stories you had no reason to even expect them in, and a very different kind of tease to get a half-glimpse of a known character in a new developmental circumstance; you feel you want to be able to ask them how they've been, but since they're now a minor character, or perhaps little more than a passing stranger in this new story, you can't. This isn't just a fun technique to play with, it can also be thematically enriching. *Photocopies of Heaven*, a collection of short stories, explores ideas relating to worlds that exist beyond the purviews of the central characters of many of the short stories, as a way of dramatizing that thematic agenda. There's no inherent reason why this couldn't have a similar role in games writing, and no reason why, even in longer form stories, you couldn't at least reintroduce previously established characters in more minor roles—for the thrill of it and because it helps keep these characters' story arcs turning, however slowly and minutely.

GRAPHIC NOVELS

Graphic novels show visual storytelling techniques that have filtered into games writing not just indirectly via movies, but also, on occasion, very directly. Games such as *Max Payne*™ and *Driver 76* are clear demonstrations of where these techniques have been harnessed. From Japan there are countless examples of manga-inspired delivery and techniques where a whole genre of manga games is still flourishing after more than twenty years.

NOVELS

In a world where a set of novels, *The Lord of the Rings*, arguably inspired *D&D*, which arguably in turn inspired a multitude of fantasy video game worlds, including *World of Warcraft*, we're far from suggesting that games need to learn to look to books for their source ideas. It is fair to say, however, that games writers should not forget to look to novels for their technical elements. After all, novels illustrate the different levels of engagement to be had. The more careful reader may dwell longer on descriptive passages, where a quicker, less patient one may skim over them in a more precursory way. This in turn gives rise to the possible generation of a story experience that can operate on multiple simultaneous levels. This can have practical application in games like *BioShock*, where stories are told not just in cinematic set pieces and in the process of the game, but also in video loops on monitors on the walls of rooms, and, for those even more invested in the world and more prepared to engage with the story, in diary extracts found on the floor and collected. Like novels, a game like *BioShock*, as discussed in Chapter 8, caters to multiple kinds of viewers/readers—from the hungriest and most patient down.

Novels are also a reminder that tackling events from different and multiple perspectives can be an effective way of exploring plots, themes, and characters. "The novel is the book of life,"[2] as D. H. Lawrence said, with its "wholeness" and its characters that "can do nothing but *live* [italics in the original]."[3] Although visual and audio-based media such as movies or games struggle to convey internal thought and emotional processes as effectively as novels, there are techniques that allow for some version of it—specific camera POV and voiceover, for example—but more importantly, novels are a reminder not to neglect experimental plot structures, where not only new (and potentially conflicting) perspectives can be examined, but where time can also be accelerated, reversed, and otherwise disrupted with considerable ease. Movies have techniques and grammar capable of exploring this area (a movie like *Inception* is clear evidence of this), but the point is, novels regularly experiment more frequently and more daringly in this area because they are less constrained by practical implications like money or running time in order to deliver on an idea. Forget to read novels and you may forget to look beyond the more conventional. We would do well to call to mind Bakhtin's "stylistic three-dimensionality" of the novel, such that it accounts for, in his terms, the "novelization"[4] of other genres, which might be interpreted as a kind of cultural python, or a Borg-like assimilator and absorber of other forms of art, which, as it feeds, increases its capacity to do so.

CHOOSE YOUR OWN ADVENTURE BOOKS

Games writers, especially those at the cutting edge of digital technology, may not feel gamebooks such as *Choose Your Own Adventure* and the *Fighting Fantasy* series have much to teach them. However, it's worth remembering they are, in their own way, demonstrations of choice-offering and branching narratives that seek to combine story-like and game-like elements, with

---

[2] D. H. Lawrence, Why the Novel Matters. *http://individual.utoronto.ca/amlit/why_the_novel_matters.htm* Last accessed May 2016.

[3] *Ibid.*

[4] *Ibid.* p. 39.

varying degrees of success. There are still lessons that can be learned from paper development, especially in more experimental fields.

GAMES

And, finally, of course, games writers should not forget to look to games themselves for inspiration; where else can you see good games writing in operation? Just as useful, if not more so on occasion to a practitioner, where you can find the opposite? But also, and in particular, the sense in which it is meant in this chapter, find games that offer new storytelling paradigms. Perhaps a little contentious, but in many ways we would suggest interactive storytelling has never really improved on *D&D*—vast, richly detailed, highly imaginative, and seemingly endless worlds conjured up with words, some numbers, and endless die rolls—a feeling of moral choice, character development, and story worlds capable of provoking and evoking a gamut of emotions—achievement, sorrow, betrayal, and more. It's very hard to think of a more elegant way to combine games playing with storytelling where each so effortlessly serves the other. It's worth keeping in mind that this kind of endeavor didn't stop altogether when digital experiences began to encroach on the time budgets of players of games like *D&D*, *Traveler*, *Runequest Tunnels & Trolls*, *Space 1889*, and countless other RPG systems of the 1970s, 1980s, and 1990s. Games like the card-based *Once Upon A Time*, its expansion deck *Dark Tales*, and *The Extraordinary Adventures of Baron Munchausen* (all three from designer James Wallis) show storytelling and games can and do go together, or can be made to go together in a satisfying, enlightening (for a games writer), and fun way. Here, players tell stories either with cards, as in the case of the first two, or without, as with the latter, and they compete to complete satisfying stories, using their own cards or their objections to either steal control of the story or to force the storyteller to refine their story and encompass a reversal or revelation in order to retain story coherency.

Likewise, board games such as *Battlestar Galactica* and *Arabian Nights* (Z-Man Games' 2009 version) are both about the theme of storytelling—one implicitly, the other explicitly—and are both excellent demonstrations of games and storytelling in harmony. In *Arabian Nights* players take part in a game where stories are to be encountered all around and as you aspire to great status you make choices, face their consequences, and create a life story for your character that sinks you deeper into the game and its mechanics. In

Battlestar Galactica you all, nominally, play as humans onboard the eponymous ship attempting to stave off attacks from the Cylons (controlled by the internal game mechanics) and find a way to Earth before the ship, and everyone on it, is destroyed. Except that at least one of you is a Cylon, no one knows who the Cylons are, and Cylons win the game by making sure the other players fail. All of which means the real story that develops through the game, and what comes to wholly define it, is who is or isn't a Cylon, how do they act, and how long does it take to discover them? Any Cylons need to be sly so no one detects them, but they also need to be active in order to ensure they do disrupt the progress of the other players. Which onboard explosions, technical failures, or dire incidents are accidents, and which are sabotage?

SUMMARY

It's far from certain what direct applications there are from these other media for games writers. It's even less certain what applications more mainstream development scenarios and agendas may yet permit. However, the point remains that games writers should actively seek to ensure their palettes of research, their frames of reference, and their experiences are as rich as possible; that means looking beyond just movies and beyond the obvious. There's a whole world of inspiration available, and if we don't know when or if ever we may get to apply it, that shouldn't prevent us from seeking it out.

EXERCISES

1. List three areas of human activity that are useful for games writers as a resource, and discuss why.
2. Take one element (e.g., character, plot, or setting) each from a TV show, book, and a board game, then—using those three elements—create a one- to two-page story outline for a game, being sure to include the following:

   A clear awareness of what platform the game is played on.

   Who it is for.

   How the player wins, or at least progresses in the world.

   How they control their avatar or actions in order to win.

3. Use music and/or sound as inspiration to create an innovative game. Write a one- to two-page design outline that answers the following questions:

   How does a player win?

   How can they tell if they are winning?

   How many players is this game for?

   Who is its intended audience?

   What games platform is it for? (Only concentrate on one lead platform.)

   How does the player control their avatar(s)? Draw up a controller configuration diagram to show which buttons on the controller do what for the lead platform. Perhaps there is no controller, or perhaps the control interface is built directly into the touch screen. In the case of the latter provide a sketch for how that control interface looks.

   Optionally, you may choose to include a story and/or character element to it.

Chapter 17 Marrying Design and Story: Driver 76 Case Study

I have an author and a game designer in me, locked in a kind of eternal death grapple. The friction generates tremendous energy . . . but sometimes I wish one of them would just choke out and die.

—Jordan Thomas, Creative Director, 2K Marin, in conversation, 2011

BRIEF TERMS

SEQUENCE A series of scenes linked by one core concept (e.g., a car chase through a city).

PAYOFF MOMENT A story moment in which the player's recent efforts are rewarded in a manner directly linked to the plot.

COMPLICATING FACTOR A story element that serves to heighten tension and conflict, thereby raising the stakes further.

As we've already explored in some detail, every project you work on as a games writer brings with it unique requirements that inform not only elements of the story, but its method of delivery. Ubisoft's

Driver 76, an action driving game released in 2007 for the Sony PlayStation Portable, features a story that takes place in the same universe as *Driver: Parallel Lines*, released the year before. Designed to appeal to a demographic similar to its parent game, a major difference is that while *Driver: Parallel Lines'* story is told primarily through lavish FMV cut scenes, *Driver 76's* story is delivered through a mock '70s comic book style. This is mainly due to budgetary, scheduling, and technological considerations—creating an FMV-driven story would have not only been an expensive and time-consuming exercise, it also would not have been as suitable for the portable platform *Driver 76* was destined for. Delivering the story in a comic book style was not only far cheaper and simpler for the developer as well as less taxing on the PSP's hardware, it was a clever way to further evoke America of the 1970s—a time when comics were arguably even more popular than they are now. Note the scripts that follow fit this new style and don't adopt a format closely resembling a movie script—they simply contain dialogue and static image descriptions designed to enable the game's artists to sketch the comic book panels destined to be navigated by the virtual camera's eye as the sequence unfolds. Each image is carefully constructed to allow delivery of story in the most efficient and pleasing manner possible, working closely with the action and dialogue.

Even with this simpler and cheaper (though arguably no less effective) story delivery system, Ubisoft's original brief stated each gameplay-bridging sequence could last no longer than sixty seconds. Despite this tight time limit, each still had to serve a variety of important functions. For a game lasting several hours, supporting gameplay with only a few minutes of story required careful thinking on the part of the writers. It's clear that, despite best efforts, the final scenes were often longer than sixty seconds, though each line of dialogue and image were subjected to intense scrutiny to justify their right to exist.

This chapter examines the range of tasks performed by each of *Driver 76's* comic book sequences, proving that with the right structuring, even a few minutes is enough time to provide a compelling, coherent story that supports and helps drive gameplay forward.

NOTE *Please note that, for the purposes of this book, the script contained in this chapter has been edited to remove any references to drugs of any kind.*

SEQUENCE 1: SETTING UP THE GAME AND STORY

SEQUENCE 1

IMAGE - NEW YORK SKYLINE.

RAY (V.O.)

I'd been in New York just six months and already hated the place. All I did was fix cars -

IMAGE - RAY WATCHES AND WE PAN TO SEE SLINK CRACK THE BREAK.

RAY (V.O.) (CONT'D)

- and shoot pool down at Elmo's with Slink.

SLINK

I'm gonna whup your ass!

IMAGE - THE UPMARKET COPACABANA CLUB.

RAY (V.O.)

Then I met Chen-Chi. And everything changed.

IMAGE - A GORGEOUS CLOSE-UP OF CHEN-CHI.

CHEN-CHI

It's Ray, isn't it? Sure, I remember those brown eyes.

IMAGE - OUTSIDE THE CLUB JIMMY YIP MUSCLES IN AND HUSTLES HER INTO A FABULOUS OPEN TOP TRANS-AM.

RAY (V.O.)

Trouble was - she already looked taken.

JIMMY YIP

You're way out your depth hillbilly.

IMAGE - RAY AND SLINK ON DECKCHAIRS ON THE ROOF OF ELMO'S BRONX BAR, CRACKING OPEN A COUPLE OF BEERS.

RAY (V.O.)

Slink spelledit out for me.

SLINK

You want the girl? Easy. Her daddy - guy named Zhou - calls the shots on who she goes out with. You make him happy - you just might get laid. He's got rich tastes, mind!

IMAGE - BIG CLOSE UP SLINK AND RAY.

RAY

Sounds good.

SLINK

Only one problem. Mister Zhou's the biggest Triad boss in town. He kills guys like you for breakfast.

RAY

Oh yeah? That's why you're gonna help.

```
GAMEPLAY: PLAYER MISSIONS CENTER AROUND
OBTAINING IMPRESSIVE GIFTS FOR ZHOU USING
ANY MEANS NECESSARY.
```


The first sequence has to fulfil several important tasks—it must introduce the player to the world, characters, and overall tone of the game they are about to experience. In the case of *Driver 76*, we're in a comic book version of '70s New York, which, while not totally divorced from our reality, is still clearly not meant to be fully realistic. The first sequence is designed not only to introduce the protagonist, Ray, but his future partner in crime capers, Slink; when the gameplay begins, the player must be in no doubt the two are good friends who enjoy one another's company, are likeable, laid back but also, in their own way, ambitious. This is important in part because later in the story, when the stakes are raised, it must be no surprise that the pair watch out for one another. Also, it wasn't enough for players to know the broad strokes of the world our heroes exist in at the beginning of the story, they must know some specifics—that Ray and Slink, while ambitious, are very much at the bottom of the proverbial food chain, shooting pool and hanging out at a seedy bar, so that by the end of the game, their newfound success feels all the sweeter.

Equally important, the sequence must provide a clear and logical motivation for the initial set of *Driver 76* missions. Any story, regardless of the medium in which it's told, has to provide its protagonist with a desire—something they want to obtain, and that can only be obtained through conflict. The key here was to identify a desire compatible with potential gameplay objectives, something that would pull the player along the story for the duration of the game. In this case, Ray's hunger to romance the intoxicating yet forbidden Chen-Chi; from the first moment of the game the player knows Ray ultimately wants her. His story-based motivation results in Slink initially suggesting the pair obtain extravagant gifts for her Triad boss father, Mr. Zhou. Quick to communicate using the comic book cut scene and, hopefully, a powerful motivation gamers can understand, Slink's idea allowed the game designers a framework to create the first set of game missions.

To help communicate a great deal of information quickly, a voiceover is added, which is also used to add flavor and character to proceedings.

SEQUENCE 2: THE FIRST PAYOFF

SEQUENCE 2

IMAGE - EXT. RAY AND SLINK ENTER ZHOU'S MAHJONGG PARLOR.

RAY (V.O.)

So we made the Zhou happy. He invited us over, said he had a job offer…

IMAGE - ZHOU'S OFFICE.

ZHOU

I wish to make a gift to Tong Elders. I need cars. No junk. Special. I give you list. Deal?

SLINK

We're the cats you're looking for.

ZHOU

Deliver, and I pay sixty thousand dollars.

RAY

Before we go Mr. Zhou, I was wondering if me and your daughter Chen-Chi… you know, she sure is lovely and…

IMAGE - RAY AND SLINK SIT IN THE STANDS OF A RACE TRACK.

SLINK

Man! That's one angry dude!

RAY

Yeah! Maybe we better just concentrate on getting him those cars. We'll need all kinds of gear, bread for bribes - the works.

SLINK

Don't you sweat on that, the Slink can hustle up some bearer bonds, baby - as good as money!

RAY (V.O.)

That night, we were in the mood to celebrate.

IMAGE - COPACABANA NIGHTCLUB IN FULL SWING. RAY AND SLINK CHILLING AT THE BAR LOOKING SLICK. A HOT GIRL CHATS TO SLINK, HER HAND ON HIS ARM. RAY SCANS THE PLACE.

SLINK

(to girl)

One day I'm gonna get me a place like this. Funky sounds, smokin' dance floor and fancy drinks with them little umbrellas. My name's gonna be in lights, baby!

IMAGE - RAY DANCES WITH CHEN-CHI, A SLOW NUMBER.

RAY

```
            Any day now, I'm gonna take
            you away from all this.

                        CHEN CHI

                        (amused)
            You going to be my white
            knight, Ray?

WE PAN TO SEE JIMMY YIP STANDING NEARBY,
WATCHING AND SMOLDERING, ROMERO BY HIS
SIDE.

GAMEPLAY: Missions center around obtaining/
stealing expensive cars for Zhou.
```


Sequence 2 had to contain a "payoff" moment for the player who has worked hard to help Ray's romantic dreams become reality—in this case, it's clear their missions have successfully gained them an audience with Mr. Zhou, though this naturally can't result in Ray's deepest motivation being satisfied (nothing is truly appreciated if it is too easy to obtain, and access to Chen-Chi is the key story catalyst for the entire game).

Two important questions that had to be asked at this point were *what does the gameplay need and how is it driven forward?* Naturally, a new quickly conveyable and easily understandable player objective must be presented. Linked to this, a further two questions asked were *what does the story need and how is it driven forward?* The answer was, something surprising, yet consistent with the world, the characters, and the theme; clearly a relatively lighthearted caper suggests action and events that can cast our characters in a comedic light. (Keeping in mind that comedic doesn't necessarily mean it makes you laugh out loud; it really means in this case how we show how our heroes are not as well-informed or aware as they might think.)

In this case, Mr. Zhou offers the pair further work, which provides the game designers with a clear framework within which to design new missions for the player—but, despite being interested in the pair, Mr. Zhou is clearly not willing to entertain Ray's interest in his daughter. Having Ray raise the subject helps to re-state his real goal, and the offscreen response suggests how far away he is from getting it.

Additionally, the sequence ends by introducing Jimmy Yip, the ultimate antagonist of the game who clearly has designs on Chen-Chi already. So, in essence, as well as rewarding the player with a payoff, the sequence contains one complicating factor, as well as two "but" elements (Mr. Zhou not wanting Ray to officially see his daughter, and Jimmy Yip clearly not happy about our protagonist's intentions either). The entire sequence is also crafted to further illustrate the game universe, a place where opportunity and danger are present, but also somewhere fun, with a lighter touch, as shown by the scene in the Copacabana where Slink reveals his dreams and Ray continues to pursue Chen-Chi, despite the increasing level of danger associated with her. This "upping of the ante" is necessary to help move the story forward. Slink's references to the club are also a way of reasserting the links and timelines between *Driver: Parallel Lines* and *Driver 76*.

In order to fund their new scheme, Slink and Ray also discuss using bearer bonds, which feature later in the story and gameplay. But why not simply use money instead? Bearer bonds allowed Slink and Ray access to funds that would eventually land them in debt to gang boss, Isaiah, without disrupting the game's upgrade and equipment-purchasing mechanic. While it was important that they need to work off that debt, it was vital that the money earned in optional side missions didn't count towards its repayment, as that would have meant the player could opt-out of completing vital core story missions. So the decision was made to use bonds, which had to be re-purchased by Ray and Slink, funded by the proceeds of the core missions, yet still tied into gameplay in an efficient and logical way. Also, this "story-specific" form of money allowed the breadth and freedom designers required to formulate the tier of missions that follow Sequence 3.

SEQUENCE 3: ADDING COMPLICATIONS

```
SEQUENCE 3

IMAGE - WAREHOUSE - NIGHT - SLINK AND RAY
STAND WAITING.

                RAY (V.O.)
          We'd done what the old man
          wanted, had sixty grand
          coming and couldn't wait.

             JIMMY YIP (O.S.)
          Hey, hillbilly!
```

PAN TO SEE JIMMY YIP, ZHOU AND SEVERAL GOONS WITH GUNS, EMERGING FROM THE SHADOWS.

RAY

What's he doing here?

ZHOU

Jimmy works for me.

SLINK

Well, whatever man. You got our money?

ZHOU

You think I do deals with punks like you? No way.

IMAGE - SLINK HOLDS RAY BACK AS WE HEAR THE TRANSPORTER DRIVE OFF. PAN TO JIMMY YIP SLIDING PAST IN HIS TRANS-AM, SMILING AT THEM.

RAY

You can't do this! Where's our money?!

IMAGE - AT THE COPACABANA NIGHTCLUB, RAY AT THE BAR.

RAY

The usual, Phil, and make it a large one.

ROMERO (O.S.)

Hey, loser! You ain't welcome here no more.

WE PULL BACK TO REVEAL CEASAR ROMERO SITTING A FEW STOOLS DOWN THE BAR, A SMIRKING JIMMY

YIP AND UNHAPPY LOOKING CHEN-CHI BESIDE HIM.

RAY

Says who, Romero? Your
girlfriend Jimmy?

ROMERO

Says me, the manager, now
get lost.

RAY (V.O.)

Things were beginning to
unravel.

IMAGE - ELMO'S BAR - RAY AND SLINK SHOOTING
POOL.

SLINK

Hey, Ray, you know those
bonds we used… I got a
little confession to make:
they were from Elmo's safe
and I kinda didn't ask
before I took them.

IMAGE - RAY AND SLINK TAKE ELMO TO ONE SIDE
TO CONFESS.

ELMO

You in serious trouble! That
ain't my money, it belongs
to Isaiah.

SLINK

The Southside Prophets'
boss?! We're dead.

ELMO

```
            Boys, when he comes to
            collect, you're on your own.

IMAGE - RAY AND SLINK STANDING ON TOP OF
ELMO'S.

                    SLINK
            We're dead.

                    RAY
            Relax man. All we gotta do
            is make the money back. With
            my ass behind the wheel and
            you hustling the streets,
            it's a home run.

GAMEPLAY: Player missions center around
getting enough money together to replace the
bonds.
```


Despite the player inevitably being successful in their missions for Mr. Zhou, it was also necessary for the mission payoff to contain a complicating 'but' moment that once again drives events forward and, usefully, thrusts Ray and Slink into deeper trouble. Again, the core four questions were once again asked: *what does the gameplay need and how is it driven forward?* Also *what does the story need and how is it driven forward?* In this case, Mr. Zhou decides to betray our protagonist by refusing to pay the agreed money, while also properly introducing Jimmy Yip in a manner that clearly illustrates he's not only someone who can't be trusted, but that he relishes Ray's troubles.

However, the loss of payment is used as the catalyst for the next set of missions—Slink's revelation that he "borrowed" the bearer bonds coupled with barman Elmo's revelation they actually belong to gang boss, Isaiah, serves to provide a new framework of missions. From a narrative perspective, it was important for at least a portion of Ray and Slink's predicament to be directly as a result of their actions in order to lend them a feeling of agency and power in the story; characters who constantly react to situations thrust upon them purely as a result of others' actions appear weak in comparison to those who make decisions—even wrong ones—and actively deal with the consequences. The main issue that arises at the end of Sequence 3 is Slink's theft of the bearer bonds and their urgent need to replace them before gang boss Isaiah discovers they're missing. Again, these provide a new need that is both quick to communicate and flexible enough to design a wide range of interesting missions around.

The initial images used in this sequence were carefully chosen in part to show the darker world Ray and Slink had chosen to enter—a place of shady deals, betrayal, and danger (as illustrated by the shadowy warehouse)—which contrasts with the bright, cheerful Copacabana Club seen later on. However, our heroes are banished even from this "safe" part of the world, an event not only designed to illustrate their worsening situation, but Jimmy Yip's growing animosity toward Ray. Again, the sequence seeks to raise the stakes wherever possible.

SEQUENCE 4: SHIFTING CHARACTER GEARS

SEQUENCE 4

IMAGE - EXTERIOR ELMO'S BAR.

SLINK (V.O.)

Isaiah'll never know my "broker" babysat these little honeys - or that he took a cut when we bought them back. Man, everyone's on the take these days!

IMAGE - SLINK AND RAY BY THE SAFE WITH THE BONDS.

RAY

You know, Slink. I got an idea... We oughta use this money to make more money...

SLINK

You been at the moonshine,
Ray?

SAME IMAGE - PANS TO RAY.

RAY

Listen. The Copacabana's
swimming in African diamonds
- some big shipment's
come in. How about we use
the bonds to hire us some
muscle, hit the Latinos and
take the whole stash?

PAN BACK TO SLINK - NOW AMAZED AND TAKEN
ABACK.

SLINK

Oh yeah, Mr. Einstein? And
who we gonna sell them to?

RAY

Zhou! Perfect, huh?

RAY (O.S.) (CONT'D)

I get the girl, we get rich,
and Isaiah's bonds still go
back in the safe. Everybody
wins.

IMAGE - RAY RUNNING WITH CHEN-CHI ON HIS
ARM AND CASH IN HIS HAND. SLINK NEXT TO HIM,
CASH IN HIS HAND TOO, ZHOU WAVING IN THE
BACKGROUND, BIG SMILE, NEXT TO HIM ISAIAH
WAVING, HIS BONDS IN HIS HAND.

RAY

You're working with a genius here Slink.

IMAGE - SLINK AND RAY, SLINK NOW STANDING, THE BONDS IN ONE HAND. (SAME IMAGE AS EARLIER)

RAY (V.O.)

So Slink took me to meet some folk in the 'burbs he'd heard of - The Thompsons, nicest husband and wife heavy protection team you could ever wish to hire.

IMAGE - THE DINING ROOM OF A SUBURBAN HOUSE - MR. AND MRS. THOMPSON, SLINK AND RAY DO BUSINESS, THE BONDS ON THE TABLE, COFFEE AND COOKIES.

MRS. THOMPSON

Would you and your friend like another cookie? They're fresh out the oven.

GAMEPLAY: Player missions center around preparation for Latino diamond theft, as well as theft itself.

Sequence 4 contains a vital change regarding Ray's character. It was important to show his internal as well as external journey—in this case, through his shifting attitude. Despite having successfully raised enough money to replace the stolen bonds, it was not only more interesting for Ray to suddenly show his entrepreneurial spirit by suggesting they use the funds to raise further cash, it was necessary to provide the game designers the logic upon which to base another set of fun missions for the player to undertake in the next section of the game. Linked to this, Ray and Slink once again actively raise the stakes by knowingly using Isaiah's bonds to bankroll the diamond theft from the Latino gang; having originally been content to steal a few cars for Mr. Zhou, the risky plan also serves to underline the growth in both Ray and Slink—they're willing to risk Isaiah's wrath to finally make some serious money and really start to get ahead. Their sensible decision to purchase protection for themselves not only serves to underline the danger they're in, but allows the writers to introduce two new characters to the story in the form of the Thompsons. Their home and, to an extent, lifestyle are, on the surface, as far from the underworld lifestyle as possible—this helps contrast the two very different worlds and makes them more interesting for the player as they're aware of the Thompsons' professional calling.

SEQUENCE 5: RAISING THE STORY STAKES

```
SEQUENCE 5

IMAGE - EXTERIOR. NY BACKGROUND. ZHOU, JIMMY
YIP (CASE IN HAND) RAY (CASE IN HAND) AND
SLINK MEET UP.

                    ZHOU
          I'm pleased you boys do not
          hold grudges. Business too
          important for emotions to
          get in way.

                 JIMMY YIP
          They're wasting our time,
          Mr. Zhou.

IMAGE - ZHOU HOLDS A PACKET WITH CHINESE
WRITING ON IT.

                    ZHOU
          How stupid are you two? This
          my stolen shipment! You
          selling me my own diamonds!
```

SAME IMAGE - PANS TO REVEAL JIMMY YIP WITH
GUN OUT.

JIMMY YIP

You've really screwed up
now…

IMAGE - MR. AND MRS. THOMPSON WITH GUNS
POINTING.

MR. THOMPSON

Hello everyone. We need to
cut in here.

RAY (O.S.)

Hey, it's the cavalry!

MRS. THOMPSON

Sorry folks, no winners
today. We'll take the
diamonds, Ray, and the cash,
Mr. Zhou. Thank you boys -
it's been fun.

SLINK (O.S.)

Aw, man!

RAY (V.O.)

We headed back to Elmo's to
figure out our next move.

IMAGE - AT ELMO'S THE BAR IS WRECKED, ELMO IS
INJURED, RAY AND SLINK LOOK ON.

RAY (V.O.)

We'd had visitors.

ELMO

The Latinos came looking for
you two.

SLINK

Oh man, ain't we popular?
We got the Latinos and the
Chinese after us. All we
need now's The Prophets…

ISAIAH (O.S.)

Oh yeah, why's that,
brother?

IMAGE - ISAIAH AND RAY.

ISAIAH

You wanna tell me how come
this safe is empty?

SLINK

Hi Isaiah. Sure. Er - here's
the thing…

ISAIAH

Who - took - my - bonds?

RAY

(thinking quickly)

The Latinos. Yeah, the
Latinos did it!

ISAIAH

Latinos, huh?

```
                RAY
        You bet. How about me and
        Slink help you take them
        out?

              ISAIAH
        You two knuckleheads do
        EXACTLY what I tell you!

GAMEPLAY: Player missions center around
taking down the Latino gang.
```


Sequence 5 had to be all about pushing Ray and Slink as deep into trouble as possible. With this in mind, Ray and Slink's plan not only totally failed from a planning perspective (they tried to sell Mr. Zhou his own diamonds), it failed in its execution when Mr. and Mrs. Thompson betrayed them. The initial scene also serves to remind the player of Jimmy Yip's presence, position, and animosity towards the pair, which foreshadows events to come later. Just when Ray and Slink think nothing else can go wrong, they discover the Latino gang has taken up arms against them, trashing Elmo's place in the process and forcing Isaiah to take a direct hand in events. Damaging Elmo's was necessary to show the player the destructive consequences of Ray and Slink's actions and the potential for yet more danger ahead; what had once been a safe place was transformed into a potential warning of worse to come.

Once again, a group of viable, clear gameplay missions had to be created from the sequence in a way that also satisfies the story. In this case, Ray and Slink, while certainly reactive in how they must accept the failure of the diamond meeting (a specific "but" moment that serves to add further conflict), actively manage to turn events in their favor when they lie to Isaiah, telling him it was the Latinos who stole his bonds—a clever and plausible lie given the Hispanic gang had just smashed up Elmo's bar in retaliation for the stolen diamonds. The following missions, concerned with dismantling the Latino gang's operations, are a clear and logical progression from what has just occurred.

SEQUENCE 6: CHANGING THE HERO'S FORTUNES

SEQUENCE 6

IMAGE - EXTERIOR - TIGHTEN ON SLINK AND RAY HAVING HOT DOGS AND COFFEE AT A STAND.

RAY

Latinos - dealt with. The Brothers - off our backs. We got star quality, man.

SLINK

We the real thing.

Chinese Heavy 1 (O.S.)

Uh-uh. This the real thing.

IMAGE - BIG CLOSE UP, A GUN BARREL PRESSES AGAINST SLINK'S HEAD.

SLINK

Be cool, man.

SAME IMAGE - PULL OUT TO REVEAL - CHINESE HEAVIES 1 AND 2 MUSCLE IN BEHIND OUR BOYS.

CHINESE HEAVY 1

Coffee break over. In the car - now!

IMAGE - WITH NEW YORK RISING IN FRAME BEHIND, THE BIG BLACK LIMO GLIDES ONTO WASTE GROUND BY WASHINGTON BRIDGE.

RAY (O.S.)

We'll hop out here if it's okay with you fellas…

IMAGE - SLINK AND RAY BEING KICKED OUT OF THE LIMO, SPRAWLING IN THE DIRT. PAN TO ANOTHER LIMO DRAWING UP.

FX: Doors open. Weapons are cocked.

SLINK

Shoot, Ray – this here's the wrong kind of Chinese take-out.

IMAGE - POV SLINK AND RAY: EXPENSIVE SHOES - PAN UP TO REVEAL ZHOU TOWERING OVER US.

ZHOU

Good news. I got my diamonds back. Mr. and Mrs. Thompson were… punished. But bad news. Before the end they tell me Jimmy behind all my troubles. He's working with Latinos. Wants to take my empire. This news, it breaks my heart.

IMAGE - CLOSE-UPS SLINK AND RAY TAKING THIS IN.

ZHOU (O.S.)

So now you my friends. You only people I trust. You work for me.

RAY

Good call, Mr. Zhou. Heck – we're almost family.

SAME IMAGE - PAN UP TO CLOSE-UP MR. ZHOU.

ZHOU

Don't push your luck,
guanxi. Go back to city and
destroy Jimmy Yip for me.
Make his soul burn.

GAMEPLAY: PLAYER MISSIONS CENTER AROUND
DESTROYING JIMMY YIP'S FLEDGLING EMPIRE.

Sequence 6 had to contain a payoff that clearly illustrates the extent to which Ray and Slink's fortunes had begun to change and that their world was starting to broaden, hence it opens with the pair enjoying food, in a large, picturesque city space. However, while the player has successfully helped Ray and Slink solve their problems with the Latinos and owing Isaiah, another issue arrives in the form of Mr. Zhou's revelation that Jimmy Yip was plotting to overthrow his empire. The forced journey to waste ground shows how vulnerable the pair still are and that Ray and Slink's efforts could still amount to nothing. Mr. Zhou's problem not only helps provide the next set of gameplay missions for the player, it begins to bring the story full-circle; Ray suddenly has a real opportunity to impress Mr. Zhou and perhaps even gain sufficient favor with him to grant official approval to date the elusive Chen-Chi. The sequence also illustrates just how far Ray and Slink have come in terms of their status—they have been chosen to spearhead the dismantling of Jimmy Yip's new operations.

SEQUENCE 7: THE FINAL TEST

SEQUENCE 7

IMAGE - NEW YORK AERIAL SHOT DAWN.

RAY (O.S.)

So Jimmy's little empire
went the way of all empires
and once again Zhou was back
running Chinatown.

IMAGE - INTERIOR ZHOU'S MAHJONGG PARLOR - SLINK AND RAY SIT FORMALLY IN FRONT OF ZHOU AT HIS DESK.

ZHOU

Foolish young men - you have done well.

RAY

Hey, thanks.

ZHOU

I have spoken with Mr. Isaiah and wiped clean your debts.

SLINK

No way.

IMAGE - CLOSE-UP RAY.

RAY

Mr. Zhou. About Chen-Chi. I would really like to -

ZHOU

You have my blessing.

RAY

Hey! No kidding!

IMAGE - RAY AND SLINK EMERGE ONTO THE SIDEWALK - PAN TO - A FAMILIAR TRANS-AM PARKED NEARBY, ENGINE RUNNING.

SLINK

What the…?!

IMAGE - RAY AND SLINK'S POV - JIMMY YIP IN THE CAR. HIS FACE AND CLOTHES BADLY BURNED.

JIMMY

Surprised, hillbilly? You know, Chen-Chi's a pretty girl. Want her to stay that way? Then keep up!

IMAGE - JIMMY'S TRANS-AM TEARS OFF DOWN THE STREET.

GAMEPLAY: Player races against Jimmy to save Chen-Chi.

Sequence 7 needed to provide the player with a taste of pure, unadulterated victory, before quickly painfully ripping it away. The first image is designed to project hope and success as the sun rises. We're taken inside Mr. Zhou's mahjongg parlor to show just how trusted Ray and Slink have become. Despite all this, while successfully completing the gameplay missions surrounding the destruction of Jimmy Yip's empire results in Mr. Zhou not only clearing Ray and Slink's debts with Isaiah, but finally granting his blessing in regards to Chen-Chi, another crisis must arise in order to fuel the next and final section of gameplay. As a direct result of Ray and Slink's actions, a badly hurt Jimmy Yip provides the final mission in the form of rescuing Chen-Chi. From a story perspective, the climax has to be tied to Ray's initial and simple goal—to get the girl. If the player fails now, all is lost as Chen-Chi might be killed. Linked to this, a clear gameplay goal arises in the simple, compelling mission to race and beat Jimmy Yip before it's too late.

SEQUENCE 8: CLIMAX AND REWARD

SEQUENCE 8

IMAGE - SLINK AND CHEN-CHI STAND ON THE SIDEWALK OUTSIDE ZHOU'S OFFICE, A COUPLE OF ZHOU'S GOONS ARE WITH THEM.

CHEN-CHI

You think he'll be okay?

SLINK

(cocky)

What, you his mom now?

SMALL PANEL INSERT - CHEN-CHI'S FACE LIGHTS UP AND WE HEAR A CAR ENGINE.

IMAGE - RAY PULLS UP BESIDE THEM, ARM CASUALLY OUT THE WINDOW, SMILING.

RAY

Miss me?

CHEN-CHI

Where have you been?!

SLINK

Yeah, man! What the heck you trying to do to us?!

IMAGE - WE'RE IN ZHOU'S OFFICE. ZHOU'S AT HIS DESK, CHEN-CHI STANDING TO ONE SIDE. RAY'S AT THE OPEN DOORWAY. SLINK SITS ON A SOFA.

ZHOU

Ray. I have surprise for you. It was to be gift for trusted lieutenant. It is now yours.

IMAGE - CLOSE-UP ZHOU HANDS RAY A CAR KEY AND AN ADDRESS IN HUNTS POINT NY.

IMAGE - FROM INSIDE A DARK GARAGE, THE DOOR RAISED, RAY'S ASTONISHED FACE.

RAY

Wow.

```
IMAGE - RAY AND CHEN-CHI IN CLOSE-UP TOGETHER
IN THE FRONT SEATS OF THE MOST BEAUTIFUL
OPEN-TOP YOU EVER SAW, THE WIND BLOWING
CHEN-CHI'S HAIR.

                    RAY (V.O.)
          I'd come a long way in a
          short time. And heck - I'd
          cut some corners to get
          there. But I had the girl,
          the car and an open road
          ahead. What else can a guy
          ask for in life, huh?

SAME IMAGE - PULL UP AND WIDEN TO REVEAL THE
CAR CRUISING ACROSS THE BROOKLYN BRIDGE OFF
MANHATTAN ISLAND. AND WIDEN FURTHER TO SEE
THE WHOLE NEW YORK CITY SKYLINE BEHIND.

THE END
```


Game story endings can be difficult to get right as they must balance climax, reward, and closure. Sequence 8 had to provide the player with the final, climactic payoff that neatly concludes the story in a satisfying, memorable way. For once, the writers don't need to consider future gameplay. Successfully completing the final mission essentially unlocks the reality briefly glimpsed by the player in the previous sequence. Ray's dreams come true—he gets Chen-Chi (with Mr. Zhou's blessing), a fantastic car, and an open road ahead of him. The initial images are designed to transmit feeling of triumph, before shifting to ones of freedom and happiness as Ray and Chen-Chi speed across the Golden Gate Bridge, a powerful symbol of change and potential. In this instance, the writers also had to make allowances for the fact *Driver 76* is a prequel to the events that occur in *Driver: Parallel Lines* – Ray and Slink, both major characters in that title, had to end *Driver 76* in a manner that allowed them to be present when TK, *Driver: Parallel Lines*' protagonist, begins his story.

EXERCISES

1. To what extent should a game title's platform define the story told? Should it be a major factor when deciding what is possible from a story point of view? Or should developers not be afraid to tell whatever story best fits gameplay, regardless of a title's platform or platforms? Discuss.
2. From a games writer's perspective, to what extent should it matter if a title they're about to begin working on is shipping across multiple platforms (handheld, console, and PC)?

PROJECTS

1. Choose a game that features cut scenes. Pick a meaningful section of the game. Create a document that describes what happens in the cut scenes and corresponding gameplay in your chosen section. Using the chapter for inspiration, analyze the content of each cut scene and list the ways in which each serves the gameplay.
2. Create the basic design and story outline for a game with the same core structural brief as *Driver 76*. It doesn't have to be a driving game, it can be any genre you choose, providing it fulfils the brief below:

   - No more than eight "scene sequences"; each should be as close to sixty seconds as possible, and each should use as few characters and locations as possible.

   - Between each "scene sequence" there must be gameplay of the genre relevant type; so seven gameplay "pots" in total.

   - In each "gameplay pot" (except the last) there must be at least three different individual "missions" supported by the same preceding "scene sequence." Voice over or on screen text can be used to further contextualize the individual missions within a "pot."

   - Each individual "mission" must have its own beginning, middle, and end.

   - The final gameplay pot should be just one mission, which helps the entire story culminate.

3. Write/design a six- to eight-page outline for a game where there are no "scene sequences" separated from the gameplay. Instead, devise a story with eight plot points that are integrated with the game design itself; consider reversals and revelations and ways to deliver them within a game system.

Chapter 18 STORYLOADING

Those who tell stories rule society.

—Plato[1]

STORYTELLING, STORYFORMING, AND STORYDWELLING

In 2005 in Chongqing, China, Jim Banister, an entertainment and technology polyglot, gave a presentation on his definitions of social narrative that would some years later lead him to what he now refers to as the *Primary Colors of Narrative—storytelling*, *storyforming*, and *storydwelling*. In these definitions he identifies the distinct intent of the creator, the audience's role, the nature of the audience's psychology, and the nature of the audience's experience. Such that, in *storytelling* the role and intention of the creator is to be an auteur or a presenter; the audience's role is as observer; the audience psychology is empathetic; and their experience is passive. In *storyforming* the creators build and manage "engines," through which interaction with the story emerges; the audience role is as puppeteer, not literally the character, but nevertheless controlling one or more avatars that perform their intended actions in the game world; the audience role has changed to be influential; and their experience is interactive. In *storydwelling* the role of the creator is to build and manage a game world or "spaces" with attendant rules that evolve in-line with what the population does, not what we anticipate they might do. The audience's role has changed to that of participant, the audience psychology is experiential, and the audience experience has become immersive. These definitions are summarized in Figure 18.1 by their creator.

---

[1] *http://www.storycon.org/quotations.htm*. Last accessed May 2016.

PRIMARY COLORS OF NARRATIVE

	TELLING	FORMING	DWELLING
PROGRAMMER'S ROLE / INTENT	AUTEUR/ PRESENTER	STORY ENGINE BUILDER/MANAGER	WORLD BUILDER/ MANAGER
AUDIENCE ROLE	OBSERVER	PUPPETEER	PARTICIPANT
AUDIENCE PSYCHOLOGY	EMPATHIC	INFLUENTIAL	EXPERIENTIAL
AUDIENCE EXPERIENCE	PASSIVE	INTERACTIVE	IMMERSIVE

FIGURE 18.1. Primary Colors of Narrative.

Of course, these definitions open up debate, perhaps in many areas. Some people strongly resist the definition of watching a movie, reading a book, or seeing a play, for example, as a passive experience when that movie, book, or play can be directly responsible for making their heart thump faster, sending a shiver down their spine, or eliciting tears or any number of tumultuous emotions besides. And, on this note, it would seem these experiences may not be best described as *interactive*, but perhaps more accurately as *reactive*. However, these initial definitions are useful for games writers to be aware of, and perhaps even use.

STORYLOADING

Considering storytelling models beyond movies, environmental storytelling, and new definitions such as storyforming and storydwelling invite a way for games writers to think of themselves and their role within development not as a storyteller at all. Instead, perhaps writers might think of themselves as someone who loads the game world with dramatic potential, and then steps away from it. Hence, the term *storyloading*. In relation to the trio of terms outlined earlier in this chapter, storyloading is perhaps a hybrid. On the one hand it's what a writer does in order to facilitate a *storydwelling* narrative construct, insofar as it is "lived" by its audience. Yet on the other hand storyloading is closer to *storyforming*, in that the creative intent can also be one of building and managing a story engine, ushering and shepherding players through an experience, albeit perhaps in increasingly deft and subtle ways.

TOP-DOWN AND BOTTOM-UP STORYTELLING

Two other terms we could also use are *top-down* and *bottom-up* storytelling. Top-down storytelling comprises developer-designed experiences in which the player journeys along a predetermined route, unlocking the right to progress through successfully overcoming gameplay obstacles. Top-down stories provide players with a controlled, focused, and planned story experience in which the game world parameters are often clearly defined. This method of storytelling can be illustrated by the "corridor shooter," an FPS genre in which the player fights their way along a predetermined landscape, with little, if any, ability to deviate from the path laid out for them. Yet, equally, top-down storytelling is also in evidence in Environmental Storytelling - players may (or may not) discover the stories, but they are still pre-set by the developers.

Bottom-up storytelling comprises story-based experiences created by players out of the game system itself, and defined by the actions and choices the player makes, not the perhaps hidden but pre-set routes or experiences the developer provides. MMOs are good examples of this kind of storytelling, where players often regale one another with stories detailing their own exploits within the game. Bottom-up storytelling is also sometimes referred to as Emergent Storytelling.

A storyteller is needed for the entire length over which a story is told. They cannot stop, leave, jump back, forward, or change tack without directly impacting the story itself and directly affecting the way that story is experienced by its audience. This is why, to a certain extent, describing a games writer as a storyformer makes perfect sense—they aren't there at every point, but they do shepherd the player through a journey, attempting to deliver a coherent story experience. Similarly, storyshaping is not bad either, since it ably confers the sense that the story's initial trajectory is set but the participants themselves then determine the way it plays out.

Storyloading is intended to convey the sense that it isn't just the story's initial trajectory that's set, but that the way it plays out will be more than partially determined at the outset too, and yet, at the same time, participants will also partially shape their own experience within this story or game and feel as if their interactions are unique and critical to the experience they get. Instead of working with the central question, *how can I tell an engaging story?* begin asking yourself *how can I load up the world with sufficient potential drama that it would be engaging to be in that world?* Instead of trying to figure out how to build a story as if at a potter's wheel with one hand behind your back, using the player as a sometimes unwilling, sometimes disinterested other hand in the process, the task becomes closer to set design. But it's more than just that because the manner in which the set is built doesn't just give the story its setting and its setup; if you can construct the set well enough, perhaps intricately enough, then the elements players encounter will have differing dramatic potential depending on who encounters them and when they are encountered. Moreover, the set can be built so as to only relinquish certain secrets at certain points, as if laden with multiple trapdoors and secret compartments all, crucially, tied to consequential events. The size of the set doesn't necessarily expand as players progress, but its dramatic potential does, without adding to art resource demands. A bank vault may always be a bank vault, but it's a substantially different dramatic proposition before a raid, during, and after, before a body is found in a locker and after, or when you're trying to break in and when you're trying to break out.

When considering games writing not as storytelling, but as storyloading, it brings to mind the difference between writing the script for the movie *Rambo* and of being Rambo and setting traps in the forest yourself. You understand the dramatic potential of the traps when they are triggered, and you understand the importance of where you place these traps in order to ensure enough are triggered to keep things interesting, but you can't necessarily determine the exact time or manner in which they will be triggered, or exactly who triggers them.

EVE ONLINE CASE STUDY

Most gamers agree Icelandic developer, CCP, takes a liberal approach when it comes to managing MMO *Eve Online*'s (literal) game universe, which provides players with a title that is ripe with the potential for "bottom-up" stories.

As discussed in Chapter 1, Eve Online's player interactions effectively take place on a single server "shard," instead of split between numerous identical worlds (which normally serves to ease population load). This means there's a huge player base interacting with one another on a massive scale—tens of thousands of players exploring, trading, cooperating, fighting, forming relationships, and completing missions—rather than a few thousand. The impact of this from a story point of view can't be understated. Many choose to join in-game corporations, formalized groups of players who band together for protection, profit, and camaraderie. These corporations often specialize in a variety of activities, both legal and illegal (by the game's virtual law enforcement standards), one being assassination. In 2005, after ten months of careful planning, a corporation called the Guiding Hand Social Club managed to assassinate one of the game's most powerful corporation heads, destroy her prize Navy Apocalypse ship, and ransack Ubiqua Seraph, her organization, seizing billions of ISK (Eve's currency) of assets in the process. All this was accomplished inside the game world, using tools created by the developers. After the event, it was revealed how Guiding Hand sleeper agents had painstakingly infiltrated Ubiqua Seraph at the highest level, patiently gaining the trust of those they planned to betray. It reads like a story from a spy novel, but was in fact an event driven entirely by a player base given the freedom they needed to create their own battle and their own victory. Though the morality of such actions is debatable, no one can deny the feat was as impressive as it was theatrical—a true player-driven bottom-up story, which captured the imaginations of gamers everywhere.

But storyloading is about more than loading environments; it's also about loading NPCs within those environments and pre-setting other triggers, such as audio and dynamic difficulty settings. And here's where it may ultimately be right to question the validity of the term given that true environmental storytelling is also about the same elements. Perhaps then, it's a matter of semantics and any sense of a shining debut into neologistic reverie on the part of the authors of this volume is ultimately somewhat premature and rather tarnished. Yet, be that as it may, storyloading can often be a far truer and far more helpful term for what a games writer is engaged in; *telling* is often very far from what is required of a games writer and the antithesis of what a player wants to experience. They invariably want to feel as if the world has been explicitly created in anticipation of their appearance into it—and this is exactly what storyloading suggests.

EXERCISES

1. List three examples of bottom-up story in video games.
2. Does storyloading benefit core gameplay in any way, or is it restricted to enhancing a title's story elements? Discuss.

PROJECTS

1. Work with a partner. Individually, devise a storyloaded environment with at least eight objects within it, then trade with your partner. Take five minutes to explore what story you can conjure from your partner's storyloaded environment, and then compare and discuss the results. Were they unexpected? Who was most responsible for each experience (the creator or the participant) and does it matter?
2. Create a story-driven video game concept document that "loads" the story instead of tells it. Be sure to do the following:

   Explore the practical potential for storyloading.

   Create a one- to two-page walkthrough document to describe the player's experience of playing for five minutes.

   Create a five-minute presentation that outlines the experience and explores the reasoning behind the creative decisions you made.

Chapter 19 Shifting Agency

Not being able to govern events, I govern myself, and apply myself to them, if they will not apply themselves to me.

—Michel de Montaigne

BRIEF TERMS

DUAL CHARACTER POV A game story in which the player, at differing times, experiences the action from two separate character viewpoints.

ENSEMBLE CAST A story within which a large cast of characters is afforded approximately the same amount of importance.

THIRD-PERSON POV Gameplay in which the action is viewed with some or all of the avatar's body in view on the screen.

DIAMETRICALLY OPPOSED MOTIVATIONS Character motivations that are totally opposite one another instead of merely different.

Games writers may frequently find themselves dealing with first- or third-person POV avatars, where player engagement is principally being courted through one central character. The player is generally acting within the story from the perspective of a constrained participant and reflecting upon it from the perspective of a passive spectator. There is nothing inherently wrong with this. But there are other ways to do things. We've seen dual character POV structures such as the one exhibited in survival horror game *Alone in the Dark: The New Nightmare*, where the two principal characters, Edward and Aline, are neatly split up at the beginning (their plane is attacked and they both parachute to safety, but land a little distance away from each other). Here, the player can choose to play as either character, with the main plot points intersecting from each path. More recently we've seen a tri-playable character structure in *GTA V*, allowing players to switch between its protagonists with a high degree of freedom. We've also seen multiple characters creating an ensemble cast effect and somewhat mosaic-like story in *Call of Duty 4: Modern Warfare* and *Modern Warfare 2*. These approaches don't only help keep things fresh and interesting for the player but, by extension, open the door to a solution for having plot reversals and player progress working together.

MULTIPLE CHARACTER PERSPECTIVES

If you play, consecutively, as two different characters that each possess diametrically opposed motivations, this gifts you a structure for doing both; for running plot reversals and player progress in tandem. If you introduce more characters with varied shades of motivation, you can make the overall narrative yet more intricate and involved. However, the price of this is living with the impact on story cohesion and player sympathy levels. Players may not always enjoy playing characters with questionable morals experiencing the game through a host of different characters. In fact, on more than one occasion within a development team, this has been categorically stated as if a point of fact. And, although cohesion and sympathy will certainly be issues to consider when adopting multiple character and multiple perspective approaches, it ultimately depends on how these approaches are constructed, so any definitive statement on the carte blanche avoidance of them can't be sufficiently endorsed. Players *can* engage with an ensemble cast—there are six playable characters in *Modern Warfare*, and as the Game Story and Character BAFTA award in 2008 would suggest, it did engage and entertain. Clearly, if characters are interesting enough people *will* engage with a variety of characters, not just those fueled by righteous fury and an arguably justifiable desire for revenge, but also characters who revel in their own evil, aware how the world might see them, but ultimately dismissive of those who brand them "bad" as a result of their morals not being compatible with the perceived norm—as seen in *Borderlands: The Pre-Sequel*™, *Star Wars: Knights of the Old Republic*, and other RPGs.

Further, stories with a larger cast of characters also bring with them other possibilities; character viewpoints can be layered for dramatic effect and identities or motivations withheld in order to build dramatic tension, introducing new questions into the story consistent with the overall gameplay and level design. Equally, not knowing who someone is or why they are doing whatever it is they are doing can be dangerous—players not knowing can easily turn into players not caring. But again, this depends on the manner in which it's handled. After all, there's a risk in the other direction too; players knowing too much, navigating a story landscape in which there remain no questions to be answered, are perilously close to players being bored, which is the same as not caring. The art is to provide a dynamic balance that moves both the game and story forward at the desired pace, while providing players with a satisfying flow of questions and answers that serve to encourage and reward progression.

BEYOND THE PLAYER AS SPECTATOR

There's more at stake than just character numbers and POV, however. What if it was possible to participate within the game in more than just a constrained way? What if it was possible to also reflect on the experience in a broader perspective than just as a spectator?

Consider this example taken from Ernest Adams' *A New Vision for Interactive Stories* talk at GDC San Francisco, 2006, in the form of a transcript from one of his playthroughs of *Façade*.

```
Audrey (the player) knocks on the front door.
Trip opens the door.

                    TRIP
                  Audrey!!

                   AUDREY
          Trip, I've been shot!

                    TRIP
                   Uh...

          Well, come on in...
          Uh, I'll go get Grace...
```

GRACE

Audrey, hi! How are you? I'm so happy to see you after so long!
(interrupted)

AUDREY
Call 911!

GRACE
Uh...

So, come in, make yourself at home.

AUDREY
OH F**K THIS!

TRIP

Ha ha! Oh I think we're going to need some drinks first if we're going to talk about sex!

Here, the player is clearly constrained—the game circumvents or ignores conversation that will lead things away from its own course and seeks to subtly influence or usher the player into following that course. Keep in mind too that *Façade* is a game that works hard to accommodate the player and make them feel the world is truly responsive to them. So much so, it's as easy to say *Façade* is an interactive story as much, if not more so, than it is a game.

Yet it is feasible for a player, in a world loaded with dramatic potential, to move more freely, choosing not just when certain actions might occur, but also what kinds of actions to effect and what the meaning of them might be, both to that player character and to the dramatic world as a whole. By way of demonstration, consider Augusto Boal's theatrical form called *Theater of the Oppressed*—which might just as readily have featured in our *More than Movies* chapter (Chapter 16) as an example of what can be learned from other forms. This encompasses a theatrical form in which the line between audience outside and actors within a play is blurred, giving us the term *spect-actors*, with spectators moving from the role of observers to act within the drama, imparting narrative structural change.

Coney, an agency of adventure and play, based in the UK and run by Tom Bowtell, Tassos Stevens, and Annette Mees, has projects showing that a physical, reciprocal, experimental, and interactive approach to storytelling is an ongoing discourse for practitioners. Coney generates their "theatrical events" through play, with a mixture of digital and non-digital resources to deliver experiences more than purely receptive, where the audience's shaping of the stories is more than purely illusory. What's more, they also explore ways to allow large numbers of people to feel this, at the same time, within the same story.

Coney's work focuses on making meaningful play for and with playing audiences. They say: "We are inspired by people and their creativity in play, and hope to help everyone see the heroism and beauty that are latent in the people and the world around them."[1] Coney's work is live and responsive to the choices and actions of their playing audience, turning ideas into play to allow audiences to encounter and explore ideas and concepts playing as *themselves*, using their own ideas and creativity to come to their own decisions. Play is open and allows for the audience to co-author the narrative. The audience is allowed and encouraged to appropriate the work for themselves and make use of it in ways that Coney, as mere authors, might never have dreamed possible. In their work it's of vital importance the choices the audience makes are *meaningful*. So, the way the audience interacts with the piece changes the course and outcome of the story; their interactions are at the core of the story's meaning.

One of the principles Coney integrates in its work is *agency of engagement*. Audiences can engage as much and as deeply as they want; they are encouraged to engage deeper as the story develops, but they are never expected or pushed beyond personal comfort levels. The intention is for the story to be a compelling experience on whichever level of engagement the audience meet it. (Rather akin to the philosophy on story layers discussed in Chapter 6, *Environmental Storytelling*, catering to multiple different kinds of audience all within the same story.)

Another principle at play for Coney is their vision on agency and reciprocity. They explain this accordingly: "If an audience puts something of themselves into the piece then the reward or gift they get in return needs to be bigger than the thing they put in. Interactive narratives are dialogues and exchanges between the makers and the audience. The makers initiate the exchange that the audiences then co-author and thus need to create a piece that gives more than it asks."

[1] Tassos Stevens, co-director, Coney, in conversation, March 2011.

Their tools are a combination of dramaturgy, game design, writing, experience, design, digital technologies, communication technologies, and a deep engagement with the themes and ideas through research and engagement with experts. "The work is about experiences and therefore plastic,"[2] says Annette Mees—"it can look different with each project, it lives in the space between art forms but uses elements of theater, live art, art, installation, games and any other form that helps make an experience. Coney's work can happen anywhere. In the past we have created work in very different spaces. Examples include *Art Heist*, an adventure about conceptual art and forgery in which the audience robs a museum. This project took place in The New Art Gallery Walsall as part of ACE West Midlands' *Art of Ideas*. We created pieces in public spaces like *Overlooked*, working with Andy Field, it was a story of love, betrayal and surveillance that started as an email exchange in the audience's inbox and completed in a grand finale in Spitalfields Market, London. *A Small Town Anywhere* was a seminal piece in interactive theater in which many strands of thinking in a wider network came to a culmination. A co-production with BAC, *A Small Town Anywhere* is a play that features no actors at all. Instead, the town Coney built inside the theater space is peopled by a playing audience, who had complete agency over the outcome of their particular town's story. Players had the opportunity to create a history for themselves in the town in advance of the show in dialogue online."[3]

THE SPACE BETWEEN PLAYER AND AVATAR

More directly apposite to video games, consider too that players and their avatars are not the same things. Of course, few players genuinely believe they are still a 105th-level frost mage when they aren't at their computers (and if they do we tend not to refer to them as players, but in other more medical terms). Nevertheless, for games developers, especially those who are at the cutting edge of explorative and new interactive story experiences, it can be helpful to keep in mind there is a space *between* player and avatar. Why? Because just maybe a project will one day come along, or perhaps you will help bring one into being, that seeks specifically to exploit this space and to reap the potential. Clearly this isn't a standard approach—removing people from their suspension of disbelief

[2] Annette Mees, co-director, Coney, in conversation, March 2011.

[3] Annette Mees, co-director, Coney, in conversation, March 2011.

by highlighting their make-believe activity while they experience it is fraught with danger. So much so that there are those who feel it should never be done and can never be done without abject failure. Again, though, such blanket views can only be dangerous and destructive. At the time of writing we've not yet developed anything serious in this regard but have long harbored ambitions to experiment with an unwilling avatar that doesn't always do what it's told precisely when it's told—rather like, instead of seeing an avatar as a car that drives you unquestionably to your destination, seeing them as horse, which is subject to its own whims and agendas. (Although perhaps it depends on the extent of your poor fortune and sympathy with automobiles.)

The contention is this: if game stories can be shorn of other storytelling conventions can they not also be shorn of the perpetual need to follow one central character with a unified POV, as well as losing a default concrete approach to player agency? Just because this default approach has been shown to consistently work, and is often absolutely the right option, doesn't mean games writers should become lazy and not keep searching and digging for new paths with less certain outcomes.

EXERCISES

1. Compare two methods through which conventional player agency in games could be subverted to create new player experiences. Based upon your analysis, which do you feel is most effective?
2. Write a one- to two-page outline for an original game story concept that uses an unconventional approach to player agency as its central element. (You could, for example, consider an unwilling avatar.)

PROJECTS

1. Research and select one specific project by Augusto Boal's *Theater of the Oppressed*, where the audience participates in dramatic experience. Create an outline of the events. Identify where participants have agency and where they do not. At which moments can they shape the drama, and to what extent? What choices are open to them? And by what means is the drama itself prevented from turning into a formless mess of chaos? Address these points in an essay.
2. Further explore Improv Everywhere by watching this TED talk: *https://youtu.be/Xl6wxnnSStI* (last accessed July 2016), and at least three other Improv Everywhere videos (*https://www.youtube.com/user/ImprovEverywhere*).

Create a two- to three-page document that proposes three scenes you think would be consistent with the Improv Everywhere philosophy of entertaining communal experiences pulling people out of their usual lives. For further research you can read *Causing a Scene*, by Charlie Todd and Alex Scordelis.

3. Write a three- to five-page paper that proposes reasons you think Improv Everywhere is useful research material for games writers.

Chapter 20 Time Gates and Act Stimulants

Every single thing changes and is changing always in this world. Yet with the same light the moon goes on shining.

—Saigyō Hōshi

Two further practical approaches for games writers to add to their toolkits are Time Gates and Act Stimulants. More familiar are Timers or Time Triggers, where gameplay features are tied to specific events with "fuses" of varying lengths, not necessarily just a short and immediate fuse. But Time Gates can be turned off as well as on, opening for set periods and closing again. Timing is a familiar element in puzzle games and this base mechanic can be played out in more complex ways to great effect (as *Portal 2*, essentially a puzzle game with FPS leanings, ably demonstrates every time the rampant AI, GLaDOS, pokes fun at the player once a puzzle has been solved). The "Gate" element need not be literal, as it is in *Portal 2*, which provides the player with a portal-making gun to solve increasingly difficult puzzles; it can be suggestive of a structural element, barring entry to further content until a certain task is completed, perhaps in a certain way within a set timeframe. Equally, the Time Gate might ease player progress at a certain juncture where players have failed often enough that they are now seriously contemplating abandoning the game in the face of its frustrations at the content being denied. As Irish comedian Dara O'Briain eloquently pointed out in BBC TV program *Gameswipe*, being denied content in a game that you've paid for isn't always a satisfactory state of affairs, and if you're denied it too often or for too long it ceases to be a spur to further progress and becomes the reason the game is abandoned. O'Briain tells of being unable to fight his way past the lumbering Berserker in *Gears of War*, despite trying several times before finally giving up in disgust.[1] Saying that, there are games that make a virtue out of their punishing difficulty curve; the popular *Dark Souls* series comes to mind.

[1] View online at *https://youtu.be/nYUng5MtTd8?t=2m40s*, last accessed May 2016.

Unlocking content through progress has long been a game design staple, and fundamentally it's still a highly effective means of building and retaining player engagement. In the case of a plot, players are often reluctant to see the time spent in making headway through the game coming to nothing. They want to be rewarded for their effort and skill and therefore, to an extent, the deeper into a game players get the more difficult it becomes to cease playing without feeling significant time has been wasted as the story and gameplay haven't been brought to a conclusion. This is no less the case in games where there is no real plot; indeed, RPG models seen in MMOs like *Warcraft* and *Eve Online* can be even harder to abandon *precisely because* there is no plot to conclude. In these types of games, it's the built-in sense of progress through levels, skill, and ability hikes, upgraded equipment, and unlocking accessible areas for your characters that helps hook you into a cycle of play-upgrade-play. This said, Dara O'Briain makes an important point, and one that an increasing ubiquity of games across broader and wider sections of society makes especially hard to ignore altogether; if the business model of your game is to sell to more than an exclusively hardcore gamer demographic, then it would seem it's time to look closer at high-level game design concepts like unlocking progress, or you may find the very people you're trying to sell the game to are the ones who abandon it soonest, frustrated and annoyed, like O'Briain.

Perhaps this is the moment to question whether the people the marketing department are trying to reach are always the same as the people the games designers are trying to make titles for. It can often be a fine line between making something for yourself, because, after all, that's what people ought to like, and making it for other people, especially when, as the skilled craftsperson, you know better than the general public. In a commercial form of art ignoring either calling, to the exclusion of the other, is ultimately doomed. We must listen to both the commercial and the artistic elements. One way of doing this is to ensure the marketing side of a game is not merely perceived as the lowbrow act of hawking wares fresh from the artist's hallowed studio, but instead is tied intrinsically to the conceptualization and development of the game throughout. Game designers should be demi-marketers, and the better designers they are the greater their sense of marketing should be; the same applies vice versa for those in games marketing. As the games market continues to broaden, it can be increasingly less acceptable for designers to see difficulty settings other than the very hardest as unavoidable flaws in their vision. It's the harder settings that must be seen as the off-track elements where fewer (although less forgiving) people will spend their time. (It's because these people are less forgiving and blog and post to forums and are generally more vociferously active in digital communities and channels that they must still be catered for.) Yet sometimes game designers and game testers are the least appropriate people to assess the difficulty levels in a game, especially when the game is not really intended for players with such high levels of skill.

TIME GATES

We don't need to abandon the unlock-progress model entirely, as it serves us well in many areas. Yet nor should we slavishly, perhaps even lazily, adopt it as a default that can never be examined and assessed before being implemented. Time Gates are one way of retaining the structure of unlocking through progress, but not restricting access indefinitely. If a player has failed too often at a task, that task could be made simpler or be eliminated entirely. Equally, in this context, dynamic or just good and responsive AI could be a better definition than a Time Gate. Here, the game is monitoring and responding to the player's activity within it. Some games feature a form of "super-easy" mode only unlocked and offered as an option if the player repeatedly fails to complete the tasks set out for them. While this is a logical design feature that ensures a broader gaming demographic will have access to a title's deeper content, some players feel playing at such a low difficulty level is a mark of shame.

A simple "skip" system can also be a very effective way of retaining the structure of unlocking through progress, but not becoming a hostage to it. We could allow players to keep trying until they themselves decide they've had enough, until *they* decide that fun is receding and their feelings are moving beyond simple frustration and into darker realms. We could still reward completionists and people who want that feeling of taking on the game and being equal to it by awarding them with more content than those who exhibit less patience and skip sections. This would seem a neat way of ensuring those who like progressing through unlocking content get what they want, and those in danger of abandoning the game completely if blocked for too long who wish to get through the experience with less difficulty also get what they want.

Time Gates could also be used in ways more deeply enmeshed in game design, and not just as mini-puzzles within a broader structure, or as safety valves to allow struggling players through. While we don't pretend to know each of the many forms this could yet take, let us outline at least one possibility by way of an example game concept. Let's call this game concept *The Delivery*.

THE DELIVERY

The Delivery is a hybrid driving, action, and adventure game for next-gen consoles with a real-time clock ticking against the storyline. It thrusts players into the role of Taylor, a highly skilled driver hired to deliver a corrupt Russian billionaire's family to a top-secret location in New Mexico. Matters quickly escalate when it seems almost everyone is out to stop Taylor making his delivery.

BACKGROUND

Not a *GTA* or *Driver* clone—the real-time clock hovers over the whole game experience—which isn't demarcated into "missions" the whole story, the whole game is a single mission. Players can invite other players online to help them in all, some, or none of the story—which adapts difficulty levels to the number of players present. These players can come with cars, or ride shotgun. Online mini-games are also available.

TECHNICAL NOTE

There are time gates that a player must reach in order to progress. This is to ensure players don't play more than a few minutes too far behind the clock. The time between gates will be balanced to ensure the player won't have to drive all-out the whole time—and in any case, the design will ensure that the player won't be able to treat the game as nothing but a simple racer—this is far from that kind of game . . .

DESCRIPTION

The game begins with an intro cut scene – a car from the city, at night, speeding along a country road. The driver checks his watch—just over four hours to make the delivery. The passengers, three children and a woman, talk among themselves—worried about who they think is hunting for them. The driver watches the road intently—then narrowly avoids a pickup truck that explodes out of nowhere, but he still has to veer off the road. The car crashes and its passengers are dragged into the pickup, semi-conscious. As dawn begins to lighten the sky, the driver, bloodied and hunched over the steering wheel, realizes what has happened.

You are the driver—Taylor; your car still works—just, your cell phone has no signal, your GPS is broken, and you have only four hours to get the family back and deliver them to your client on-schedule. Open roads stretch ahead of you in several different directions. Immediately you have some major decisions to make. Which way first?

When you get to your first roadside café and get the chance to re-fuel, speak to your client on the temperamental payphone, and ask a few questions of the locals to get your first clues as to where the family have been taken—at this point you also get the backstory in flashback—how the family aren't yours, how you were hired by a Russian billionaire, why the police want to stop you, and where you have to go—and why you have to get there.

As you drive, shoot, and stealth your way across the arid, mostly deserted land, collecting all the members of the family, the clock is always against you—the game responds to you, filling your journey with events, surprises, story, spectacles, and obstacles—it responds to you, and your decisions have repercussions—shoot someone and their brother might not take too kindly to it when you see them an hour later . . .

If your speed has barely dropped and you've been going flat-out for a while a tire might blow. When that happens, a building might be nearby, or a caravan might sit just off the road up ahead, or a car could come the other way. Or perhaps there'll be a police chopper coming from the west, or a farmer's plane coming from the east.

If the only thing around is a building—perhaps it's where's Old Man Haines lives alone with his sawed-off shotgun and bitter madness. Or it's a desolate gas station—in the middle of being held up. Or it's an old cereal processing plant—and there's some guy out of *The Texas Chainsaw Massacre* in there. Or a motel, where a woman with a suitcase of money is staying. Maybe you take the money. Maybe you don't.

Maybe you see a worn-out caravan. Inside it could be an old guy flipping burgers, or a bored prostitute, or a minister with amnesia, a beat poet off his head, a cheerleader who ran away from the guy who just kidnapped her, a rock band skinning up, or a sun-fried Asian selling crickets in cages. They can tell you which direction to go to get hold of a car. But then again, maybe you'll just take the caravan. Maybe you'll leave them alive. Maybe you won't.

Maybe you see a car. Maybe this time it's the O'Reilly Brothers, running from the law and hiding out in the wasteland this side of the Mexican Border. Or a runaway bride from a shotgun wedding, or a hit man with a body in the trunk, or an escaped convict in a stolen vehicle, or a Japanese couple on vacation, or a rogue trader from Wall Street with a suitcase full of cash in his trunk, or a Mexican drug runner, or a cop. Out here some people won't stop just because you step in front of them—you might have to use your gun. Hit the gas tank or the engine or the tires and the car will only get you so far before you need to swap it again. Kill the driver and that might come back to bite before the game's over. Let the driver go and it might be worse.

If you've already blown a tire you'll see a police roadblock up ahead—you might want to think about turning around . . .

If you've hit a roadblock before, you might hit a dead end—the bridge is down, or it's a rock slide, or a jack-knifed truck, or you run into a pack of Hells Angels, or a psycho in a big rig's behind you, or the engine overheats—it must be over a hundred degrees out.

If you've had no run-ins with Hells Angels in the past, they'll ride on by. If you messed with them before, they won't—unless you took the money from the woman in the motel . . .

If you're stuck and do nothing there'll be a drifter coming along the road to help or provoke you, or a Jamaican ice hockey team lost and going the same way as you, or a serial killer convinced it's your birthday, or there'll be an explosion in the distance. You won't get that "what am I supposed to do next?" feeling.

The land between San Antonio and Mexico is heaving with hicks, deadbeats, killers, kooks, and freaks. Some of them want to stop you because you're you—Taylor has never been a popular guy. Some of them don't care who you are—but don't like you already. This is *From Dusk Till Dawn* before the vampires come in. This is *North by Northwest* with a clock on it. This is the second half of *Psycho*—and at every stage you're making decisions that define the game world you travel across. And the whole experience is shot through with an off-the-wall, quirky humor, a little touch of *My Name is Earl* and lots of American stereotypes re-fitted and spun out to make the familiar seem fresh and surprising.

And of course, there's also a story to unravel. What did the Russian billionaire do to bring the cops on your tail? Why are people trying to stop you getting his family back to him? And is the real delivery the family, or something else?

The point *here* is not that we should keep looking for new, interesting, and fresh ways to mesh story and game design, rather that we shouldn't forget sometimes the simplest and most common of game mechanics, such as achieving something distinct and easily measurable within a set (and, if need be, easily modifiable) time range, can open the door to achieving this.

ACT STIMULANTS

If Time Gates could also be termed Time Triggers or AI Triggers, then the same could be said of *Act Stimulants*, in so far as they are fundamentally events, in the broadest sense, triggered at specific moments in relation to an avatar's location, achievements, actions, and/or time spent performing, or not performing, specific tasks. However, Act Stimulants are different in that they are a tool for writers to allow them to think in purely structured plot terms within a game environment that could be largely structure-free—an environment such as a sandbox game. In a sandbox game you may roam around the world either unaware or uncaring of the many missions or mini-games available to you. You are free to do as you desire when you're in the right place at the right time, perhaps also with the right object or preceding sub-missions completed. Act Stimulants allow you to impose a plot structure on this game world without suffering the worst excesses of this freeform environment and to re-engage with players who may be tiring as a result of the lack of compulsion to do anything at all when faced with the paralyzing array of seemingly everything. It also allows you to do this without a sequence of structural node scenes trying vainly to retain story cohesion, which end up being the analogous equivalent of straining buttons on the jacket of a man much too big for it: a perhaps noble, but still futile attempt at a fit. Why would you want to do this? You wouldn't necessarily—not if the sandbox model is working well for you and you don't want more plot cohesion, but less. It's a question of intention. If you want more from a story, if you want more of what a story can give a game, then Act Stimulants are an option.

So what are they and how do they work? If you know the story you want to tell and you've broken it into an act structure, Act Stimulants can be tools to re-impose or re-energize that plot without necessarily resorting to a cut scene. An Act Stimulant can be more than just a triggered reminder of a task yet to be completed; it can also be a dynamic response from the game as it makes something happen that you have no option but to deal with. If your story and game world are intended to reflect the atmosphere and experience of a taut conspiracy thriller, for example, your response to external stimuli is part of what keeps things interesting and exciting and conveys that intended atmosphere; there may be occasions when you need to bring or force story onto the player to create the effect you require, perhaps with effects such as surprise, claustrophobia, a sense of the net tightening, that you're being watched, and are not always free to do as you choose. Again, there are plenty of reasons why you wouldn't do this, and forcing anything on a player always carries risks. Nevertheless, this can still be a very valid option, and we would do well to remember that allowing a player to become bored by the game is no less of a risk. The important task is to keep the player engaged, and that doesn't just mean surprises or apparently unrestrained freedom. Players often respond poorly to surprises that move beyond a consistent rule set, so if players become accustomed to moments where the story comes to them and you make this a coherent part of the game, players will not reject it out of hand. As noted earlier, apparently unrestrained freedom (because the role of smoke and mirrors to create this effect can't be underestimated) has its own drawbacks, including a lack of clear motivation or compulsion.

A game world can be, and often is, designed so players can arrive at a specific location to perform a specific mission, yet that mission can potentially then be hijacked to make an event happen that is vital to the plot unfolding in a clear and compelling manner. In such a case, this is really an embedded story element, which may also involve an AI Trigger or Time Gate. Similarly, a game world could be designed such that players have their other mission options reduced or withdrawn. RPG titles such as *Witcher 3*, *Fallout 4*, and RPG-centric shooters like *Borderlands* often provide a wide selection of optional secondary missions for the player to undertake, should they choose; these serve to deepen the world, provide extra gameplay, and allow characters to improve themselves in a variety of ways (e.g., gathering more potent weapons, better clothing, and more experience points), but it's noticeable that there are a finite number of them, as eventually, the core game story has to be tackled. Still, the player is given a sense of freedom insofar as they can choose to approach core missions as soon as they become available, or once they've spent some time exploring other, more "orbital" content.

Or perhaps the design structure is such that players are led to the top of the mission section pyramid to find only one option remains. In all these cases they'll find that, although free to roam around the sandbox world as much as they like (perhaps with some geographical restrictions), they are effectively blocked from progressing until they complete a nodal mission and unlock more content. An Act Stimulant is different insofar as it doesn't necessarily wait for the player to select or to complete the required mission; it can be activated outside of these limitations—perhaps while the player is doing very little of structural significance within the game, or even while they are attempting to complete a sub-mission. A good example of this can be seen in Firaxis' excellent turn-based strategy game *XCOM 2*™, which features DLC that occasionally drops random alien boss-level creatures into a map, regardless of the current state of the player's mission. As noted, such an approach carries risk. But engagement is the critical objective and we should limit the things we *never* or *always* do in game design to the bare minimum to ensure we maximize our chances of engagement. The question is whether what the player loses in this approach is outweighed by what they gain. The answer lies in the kind of game you are trying to make and whom it's for. That will provide you a clue as to what their expectations are and how they might respond to unconventional approaches in game design.

To demonstrate Act Stimulants let's formulate an example concept: imagine a game where your avatar is on the run. Let's up the ante and have them being hunted by the law, so there's nowhere for them to hide, then splice in a little sympathy and have them wrongly accused too. At first glance it seems quite hard to reconcile this setup with a sandbox world of meandering and broad freedoms. But let's introduce other gameplay, design, and personalization elements, and say that creating your own disguise is also part of what makes the game fun. Now the player's avatar can move more freely and approach the game world, and the enjoyment contained in it, more on their own terms. Except that if we let this state of affairs carry on for too long, undisrupted, the game may start to overly resemble other sandbox worlds and we'll start to lose most of the advantages of the plot we initially signed up for. So perhaps, after an hour of the player performing various missions, perhaps with varying degrees of success, we employ our first Act Stimulant. We might decide that the authorities have tracked down the avatar's current hideout—wherever it may be—so the moment the location, and the means by which the avatar is attacked, snared, or otherwise endangered by the police, FBI, or whatever could be different for different players or on different playthroughs, keeping player engagement (and replayability) high. Further, in this example, this Act Stimulant delivers a plot point without a cut scene—the action is wholly contained within the game, not a moment in which the player is frozen temporarily out of it. Following a successful evasion of the police we might then return the avatar to the sandbox world, only to introduce another Act Stimulant later on which sends the plot in another direction, as they perhaps learn information that allows them to begin to clear their name, again in such a way that feels like a mission, or something integral to gameplay—giving us plot development through gameplay, not to the side of it.

Act Stimulants don't have to be tied specifically to acts; they can be subdivided into Sub-Act Stimulants, and it really starts to become semantics at this point. But fewer effective, engaging, and memorable uses are likely to be received better than more watered down, too overly anticipated uses.

Finally, here, to recap—Act Stimulants are *not* different from an event, time, and/or AI Trigger, except that they are a way for writers to view these triggers when trying to keep a plot moving in a free game-world environment without resorting to play-stopping cut scenes.

EXERCISES

1. Which three genres do you feel are particularly suited to either Time Gates or Act Stimulants? Discuss.
2. Can either Time Gates or Act Stimulants be of any use in multiplayer games? If so, how?

PROJECTS

1. Taking the concept of *The Delivery*, create a two- to three-page player journey document to show how you think an act stimulant could deliver an

exciting experience for a player. Consider practical details and, in a separate, one- to two-page design note document, discuss solutions to the problems caused by imposing an act stimulant on a player, rather than them allowing them to choose when to embark on the next story section. If you think there are no workable solutions to any of the problems, list them out and provide the reasons why.

2. Either individually or in groups, create a three- to four-page story-driven game concept document that utilizes Time Gates and/or Act Stimulants. Explore the practical potential of these concepts by creating an integrated design and story outline.

   State what game mechanics you have chosen to work with and include sections relating to:

   How does a player win?

   How can they tell if they are winning?

   How many players is this game for?

   Who is its intended audience?

   What games platform(s) is it for?

   How does the player control their avatar(s)? Try drawing up a controller configuration diagram to show which buttons on the controller do what for the lead platform. Perhaps there is no controller, or perhaps the control interface is built directly into the touch screen. In the case of the latter provide a sketch for how that control interface looks.

   If using act stimulants you should also include a structure diagram illustrating as clearly as you can how the structure and gating of player's experience works.

Chapter 21 Aristotle, Games Writing, and Games

The pursuit of what is true and the practice of what is good are the two most important objects of philosophy.

—Voltaire

BRIEF TERMS

ARISTOTLE Greek philosopher and polymath of the 4th Century BC, student to Plato, teacher to Alexander the Great, one of the most influential and important thinkers of the ancient and medieval worlds, is still studied to this day.

Poetics, as Aristotle's collected thoughts are generally known, are quite remarkable. They're roughly forty pages of notes that not only gave birth to the field of literary theory, but, arguably, sketched out much of its course over the last 2,000 years. It's difficult to conceive of literary theory as we know it without them.

So what's this chapter about? As this book illustrates, the fields of games writing and games design are both fascinating and problematic areas that are constantly evolving, being scrutinized, redefined, and explored. While the growing number of academics and professionals involved in the various debates inevitably disagree on a number of points, one thing cannot be disputed—these fields are cutting-edge places highly conducive to flux and counter-arguments. The field is open to anyone with a coherent, compelling opinion. And this is a good thing. However, given the relative youth of modern games writing and design when compared to film and television, to give two obvious examples, it's tempting to look forward, or perhaps sideways, when trying to answer the many fascinating questions that appear when something new calls for definition and refinement in order to aid the writers, producers, and designers of this brave new world. But what about looking back in time, into the eye of the storm itself? It is not only logical but perhaps necessary to ask ourselves: *does Aristotle have anything to tell us as games writers and makers of games?*

WHY WATCH A PLAY/PLAY A GAME?

In *Poetics* he explores people's motivations for watching plays, particularly in relation to our desire to imitate and to see things from our lives and from our imaginations presented before us and about how we have a yearning for rhythm. But let's focus on a couple of other points he makes. First, catharsis. This is a familiar Aristotelian term—though it's provoked considerable debate in academic circles as, in truth, it's a more complex issue than the way we're going to look at it here, and part of the reason the term causes so much controversy is the infrequency with which it's used—as well as its opaqueness.

He says:

Tragedy . . . is a representation of . . . action . . . by means of pity and fear bringing about the purgation of such emotions.[1]

Aristotle believes this is what tragedy *is*—not this is one of the things it does—but *this is what it is*. Now, if catharsis is utterly essential for stories, consider how much more relevant it could be for games—and how much more important it is for us to consider its implementation. We could view games as a deeper manifestation of tragedy rather than a merely receptive drama—by offering players the opportunity to *participate* in the pathos and fear of an environment. We can offer players the opportunity to enact their own catharsis, perhaps—quite literally—to pull the trigger themselves.

Aristotle considers the very processing of emotions a key reason people watch plays, and thus central to the creation of good drama. This processing has important applications in game design—where players expect to experience a range of emotions that feed into the core desire to win.

We could theorize that what Aristotle argues is that asking yourself what emotions your potential players might experience at any point in the game ought to be as commonplace as asking what will they see on-screen at any point.

Aristotle also uses the term *rhaumaston*—meaning wonder, or the marvelous. He talks of representing things not as they are, but as they should be, of telling untruths the way they should be told, and the aim of creating wonder as the purpose of poetic art itself, cautioning that . . .

As far as poetic effect is concerned, a convincing impossibility is preferable to an unconvincing possibility.[2]

Games, no less than other forms of entertainment—or dare we say "art"?—consistently strive for wonder—for people to say they thought a title was "amazing" or "fantastic," or whatever other adjective or phrase best captures that feeling of awe at something so enthralling it inspires wonder at its very creation.

---

[1] Aristotle, "On the Art of Poetry," *Classical Literary Theory*, Aristotle/Horace/Longinus (London: Penguin, 1965), 38–39.

[2] Ibid., 73.

STORY AND PLOT

Regarding story and plot, Aristotle uses the word "mythos." This means story, legend, or plot—and depending on the context, he appears to use it to mean plot, story, or, in some instances, something later thinkers have called Narrative or Discourse, or Narrative Discourse. Why does this matter, other than for academics? Because careful delineation of these terms throws up some extremely important distinctions that aren't only helpful to our understanding of what's going on in something we're watching or playing, but also to our understanding of how to construct these things ourselves—giving us tools we can use, or would do well to be reminded of.

Aristotle says:

Every tragedy has six constituents, which will determine its quality. They are plot, character, diction, thought, spectacle and song . . . Of these elements the most important is the plot, the ordering of the incidents.[3]

He defines plot as:

the arrangement of incidents . . . complete action.[4]

In other words: *the things that happen.*

He makes reference to story in a different context, linking thought (dianoia) to theme, that is, to *meaning*. And he also highlights diction—or discourse—having this to say about it:

The greatest virtue of diction is to be clear without being commonplace.[5]

So here he's really discussing the manner in which things that happen are presented. (The keen-minded among you might notice the similarity between this expression and what the formalists of the early twentieth century had to say, who felt defamiliarization was the key to literary value—brutally put, something's literary if it's not in a familiar form.)

Although not something Aristotle explored in detail, this distinction between plot and story can be one of the most helpful tools any storyteller in any medium can ever have.

Ask yourself what occurs in the tale you're working on—this is the plot—the sequence of things that happen. Then ask yourself what it's *really* about—and what

[3] Ibid., 39.

[4] Ibid., 39, 41.

[5] Ibid., 62.

it means—not who does what to whom, who goes where, who sees what and what happens—that's all plot. When you rip that away you're left with what it means.

To illustrate this point—how about a couple of examples? Here's one possible interpretation of the *plot* of a well-known game:

The protagonist's flight crashes, he discovers an underwater dystopian city, battles his way through a variety of districts in a bid for freedom, ultimately destroying two key figures of the city's civil war along the way as well as uncovering the truth of his origins.

And here's one possible interpretation of its *story*:

The best of us, with the best of intentions, can unwittingly create hell, rather than heaven.

The game? *BioShock.*

And here's another game. One possible interpretation of its *plot* might be:

You're born after a terrible nuclear war, escape the bunker, discover a town, track down your father, battle the area's denizens, help or hurt a wide variety of characters, and uncover a deeper conspiracy involving forces vying for control of the area.

And a possible interpretation of its *story*:

Even from the deepest despair, hope can still spring.

The game? *Fallout 3.*

How might this help games writers, producers, and designers? It's useful in two key ways:

1. As a development tool—not just in writing stories and plots, but also in design—being clear about what the story is—because that's something reflected in the rest of the game, and the rest of the game contributes towards, and helps generate a common language between, writers, designers, and others on the team. Writers might be used to thinking in terms of plots, stories, and discourse, but other people often aren't, and it can help everyone to be clear about these distinctions. In general, developers can lump everything together and call it plot—which as a critical and analytical tool, is rather like selecting a shovel to break an egg. It will work, to an extent, but is messy and clumsy at best.
2. As a marketing tool—being able to distinguish between plot and story can be useful for publishers as they try to tease out the optimum way of presenting the game to potential future players, or of making sure it's properly targeting its intended demographic. In the minutiae of plot details a story's meaning can often get lost—and it's good practice to be clear early on in the process what kind of meaning you want to present to potential customers—and to ensure you're still on-message. And if you know what your message really is—that can help when trying to project and sell it.

PLOT STRUCTURE

Let's examine Aristotle's thoughts on plot structure. He raises a couple of key points. One is this:

Now a whole is that which has a beginning, a middle, and an end. A beginning is that which does not necessarily come after something else, although something else exists or comes after it. An end, on the contrary, is that which naturally follows something else either as a necessary or as a usual consequence, and is not itself followed by anything. A middle is that which follows something else, and is itself followed by something. Thus well-constructed plots must neither begin nor end in a haphazard way, but must conform to the pattern I have been describing.[6]

This can sound so platitudinal it doesn't appear to really mean much and one's mind can find itself wandering onto other things—it's almost like Lewis Carroll's storytelling advice in *Alice in Wonderland*: "Begin at the beginning," the King said, gravely, "and go on till you come to the end: then stop." However, it is fundamentally how plots work—*sequentially*—moving from one state to another. And without that sense of change in states, even if it is ultimately to return, ostensibly, to an initial state, that is still tracking a process through stages—a plot *must have* phases of development: *things happening that lead to other things.*

Aristotle also explores how events don't just sit in sequence, but follow according to what's "necessary" or "usual" —that is to say "probable"—they should conform according to logic. Even if you're in a fantasy world, events after your first imaginative leap must follow according to the logic of the characters and the circumstances in play.

Another point to note is the two most important means by which tragedy plays on our feelings, "reversals" and "recognitions," are both constituents of plot.

A reversal –	for example, the person you thought was trying to kill you proves they've been trying to save you.
A revelation –	for example, an unexpected message from an ally you thought to be conquered offers hope and the promise of troops.
Both together –	for example, Ganymede's a man—but it turns out it's Rosalind in disguise (Shakespeare's *As You Like It*).

---

[6] Aristotle, "On the Art of Poetry," *Classical Literary Theory*, Aristotle/Horace/Longinus (London: Penguin, 1965), 41.

There aren't any diagrams in the *Poetics*, but, if we were to extrapolate from this a diagram from the text on structure, Figure 21.1 illustrates one possible way.

White squares = reversals

Black ovals = recognitions

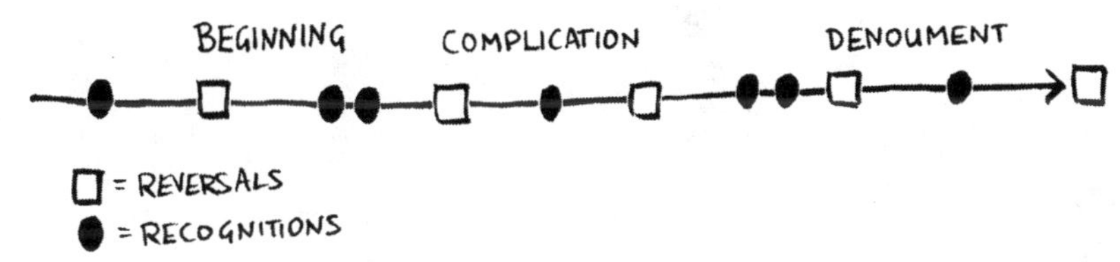

FIGURE 21.1 Linear plot route.

This diagram is interesting in comparison with other more recent models from Syd Field, Seymour Chatman, and Joseph Campbell, among others. The models they present are more detailed because they are often being more specific—either inspired by a particular medium, such as a novel, or exploring a specific plot archetype. Within the context of what they illustrate, and their authors' specific story perspective, these models have their uses. But, in a certain sense, the more detailed these models are the less useful they are, at least for games writers. In the context of games, they are reminiscent of the Franz Kafka parable, *Der Kreisel*, or *The Top*, about a philosopher whose obsessions lead him to attempt to understand a child's spinning top. So he picks it up to study it. Whereupon it stops spinning, and so therefore makes it impossible for him to further study it or understand it.

If we bring Aristotle's model back and maybe depict it a little differently—to emphasize the crest and trough nature of the reversals, and moments of interactive choice—we arrive at the structure illustrated in Figure 21.2.

Aristotle is really saying that as long as one uses reversals and revelations—especially reversals—a plot will possess a coherent, compelling shape. The organizing principle of the importance of reversals within a very simple, very loose but unified model like this can be more helpful to games writers than many more recent and detailed plot structure models. It allows them to clearly identify moments where they may wish to furnish a player with choice and provides a macro view of the plot development along multiple, potentially parallel paths. One can quickly see if one's plot's going nowhere if there are no reversals or revelations along its course.

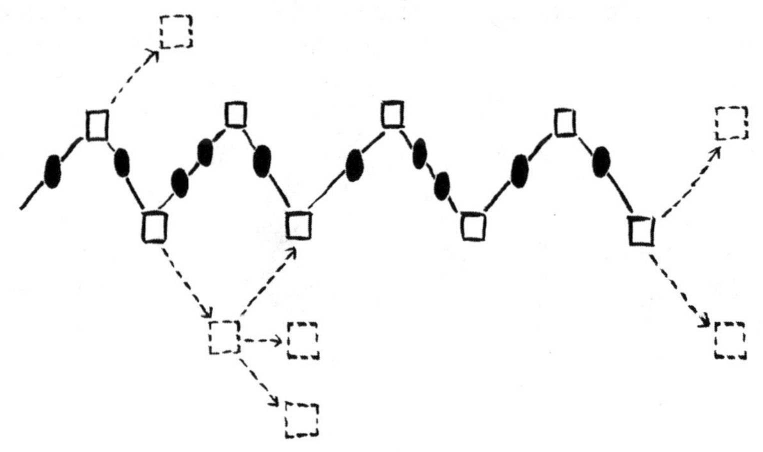

FIGURE 21.2 Plot route with reversals.

PLOT UNITY

Aristotle has more to say about plot when it comes to unity.

A plot does not possess unity . . . merely because it is about one man. Many things . . . may happen to one man, and . . . not contribute to any kind of unity . . . he may carry out many actions from which no single unified action will emerge . . . the plot . . . being the representation of an action, must present it as a unified whole; and its various incidents must be so arranged that if any one of them is differently placed or taken away the effect of wholeness will be seriously disrupted. For if the presence or absence of something makes no apparent difference, it is no real part of the whole.[7]

This says something important, not just about good writing, but good game design. If we extrapolate out from the same principle—that a whole needs to be integrated to have unity—then we might consider this tells us gameplay isn't everything—not because story matters more, or that any other single element matters more, just that everything is subservient to the overall experience of playing the game. There are occasions when the theme may surface, or artwork may sparkle, or sound effects carry the experience—there are countless times when elements often (and ideally) pass the baton of primacy between each other seamlessly and unnoticed. It's possible Aristotle cautions us here about things occurring in game design simply because they're "cool,"

[7] Ibid., 42–43.

or because the designer's "always wanted to do it," or the tech allows it, or the artist wanted "to make it that way" and it made them happy if they were left alone to get on with it. We must be faithful to integrated, unified creative visions—not respond to the whims of the individual (unless they happen to be the game's vision holder, and even then something more than a whim needs to be offered).

This is arguably something writers have a history with, and it's generally known—they even have a phrase—"kill your darlings"—to remind them to remove anything they're clinging to for perhaps sentimental reasons. In his *The Art of Dramatic Writing*, Lajos Egri tells the story of Rodin's statue of Honoré de Balzac as a means of imparting this advice to writers. Having just completed the statue the sculptor wakes his students in the night to ask their opinions. In turn they all praise it—and, beyond anything else, Balzac's hands most impress them. As each student heaps further praise on these hands, Rodin's mood darkens, until, finally, he takes an axe and chops them off. His students are dumbfounded and think him mad. But he tells them all to remember that no one part of a composition is more important than the whole.

The point is writers and artists in general are aware of this principle of unity, even if they don't always apply it. Games designers should be aware of it too—and should seek to apply it.

Remember the Gravemind scene in *Halo 2*? The rhyming couplet-spouting tentacled plant-thing that captures Master Chief? The creature's rhymes might be nice—but is it part of the whole? Does it fit the universe depicted in *Halo*, which so many people bought into? Or does it pull you out of the world you thought you were in? There were admittedly those for whom the answer to that question was a resounding "yes."

On the other hand, popular platform game *Little Big Planet* makes a virtue out of how almost anything can fit within it. It's a universe where the whole is all about how the disparate, peculiar, personal, and idiosyncratic can all fit together. It's a universe that's very hard to break—play a Metallica album in the background and the sweet, cute game still works despite existing beside a crunching guitar riff and pounding bass line—you might even feel inspired to dress your characters in black leather and studs—everything still fits.

LINEARITY AND ALTERNATIVES

As for linearity, plots are, by definition, linear. Either in the top illustration, or the bottom, each depiction of structure is linear, as illustrated in Figure 21.3.

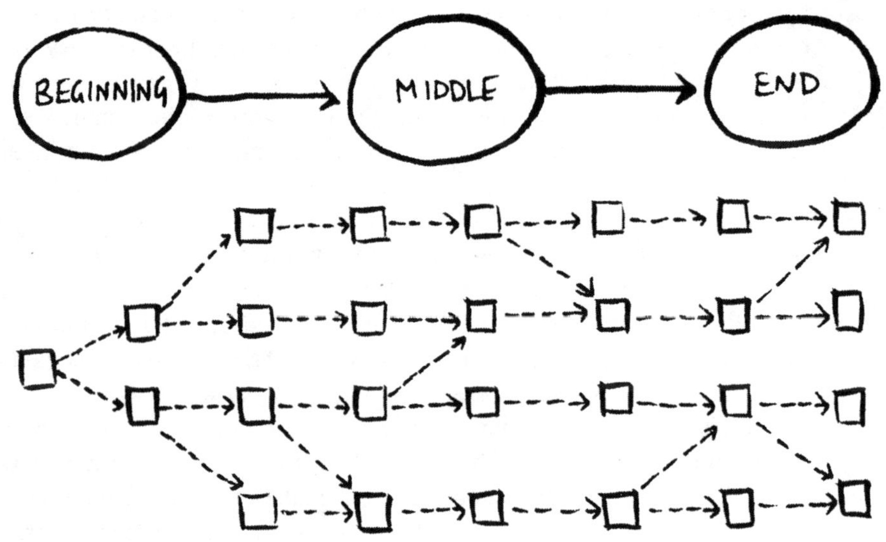

FIGURE 21.3 Linear nature of plot.

Talk of non-linear plots is really obfuscation, or a misnomer, and in reality non-linear plots should more truly be considered meta-linear or multi-linear—with many different paths possible and many different plots—and yet the linearity is still there, and this is by necessity. If a plot still tracks from one state to another and each state is consequential to the next, then it is still linear—even if it is multi-tracked.

When it comes to genuinely non-linear tools for games writers, that distinction between plot and story can help. Remember Aristotle was commenting on the contemporary plays he was watching—but he lists five other elements that contribute to them that are additional to Plot: Character, Diction, Thought, Song, and Spectacle.

These elements may help in the telling of a story, or the creation of a world, or an atmosphere, or an experience players may want to be involved in—and they are not bound by linearity. And all of these elements are things games makers should have in their armory.

There are some characters that only need to be heard, seen, or have their name read out for an expectation of a story world to erupt, pre-packaged in the minds of players—suggesting an atmosphere, values, themes, tone of voice. This is why archetypes (and of course—though also for obvious commercial reasons, licensed characters) are so useful for games writers—they don't need the backstory and setup. But that's not to say new characters can't ever be just as useful—fresh, carefully designed characters can also conjure expectations of tone, theme, and atmosphere.

Of course, what can you really do with a character unless you combine it with plot (and is it really a character until it is hooked with plot)? But a games writer could explore finding ways to use the expectation latent in a player's mind—and that expectation comes without being necessarily tied to linearity; one might, for example, tie characters (and the expectation that comes with them) to environments—a wannabe driver at a racetrack, or a playboy at an expensive nightclub, for example. Or perhaps you might subvert these expectations to good effect and place a prince, in disguise, in a den of thieves, or a respected scientist in an alley in the slum part of town.

Show don't tell is a well-known mantra for writers. For games writers there is a different hierarchy: *do—then show—then tell.* But while *telling* may be the peasants of that feudal system hierarchy, it shouldn't be ignored completely—even great kingdoms need to feed the nobility—and even extended metaphors such as this one suffer their own Black Death—giving rise to labor becoming more valuable—and the devaluation of castles through the use of gunpowder—which therefore need to be abolished. So, although only using an audio track is clearly not the best means to deliver plot, it nevertheless *is* a means. And it is a perfectly good place to deliver character through diction—which may be instructional—"Turn left!" "Ammo up ahead!" and so on—or may be tonal or thematic. In *Left 4 Dead*, in the process of working your way through an office block, Zoey—one of the survivor characters, as whom you may or may not be playing—gives the feed line to a *what do you call so many dead lawyers* joke—and it's possible her punch line is never delivered in-game. ("A good start" is often the line.)

The point here is that when using an audio track on its own you are not restricted to only using it in a purely linear fashion as part of a sequence of mini radio play scenes; it can be tied, once again, to environments or moments within the gameplay itself; *Portal* is an excellent example of this.

Provoking thought does not have to be tied to linearity. You can provoke thought in bubbles of environments, allowing the player to choose which environment (and so which thought) to experience in whichever order they choose. Or you can provoke thought as the game runs, not just in speech in the audio track, but using imagery and, if possible, within the gameplay itself; try encouraging thoughts such as what is this place? what happened here? should I save her, or harvest her?

Song can, of course, be playing just through an audio track while the game is still running, and it can contain a great deal—not just the meaning, character, tone, and theme in the words, but also the atmosphere, tone, and theme in the music too.

You only need to hear a track like the Go! Team's *Get It Together* and you know what world you're in, and when you're playing *Little Big Planet*, it reaffirms your sense of place and helps bring the whole world to life.

With sound and visuals games are well equipped to deliver spectacle and, further, put you in the middle of it. Of course—spectacle does not have to be tied to linearity like the impressive and spectacular opening to *Mass Effect 2*. Spectacle can also be inside the gameplay, or tied to an environment bubble.

ENDINGS

Regarding endings, Aristotle has this to say:

Every tragedy has its complication and its denouement . . . By complication I mean the part of the story from the beginning to the point immediately preceding the change to good or bad fortune; by denouement the part from the onset of this change to the end.[8]

He's emphasizing two key points here—one is plots are about change, the transition from one state to another. The other is that plots must unravel. The English language word "denouement" comes from the Old French verb "denoer"—to untie, and "nodus"—knot—literally to untie the knot. So this further emphasizes the former point; you can only unravel a knot that has become tied. In its purest form a plot is about creating a problem, then resolving it—or, as is often said in writing circles—get the cat up the tree, then get it down again! It is important to remember stories are shorn of their meaning if plots don't end—because endings are ultimately where the meanings of stories reside. Again, this isn't news to writers, but this same methodology appears applicable to game design, and is something game designers should consider. Many developers concentrate their effort at the beginning of a game, and many players do not finish games. But could a greater emphasis on game endings (and perhaps a compression of length) lead to a more satisfying, and ultimately more "meaningful" end product?

---

[8] Ibid., p.56.

SUMMARY

Aristotle's *Poetics* has a number of useful lessons to impart to us as games writers and designers:

- People play games because we have an instinct for imitation, harmony, rhythm, and catharsis.
- Story is not Plot; the sequence of events—the story—is *what* happens; the *way* you deliver it/*how* you deliver it is plot.[9]
- Plot Structure must have revelations and reversals.
- Plot Structure must move from a beginning, to a middle, to an end.
- Plots need unity. A whole needs unity. Nothing is greater than the whole.
- If it's not part of the whole, chop it off or cut it out.
- Plot is linear, but other story elements are not, and you can use character, diction, thought, song, and spectacle to achieve non-linear story goals.
- Plots need change.
- Plots need endings or your story lacks meaning.

EXERCISES

1. Choose a game, a movie, and a book. For each of your choices write a summary of their plot in no more than a paragraph. Using no more than four sentences, write down your interpretation of the meaning contained in each.
2. What other definitions would you offer for the term "plot"? How would you distinguish this from the "story," or the "meaning," or the "theme"?

[9] This is an extrapolation from Aristotle, informed by readings of other literary criticism, not what Aristotle says directly in *The Poetics*.

Chapter 22 CHOICE OR ENLIGHTENMENT?

The foot feels the foot when it feels the ground.

—Buddha

BRIEF TERMS

ID The (theoretical) part of human personality concerned with basic and instinctive urges and desires.

EGO The (theoretical) part of the human personality that seeks to satisfy the id in realistic ways to its long-term advantage.

SUPER-EGO The (theoretical) part of the human personality that governs self-critical and moralizing agendas.

APHORISM An original thought presented in a memorable form, often concise, pithy, cleverly observed or turned, and subjectively true.

ENLIGHTENMENT

Interactive storytelling is distinct from non-interactive storytelling with regard to the choice it offers its audience. But what is the *meaning* of the choice offered to the audience? Given that they come from a prescribed and pre-limited set, these choices can only be as profound and meaningful as the original design allows. In fact, given they are limited choices, the act of choosing one is no more an indication of meaning than if there were no choices at all. You cannot prove free will by choosing from a predetermined set of options, no matter what the detail of those choices really are. *Mass Effect 2* at one point forces the player to choose between destroying a race of sentient enemy robots or reprogramming their belief systems to turn them into allies. No other options are presented beyond a form of mass brainwashing or, in essence, genocide.

In this sense choices made in an interactive medium can tell us nothing beyond the confines of the world created for us to play in. Worse than that, this dramatic world, because it consists of a set of predetermined options, has no innate meaning of its own. Its plethora of choices undermines any meaning it may have; the more options available, the less can be meant. The only meaning an interactive world may have is either held in its non-interactive elements (so the less interactive, the more meaning) or in the meaning perceived by the players engaged within it. Yet choices a player makes can, at most, only ever tell this player something about themselves, about their own id or super-ego. An essentially good-natured person may choose to play to type in a fantasy world that allows them to be a healer and practitioner of benevolent magic who uses their abilities for "good," or they could explore darker impulses, playing instead a chaotic character who uses their powers to wreak havoc and destruction; a male gamer playing MMO *Guild Wars* using a female avatar might perhaps be expressing something of importance about himself, but equally, the meanings behind his choice could all too easily be inflated beyond any significance. In any event, these *meanings* would seem to be extremely limited; they can only tell us about, or cause us to reflect upon, something already within us—they cannot bring meanings from outside of ourselves. They are cannibalizing meanings, feeding off the players themselves, not providing offerings from elsewhere that are internalized and consumed within.

In contrast, non-interactive storytelling can, at its best, be the metaphorical equivalent of Moses coming down from Sinai bringing forth the word of God. This kind of storytelling can bring us views, insights, and new ways of understanding the world and our lives beyond the limitations of our own individual or social vistas. Where interactive storytelling can offer *choice*, non-interactive storytelling can offer us *enlightenment*, enriching us precisely because it is not something that originates from us and is re-fed back into us. To be open to enlightenment we must accept that not all truths and insights are equal. It may be fascinating to learn more about ourselves, and as an entertainment medium that is far preferable to learning nothing. Yet a writer is substantially more limited in their scope as a result of working with interactivity, and as consumers, with each increase in interactivity, our horizons to absorb the new and insightful are considerably restricted. We must look to the inspired to be enlightened.

FIGURE 22.1

CHOICE AND ENLIGHTENMENT?

Good interactive storytelling (and integrated technology, game design, art, and other resources) is not limited to the choices prescribed by the developers. In sandbox games, players can make choices not legislated for, using unusual weapons to perform set tasks, or using vehicles in an unusual way. Sandbox action-adventure game *Grand Theft Auto III* contains a mission in which you must kill a target at a golf course. When you arrive to do so, your victim will try to escape, so you must chase him around the city until you manage to run him off the road. However, as he attempts to flee the scene in a golf cart, it's possible to give chase in one of your own and to run him into a lake on the golf course, thereby drowning him without the whole second part of that mission ever taking place. In a similar way, more responses, and so more meanings, can be created from a sum of limited parts than those prescribed and those expected. Games and *games systems* could be seen as a conduit through which meaning is conveyed from a single person to one or many others. We've seen this in games such as *D&D* and the more recent *Sleep Is Death*, where the "Games Master" projects and conveys a worldview via the game itself. In *Sleep Is Death* the player interacts with considerable freedom within the simple 2D world the Games Master has created, typing in their conversations or action intentions direct from the keyboard in English, for the Games Master to respond to in real time (within 30 seconds), either by replying with NPCs or by telling them the results of the intended actions with any context, effectively creating an environment that replaces AI with human intelligence and so is malleable to the Games Master's own psyche.

What does it matter if the choices present have meaning on a personal level? Where do meanings operate within us if not at this level? All meaning must ultimately be a personal response. Is not *know thyself* an aphorism dating back to the Ancient Greeks? It's an aphorism suggesting humans should seek to know themselves, and there can be no truer path to enlightenment. Further, can we not learn unexpected things about ourselves and find enlightenment that way? If games permit our ids or super-egos to take over, shouldn't that be encouraged? Sometimes we may need to circumvent ourselves in order to see who we really are.

Additionally, can game worlds and game systems not be environments for expression within themselves that go beyond words? What might be the difference between a language with its fuzzy limits, where artists and the people who use it daily push at the fringes of what it offers by way of expression, and a game world, with its own fuzzy limits that can be updated and patched? Can a game world sufficiently rich and complex not offer the same level of opportunity for expression, and, in effect, become a language in its own right?

In any case aren't stories *experienced* worth more than those merely received? And don't interactive story worlds allow for greater interconnectivity and social experiences than any other kinds of story worlds? The world in which we live is not passive, so is it not true to say that interactive storytelling, benefiting from the input of others, can more truthfully render life in all its multi-perspective complexity? There are occasions when our choices appear to be limited, and others when we feel as if more open up for us. There are times when we make choices to which we can't possibly understand the full gamut of consequences. Perhaps the development of a title such as *Heavy Rain* is reason to believe there is interest in a playing experience beyond the usual definitions of what a game is; it may be *less* a game than *more*, but it is bringing interactive storytelling to the fore, and if the medium is to be more than mere choice and genuinely offer the possibility of enlightenment, then this can only be a good thing.

Alternatively, we may resist the quasi-religious tones in *enlightenment*, and consider that games, whether in combination with interactive storytelling or not, have the potential to offer *understanding*. So much so in fact that educationists have been championing the benefits of games playing for some time now. In addition, scientists have been adding to the discussion as the benefits to recovering patients and practicing and even operating surgeons have also become evident. The military too have been vocal about the clear benefits of gaming, and not just as a recruiting tool; as far back as 2005, there was talk at the Serious Games Summit in Washington, DC, of the game *America's Army* being a training tool. For historians too there can be real benefits, with simulations helping them to not only understand their subject through digital environments, but also helping them convey their subject, helping students to, in turn, understand and engage with it. There can surely be no better way to understand military history than through simulations that present similar choices to the ones faced by the commanders and key participants; this encourages and enables *understanding through participation*. Of course, war games themselves have a history of not merely being the pastime of middle-aged men, but of being the proving ground of plans before they are rejected or put into action in real life. The Prussian Army trained officers through war games, or *kriegsspiel*, during the nineteenth and early twentieth century. The German pocket battleship, Admiral Graf Spee, was sunk in 1939, according to the predictions made by British war game simulations. In one curious incident in the winter of 1944, the staff of the German 5th Panzerarmee were war gaming the U.S. offensive through the Ardennes, and before the game had been completed the Americans did indeed launch an attack in the same area. The Germans began to repulse the attack, but also carried on playing the game simultaneously. In the game, the German commanders identified when and where reserves would be needed and were able to replicate the order in reality to ensure the reserves were committed in the shortest possible time, ultimately ensuring that the American attack was beaten back. Whether you call this enlightenment or not, it is clearly the kind of *knowledge* that is well worth having and knowing how to access and disseminate.

In any event, is story not conflict? And is conflict not better delivered and understood interactively rather than reactively?

EXERCISES

1. Consider the discussion within this chapter. Do you think it is possible for a games writer to bring meaningful enlightenment to players? Can you envision future forms of game-based enlightenment not mentioned in this chapter? Discuss.
2. Choose a game that features story as a core element. Analyze its story to answer the following questions:

   What choices does it present the player with, if any?

How does it allow the player to express themselves?

Does the game story primarily present the player with choice, enlightenment, or both?

3. Investigate *Sleep Is Death*. See *http://sleepisdeath.net/* and *https://youtu.be/BYdVDmfbwjI*. (Both sites last accessed July 2016.)

   Do you think this game offers the real potential for you to express yourself in meaningful ways? Discuss.

PROJECT

1. Choose a paper RPG system and run a pre-designed adventure for a group of players that lasts no longer than two hours. How does the experience of running and playing a paper RPG adventure compare with designing and playing video games in terms of the *story experience*?

Chapter 23 THE FUTURE OF GAMES WRITING

Study the past, if you would divine the future.

—Confucius

BRIEF TERMS

UNCANNY VALLEY A term used to denote the emotional space occupied by something that is close to being perceived as human, but still clearly not.

GAMIFICATION The process by which game mechanics permeate other, normally unrelated sections of life.

PROCEDURAL STORYTELLING The process by which a coherent game story and characters are created spontaneously while the player is playing, using systems designed to mimic narrative structures.

How can we be sure we're going anywhere if we don't look back to where we've been? Mapping the past can describe a trajectory for the future. Since the days of *SpaceWar!* the universe of games development has certainly traveled some distance. But where might we be going? What follows are some suggestions of coordinates that may be on that future trajectory.

NEW OPPORTUNITIES FROM GRAPHICAL FIDELITY

Game stories will acquire another dimension with increased graphical realism. In 1970, Japanese roboticist, Masahiro Mori, coined the term "The Uncanny Valley," stating that something that looks or acts in a manner close to human-like will cause revulsion in the viewer, who reacts against a combination of "lifelikeness" still tempered with "otherness." Since titles such as *Half Life 2* and *Heavenly Sword* began to appear, games graphics have been in the vicinity of this valley. However, games such as *The Order: 1886*™ are continuing to push graphical boundaries further. But it's not only how elements inside a game world look that's vital to breaching Mori's famous valley; movement is also a key factor. Once something or someone artificial actually moves we receive a huge amount of data that can serve to pull us down into the same dip. But once again, *The Order: 1886* wears down this revulsion though the use of high-quality motion capture.

Quantic Dream's interactive drama action-adventure game *Beyond: Two Souls*™ features expressive characters who appear lifelike as they frown, shout, cry, whimper, and laugh inside the body of the game world. Again, cutting-edge motion capture techniques have been employed to achieve this level of visual fidelity. It's only recently that games have been able to feature *moving* characters who look so realistic facially. The ability to project emotion through expression will become a feature increasingly available to games, hopefully wielded by writers skillful enough to weave a story that's as compelling as the technology is impressive. Currently only big-budget games can afford to furnish players with characters as visually realistic as the ones presented in *Beyond: Two Souls*, but as technology becomes more affordable that will change. Smaller-budget developers are already empowered to create impressively realistic worlds, such as the one portrayed in Lucky Pause's exploration-puzzler, *Homesick*™. It therefore stands to reason it won't be too long before even small studio titles can feature almost totally realistic characters, affording them greater possibilities in creating levels of sympathy and empathy and therefore ways of extents of emotional engagement. But even totally lifelike characters moving realistically through a convincing game world can't provide a compelling experience unless the quality of games writing matches that of the technology.

More recently not just graphical fidelity but virtual reality (VR) looks certain to have an increasing bearing on game development and storytelling within games because it also touches on the sensation of sight in conjunction with our senses enhancing the overall game experience; expect the emotional experience to become more immersive and themes within storytelling to continue to encompass and explore the nature of virtual reality intellectually, spiritually, and philosophically.

INCREASE IN RELATIVE VALUE

Game stories will come to matter more. As technology becomes increasingly ubiquitous it will drive innovation into other areas of game development. The increase in middleware, and a select few market-leading game engines with tech support, will result in game development not always hinging on rapacious technological innovation. Instead, game design, with a stabilized set of grammar arising from an increasing number of professional games being released, will come to be the main force that drives game evolution. Games developers, currently arguably more focused on using design and technology to sell their games, will come to view game story as an even more potent unique selling point than it is now. This is not to say that a game's story—and all the elements it entails—is not currently valued by many developers and marketing departments, but the projection is that in the future, story will be used as one of the main differentiators between IP, which, at the upper end of the production ladder, in terms of graphical and audio fidelity, will be increasingly difficult to tell apart. Following the story of a favorite game character or set of characters, while not unknown today, will become a primary marketing tool in much the same way as following a favored television series has now. Most viewers of a soap such as *The Young and the Restless*© will care far more about the characters and relationships unfolding on the screen than the quality of the lighting or shot composition. While the latter two elements are vital to the show's integrity, they are likely only to be commented upon if they fail to meet an expected standard.

DEEPENING PRESENCE IN SOCIETY

Games will seep deeper into society. Games are becoming increasingly popular and, as technology improves, they are finding their way onto a greater variety of devices. Game designer and owner of Schell Games, Jesse Schell, gives an interesting and informative talk titled "Gamification" in which he explores this idea. His basic, but profound, main point is, game makers (and, let's not forget, marketers) are always seeking new ways to get people playing—and paying. Whereas today a person might purchase a toothbrush because they like the design, trust the maker, or like the price, in the future that same person might base their choice on what game they play, as the developer and dental brand got together to offer a special award scheme that granted the user MMO money for each brush stroke. And if that happens, what's to stop game designers from seeking new ways for players to be experiencing the game story even when they're not at their computer, actively playing? In 2010, *World of Warcraft* MMO developer, Blizzard, released a *Remote Auction House* app which, for a small monthly fee, allows players to manage in-game auctions on their phone or Apple iPad. This use of remote technology will continue to blossom in as many ways as designers and marketers can make possible. Games, already available on numerous handheld devices, will find ways in which to provide players indirect avenues through which to experience a game world. In this case, Blizzard has provided players with an intriguing tool. As developers find more ways for us to interact with games across a variety of platforms and technologies, they'll find, connected to these, an increasing number of ways for a game's story to interact with us in our everyday lives. Buying into a character in a game could result in a host of other media opportunities opening up, each of which offer alternative ways in which to experience the game story. If you purchase a movie ticket to watch a film linked to the game's IP, for example, this could allow you to, at the very least, unlock items in-game that otherwise would not be available to you. However, reversing this idea is where things get interesting—in the future the manner in which a game story is played, the choices made by its player base, could directly influence what happens in a movie based on its IP. This would go beyond any form of contemporary market research that is used to determine basic trends, such as knowing which race in an MMO is the most popular, or how many players opted to save the princess, risking their own virtual lives in the process. Our increasingly connected world could enable the player base to influence large sections of a film, based on their interactions with the game story. And why stop there? The ability for developers to track story interaction could influence the IP across the spectrum, which would in turn encourage players to see their gameplay as a real way to influence the direction of the IP as a whole (a form of digital vote, open to all who choose to participate).

INCREASING REACTIVITY

Games and game stories will become more adaptive and capable of generating experiences more procedurally. Technology will not only have the potential to affect how we react to stories, it will also help stories begin to react to us, as players, in ways that might sound a bit frightening at first. The beginnings of this can already be seen in *Left 4 Dead*, which contains AI designed to change gameplay, depending on players' behavior. Valve's Gabe Newell foresees a time when games will change how they play depending on how a player is feeling at that specific moment. With a wealth of possible ways to sense emotion—heart rate, pupil dilation, rate of breathing, sweat, eye motion, posture, and expression are all indicators that are already measurable by today's technology—it's just not built into our mice, keyboards, monitors, and gestural controllers. Yet. A game story might choose to drive a player hard for twenty minutes and raise their heart rate with a series of high-stakes puzzles against the clock before giving them respite, providing a simple, more relaxing, exploratory mission that brings down the heart rate. Perhaps game stories will one day not even require a games writer—the history of games development already beautifully demonstrates how software exponentially develops. With AI improving all the time[1] we can imagine programs being sophisticated enough to merge narrative elements from a wide variety of sources, weaving a procedural story that reacts to the player's responses differently every time, even remembering prior choices made months or years ago in a previous version of the series, and to react accordingly, linking the two titles, shifting the world in a way that illustrates the nature of consequence (*Mass Effect 2* illustrates this, to a limited extent). Playing *Final Fantasy XXII*, if it ever came to exist - might be a radically different experience for two players who play in radically different ways, perhaps seeking very different stories (one preferring to primarily explore a games world, the other enjoying more immediate conflict).

Whatever options continue to open as technology becomes both more powerful and more accessible, the way in which game stories evolve will ultimately be dictated by the most important people in the equation—the players. Developers and publishers can create a host of fascinating, clever, and hopefully even useful technologies through which increasingly potent game stories can be told, but if a new technology does not meet with approval by the gaming public, it will be quietly shelved. This basically means the future is in your hands. Be adventurous.

EXERCISES

1. Discuss three technological evolutions you would like to see in game story.
2. Which in your opinion is the main challenge to good storytelling—the development of AI or harnessing multiplayer activity? Why?

---

[1] See this article on Japanese AI that co-authored a short novel: *http://www.digitaltrends.com/cool-tech/japanese-ai-writes-novel-passes-first-round-nationanl-literary-prize/*, and this short movie written by AI called Sunspring, *https://youtu.be/LY7x2Ihqjmc*, both last accessed September 2016.

3. Imagine you're in a future where there are no technological limitations to game design and story. Discuss which game story feature you would invent and use on your new global game.
4. As a group discuss the impact of VR. Will it ultimately offer little more than graphical enhancement? Do you think VR offers designers and players paths to potential new gameplay and storytelling experiences?

PROJECT

1. Consider what design parameters you would need to establish in order for an AI program to write stories. Either alone or in groups, design a hypothetical AI to write a certain kind of story (of your choosing). Present your hypothetical design to the class. (Bear in mind, for this exercise, it doesn't matter if you know how to program AI or not—it's the thinking behind the programming that matters here and delivers a sense of how you view "story design" as a whole; consider what routines your AI should include, how frequently it should run these routines, and with what priority over other routines.)

Part IV What's It Like Being a Games Writer?

Authors' Note

Although we could have used this section to outline our own thoughts on what it was like to be a games writer at this most exciting, evolutionary, frustrating, interesting time, we decided this would only be of limited value. Two thoughts, we realized, would not be as interesting as hearing many, giving a greater sense of perspective, and covering a broader reach of experiences and opinions. Not only that, but we also found ourselves wondering what games writers as a broad community would have to say on this subject and if that might lead us to draw hitherto unexpected conclusions from the multiplicity of views expressed.

So, we approached our friends and colleagues who are also games writers and asked them this question: *What is it like being a games writer? Please could you tell us something good and something bad, even just a sentence or two on each. Or—perhaps just something good, or only something bad.*

We also offered them the possibility of anonymity, given that, as practitioners, they might not have felt too comfortable about disclosing their views within an industry on which their livelihoods depended. What follows is the sum of the responses to that question, updated in this Second Edition with additional voices.

Chapter 24

What's It Like Being a Games Writer?

OBSERVATIONS OF GAMES WRITERS

The following comments are from some of the leading writers in the industry.

*Being a games writer was, for me, a matter of getting to do some of the weirdest and most fun things I'd ever done creatively, while also having a *ton* of constraints to work with—from production, to design, to typical office politics. If* *you like working in teams and dealing with all kinds of difficult, but fun-to-solve problems, then maybe you'll dig games writing.*

Anthony Burch
Lead Writer for Gearbox on *Borderlands 2*

I really like the challenge of scoping the writing to fit the game's technical or budget constraints. Those moments of thinking around problems or finding interesting ways of presenting story that fit the project spec are also rewarding.

It's frustrating when you work hard to hit deadlines and then see them get moved back. More time means more editing and maybe some adding, but it's hard not to think about what you could have done if you'd known there was going to be more time available. It's similarly frustrating when content gets cut to fit new timelines and you end up trying to stitch plot back together, especially when you're trying to navigate the opinions of everyone from the publisher to the tester about how the writing should be done.

Dan Mayers
Game Director at Firelight Games

Good . . .

For me the joy of writing for games is that they incorporate so many different styles and disciplines, it can be part novel, part film, part TV series. You get involved in every aspect, from character creation and dialogue, or longer form narrative and cinematic scenes, to environmental storytelling. You get to put together the pieces of a whole world and see it come to life on screen.

Not so good . . .

You can't be precious. I've written what I thought were the wittiest, or most deeply dramatic character or scene but, for gameplay reasons, they've had to be cut. Story and gameplay have to work together and letting go of even your brilliant ideas for the good of the game as a whole is a hard lesson you learn early.

Kristen McGorry
Writer at Lionhead Studios

I got started in games as a level designer rather than a writer. I'd always written, but while growing up video games were my medium, and video games didn't have writers. To make games I learned to code, I learned to script, I learned how geometry affects player behavior and emotion, I learned the psychology of play. And then it turned out video games do have writers after all.

But all that, I think, has left me a better games writer. AAA game dev is a highly collaborative exercise, and no-one gets the most out of their individual work without understanding the other disciplines involved. Writing for games is unusual, demanding a lot of anticipation and contextual understanding. For example, I've had times where we've had to pull apart a beautiful scene because the fear and refusal being played out was totally at odds with the feeling of empowerment and excitement the player was going through at that moment. As storytellers we weren't in sole control of that moment—the player works alongside you as an active participant. We were able to make our writing better through thorough understanding of the gameplay in the background.

I'm also lucky in that I've worked with people who take narrative design very seriously—not all writers are so fortunate. I've had to do huge rewrites because design pillars have changed (your end boss is invincible? OK, I'll weave that theme nicely through the game. What do you mean you've changed your mind? We've already recorded half the script!) but I've also been on the inside, able to shape game and story side-by-side, and have never had to 'just come in and do the words.' Sadly, that doesn't get you out of having to write huge lists of variants on "I'm casting a spell!"

For all its quirks, games writing is immensely exciting: players who have genuine agency can participate in your story and take partial ownership, becoming deeply engaged. It's also immensely frustrating: players can literally ignore everything you've done, no matter how unskippable you make your cutscenes. But whatever you write, it's never going to work for everyone. Surrendering a bit of control can mean those who click with your work have a truly memorable and engaging experience.

And if that doesn't work, you can always fall back on filling item descriptions with innuendo.

Ben Brooks
Lead Content Designer at Lionhead Studios

What's it like to be a games writer?

On a good day, you'll be writing scripts, brainstorming mission ideas, and even sitting in a VO booth/at a mocap stage watching your words come to life. On a bad day, you'll be endlessly chasing bugs to figure out why a conversation isn't playing, wrestling with whatever tool is being used to manage all of the text, and banging your head against your desk because the mission you've already written six times needs to be re-written yet again.

William Harms
Lead Writer on Mafia III

When you write dialog for a character—and it doesn't matter how major that character is—you become that character. You repeat a line over and over in your head (and sometimes out loud) until you start to truly believe what you've written. Doesn't matter if it's a short yelp of pain or an impassioned speech by the hero, over time you develop a kind of schizophrenic ability to switch between different personalities and mindsets at the drop of a hat. You end up having heated discussions with yourself.

Ant Orman
Senior Narrative Designer at 2K Australia

Getting to live something you've dreamed about for a long time is kind of bittersweet—it's everything you wanted, but it's also hard.

Much harder than you think it's going to be. Something you used to do for fun becomes a matter of life or death. At least, that's what it seems like sometimes! Inevitably, you are going to run into someone that hates what you do. A coworker, a fan, someone is going to try and tear you all the way back to where you came from. It's important not to give up. You did work hard. You DO know what you're doing. You can't please everyone, so do your best to please the people that matter the most. Let me reiterate: DON'T GIVE UP.

Kirsten Kahler
Writer at Gearbox Software

I've written for a lot of different narrative media—film, TV, theater, comics, song writing, etc.—and, without a doubt, writing for games is the most challenging.

First, there's no way to become a good writer writing only games; the ratio of thinking/planning to writing is even more tilted toward the former than in other media, because games don't require that many actual spoken or read words, and thus, to use a workout metaphor, you simply don't get enough reps in to improve. So you have to first become a serviceable writer in another medium (the two most common are fiction and screenwriting, although I've known some former journalists, playwrights, and even poets who transitioned to game writing, too).

Second, there's no beaten path to get into the games industry as a narrative specialist. Ask ten working game writers how they got into the business and you'll get ten disparate origin stories. The job didn't really even exist before the mid-Aughts; it took the industry that long both to achieve the technical means to tell stories in any but the most bare-bones way and to realize that, having done so, the need now existed for people who were specialists in storytelling. (Some in the industry still have yet come to that realization.)

Most dauntingly, the task itself is sui generis. Game narrative differs from every other form of storytelling devised by humans in that it is often non-linear and it gives control over the speed with and sequence in which the story unfolds to the audience. The human mind evolved to use storytelling for a brilliant array of purposes, from passing down the skills needed to hunt for food, to depicting our relationship with our gods, to expressing the emotional experience of living our tiny lives in a big universe. For millennia we told stories in an orderly fashion: this happened (creating a problem), then this happened (an attempted solution to the problem), then that happened (the problem was solved, or it wasn't solved and so demanded a new solution). We told stories that mimicked our subjective experience following time and Newton's Second Thermodynamic Law's linear, one-way flow. Why would we tell them any other way?

And then fiction writers and screenwriters got all sassy and invented things like flashbacks and flash-forwards and dream sequences and whatever the heck it is Tarantino was doing in Pulp Fiction, and our stories started getting less linear. And then we created a brand new medium in which we put 90% of the power to dictate how a story unfolds in the hands of the consumer—or, here, the player (a vital distinction). All the tools in our writer's toolkits having to do with what information the audience knows when, and in what order, and at what pace, were removed, and, with them, things like suspense and dramatic irony.

I'm here to report that telling meaningful, emotionally resonant stories without those tools is hard, man, harder than anything I've ever had to do while writing a screenplay. You have to figure out how to get story across in discrete little quanta:

a piece of codex text here, a bit of voiced dialogue there, a trace of environmental world building over there. And how to present it in such a way that it doesn't matter, or at least matters far less than usual, what order the player receives and ingests those quanta of information in. I often described my first major game narrative gig, writing the first Destroy All Humans! as being asked to draw a picture, cut it up into jigsaw pieces, and put the pieces back together, all with my hands in a black bag so I couldn't see what I was doing. And, frankly, that undersells the degree of difficulty of the job.

But that's why those of us lucky enough to make a meager living at it love it so. It's devilishly difficult in the most satisfying way. So much so, in fact, that we opt to endure all sorts of obstacles and indignities—including the data-supported fact that the gaming public cares a lot more about the narrative dimension of the games they play than do many of the non-narrative people making those games. We are frequently disrespected in our own industry, because the technical skills needed to do our jobs well can seem invisible, even at times to the people we work with. Everyone talks; everyone writes emails and texts; everyone watches Game of Thrones. What could be so hard about writing stories, then? (It reminds me of how, back in my long-ago days as a professional actor, the most urgent question people always wanted to ask me was how I managed to learn all those lines, as if that was the hardest part of acting, as if there were no other skills or technique or craft involved. But, of course, if you approach your work as an artist in the proper way, it should look invisible, effortless, to those on the other end. Try watching to ballet dancers rehearse without music; you'll come away with a renewed appreciation for how hard they work, to be sure. But athletes work hard, too. The alchemy that turns craft and effort into art is and should be more inscrutable and mystified, for storytellers just as much as for dancers, in order to have its desired effect. Unless we're talking about Brecht. Let's not talk about Brecht.)

Anyway, the point is, being a game writer is, like all things worth doing, hard and punishing and soul-crushing and frustrating and infuriating and very, very occasionally, transcendently, ecstatically satisfying. Working that hard, for that long, can seem too daunting to persevere at . . . until you see a fan at a con dressed up as a character you cooked up in your own little imagination. At that moment, seeing how something that started as an idea in the back of your mind matters so much to a human being you've never even met that they would want to inhabit it, to take it fully into themselves and remake themselves in its image, you are powerless to deny how very fortunate you are to be one of the relative handful of people who have been able to make the creation of such a thing your livelihood. It's an incomparable experience, and everything you've suffered to get there blows away like dandelion wisps in that moment and ceases to matter. Such is art; such is life.

Tom Abernathy
Writer/Director/Narrative Designer

What's it like being a game writer?

If you come from another medium like television or film, game writing can be profoundly frustrating as narrative is usually, if not mostly, secondary to gameplay. The constraints on writers tend to run counter to what it takes to tell a good or, more likely, coherent story. Compelling dialogue and taut structure can be easily compromised by the demands of UI, art, animation, sound, design, and programming. Equally as constrictive are the requests from Up Above (read: the publisher) who often pushes for a last-minute "scoping down" of the project for budgetary concerns or requires holistic changes to meet ambiguous business needs.

However, if you have an adaptable spirit and love collaboration, there is no greater outlet for a writer than games. The demands of innovation force people from various skill-sets and expertise to work together on a daily basis to solve insurmountable creative and technological problems. It's interesting to witness the melding of these minds, both left- and right-brain dominants, racing toward a solution. But it's exhilarating to be a part of it.

I often forget that video games are software. The entertainment experience that is married to it is not immune to matrimonial struggles. As a writer in this field, I have found that, to abate those struggles, I can't be precious about what I write. If there are changes that need to be made that do not meet my standards of good story-telling, I will do whatever it takes to make those changes work to satisfy both the standards of solid story-telling and the latest creative vision. Making games is extremely difficult. Racing toward the deadline of your game's release is a long, grueling process. The last thing a writer needs to be is a stick in the mud for no other reason than to satisfy a narrative vision that is no longer in line with the game's creative direction.

The release of the game isn't the end of the game development experience . . . at least, not for those who are anxious to hear what people have to say about the final product. Beware of the noise machine on Twitch, Reddit, and other havens of the core gamer. It is often gut-wrenching to see/read them lambaste the fruits of your labor with inane, profane, and childish comments. Yet, these frustrations are fleeting. When you happen upon your final product—an actual piece of innovation that you worked on!—sitting on the shelves of a Best Buy or appearing in the digital queue on Steam, the App Store, or Google Play, there is nothing more rewarding.

Ross Berger
Screenwriter/Producer/Transmedia Strategist

The Good: Collaboration

It's not uncommon for projects to have more than one writer, especially when branching narrative is involved. Being able to bounce ideas off other writers is a great way to get out of a rut and explore new options. Even on projects with a single writer the rest of the team will have input on the story. I love collaborating with designers and artists as their innovative features and awesome art always inspire me. It makes me work extra hard to inspire them in return.

The Bad: Collaboration

Yes, there are two sides to this coin. Having everyone dump their feedback on you in form of countless notes in Google Docs or during endless "brainstorming" sessions and being expected to integrate them without an understanding as to why something may be a bad idea or cause structural or dramatic issues can be challenging at best. These are the days when you really wish you were a novel writer. But finding a way to "make things work" is part of your job and it pushes your creativity to new limits. So learn to take a deep breath and roll with it.

Dorian Richard
Writer and Narrative Designer

What's it like being a games writer? Most of the times, I feel like a fraud. I could blame my impostor syndrome for this (yes, according to the American Psychological Association, that's really a 'thing'), but it's most probably the fact that I've had zero academic background and zero experience when I started doing this, a year ago.

Writing for games feels like being a criminal defence lawyer sometimes. I have to defend my stories or characters against editors or producers who accuse them of different offences ("Too many characters!" "Too long!" "Too short!"), while trying to keep my texts from being thrown in the ultimate jail—the recycle bin.

At other times, I feel like a negotiator trying to convince the 'madman' to give me three extra days for writing that synopsis or one extra bad guy in the story. The negotiation doesn't always go my way and the hostage/text sometimes ends up deformed beyond recognition.

Writing for games also feels like being a belly dancer. You have to be flexible and ready to adjust your "dancing routine" whenever the art or design team change the "music"—and they seem to have a thing for "rhythm changes."

Why do I do it, then, if it entails so many limitations and frustrations? For the sheer pleasure of creating a universe with which people can interact. Because I think it's a privilege to learn something as complex as creating a game from scratch and also getting paid for it. Because working with a bunch of talented people has enriched my experience immensely. And, let's be honest, in an industry created for men and dominated by them, being a female games writer feels pretty badass (and turns out, it's a great pick-up line, too).

Ina Hofnar
Games Writer

Positive

A gripping storyline can be the making of a game, and you have the power to orchestrate that. Wield it well!

Games can make players laugh, cry, or scream in terror as much as any other art form, if not more. Watching someone play your game and experience the intended emotions can make all the pain worthwhile.

Negative

It is inevitable that you will have to compromise your vision for reasons of budget, time, or conflict with others on the project.

Get used to people thinking you can be called in at the last minute to magically create a compelling narrative around an almost-finished game.

Everyone fancies themselves a writer. This can make actually being one a frustrating process.

Jackie Tetley
Game Designer and Writer

Being a game writer, narrative designer, or story developer can be one of the most rewarding jobs within the creative writing industry. Often you'll get the chance to see your writings come alive and working with so many different professionals from all kinds of expertise is just a tremendous enrichment while creating new worlds and stories. On the downside one has to consider that not all companies, but luckily this number is decreasing, see the need for professional game writers, which can make it a bit hard to get yourself established as one.

Usually it is always a good idea to learn a second area of expertise like level design besides writing, if you want to become a game writer or narrative designer.

Tobias Heussner
Game/Narrative Designer for Bigpoint GmbH on *Drakensang Online*

What's it like being a writer for games? It's unlike any other type of writing out there, in that you're an intimately connected part of a much larger team, with dependencies upstream and downstream from you. Your work impacts and is impacted by so many other developers, it's collaborative in a way that I don't think exists anywhere else. That's got its good and its bad—the constraints can be tight, can be imposed from the outside, and are often driven as much by technology ("No, we can't have the characters embrace. Would you settle for a curt nod?") or budget/schedule ("Sorry, you only get four bad guys. Make them count.") as creative concerns. To someone used to using the broad canvas of, say, novel writing, where you can put a million zombies on the stage because all it takes is writing the word "million," that can be an odd feeling. On the other hand, seeing something you've written fully realized—and seeing players get a kick out of it—is an amazing feeling of shared accomplishment.

Richard Dansky
Central Clancy Writer for Ubisoft/Redstorm on *Tom Clancy's Splinter Cell: Conviction*

Writing games is the best job in the world. You get to work with amazing teams of talented and passionate people to bring the coolest form of entertainment to the world. The only real downside is the heartbreak of a game being cancelled while still in development, which happens far more often than most people know. It makes the triumphs that much sweeter.

Matt Forbeck
Writer on 505 Games' *ArmA: Armed Assault*

The Good: The opportunity to write stories for an audience that will experience them vicariously through games.

The Bad: Coming into a project at the last minute to write barks, character background, story arcs, and flavor text.

The Ugly: The spelling, punctuation, and grammar of the people who think they are writers, but aren't.

Chris Keeling
Writer on the U.S. Army's *America's Army: Soldiers*

Something good: I feel like a new type of writer. These are not like books and movies, here I can move people through interactivity, it is a new dimension of storytelling.

*Something bad: Like a man of anguish, I am always facing the design limitations of **a** game system which cannot totally reflect my story.*

Anon
Japanese RPG Games Writer

The player notes every word. If I describe a pipe as "old and broken," they'll spend an hour trying to repair it. Everything is seen as a clue. If the pipe was never meant to be repaired, they'll quit in tears and rage. A simple adjective can guide them to a solution, or accidentally drive them mad.

Gene Mocsy
Writer on Autumn Moon Entertainment's *Ghost Pirates of Vooju Island*

Being a games writer is for me the chance to combine a lifetime interest in interactive technology with a love of story. My most delicious challenge is in the limitations presented by the genre. The purpose is to game, not take in a passive story experience, so the story must be integrated into whatever movement and action and interactivity make up the core of the game. The downside to being a games writer is that not all developers understand that story is not something you "plug in" after the fact.

Anon

Something good: Nothing compares to having your friends gush about a game you worked on. Besides bragging rights, though, the process of working with talented people of diverse disciplines and perspectives can be incredibly rewarding.

Something bad: Creative edits after you've handed in a script are sometimes vexing but that's part of the life for a professional writer. You can never grow too attached to a project, especially a work-for-hire.

Jason L. Blair
Writer on Sega/High Voltage Software's *Conduit 2*

Good: You play god—building and destroying empires and creatures at your whim. Writing is basically the ultimate sandbox game.

Bad: Except when you're being constrained in your writing style by a pre-existing IP, or a decision from management.

Dan Rosenthal
Narrative Designer on Simutronics' *DragonRealms*

Giving the player as much control (or feeling of control) as possible is simultaneously one of the best and worst things about writing for games. Player agency is a unique aspect of games and presents challenges and opportunities that you can't find anywhere else. But it is also extremely difficult to pull off, and you're reliant on the success of many other team members in order for that to happen. All it takes is a sloppy audio programmer (for example) to make your dialogue go from brilliant to grating.

Anon

The Good

1. *You get paid for writing fiction. Upfront. Regularly. This is not at all like writing novels or short stories that you then shop around, or like writing screenplays that gather dust on an agent's desk in a folder labeled: "After Hell Freezes Over." You get to create great characters and stories that tens or hundreds of thousands or even millions of people are going to experience. That is awesome.*
2. *The fans are great. When you start hearing your own lines quoted on forums, and get fan questions about the story and characters through your website, and*

*run across people who say, "You wrote that game? I *loved* that game!" . . . as a creative worker there is nothing quite as fulfilling. Except maybe winning the lottery, which hardly is a direct outcome of your own genius and the Protestant Work Ethic, but speaking for myself I'm pretty sure I'd still enjoy it.*

The Bad

1. *The problem with being a game writer is that you are not in a position of power. In fact, on the totem pole of game development, the only thing lower than the game writer is whatever firm surface is necessary to support the weight. Design, art, animation, sound, music, marketing, accounting, the mailroom, janitors, the cafeteria lady, and the panhandler out front all have opinions that carry more weight with management than yours. Get used to that, and pick your battles with extreme care. Your role is critical to the success of the game, and sometimes it takes sheer bull-headed stubbornness to see that it is done right.*
2. *Any human being blessed with both a functioning nervous system and a keyboard assumes that they know how to write. See? Words in a row! I can write, too! They do not believe that it is not that simple, and that every single word explains something about the character, what they are saying, why they are saying it, and who they are saying it to. Every piece that you put into the story is in there for a reason, and cutting or adding random chunks is sort of like turning an F1 car over to an eager kid with modeling clay to do repairs.*

The Ugly

1. *It is an iterative process, and your stories and plots and characters are going to take a lot of abuse. You'll have a lot of time and opportunities to fix things that weren't so great in the first draft, because there will be about three hundred and eighty-seven drafts by the time the game actually ships.*
2. *Game development is (in theory) a for-profit enterprise that (generally) has production schedules that are (pretty much never) rigorously adhered to. However, what is true is that the writer is one element of a long chain that starts in pre-production and ends on a gamer's system after passing through a factory or web cloud. There are a lot of other pieces to the game both upstream and downstream of writing, and everyone involved has to be flexible and creative to make sure that the best possible result comes out at the end. No, I do not believe that an analogy that involves the digestive system is appropriate here.*

Jeff Spock
Lead Writer on Ubisoft's *Heroes of Might and Magic V*

It's exciting, complex, thrilling, precarious, and needs a whole team working together to get anything of quality.

It's also immensely difficult when you're not respected, cut out of meetings, felt to be pointless or, at best a nuisance.

Anon

The good: There's nothing like the feeling of knowing that you helped create this amazing experience for a player. I fall in love with every game story that I work on, enough so that I can envision countless stories, sequels, movies, and books all emanating from within this one world. You have to love games to be in game development. But I also love the adventure. Who knows what kind of story we'll be working on next? Each game is an opportunity to learn about so many different things. We hadn't read Sapkowski before working on The Witcher, *but we soon learned why his books are considered* The Lord of the Rings *of Eastern Europe.*

The bad: The game industry as a whole has become more cognizant of the importance of good writing in video games. However, writers are still sometimes brought in as an afterthought, as if story aspects of the game can be divorced from gameplay, artwork, and other elements.

Sande Chen
Writer on Atari's *The Witcher*

Something good: I can feel like a very important person who takes responsibility for the main part of a game.

Something bad: But other times feel like the game producer's dog, actually.

Anon
Japanese Action Games Writer

How does writing for the games industry treat you? I've been wined and dined in London and LA, I've won awards and felt like a king. I've had companies that haven't paid me for close to a year and who gave the lead programmer's dog a credit on the game, but not me. Remember the good things, because they get you through the bad times.

A lot of people ask how to get into the industry, how to become a writer. The answer is simple. Write, play games, and keep at it. Beyond that all you need is the mental stamina of a marathon runner, the patience of a saint, and the creative dexterity of three professional screenwriters. You will constantly be asked to do the impossible and often in less time than you could deliver the feasible. But then if you love the adrenalin of extreme sports, but prefer the comfort of an office chair, then it's a rush that's hard to match.

Anon

Something good about being a games writer:

- *Every day that you wake up; every word that you write; every game that you publish . . . you're helping to define an entirely new form of art.*
- *You can often work in your underwear.*

Something bad about being a games writer:

- *Every party; every family Christmas; every new person that you meet . . . you will have to explain that being a games writer does not mean you are a programmer.*
- *Following this you will hear, usually accompanied by a quizzical/pitying expression, multiple iterations of the phrase "I didn't know games had stories!"*

Tom Jubert
Writer on Paradox Interactive's *Penumbra: Black Plague*

A game in development is a shape shifter. Constant changes in design and gameplay make writing for games a never-ending story until the day before shipping. What you wrote—and worked—yesterday might not work today. Be prepared to often say goodbye to one month's work, erase and rewrite: it's the games writer's curse. A Sisyphean task for a mythic job on paper. Being a scriptwriter is like living on a rollercoaster. Oh, did I mention that I actually—and totally—love it?

Cristina Nava
Scriptwriter for Ubisoft's *We Dare*

In my experience with indie games, my role as game writer has spanned from writing character tales from nothing more than a sketch to writing tutorials which have accented holes in gameplay functionality, leading to further development iterations. You sometimes act as babysitter for team members who can't seem to meet deadlines or play nice with others. While writer is the title and launching the game is exhilarating, there are many unseen roles you will need to step up and fill to see your name in the credits of a published game. While I enjoy it, only you can decide if this is a fun process for you.

Drew McGee
Writer on Conjured Realms' *Bumble Tales*

I love story. I love games. Always have. So being a games writer enabled me to bring two genuine passions together. It has also miraculously enabled me (so far) to always be working on the next, new thing. Some of my first writing was for games—old-school boardgames and roleplay. That was great training for the plotting necessary to write a novel. Now, that I can do both, I am a happy camper. Or writer.

And something bad? There are projects that you put your heart, soul, and talent into that simply vanish. (That doesn't happen with novels.) And sometimes you are asked to only use your skill in carefully circumscribed areas, like creating the major story arc or scripting dialogue when, in my case, I'd want to make story and gameplay fuse together. And . . . occasionally you get in a situation where there are a lot of cooks sending their queries and edits on the evolving story. Patience and diplomacy helps in dealing with that.

Matt Costello
Writer for id Software's *Rage*

What is it like being a games writer? The only job better than games writer is astronaut, and only because NASA doesn't care about Metacritic scores.

Something good: Most of my prior writing was done in a vacuum and at odd hours, but not so with games. We've developed a tight dialogue iteration loop at my studio—what I write in the morning is recorded that afternoon and implemented by the designers for review the next day. Within 24 hours, I can hear and play the results.

Something bad: Because it is so expensive to develop an AAA title, final creative control does not rest with the writer, the lead designer, or even the creative director. Publishing executives sometimes demand drastic changes based on market research, a desire to avoid controversy, or their own whims.

C. J. Kershner
Writer on Kaos Studios/THQ's *Homefront*

The diversity of games, genres, and platforms means that, as a writer, you are constantly being challenged. You have to adapt and be flexible. You can't become complacent. There's something strangely exhilarating about that. You have to feel the texture and the grain of the barrier you're trying to push. On the downside, many companies still don't know how to use writers properly and often shamefully undervalue and underuse them. We are still kicking back against the residual feeling (largely caused by years of writing being done by non-professionals) that "anyone can write for a game" because "anyone can write." Being able to write words does not make someone a writer, just as being able to draw stick figures doesn't make me Rembrandt.

Rhianna Pratchett
Lead Writer on Crystal Dynamics' *Rise of the Tomb Raider*

Something good: I feel like a hero if our game is successful.

Something bad: I feel terrible the game is not successful, and my story always becomes the cause of any failure.

Anon
Japanese Action Games Writer

Something good about being a games writer is working in a team, with people with so different skills and competencies: the team work is a great thing for a writer, since we can get inspiration both by other peoples' ideas and the limitations and constraints we may have in the game structure (from a game design, coding or graphic point of view).

Something bad, instead, is that sometimes marketing impositions are a bit too tight and that good ideas are dismissed only because they do not match a certain market expectation or projection: of course the target of the game and marketing research should always be taken into consideration, but maybe also giving some vent to the writer's and team's creativity would not be totally bad!

Valentina Paggiarin
Writer on Ubisoft's *My Secret World*

Something good: It's like being a shadow producer, because I have to manage how my story affects the game's development budget and schedule, etc.

Something bad: It's also like being a slave to the game engine, budget, and schedule.

Anon
Japanese Action Games Writer

---

*It's tough to answer the questions "What is it like being a games writer?" when the truth is, it's not *like* anything. It's a bit like writing for TV, except it's not. It's a bit like writing for radio or comic books or the stage, except it's not. It's games, and it's new and it's changing, so it's not anything else—and that makes it cool. Not since TV took off in the 40s has a new medium come down the pipe for writers to get their teeth into, and we're only just scratching the surface. This is an exciting time to be a writer in games; the wave is breaking as technology reaches a plateau and the razzle-dazzle of great graphics and gimmicky game play start to ring a little hollow. We're at a point where players want story that matches the potency of the rest of their gaming experience.*

It's a great thing and it's a terrible thing, because like it or not, we who write game stories right now are the pathfinders. We're moulding the future of this medium with every choice we make, and that's a big responsibility. It's important we embrace it, though, that we go in clear-eyed and steeled for the challenge. We must be craftsmen and be artists, willing to fight our corner and give narrative the room it needs to grow and mature—because games are changing the way we tell stories, and they are changing the way audiences experience them. And who wouldn't want to be a part of that?

James Swallow
Writer on Ubisoft's *Deus Ex: Human Revolution*

---

*The Good: It's like no other form of writing. We get to write stories and scripts which people won't just watch, or read; they'll *play* them. We're still in the medium's infancy, and writers are helping to define how games develop and evolve. If you can't step back and see how tremendously exciting that is for a storyteller, you may as well go home.*

The Bad: It's like no other form of writing. No other medium rips apart, rewrites and trashes its stories and scripts so extensively, as a matter of routine. It's frustrating, because it can feel like you're doing ten times as much work as other writers just to keep on top of the constant changes. Games writing isn't for the faint of heart.

Antony Johnston
Writer on EA Redwood Shores' *Dead Space*

Something good: Games writing always keeps me sharp about topics like as history, politics, economics, technology, philosophy, ethics and world affairs, etc.

Something bad: The work is too hard at times. There can be no time to sleep.

Anon
Japanese RPG Games Writer

Something Good: The opportunity to work collaboratively with gifted, enthusiastic souls in a creative environment that's still evolving its boundaries at a frightening rate—strap on your big-boy hiking boots, ladies and gentlemen, we've an exciting ways to go yet!

Something Bad: Having designers tell you how to write, or confidently instruct you to change or edit elements of a story (when they don't negatively impact game design) whose sole qualification to do so is having watched some films. One does not have to be a gifted wordsmith to have a useful opinion, but story finger painters should know their limits and stick to what they're good at.

Anon

The Good: As a writer for Alternate Reality Games, I've felt essential to the gameplay. I've found many opportunities to write from a first-person perspective and really get a feel for characters, since they often have to keep the attention of players for a span of six months or longer. I appreciate the accessibility factor of ARGs and that people from many backgrounds interact with my writing.

The Bad: However, writing for video games can be a different experience. Times are getting better, but we still have a lot of work to do with out-of-house involvement and communication. Sometimes a writer is unintentionally (or intentionally) left out of the design process, which is fatal for strong, interconnected writing.

Beth Aileen Lameman
Writer on Aboriginal History Media Arts Lab's *Techno Medicine Wheel*

Good: Interdisciplinary, collaborative nature; involvement in a young industry—feeling like you are contributing to an industry in its early development, the narrative pathways, modes, and structures generated by the addition of interactivity to established modes of storytelling, and the excitement of creating a world and space that allows the final collaborator—the Player—walls on which to throw their graffiti.

Bad: Same as above.

Daniel Manley
Writer on 2K Marin's *BioShock 2*

The good thing about being a games writer is that it's an emerging art-form with very few set "rules"—there is only pure potential.

That said, it is very difficult to find more than a handful of standout achievements in games writing. Call of Duty: Black Ops is nominated for a 2011 BAFTA in this category. That should tell you something about the quality of stories, character, and dialogue in games, and the standards by which they are judged.

The main reason why, more often than not, writing in games seems to come out of deriva-tins rather than creative minds, is because the games industry still doesn't fully embrace individual creatives like the film industry.

The industry today operates like Hollywood in the 20s. Creatives are anonymous employees rather than individuals. In films today, writers are usually billed and valued as highly as directors and partake in their work's profits, their contribution in games is forgotten, bought out and stilted.

The games industry will see originality—and their proceeds—flourish again, when craftsmen and women are both allowed to fully express themselves and are properly compensated for it, too.

Whether you like it or not, it all comes down to story in the end.

Anon

Subject: Games Writer needed

Hi!

We're currently looking for a writer to join our team to put the dialogue in place. I've been given your name and had a quick look at the credits on your website. I was wondering what your current availability and rates are?

P. M. Schedule

Producer - totalcrunchtimegames.

Subject: Games Writer needed - Interested scribe

Hi!

Thanks for contacting me. I am just finishing off a project so would be able to talk to you about coming onboard with totalcrunchtimegames. Could you let me have a few more details about the project so I can give you an accurate answer to your questions? For instance, would you let me know the scale of the project, the timescale you have in mind (deadlines etc.), and the role you'd need me for (narrative design? dialogue? voice direction?)? Thanks in advance, I look forward to hearing back from you and to learning more about the game.

Have a great day.

Eager scribe

Subject: Games Writer needed - additional details

Hi!

We've already written the script (Paul the lead artist wrote some, Derrick in design and Jon from accounts—who did a Creative Writing module in 1991—did the rest). We've also completed some of the cutscenes (but ran out of budget, so we only got 3 out of 18 made, you'll have to do the rest in level dialogue). In total there are 28,300 lines of dialogue in the game, with 140,000 AI lines. We need you to *just polish them up a bit (make them great but try not to change anything). Our budget is $27.45 for the whole writing package and we need all the lines back by Friday.*

Let me know what you think.

P. M. Schedule

Producer - totalcrunchtimegames.

Games are great. Writing is great. Putting story into games is a technical challenge to a writer's craft. What's often a bigger challenge is helping a team to understand how difficult writing is and the immense challenges of getting that writing into the game in a form that works. Often the first job a writer has to do on a project is to persuade a team (or elements of it) that there is a point to a professional writer being there. There are still many development teams that either don't want a story in their game (but still hire a writer), or who think that anyone can do the job (so hire a writer to tell the team how great they've done writing the story without them). Any writer hoping to work in the industry should walk into it knowing that they are going to get emails (and projects) like the one above on a regular basis.

So, why do it? Simple—because when it does work it's great. There are an increasing number of companies who recognize that emails like the one above are out of place and out-dated. These progressive companies set up dedicated story teams, or schedule sensible time for each discipline to support the story, so that narrative becomes a valuable part of the game experience. When these measures are put in place, a writer's discussions switch from justifying the principle of stories in games and become all about how to make the story better, the ways to integrate this particular story with the gameplay, and how each part of the team can make the other's lives easier.

So, writers should enter the industry knowing they will face resistance from people who either don't want a story in the game, or who don't perceive value in someone who has made writing their job, but to keep going they need to remember that there are good companies out there, that the industry and its view of storytelling are changing.

Andy Walsh
Writer on Ubisoft's *Prince of Persia*

As a writer who spends a lot of time procrastinating by playing video games, writing for video games offers a guilt-free way of combining the two. I've always loved games with decent plots and dialogue, and it's exciting to be part of what is still very much a fledgling industry, which has seen many changes even in the few years I've been involved.

On the downside, you don't always get to be involved in the planning stage—writers are often called in relatively late in the design process. Being asked to punch-up a script based on a fundamentally rubbish premise can be a bit depressing—it feels like vacuuming the carpet while the house is on fire.

Tim Clare
Writer on HD Interactive's *Nexus: The Jupiter Incident*

It's evolving too fast for any description to remain apt for more than a week, and that's precisely, for me, what makes it so electrifying. But for my generation, most of what we know about story applies best to manipulative, authored push content. That is to say expository drama, Clockwork-Oranged into the player's agonized, swiftly drying retinas . . . inelegantly grafted onto what essentially wants to be a deeply participatory, personal vision quest. A goddamn thing of the body, hunting a white elk in a peyote fugue, ending in some ecstatic sun dance you might not survive.

The player's a kind of schizoid, causal tornado—and as a writer in any game worth its salt weight, you're struggling to provide emotional context for a protagonist who could be anyone, inwardly. It's like writing and directing an iterative play, where your lead actor is an amateur capable of sublime personal truth, but they've never seen the script. This beautiful freak could execute any manner of Dadaist improv stunt in the middle of your big fat self-important melodrama at any time. And each time you put on the show—it's someone new.

So yeah. If you haven't run screaming from that mutant analogy . . . call me.

Jordan Thomas
Creative Director on 2K Marin's *BioShock 2*

Appendix A RATING SYSTEMS

ESRB RATING SYSTEM

http://www.esrb.org/index-js.jsp

Rating	**Abbreviation**	**Age Suitability**
Early Childhood	EC	Ages 5 and below
Everyone	E	6 and above
Everyone 10+	E10+	10 and above
Teen	T	13 and above
Mature	M	17 and above (may contain intense violence/blood/sexual content/strong language)
Adults Only	AO	18 and above (may contain prolonged scenes of intense violence/blood/sexual content/strong language)
Rating Pending	RP	Could apply to any game

PEGI RATING SYSTEM

Age ratings combine with content descriptions

http://www.pegi.info/en/index/

Rating	**Abbreviation**	**Age Suitability**
3	n/a	All ages
7	n/a	7 and older
12	n/a	12 and older
16	n/a	16 and older
18	n/a	18 and older

CONTENT DESCRIPTION

Violence (game contains depictions of violence)

Bad language

Fear (game may be frightening or scary for young children)

Sex (game depicts nudity and/or sexual behavior or references)

Drugs (game refers to or depicts the use of drugs)

Discrimination (game contains depictions of, or material which may encourage, discrimination)

Gambling (game encourages or teaches gambling)

Online game

SAMPLE NON-DISCLOSURE AGREEMENT

MUTUAL CONFIDENTIALITY AGREEMENT

THIS AGREEMENT is made on the day of 2016

BETWEEN

________________________ whose address is at ____________________

____

AND
ABC Games Writing Company, whose address is at **99 Dawson Street, Denver, 80210,** hereinafter jointly referred to as the "Parties" or individually as the "Party"

INTRODUCTION

(A) The Parties wish to discuss **possible transactions between the parties**. The discussions will necessitate the disclosure of information concerning the business and affairs of each other and of other companies in the same group of companies as each of the Parties ("the business and affairs of the parties").

(B) Each party requires such disclosures to be treated in confidence and to be protected in accordance with the terms of this Agreement.

IT IS AGREED as follows:

1. Information disclosed under this Agreement will include, but not be limited to, commercial, financial, technical, operational, or other information in whatever form (including information disclosed orally) which concerns the business and affairs of the Parties and is of a confidential nature, including any such information disclosed prior to the date of this Agreement ("Confidential Information").

2. Each party will:

   2.1 keep in confidence any Confidential Information disclosed to it by the other party and will not disclose that Confidential Information to any person (other than their employees or professional advisers, who need to know the Confidential Information) without the written consent of the other Party;

   2.2 use the Confidential Information disclosed to it by the other Party only for the purpose for which it was disclosed;

   2.3 ensure that all people to whom the Confidential Information is disclosed under this Agreement are aware of the terms of this Agreement; and

   2.4 make copies of the Confidential Information only to the extent strictly necessary to the purpose for which it was disclosed.

3. The parties will keep the existence, nature, and content of this Agreement confidential, together with the fact that discussions are taking place concerning the business and affairs of the Parties.

4. Paragraphs 2 and 3 will not apply to:

   (a) information which has been published other than through a breach of this Agreement;

   (b) information lawfully in the possession of the recipient before its disclosure under this Agreement took place;

   (c) information obtained from a third party who is free to disclose it;

   (d) information independently developed by a Party;

   (e) information which a Party is requested to disclose and, if it did not, could be required by law (including a regulatory body) to disclose.

5. No licenses or any rights under any patent, registered design, copyright, design right, or any similar right belonging to either Party are implied or granted under this Agreement.

6. The obligations and restrictions in this Agreement will last for a period of 2 years from the date of the last disclosure of Confidential Information under this Agreement.

7. The receiving Party will on request either:

   (a) return all copies of the Confidential Information to the disclosing Party; or

   (b) destroy it and confirm in writing to the disclosing Party that this has been done.

8. The disclosure of Confidential Information under this Agreement does not oblige either Party to enter in to any further agreement with the other Party.
9. Neither Party will export directly or indirectly any technical data acquired under this Agreement or any products produced utilizing any such data to any country to which the U.S. Government or any of its agencies requires an export license or other government approval, without first obtaining such license or approval.
10. This Agreement is governed by the Law of The United States.

SIGNED on behalf of

SIGNATURE

NAME

POSITION

SIGNED on behalf of ABC Games Writing Company

SIGNATURE

NAME

POSITION

Appendix C Sample Writing Services Contract

CONFIDENTIAL

SERVICES AGREEMENT

THIS AGREEMENT (this "**Agreement**") is entered into as of __________, 2016, by and between (1) **BIG CLIENT** of Glass Building Centre, 145 Long Street, Los Angeles, CA 90255, United States of America ("**Big**"); and (2) **ABC GAMES WRITING COMPANY** of 99 Dawson Street, Denver, CO 80210 ("**ABC**").

1. RECITALS

1.1 Big is a developer of high quality video game software.

1.2 Big is considering the possible development, publication and release of a currently untitled quiz-based video game featuring quiz show questions (the "**Game**") for play on console platforms.

1.3 Big wishes to engage the services of ABC to create two sample story proposals to help Big to decide whether to proceed with the development of the Game and for possible utilization in the Game. ABC has agreed to provide these services upon the terms and conditions set forth in this Agreement.

2. ADDITIONAL DEFINITIONS

"**Acceptable Form**" means that all of the Deliverables are: (a) in the reasonable opinion of Big are of a nature and quality that are suitable for the proposed Game; and (b) free from typographical and grammatical errors.

"**Commencement Date**" means the date of this Agreement set above.

"**Deliverables**" means two distinct and appropriate story proposals, to be prepared by or on behalf of ABC and provided to Big in accordance with this Agreement.

"**Fee**" means the sum of four thousand dollars ($4000).

"**Services**" means the preparation and supply of the Deliverables in accordance with this Agreement.

"Target Completion Date" means the date of the fifteenth day after the Commencement Date.

"Term" means the period commencing on the Commencement Date and expiring on the first anniversary of the Target Completion Date.

3. SERVICES

3.1 With effect from the Commencement Date, Big engages ABC to provide the Services in accordance with the terms and conditions of this Agreement.

3.2 ABC shall prepare and supply the Deliverables to Big in Acceptable Form no later than the Target Completion Date.

4. INTELLECTUAL PROPERTY RIGHTS

4.1 ABC unconditionally and irrevocably assigns to Big with full title guarantee all present and future legal and beneficial right, title, and interest, including all copyright and other intellectual property rights, in and to the Deliverables throughout the world absolutely to the fullest extent permitted by law.

4.2 ABC shall procure unconditional and irrevocable waivers in writing for the benefit of Big of any and all moral rights existing in or relating to the Deliverables throughout the world absolutely to the fullest extent permitted by law.

4.3 ABC agrees that it shall not have, nor claim to have, any right, title, or interest in or to the Game or the Deliverables, nor any advertising ideas, announcements, phrases, titles, music or words originated, supplied and/or used by Big in conjunction with the Game, and that all such rights in the Game and the Deliverables are recognized to be in Big.

4.4 ABC agrees to do any and all such acts and things and execute any and all such documents as Big may reasonably require in order to give effect to the intended operation of the provisions of Clauses 4.1, 4.2, and 4.3, including where necessary to vest in Big any right, title, or interest in or to the Deliverables.

5. FEE

5.1 In consideration of the full and proper performance of the Services by ABC in accordance with all of the terms and conditions of this Agreement, Big shall pay the Fee to ABC in accordance with this Clause 5.

5.2 Upon supply of the Deliverables to Big in Acceptable Form, ABC may submit a written invoice to Big for the Fee. Big shall pay the Fee to ABC within thirty (30) days following Big's receipt of such invoice. Big shall have no obligation to pay the Fee if ABC fails to supply a written invoice to Big. Big shall pay the Fee by bank transfer into ABC's bank account, details of which are set out below:

Account number: **12341234**

Sort code: **12-23-12**

Bank: **Writing Bank of California**

Branch address: **1223 South Vermont Avenue, Los Angeles, CA 90054, USA**

5.3 The parties acknowledge and agree that the Fee and any other sums expressed to be payable under this Agreement shall be inclusive of all taxes, including value added tax.

6. FIRST REFUSAL RIGHT

6.1 The parties acknowledge that Big has engaged ABC to supply the Deliverables solely for the purpose of helping Big to decide whether it wishes to proceed to develop and publish the Game. Accordingly, Big is under no obligation to develop and publish the Game, nor is it under any obligation to use the Deliverables (or any of them) within the Game should it decide to develop and publish the Game.

6.2 Notwithstanding Clause 6.1, and provided that ABC supplies the Deliverables to Big in Acceptable Form, if Big decides during the Term to proceed to develop and publish the Game, then:

(a) ABC shall have a right of first refusal to create appropriate text for the Game (the **"Writing Services"**) in accordance with this Clause;

(b) promptly following the date on which Big decides to proceed to develop and publish the Game (whichever is the later), Big shall notify ABC and for the period of thirty (30) days following the date of that notice (the **"Exclusive Negotiation Period"**) Big and ABC shall negotiate in good faith the terms on which ABC shall provide some or all of the Writing Services for Big; and

(c) during the Exclusive Negotiation Period, Big shall not negotiate with any third party for the provision of the Writing Services. If, at the expiry of the Exclusive Negotiation Period, the parties have been unable to agree commercial terms on which ABC shall provide the Writing Services to Big for the Game, then Big shall be free to negotiate with any third party for the provision of Writing Services and to appoint any third party for the provision of the Writing Services.

6.3 Nothing in this Clause 6 shall operate so as to prevent or restrict Big from: (a) discussing or negotiating with any third party or engaging any third party for the provision of services with respect to the Game that are not Writing Services; or (b) discussing or negotiating with any third party or engaging any third party for the provision of Writing Services at end time following the termination or expiry of this Agreement.

7. TERMINATION

7.1 *Term.* This Agreement shall commence on the Commencement Date and, subject to earlier termination as provided in this Agreement, shall continue for the Term. This Agreements shall automatically expire upon the end of the Term.

7.2 *Breach.* If either party commits a material breach of this Agreement, and if such material breach is capable of remedy and not cured within thirty (30) days after written notice of the breach is given by the non-breaching party to the breaching party, then the non-breaching party may give notice to the breaching party of its election to terminate this Agreement. However, such right of termination shall not be exclusive of other remedies available to the non-breaching party.

7.3 *Survival.* The following Clauses shall survive the termination or expiration of this Agreement: Clauses 4, 7.3, 8, and 9.

8. WARRANTY AND INDEMNIFICATION

8.1 *Authorization.* ABC warrants and represents that it has the right and power to enter into and perform this Agreement, that ABC is free to enter into this Agreement and provide the Services pursuant to this Agreement, and that ABC is not under any agreements or obligations to any third parties that would preclude or interfere in any way with its entering into and fully performing its obligations under this Agreement or the full and unrestricted exercise by Big of the rights granted to Big under this Agreement.

8.2 *Deliverables.* ABC warrants and represents that: (a) none of the Deliverables shall be libelous, defamatory, or obscene; (b) the supply of the Deliverables shall not infringe the rights (including intellectual property rights) of any third party; and (c) the Deliverables shall be free from all known viruses, spyware, and other malicious software.

8.3 *Indemnification for Breach.* ABC shall indemnify and hold Big harmless against all losses, claims, demands, liabilities, and expenses, including reasonable attorney fees, which may arise from its breach of any term, covenant, representation or warranty of this Agreement.

9. GENERAL PROVISIONS

9.1 *Recitals.* The recitals in this Agreement constitute an integral part of the Agreement reached by the parties and are to be considered as such.

9.2 *Captions.* The captions contained in this Agreement have been inserted for reference and convenience only, and do not define, limit or describe the scope of this Agreement or the intent of any provision.

9.3 *Independent Contractor.* The parties, by this Agreement, do not intend to create any partnership, principal/agent, master/servant, franchisor/franchisee, or joint venture relationship and nothing in this Agreement shall be construed as creating such a relationship. Neither party nor its agents or employees are representatives of the other party for any purpose except as expressly set forth in this Agreement, and neither party has the power or authority as agent/employee or other capacity to represent, act for, bind or otherwise create or assume any obligations on behalf of the other party for any purpose whatsoever.

9.4 *Non-assignability/Sublicensing.* ABC shall not sell, assign, delegate, charge, sublicense or otherwise or transfer or encumber this Agreement or the rights granted in this Agreement or the obligations undertaken in this Agreement, without the prior written consent of Big.

9.5 *Waiver.* The waiver by any party of a breach or default of any provision of this Agreement by the party shall not constitute a waiver by such party of any succeeding breach of the same or other provisions; nor shall any delay or omission on the party of either party to exercise or avail itself of any right, power, or privilege that it has or may have hereunder, operate as a waiver of any such right, power, or privilege by such party.

9.6 *Governing Law and Jurisdiction.* This Agreement shall be governed by, subject to, and construed under the laws of the State of California. The parties shall submit to the exclusive jurisdiction of the courts of the State of California.

9.7 *Unenforceability.* In the event that any term, clause, or provision of this Agreement shall be construed to be or adjudged invalid, void, or unenforceable, such term, clause, or provision shall be construed as severed from this Agreement, and the remaining terms, clauses, and provision shall remain in effect.

9.8 *Notices.* All written communication under this Agreement (**"Notices"**) shall be considered given when the same is: (a) delivered to the party(ies) entitled to such Notice, (b) deposited with a guaranteed courier service to the person(s) and address(es) stated at the beginning of this Agreement; or (c) transmitted by facsimile with an original sent concurrently by a guaranteed courier service. Notice shall be deemed effective upon the earlier of actual receipt or two (2) business days after mailing or transmittal.

9.9 *Confidentiality.* The parties are to maintain the existence of this Agreement strictly confidential unless and until an appropriate formal announcement of this Agreement has been released by Big. Also, the parties are to maintain the underlying terms of this Agreement strictly confidential at all times unless the parties agree in writing to release such information. However, to enable Big to carry out the terms of this Agreement, Big may discuss the present Agreement in confidence with other companies in the group of companies of which Big is a member, the game development companies that will assist Big in the development of the Game, and Big's public relations firms.

9.10 *Integration.* This Agreement constitutes the entire agreement between the parties relating to the subject matter of this Agreement. All prior negotiations, representations, agreements, and understandings are merged into, extinguished by, and completely expressed by it. Neither party shall be bound by any definition, condition, warranty, representation, modification, consent, or waiver other than as expressly stated in this Agreement, unless set forth in writing executed by the party to be bound.

[Signature to Follow]

[Signature Page – Services Agreement]

IN WITNESS WHEREOF, the parties have caused this Agreement to be executed by the respective corporate officers or agents hereunto duly authorized.

BIG	THE ABC GAMES WRITING COMPANY
Signed: ____________________	Signed: ____________________
Print name: ____________________	Print name: ____________________
Title: ____________________	Title: ____________________
Date: ____________________	Date: ____________________

Appendix D

Selected Exercise Solutions (Chapter 10)

Chapter 10

TABLE 10.3. Death in Shadow Bay Dialogue Edit – COMPLETED

Original	Edit	Designer Notes
Morning! Are you ready for a cool day of adventure?	Morning! Ready for a day's adventuring?!	Missy, greeting player (happy)
Oh, hi. I slept really, really badly last night.	Hi. I had an awful night's sleep.	Missy, greeting player (unhappy)
Urgh! It's impossible to sleep in this terrible, yucky town!	Urgh! I can't get any sleep in this horrible town!	Missy, greeting player (unhappy)
"Good morning". Not sure if I'm feeling pretty today.	Morning. Am I pretty today? Not sure.	Missy, greeting player (neutral)
Did you sleep ok or did you have nightmares?	You sleep okay? Any nightmares?	Caleb, greeting player (happy)
Hey. I'd say "good morning" but that'd be a total lie.	I'd say "good morning" but that'd be a lie.	Caleb, greeting player (unhappy)
I'm having, like the worst morning ever!	This is the worst morning ever!	Caleb, greeting player (unhappy)
Morning. Ready to face the world, are you?	Morning. Ready to face the world?	Caleb, greeting player (neutral)
There's definitely something sright there!	There's something!	Missy, spotting clue
I just saw something, do you see it too?!	See that?!	Missy, spotting clue

(Continue)

TABLE 10.3. Death in Shadow Bay Dialogue Edit - COMPLETED *(Continued)*

Original	Edit	Designer Notes
I'm pretty sure that's a clue over there!	Is that a clue?	Caleb, spotting clue
Ah ha! See you have to pay attention! I think there's something of importance here!	Check that out—a clue!	Caleb, spotting clue
You can't be serious about that, can you?	Are you serious?	Missy, player guesses wrong
Nope, that's not going to be the right answer!	Uh—so wrong!	Missy, player guesses wrong
I'm afraid not, dearest of cousins.	Wrong answer, cuz.	Caleb, player guesses wrong
Ah, no. That's not any-where close to correct.	Not even close!	Caleb, player guesses wrong
Huh. What a lucky guess.	Lucky guess.	Missy, player guesses wrong
Okay, that sounds like it's right.	You just might be right.	Missy, player guesses right
Yes! A great deduction indeed!	Excellent deduction!	Caleb, player guesses right
You really mastered that in no time!	Good thinking!	Caleb, player guesses right

INDEX

C

M

N

O

P

U

V

W